# Microsoft Dynamics GP 2013 Implementation

Successfully implement Microsoft Dynamics GP 2013 with easy-to-follow instructions and examples

**Victoria Yudin**

[PACKT] enterprise
professional expertise distilled
PUBLISHING

BIRMINGHAM - MUMBAI

# Microsoft Dynamics GP 2013 Implementation



First published: November 2010

Second edition: September 2013

Production Reference: 1160913

Published by Packt Publishing Ltd.
Livery Place
35 Livery Street
Birmingham B3 2PB, UK.

ISBN 978-1-78217-784-5

www.packtpub.com

Cover Image by Aashish Variava (aashishvariava@hotmail.com)

# Credits

**Author**
Victoria Yudin

**Reviewers**
Frank Hamelly
Vaidhyanathan Mohan
Jivtesh Singh
Leslie Vail

**Acquisition Editor**
Saleem Ahmed

**Lead Technical Editor**
Sweny M. Sukumaran

**Technical Editors**
Dylan Fernandes
Monica John
Mrunmayee Patil

**Project Coordinator**
Kranti Berde

**Proofreader**
Amy Johnson

**Indexer**
Monica Ajmera Mehta

**Graphics**
Ronak Dhruv

**Production Coordinator**
Nilesh R. Mohite

**Cover Work**
Nilesh R. Mohite

# About the Author

**Victoria Yudin** has been designing, implementing, integrating, and customizing business management and accounting systems for over 20 years. She has been a user of Microsoft Dynamics GP (and its Great Plains Software predecessor) since it was available on DOS and has been a Dynamics GP consultant for almost 15 years.

Victoria has the distinction of being the only person in the world named a Microsoft Dynamics GP Most Valuable Professional (MVP) each consecutive year since 2005. She has also been on the DynamicsWorld's Microsoft Dynamics Top 100 Most Influential People list each year since 2010. Victoria has also been in the top 10 of Doug Pitcher's "most famous, awesome and totally influential Dynamics people" list for all 3 years it has been published. (`http://bit.ly/18UaKkL`)

Victoria has an undergraduate degree from the Wharton School of Business at the University of Pennsylvania, and has numerous certifications for Microsoft Dynamics GP and related technologies.

In November 2000, Victoria started Flexible Solutions, Inc. to bring together her experience in accounting and business with her love for technology. Flexible Solutions (`www.GPReportsViewer.com`) is a Microsoft Dynamics GP Partner, offering the GP Reports Viewer add-on for Dynamics GP, as well as Microsoft Dynamics GP implementation, reporting, and support services.

In September 2008, Victoria started her blog, called Ramblings and musings of a Dynamics GP MVP (`http://victoriayudin.com`) to share her experiences and thoughts with the Dynamics GP community. Currently Victoria's blog gets more than 45,000 hits per month. Victoria also regularly helps fellow Dynamics GP users and consultants on many of the Dynamics GP online forums, including Experts Exchange, where she has earned the rank of Wizard.

Victoria previously authored the *Microsoft Dynamics GP 2010 Implementation* book and has had articles published on `MSDynamicsWorld.com` and in the GPUG Magazine.

---

To my parents, Alexander and Svetlana, thank you for your unconditional and unwavering love and support. None of this would have been possible without your sacrifices and hard work.

Thank you to Mickie Stamm for being so amazing to work with and for teaching me everything I know about SQL.

To Leslie Vail, thank you so much for agreeing to review this book—you have added tremendous value to the content and helped clean up my writing. Thanks to Frank Hamelly for your ideas and for finding all my typos. To Jivtesh Singh and Vaidy Mohan, thank you for your insights.

Thank you to all the hard working folks at Packt Publishing for helping me stay on schedule and guiding me through the process.

---

# About the Reviewers

**Frank Hamelly** is a business and technology professional with over 25 years experience implementing and supporting various ERP systems and business process re-engineering initiatives across all organizational areas and various industries, from mid-sized to Fortune 500 companies. He has held executive positions in Accounting and Finance, and Information Systems. Application experience includes SAP, SAP Business One, Baan, Fourth Shift, and Microsoft Dynamics GP. Industry experience includes manufacturing, telecom, aerospace, life sciences, utilities, and media. He holds a degree in Business Administration with an Accounting concentration from the University of Pittsburgh. He is a Microsoft Certified Professional (MCP), a Microsoft Certified IT Professional (MCITP), a Microsoft Certified Trainer (MCT), and has been a Microsoft Most Valuable Professional (MVP) since 2008. He is the author of numerous articles for Dynamics-related websites and a speaker & moderator at Microsoft Dynamics Convergence (2011, 2012, and 2013), GPUG Summit (2011, 2012, and 2013) and MSDynamicsWorld's Decisions Spring 2010, 2011, and 2012. He is the author of the blog GP2themax with over 5,000 page views per month.

**Vaidhyanathan Mohan** is a Microsoft certified freelance Microsoft Dynamics GP consultant with expertise on Microsoft Dynamics GP and related technologies. Starting his career as a GP developer, he slowly and steadily enhanced his skills on Microsoft Dynamics GP, both on the product and technologies, and became a complete product consultant.

He has worked on various challenging customization developments and Dynamics GP implementations. He is an active participant on all Microsoft Dynamics GP community forums; Microsoft Dynamics GP technical blogger, namely Dynamics GP—Learn & Discuss (`http://vaidymohan.com`), which is listed on Microsoft's official Dynamics GP blog space.

He is who he is now because of his devoted parents, his brother and family, his wife and his daughter. He is an avid photography enthusiast (`http://500px.com/seshadri`), music fanatic, coffee addict, and immensely fond of anything about Microsoft Dynamics GP.

**Jivtesh Singh** is a Microsoft Dynamics GP MVP and a Microsoft Dynamics Certified Technology Specialist for Dynamics GP. Through his blog, which is widely read in the Dynamics GP community—he covers Dynamics GP Tips and tricks and news.

Jivtesh is a Dynamics GP Consultant and Systems Implementer and has been associated with the Microsoft Technologies since the launch of Microsoft .Net framework. Jivtesh has over 10 years of experience in development and maintenance of enterprise software using coding best practices, refactoring and usage of design patterns, and Test Driven Development. Jivtesh recently built a Kinect interface to control the Microsoft Dynamics GP 2010 R2 Business Analyzer with gestures. Later he built a part of the GP Future demo for Convergence GP Keynote.

Jivtesh has setup a custom search engine directory for Dynamics GP Blog at www.gpwindow.com to help with easier access of Dynamics GP resources for the GP Community. With MVP Mark Polino, he has also set up a Dynamics GP product directory `www.dynamicsgpproducts.com`

Jivtesh's Blog on Dynamics GP—`www.jivtesh.com`

Jivtesh's Custom Search Engine for GP Blogs—`www.gpwindow.com`

Dynamics GP Products Website—`www.dynamicsgpproducts.com`

**Leslie Vail** is a CPA and has been working as a Microsoft Dynamics GP consultant for 20 years. She began with Dynamics GP Version 1.0 in 1993. During this period, she has completed numerous implementations, conversions, and custom development projects. She presents at many partner and customer technical conferences and conducts training classes throughout North and Central America.

Leslie is recognized throughout the industry for her product expertise and contributions to the Dynamics GP community. She has been identified by Doug Pitcher from Rose Business Solutions, Inc. as the third most famous, awesome, and totally influential Dynamics GP people for 2013 (`http://tinyurl.com/kjvxh3m/`). Leslie's home base is Dallas, TX.

As a Microsoft Certified Trainer (MCT), she serves as a Subject Matter Expert (SME) for the Microsoft Assessments and Certification Exams (ACE) Team. She is a member of the US MCT Advisory Council and has been named a Microsoft Most Valuable Professional (MVP) since 2007. She is one of the top contributors to the Microsoft Dynamics GP Community forum and she maintains the popular Dynamics Confessor BlogSpot (`http://dynamicsconfessions.blogspot.com/`).

She has reviewed and developed Microsoft Courseware, authored the book *Developing Microsoft Dynamics GP Business Applications* and co-authored the book *Confessions of a Dynamics GP Consultant*. She has been the Technical Editor of several books dedicated to Microsoft Dynamics GP.

Leslie provides implementation and consulting services for companies ranging from a high-net-worth individual to a multi-national manufacturing firm. She is certified as a Microsoft Certified IT Professional in Microsoft Dynamics GP Applications, Microsoft Dynamics GP Installation and Configuration as well as Microsoft SQL Server. She holds Microsoft Certified Technology Specialist certifications in Dexterity, Modifier with VBA, Integration Manager, Report Writer, HR/Payroll, Financials, Inventory and Order Processing, FRx Report Designer, SQL Server 2008, and Microsoft XP Professional.

A skilled developer, Leslie uses Dexterity, Modifier with VBA, Integration Manager and eConnect to provide custom solutions for her clients. She is a Certified Integration Developer (CID), a Dexterity CID, a Dynamics Tools CID, and a Dexterity Certified Systems Engineer.

Her training expertise spans the entire Microsoft Dynamics GP product line. She is an experienced trainer and teaches classes for Dexterity, Financials, Inventory & Order Processing, HR/Payroll, Integration Manager, Modifier with VBA, FRx Report Designer, SQL Server Reporting Services, Report Writer, Crystal Reports, SmartList Builder, Excel Report Builder, Integrated Excel Reports, Extender and System Manager.

Prior to working with Microsoft Dynamics GP, Leslie was the tax director for a large financial institution; before that, she worked for one of the original Big Eight accounting firms as a senior tax accountant.

# www.PacktPub.com

## Support files, eBooks, discount offers and more

You might want to visit www.PacktPub.com for support files and downloads related to your book.

Did you know that Packt offers eBook versions of every book published, with PDF and ePub files available? You can upgrade to the eBook version at www.PacktPub.com and as a print book customer, you are entitled to a discount on the eBook copy. Get in touch with us at service@packtpub.com for more details.

At www.PacktPub.com, you can also read a collection of free technical articles, sign up for a range of free newsletters and receive exclusive discounts and offers on Packt books and eBooks.

PACKTLIB™

http://PacktLib.PacktPub.com

Do you need instant solutions to your IT questions? PacktLib is Packt's online digital book library. Here, you can access, read and search across Packt's entire library of books.

## Why Subscribe?

- Fully searchable across every book published by Packt
- Copy and paste, print and bookmark content
- On demand and accessible via web browser

## Free Access for Packt account holders

If you have an account with Packt at www.PacktPub.com, you can use this to access PacktLib today and view nine entirely free books. Simply use your login credentials for immediate access.

## Instant Updates on New Packt Books

Get notified! Find out when new books are published by following @PacktEnterprise on Twitter, or the *Packt Enterprise* Facebook page.

*This book is dedicated to Joseph Puntasecca, the love of my life.*

# Table of Contents

# Preface

*Microsoft Dynamics GP 2013* is a sophisticated Enterprise Resource Planning system used throughout the world. Implementing Dynamics GP for an organization can be a daunting task, requiring thorough planning and understanding of the available features and options. This book provides guidance for the planning, installation, and setup of Microsoft Dynamics GP 2013 with examples, advice, step-by-step guides, illustrations, and links to useful resources.

While it is specifically written for Microsoft Dynamics GP 2013, most of the concepts and explanations will apply to any Dynamics GP version. The implementation methodology in this book is geared toward small to mid-size companies, and can be useful to both Dynamics GP consultants and end users. Even experienced Dynamics GP consultants will benefit from having detailed instructions for the installation and setup of the core Dynamics GP modules.

By the end of this book, you will have a better understanding of the licensing and the application structure of Dynamics GP, be able to put together an implementation team, install, and set up Microsoft Dynamics GP 2013. You will also learn how to install and configure SQL Server maintenance for Dynamics GP and how to import data using Integration Manager.

## What this book covers

*Chapter 1, Application Structure and Licensing*, serves as an introduction to the Microsoft Dynamics GP structure, covering module and series, how Dynamics GP works with Microsoft SQL Server, and the Dexterity development environment that Dynamics GP is written in. New Perpetual Licensing for Dynamics GP will be explained.

*Chapter 2, Planning – Business Requirements*, discusses putting together an implementation team and steps for starting to plan a Dynamics GP implementation, including data that needs to be populated during the implementation and the tools available to do this.

*Chapter 3, Planning – Dynamics GP System*, details various components of the Dynamics GP system that need to be planned for, including how many companies to set up, integration with other systems, General Ledger account framework and account format, and numbering schemes for master records. Other topics covered include fiscal year and period setup, users and security planning, tax setup, multicurrency, and posting setup.

*Chapter 4, Planning – Infrastructure*, covers general concepts for infrastructure planning, including minimum requirements and recommendations for Dynamics GP 2013, considerations for virtual environments, Remote Desktop Services, and networks. Alternatives for placement of shared files and data backups are also discussed.

*Chapter 5, Installation of SQL Server, Dynamics GP, and Integration Manager*, is a step-by-step guide for installing SQL Server 2012, Dynamics GP 2013, and Integration Manager 12.0. Post-installation steps, including creating Dynamics GP companies and setting up SQL Server maintenance plans, are included.

*Chapter 6, System and Company Setup*, covers setting up the Dynamics GP 2013 system and companies with detailed step-by-step instructions and recommendations. Topics include multicurrency, account format, taxes, fiscal periods, credit cards, and posting.

*Chapter 7, Module Setup – General Ledger, Bank Reconciliation, Payables, and Receivables*, includes steps for setting up the General Ledger, Bank Reconciliation, Payables Management, and Receivables Management modules in Dynamics GP 2013. Detailed explanations and recommendations are provided for available setup options.

*Chapter 8, Module Setup – Inventory, SOP, and POP*, includes steps for setting up the three distribution modules in Dynamics GP 2013. Detailed explanations and recommendations are provided for available setup options.

*Chapter 9, Populating Initial Data*, is a step-by-step guide to using Integration Manager to import data into Dynamics GP. An introduction to Integration Manager terminology and illustrations of destination mappings for various imports are included.

*Chapter 10, Training, Tools, and Next Steps*, covers topics such as planning and best practices for training, the various tools available from Microsoft for Dynamics GP 2013, and additional resources available for troubleshooting and maintaining Dynamics GP.

*Appendix, General Ledger Account Categories*, contains a list of the default General Ledger account categories in Dynamics GP.

## What you need for this book

To run the examples in this book the following will be needed:

- Microsoft SQL Server 2012 (SQL Server 2008 or 2008 R2 can also be used, but you may not be able to follow some of the step-by-step instructions in the SQL Server installation section)
- Microsoft Dynamics GP 2013
- Basic understanding of accounting/ERP software and some Dynamics GP terminology may be helpful
- Many of the web links in this book require access to Microsoft's CustomerSource or PartnerSource

## Who this book is for

Companies looking to implement Microsoft Dynamics GP will find critical information for their implementation in this book. Even if you have an outside company performing your implementation, this book will give you useful ideas, options, and insight.

New or existing Microsoft Dynamics GP consultants, administrators, and power users will benefit from the step-by-step installation instructions, explanations of all the setup windows for the core modules of Dynamics GP 2013, and guides for using Integration Manager to import data.

## Conventions

In this book, you will find a number of styles of text that distinguish between different kinds of information. Here are some examples of these styles, and an explanation of their meaning.

Code words in text are shown as follows: "If there are no modifications to windows or reports, the `Forms.dic` and `Reports.dic` files will not exist."

**New terms** and **important words** are shown in bold. Words that you see on the screen, in menus or dialog boxes for example, appear in the text like this: "Detailed navigation will be provided for each setup window, or you can keep using the setup checklist (**Microsoft Dynamics GP | Tools | Setup | Setup Checklist**).".

> Warnings or important notes appear in a box like this.

> Tips and tricks appear like this.

# Reader feedback

Feedback from our readers is always welcome. Let us know what you think about this book—what you liked or may have disliked. Reader feedback is important for us to develop titles that you really get the most out of.

To send us general feedback, simply send an e-mail to `feedback@packtpub.com`, and mention the book title via the subject of your message.

If there is a topic that you have expertise in and you are interested in either writing or contributing to a book, see our author guide on `www.packtpub.com/authors`.

# Customer support

Now that you are the proud owner of a Packt book, we have a number of things to help you to get the most from your purchase.

## Errata

Although we have taken every care to ensure the accuracy of our content, mistakes do happen. If you find a mistake in one of our books—maybe a mistake in the text or the code—we would be grateful if you would report this to us. By doing so, you can save other readers from frustration and help us improve subsequent versions of this book. If you find any errata, please report them by visiting `http://www.packtpub.com/submit-errata`, selecting your book, clicking on the **errata submission form** link, and entering the details of your errata. Once your errata are verified, your submission will be accepted and the errata will be uploaded on our website, or added to any list of existing errata, under the Errata section of that title. Any existing errata can be viewed by selecting your title from `http://www.packtpub.com/support`.

# Piracy

Piracy of copyright material on the Internet is an ongoing problem across all media. At Packt, we take the protection of our copyright and licenses very seriously. If you come across any illegal copies of our works, in any form, on the Internet, please provide us with the location address or website name immediately so that we can pursue a remedy.

Please contact us at `copyright@packtpub.com` with a link to the suspected pirated material.

We appreciate your help in protecting our authors, and our ability to bring you valuable content.

# Questions

You can contact us at `questions@packtpub.com` if you are having a problem with any aspect of the book, and we will do our best to address it.

# 1
# Application Structure and Licensing

As a start to your Microsoft Dynamics GP implementation, we will go over some key concepts to help you plan and carry out the best implementation possible. Some of the terminology within Dynamics GP may be new to you, so we will start with some key definitions in this chapter. We will also go over the Dynamics GP licensing and application structure, so that you can make sure you have all the components you need as you start your implementation.

In this chapter you will learn about the following:

- The structure of Dynamics GP: What modules and series are, and how they all work together
- Dynamics GP licensing
- How Microsoft SQL Server and Dynamics GP work together
- The definitions of Dexterity and product dictionaries
- Financial reporting choices: Management Reporter, AFA, and FRx

# Structure of Dynamics GP – modules and series

Microsoft Dynamics GP is a modular application. In this case, a module refers to a set of related functionality within the application. A module can be as robust as **Payables Management** (typically referred to as **Accounts Payable**), which contains all the details about your vendor transactions, has over fifty windows and tables, and hundreds of stored procedures. A module can also be as narrow in scope as **Customer/Vendor Consolidations**, which allows you to define relationships between vendors and customers and only has a few windows, tables, and stored procedures.

When implemented together, the Dynamics GP modules integrate to provide a fully functional **ERP** (**Enterprise Resource Planning**) application. There are over one hundred modules available for Dynamics GP and it is sometimes tempting to simply install them all, or install every module included in your licensing. Don't do this! Installing modules that you do not need may result in adverse behavior in other modules, and may make administration of Dynamics GP more cumbersome than it needs to be. Best practice is to keep it as simple as possible, plan for and implement only the modules you need.

In Dynamics GP, modules are grouped into series by related functionality. For example: Payables Management, Purchase Order Processing, Purchase Order Enhancements, and Scheduled Payments modules all deal with vendor transactions and are grouped into the Purchasing series. Navigation in Dynamics GP is performed by series, as are many setup and maintenance tasks.

# Dynamics GP licensing

Before you start your Microsoft Dynamics GP implementation, it is important to understand what modules you own and how the licensing structure works. This may change some of your plans for Dynamics GP or help you determine additional purchases needed prior to implementation.

The licensing structure has been drastically changed starting with Dynamics GP 2013, so even if you were familiar with Dynamics GP in the past, you may need to take some time to familiarize yourself with the new options. If you are upgrading to Dynamics GP 2013 from a previous version, you will need to upgrade your license with Microsoft.

The new licensing model for Microsoft Dynamics GP 2013 is called **Perpetual Licensing** and is intended to greatly simplify purchasing Dynamics GP. The core components of the new licensing are the **Starter Pack**, the **Extended Pack**, the **Full User**, and the **Limited User**. Additional modules and options are available for purchase separately. Description of the Perpetual Licensing components are in the following table:

| Component | Description |
|---|---|
| Starter Pack | The Starter Pack is the only required part of a Dynamics GP license and includes many core financial and distribution modules plus three Full User licenses. All the modules covered in this book are included in the Starter Pack. For those familiar with previous Dynamics GP licensing, the modules offered with the Business Essentials edition, plus a few additional ones, are included in the Starter Pack. |
| Extended Pack | The Extended Pack includes modules with advanced functionality such as Manufacturing, Project Accounting, Contract Administration, and the Distribution Suite. Compared to the previous Dynamics GP licensing, the Extended Pack is similar to, though not quite the same as, the Advanced Management licensing edition. |
| Full User | The Full User license allows users full read and write capability to all modules licensed. |
| Limited User | The Limited User license allows full read capability to all modules licensed. The Limited User also includes write capability to the Time and Expense functionality. |

Full Users and Limited Users are sold on a concurrent user basis—you can have an unlimited number of users set up in the system, as long as the number of users logged in at any one time does not exceed the number of licenses you own.

**Module Based Licensing** is no longer sold to new customers. **Business Ready Licensing** will be sold to new customers until June 2014 if they are purchasing Microsoft Dynamics GP 2010.

# Core modules explained

There is a set of core modules that will be found in almost every installation of Dynamics GP. These are key modules that perform basic accounting functions and are the modules we will focus on in our implementation planning and examples throughout this book. The following are descriptions of the core modules that will be found in most Dynamics GP implementations. All of these modules are included in the Starter Pack under Perpetual Licensing:

- **Dynamics GP System Manager**: The **System Manager** is the mandatory core module that controls the Dynamics GP application, users, companies, and security.
- **General Ledger**: Everything in accounting ultimately ends up in the **General Ledger** (**GL**). This module is the final stop for all other modules and controls the chart of accounts as well as the individual General Ledger transactions and account balances. While technically possible, it would be extremely difficult to implement a functioning Dynamics GP system without the General Ledger.
- **Payables Management**: Commonly referred to as **Accounts Payable** (**AP**), this subledger holds the details for all vendors and vendor transactions.
- **Receivables Management**: Also called **Accounts Receivable** (**AR**), this subledger holds the details for all customers and customer transactions.
- **Bank Reconciliation**: This module holds details for all cash transactions and bank accounts (called **Checkbooks**). Cash movements from other modules, such as Payables Management and Receivables Management, are posted to Bank Reconciliation.
- **Fixed Assets**: All the capital assets of a company can be tracked in this module. Depreciation and amortization of assets is performed in **Fixed Assets** and sent to the General Ledger.
- **Inventory Control**: This module holds the setup for any items sold or used by a company. This can include items stocked in inventory, services that need to appear in detail on customer invoices, or internally used items that need to have quantities tracked. Inventory Control allows for multiple warehouses or locations, serial number or lot tracking, unit of measure setup, and cycle and physical inventory counts.
- **Purchase Order Processing**: Detailed purchase orders with line items are entered and printed in this module, which allows for a transaction flow from purchase order, to receipt of goods, to invoice. The Purchase Order Processing module helps integrate Inventory Control and Payables Management, and also works with Sales Order Processing.

- **Sales Order Processing**: Detailed sales transactions with line items are entered in Sales Order Processing, which allows for a transaction flow from quote to order, to back order, to fulfillment order/invoice. Customer invoices and returns with line item detail are created and printed in Sales Order Processing. This module integrates Inventory Control and Receivables Management, and also works with Purchase Order Processing.

The interaction between these core modules is illustrated in this diagram:

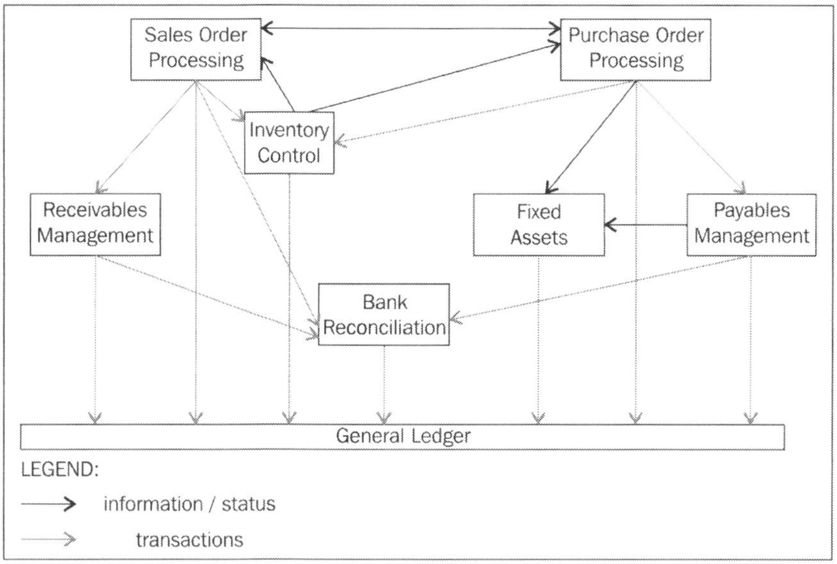


# Dynamics GP and Microsoft SQL Server

Older versions of Dynamics GP, when it was still called Great Plains, supported installation on three different database platforms: c-tree, Pervasive PSQL (previously called Btrieve), and Microsoft SQL Server. Starting with version 8.0, Microsoft Dynamics GP is only supported on Microsoft SQL Server. With Dynamics GP 2013 the supported versions of SQL Server are 2008, 2008 R2, and 2012.

# What you may not expect from a SQL Server Application

While I have not heard a single complaint about not being able to support Dynamics GP on c-tree and Btrieve anymore, there are some legitimate complaints about Dynamics GP not taking full advantage of Microsoft SQL Server. Understanding the evolution of an application helps explain the reasons for this and, with every new version, Microsoft has been enhancing Dynamics GP to make more use of SQL Server functionality. However, it is important for implementers to have an understanding of the aspects of Dynamics GP behavior that do not always take full advantage of Microsoft SQL Server.

> An excellent discussion on this topic can be found on the Developing for Dynamics GP blog:
>
> Understanding how Microsoft Dynamics GP works with Microsoft SQL Server: `http://bit.ly/18fvKo3`
>
> Understanding how Microsoft Dynamics GP works with Microsoft SQL Server continued: `http://bit.ly/18fvTrE`

# Application security and SQL Server authentication

One key aspect that you may find surprising if this is the first time you are working with Dynamics GP is that it only uses SQL Server authentication. User logins created in Dynamics GP are automatically created in SQL Server and the passwords are encrypted. Security for all Dynamics GP functionality is handled inside the application itself and, as the SQL Server passwords are encrypted by Dynamics GP, you are not easily able to use the same SQL Server logins for any other purpose. While good for security, this makes it more difficult when integrating other applications and is important to keep in mind when planning your infrastructure.

Some tasks within Dynamics GP must be performed while logged in as the SQL Server sa (system administrator) user. Examples of these tasks are creating new Dynamics GP users, installing and initializing additional components and third-party add-ons, and running various tools provided by Microsoft for Dynamics GP. There are workarounds available for some of these, but they do not completely take away the need for using the SQL Server sa user in Dynamics GP.

Another remnant of the older database platforms is a SQL Server and Dynamics GP user called `DYNSA` that gets created automatically during the Dynamics GP installation process. This user does not need to have any rights within the application, but it is critical for this user to be the database owner of all the Dynamics GP databases. Even though day-to-day operations do not typically rely on the database owner, installation of new modules, creation of new companies, and upgrades or service packs may fail if the database owner is not `DYNSA`.

A Dynamics GP ISV, FastPath, has a whitepaper on minimizing the use of sa in Dynamics GP which is available at `http://bit.ly/15YoCLs`.

# SQL Server databases created by Dynamics GP

When you install Dynamics GP, a global system database is created. In prior versions of Dynamics GP this database was forced to be called `DYNAMICS`. Starting with Dynamics GP 2013 you can change this name for new installations. The system database holds all system-wide settings such as users, companies, security, multicurrency settings, exchange rate tables, intercompany setup, and any other information that needs to be shared globally in Dynamics GP. Active processes and logins are also stored in the system database.

There is no limit on how many companies you can create in Dynamics GP. Every new company will be a new SQL Server database. The only restriction is for the SQL Server database ID to be five characters or less and to not start with a number.

A sample company is available to be installed with sample data for many of the Dynamics GP modules. The sample company is called Fabrikam and in versions prior to 2013 the database ID used to be `TWO` (because in older versions of Dynamics GP the sample company was called The World Online). Starting with Dynamics GP 2013 you can change this database ID to be whatever you would like within the naming restriction of five characters or less and not starting with a number.

# SQL Server sort order options

Only two Microsoft SQL Server sort orders are supported by Dynamics GP:

- Binary: Sort order 50.
- Dictionary Order, Case-Insensitive (DOCI): Sort order 52.

The recommendation for new installations is to use the DOCI sort order. It will make Dynamics GP easier to work with for both users and administrators, and it will also remove some limitations on integrating products.

# Where is the application server?

Dynamics GP is a client/server application. All the data is centrally stored in Microsoft SQL Server databases (and, optionally, some shared files on the network) and the SQL Server must be running and accessible to all client machines running Dynamics GP. The Dynamics GP application itself does not need to be installed or running on a server and administrative functions can be performed from any client machine where the application is installed.

# Dexterity and product dictionaries

Microsoft Dynamics GP is written in a proprietary application development environment called **Dexterity**. Over the years there have been many questions raised about when Dynamics GP will be rewritten in a different language. There was even an announcement about 12 years ago that Dynamics GP 7.0 would be rewritten in C#. The reality is that Dexterity is here to stay. While implementation and day-to-day operation of Dynamics GP does not require any knowledge of Dexterity, it is important to understand the terminology and structure of the Dexterity environment.

## Dexterity components

Dexterity is a 32-bit environment with a number of components that work together:

- **Application Dictionaries**: These are files with the extension of `.dic` that store code and resources. Resources are objects such as tables, windows, and reports.
- **Runtime Engine**: This combines and interprets code and resources in application dictionaries to result in a functioning user application.
- **Dexterity Dictionary** (`Dex.dic`): This includes resources used by the runtime engine to translate the application dictionaries.

## Dynamics GP products

In any installation of Dynamics GP, you will find multiple products. Products can be installed and used independently even though they may integrate with other products. Typically, each Dynamics GP module will be a separate product. The major exception to this is the Microsoft Dynamics GP product, which includes most of the core Dynamics GP modules.

Each product has the following unique characteristics and components:

| Component | Example |
|---|---|
| Product Name | Microsoft Dynamics GP |
| Product Number | 0 |
| Product Dictionary | `Dynamics.dic` |
| Forms (or Windows) Dictionary | `Forms.dic` |
| Reports Dictionary | `Reports.dic` |

A **Window** in Dexterity is an actual screen used in the application to enter or view data. A **Form** is a combination of windows, menus, and other resources that work together. For example, the **About Microsoft Dynamics GP** form shown in the following screenshot has two windows: **About Microsoft Dynamics GP** and **Microsoft Dynamics GP Options**. Together these two windows make up the **About Microsoft Dynamics GP** form.

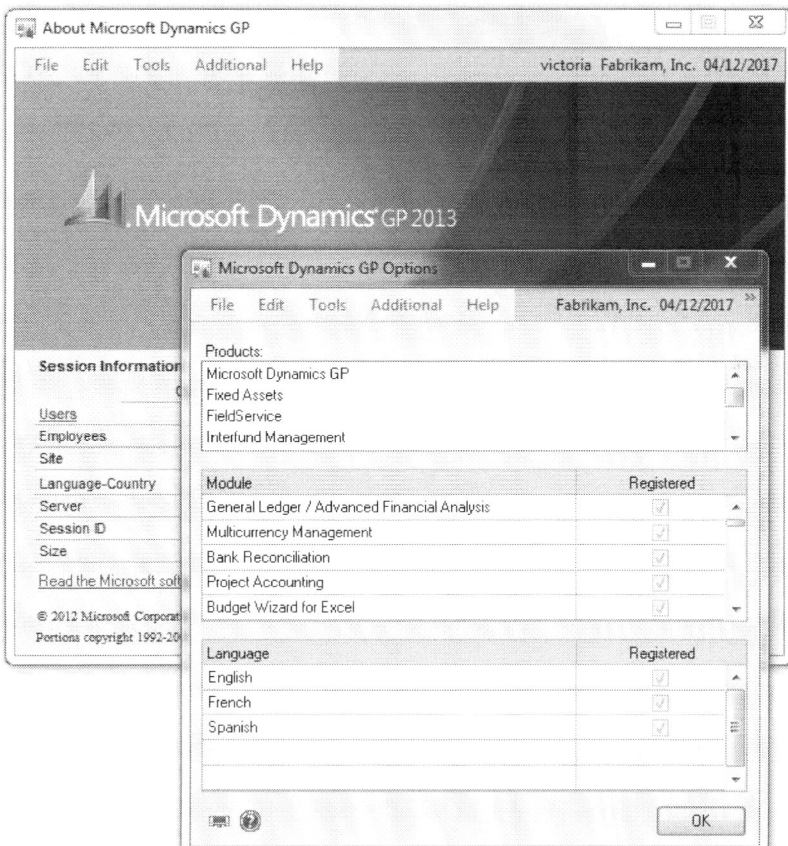

The product dictionary contains all the core forms and reports for each product. If there are no modifications to windows or reports, the forms and reports dictionary files will not exist. If the forms or reports dictionary is found, the Dynamics GP application will look to them first when opening a modified window or report. This allows any modifications made to windows and reports to supersede the out-of-the-box code, while keeping the original product dictionary intact.

In a typical Dynamics GP installation, the product dictionary is installed locally on each workstation. The forms and reports dictionaries can be installed either locally on each workstation or located on a network share, accessible by all workstations. For implementations with no modifications to the out-of-the-box windows or reports, it is recommended to install all the dictionary files locally for improved performance.

## Report Writer and Modifier

Report Writer and Modifier are tools that allow reports and windows in Dynamics GP to be modified.

Report Writer is a Dexterity reporting tool that is included with the Dynamics GP System Manager. With Report Writer, you can modify existing reports or create new custom reports. In a standard Dynamics GP installation, there are over 800 Report Writer reports. Typical modifications to reports include adding a company logo, changing the alignment of reports to fit a pre-printed form (for example, for payables checks), and removing or adding columns on reports. Modified reports for the Microsoft Dynamics GP product are stored in the `Reports.dic` file.

Modifier is a Dexterity tool for customizing the appearance and behavior of Dynamics GP windows. With the new Perpetual Licensing for Dynamics GP 2013, Modifier is included with the Starter Pack purchase. Typical modifications to windows include making fields required, hiding fields, changing the name of field prompts (or labels), and changing the tab order of fields. Modified windows for the Microsoft Dynamics GP product are stored in the `Forms.dic` file.

# Financial reporting: Management Reporter, AFA, and FRx

When Dynamics GP was originally released, a financial reporting tool called **Advanced Financial Analysis** (**AFA**) was included for the General Ledger. This is a Dexterity based tool that includes some basic financial reports and allows users to modify and create financial statements such as Balance Sheets, Profit & Loss Statements, and Cash Flows.

It quickly became apparent that AFA was not a robust enough tool for many user requirements, so Great Plains Software, several years prior to Microsoft's acquisition of it, purchased **FRx Software** to accommodate the need for more functionality and flexibility for financial reporting. FRx Software made a financial reporting package called **FRx Reporter** (commonly called **FRx**) that works with many General Ledger packages in addition to Dynamics GP. If you have implemented previous versions of Dynamics GP, you have most likely worked with FRx, as this was the financial reporting tool of choice for Dynamics GP.

Starting with Dynamics GP 2010 a new product, called **Management Reporter**, was introduced by Microsoft to replace FRx. Management Reporter is now the only financial reporting package supported for Dynamics GP 2013 and licensing for Management Reporter is included in the Starter Pack. There are migration tools and guidelines available for moving from FRx to Management Reporter.

> While not officially supported, if you are upgrading from previous versions of Dynamics GP and are using FRx, in my testing, FRx will still work as it did previously with the new Dynamics GP 2013.

# Summary

In this chapter we introduced some Dynamics GP specific terminology and concepts, and discussed the new Perpetual Licensing model and core modules. We outlined the structure of Microsoft Dynamics GP and briefly discussed how Dynamics GP and Microsoft SQL Server work together. The Dexterity system and financial reporting packages were introduced. You should now have a basic understanding of the Dynamics GP structure and terminology that will help you as you start your implementation.

In the next chapter, we will discuss how to start planning for your implementation.

# 2
# Planning – Business Requirements

Good planning results in successful implementations. Planning can be broken down into three distinct phases:

- Business requirements
- Microsoft Dynamics GP system setup
- Infrastructure

This chapter will go over the business requirements planning phase, detail important planning concepts, and give some real life examples.

In this chapter, you will learn the following topics:

- Putting together an implementation team
- How to start planning your Dynamics GP implementation
- Different reporting requirements and steps to identify them
- Considerations when deciding whether to run two systems concurrently
- Data that may need to be populated during your implementation and the tools available for importing data into Dynamics GP
- How to start putting together your implementation timeline

# Implementation team

At the start of any implementation, you should identify the team that will ultimately be responsible for the implementation. Some companies believe that they can hire an external consultant or a new employee to complete a Dynamics GP implementation with minimal involvement from other company resources. This typically results in frustration, unrealized expectations, and a poor implementation. There can be no successful implementation of an **ERP** (**Enterprise Resource Planning**) system without active involvement from the end users and company management.

# Who should be on the implementation team

Involving the end users does not mean all end users of Dynamics GP must actively participate in the implementation. However, one or more core end users need to be identified and involved in the process from the very start. Typically, this will be the controller or a senior accountant who has been with the company for some time and knows all aspects of the operation from the accounting perspective.

In addition to having someone with knowledge of the company's accounting practices, the implementation team should include someone who understands the business very well from an operational standpoint. That is, a person who comprehends the overall vision for the company's products and services, as well as the detailed flow of the company's operations and transactions. This role may be filled by one or more persons, depending on the size and complexity of a company.

Another key component of the implementation team is a knowledgeable IT resource in the company. This should be someone that has a good understanding of the company's infrastructure and the systems that are currently in place, as well as what future IT projects and changes are planned. The IT resource should be one that has appropriate permissions and passwords for the systems needed during the implementation, whether or not this team member will be the one performing the actual installations. Often this will also be the person in charge of maintaining the Dynamics GP system after the implementation.

Typically, a company will not go forward with a Dynamics GP implementation without the direction of the owner, president, or someone at a high position in the organization. It is important to have this person on the implementation team. They may not be closely involved with many details of the project, however, this team member, frequently called the project champion or sponsor, is the one ultimately responsible for motivating the staff and getting the company employees to accept the inevitable changes that come with switching to a new system. This team member will be the resource to go to if there are issues or roadblocks during the implementation.

When an external consultant performs the Dynamics GP implementation, the assumption is that you chose this consultant for their experience with Dynamics GP. However, if someone with limited or no experience with Dynamics GP is performing the implementation internally, it is important to have access to a knowledgeable Dynamics GP resource. This can either be a consultant provided by your Dynamics GP partner or someone that you contract with independently. No book or manual can cover every scenario and situation, so having this resource will help fill in any gaps in understanding and knowledge. It will also provide a security blanket—the implementation team will know they have a resource available for any Dynamics GP questions that come up.

# Project manager

After you assemble the individuals on the team, you must identify the project manager. The project manager may be one of the people we have already talked about or an additional resource. While the project manager may not be the one performing many of the implementation steps, they absolutely must be involved with all the details of the implementation, from beginning to end. Because of this, the project manager should not be the company's president or someone that already has numerous demands on their time; this should be someone who has the time necessary to delve into the minutiae of your Dynamics GP implementation.

What's coming next may be a somewhat radical idea. If an external consultant or company is performing the Dynamics GP implementation, the project manager should be an employee of the company, not an external consultant. An alternative to this is to have two project managers working together—the consultant and a company employee. The reason for this is that the project manager must internally drive the project and make sure it keeps progressing as planned, getting all the company resources to do what they need to do. Very rarely will an external consultant have the same ability to command resources within a company that an internal employee will.

# The team and practical considerations

To sum up, the implementation team will consist of the following:

- **Project manager**—internal
- **Co-project manager**—optional/external
- **Accounting resource**—internal, controller, and/or senior accountant
- **Operations resource**—internal
- **IT resource**—internal

- **Champion/Executive** – internal
- **Dynamics GP resource** – may be another team member or an additional, external resource

Depending on the size and complexity of a company, the Dynamics GP implementation team may be just a few people or could be comprised of up to 10 people or more. There are a few thoughts to keep in mind as you are putting together your team:

- When in doubt as to how many people should be on the implementation team, err on the side of having a smaller team. If there are three people that make up the accounting resource, select one for the team and consult the others as needed. Often, the implementation time frame grows as the team grows. For a company of 20, the implementation team should not be 10 people.
- Put together a list of all the contact information for the implementation team and distribute it to all the members of the team at the start of the project. Getting this out of the way upfront will save time as the project gets going.
- Put together a list of additional resources and support staff that may be important for the team to have access to, and distribute it to all the members of the team at the start of the project.

# To plan or not to plan

This should not really be a question, but we will answer it anyway, once and for all. Planning is not optional. You might think that you have a small and straightforward implementation and, to save time and money, you should just get the software installed and start using it. There may be some software for which this approach works. This will not work for Dynamics GP. In the long run, you will spend more time and money fixing things if you do not plan your implementation. You may also never get the intended results from Dynamics GP without proper planning upfront.

# How to start planning

Planning does not have to be a scary prospect, or something that takes an inordinate amount of time and produces a 200-page document. There is a fine line between not enough planning and over-planning. For a typical implementation in a small to mid-size business, planning every detailed step of an implementation is not warranted. You should plan for key steps, dates, and deliverables.

Many companies find that planning to implement a new ERP system can provide an unexpected opportunity: a chance to re-examine some of the current workflows and reporting and improving both. While it may require some additional effort during the planning process, that effort will more than pay for itself very quickly with resulting efficiency and better reporting. As you plan, do not simply accept that things should be done the way they always have been. Take time to understand the reasoning, and to question any reasoning that does not make sense. Don't be afraid to suggest improvements.

Keep in mind that the business requirements should drive planning, not the infrastructure. Certainly, planning the infrastructure is a critical step, but understanding and planning for the business needs should be the first priority. As you plan your implementation, there are five main topics to understand and document:

- **Start at the beginning**: Have a good grasp of what the company does at a high level. You may have worked with the company for five years and already know this—that is great. However, if you are new to the company, take the time to understand the basics; it will help put the implementation into perspective.
- **Understand the vision**: What are the plans for the next one to five years? Is the plan to keep offering the same products and services that are offered now, but double the volume? Or is there a plan to go in a new direction? Understanding the vision will help you properly size the infrastructure, as well as give you an idea about what future requirements you may need to keep in mind as you are implementing Dynamics GP.
- **Identify current issues and limitations**: Find out the driving factors behind the decision to implement Dynamics GP. Is the current system not meeting critical needs? Is it simply not able to handle the volume? Often the answer to both of these questions is yes. A good understanding of the current issues will help you make sure that the newly implemented system will address them. Your understanding of the issues will increase as you delve into the planning, but you should know the critical complaints upfront.

- **See the finish line**: What are the expectations at the end of the implementation? While this goes hand-in-hand with understanding the reason to implement a new system, it is worth separating. Many companies will have clear-cut goals that they want to achieve once Dynamics GP is implemented, for example:
  - Close each month by the tenth of the following month
  - Present financial reports in a particular format to the management or investors
  - Allow tracking of processes or transactions in a multi-user system, instead of entering details in Excel spreadsheets maintained manually throughout the organization
  - Allow for faster processing of transactions
  - Allow for faster searches of transactions and balances to better address customer and vendor requests
  - Allow for more concurrent users working on similar tasks
  - Allow remote users to enter transactions or run inquiries and reports

  Similar to the current issues, you may add more items as you continue with your planning, but the key deliverables should be clear from the beginning. As you identify these goals, prioritize them—some may be the key reasons for the Dynamics GP purchase, while others may be incidental. Know what the foremost objectives are so that you can make sure you meet them.

- **Document the workflows and gaps**: What are the steps taken for each transaction type and are there any gaps in the Dynamics GP functionality? This is perhaps the most challenging of the planning steps as it requires not only understanding existing accounting and business workflows, but also identifying what is currently done that may not have corresponding functionality in Dynamics GP.

  To identify and document all the current workflows, first spend time with the accounting and operations resources on your team, then briefly visit some of the users actually performing the day-to-day work. Once you have documented the workflows, use your Dynamics GP resource to identify any gaps between the needed functionality and Dynamics GP. The Dynamics GP resource can also help to come up with alternatives or solutions to bridge those gaps.

# Not Just Widgets, Incorporated—a sample company

We are going to introduce a company called **Not Just Widgets** (**NJW**) to use as an example throughout this book. NJW resells software and hardware products, and offers some limited services to its customers. It is currently using a combination of an old small accounting package and many Excel spreadsheets. Let's go through the list in the previous section for NJW:

- **Start at the beginning**: What does the company do? NJW has been in business for five years and it resells software and hardware products that it purchases from other companies or distributors. It keeps many smaller or faster moving items in a small warehouse on premises, and larger or infrequently sold items are drop-shipped directly to customers. Some consulting services, such as system audits, network planning, and implementations are performed either by employees of NJW or independent contractors hired as needed.
- **Understand the vision**: What is the plan for the next few years? There are currently no plans to do anything differently. NJW will offer the same products and services. However, as the volume has been growing steadily over the last few years, NJW anticipates that steady growth to continue.
- **Identify current issues and limitations**: What is driving the Microsoft Dynamics GP implementation? NJW currently has a few major complaints/limitations:
    - The current system often crashes or performs extremely slowly when multiple users are in it at the same time.
    - The current financial reporting is not adequate for management.
    - The current inventory and sales reporting is not adequate for management and users.
    - Sales commission reports are currently put together manually and take a long time every month.
    - The existing system has no fixed assets functionality, and fixed assets are currently tracked in a complex Excel spreadsheet.
    - The existing system has no budgeting ability.
- **See the finish line**: What are the deliverables? Here are the goals that NJW has set for their implementation, with priorities on a scale of 1 to 5:
    - Allow up to 10 concurrent users in the system to start, with the possibility of up to 15 or 20 concurrent users within three years (Priority = 1).

  - Track fixed assets in the new system, not in Excel (Priority = 3).
  - Start using budgets (Priority = 4).
  - Allow some employees to access the system remotely (Priority = 5).
  - Create better reporting to help key personnel manage the company. This includes financial reporting as well as management and commissions reports (Priority = 1).
  - Create better numbering schemes for inventory items, vendors, and customers. There are currently many duplicates and some cleanup is needed (Priority = 2).

- **Document the workflows and gaps**: What are the steps taken for each transaction type and are there any gaps? Four gaps were identified for NJW:
  - Sales commissions are currently not entered as a payable or expense until the end of the month. Using the commissions functionality in Dynamics GP would allow commissions payables and expense entries to be recorded with each sale. NJW has determined this should be fine and will stay with the Dynamics GP functionality without any workarounds.
  - Customer invoices and statements available out-of-the-box in Dynamics GP will not meet NJW's requirements. Custom invoices and statements will be created in either Crystal Reports or SQL Server Reporting Services as part of the implementation.
  - For internal management purposes and collections, NJW wants to see the Receivables aging reports by due date. They also need to be able to send monthly aging reports to their lending bank, and the bank wants to see the aging by invoice date. Both cannot be set up at the same time in Dynamics GP—aging is either by due date or invoice date, but not both. As NJW internally may need variations on the aging reports and the bank report is static and once a month, the suggested solution to this is to set up Dynamics GP with aging by due date and create a custom report for the bank using either Crystal Reports or SQL Server Reporting Services.
  - While drop-ship functionality exists in Dynamics GP, it does not allow for invoicing a customer prior to posting the vendor invoice. This does not work with NJW's workflow. A tool called **Shipment Notification** is available from Microsoft to allow transferring drop-ship sales orders to invoices prior to receiving the vendor invoices. The tool will need to be tested, but should address this gap. Your Dynamics GP partner can help obtain this and other similar tools on PartnerSource: `http://bit.ly/13TIhe7` (requires **PartnerSource** access).

Depending on the length and complexity of the deliverables list that you identify during your planning, you may decide to split up your implementation into phases. For NJW, the implementation will be a success without budgeting capability and remote access. While they should plan for both budgeting and remote access, they can add them later after **Go Live**. In addition to this, while the fixed assets functionality is a priority, they can add it as a separate phase after Go Live.

# Identifying reporting needs

Reporting is often looked at as a by-product of an implementation, something that may need to be tweaked after the implementation is completed. Your implementation will be much more successful if you identify the reporting needs upfront and include reporting in your planning. There are three types of reports to consider: **financial statements**, **management reports**, and **business forms**. Let us look at each of these in more detail.

## Financial statements

Financial statements typically are run monthly, once the month is closed. Some companies also like to see interim financial statements throughout the month. The basic financial statements are **Balance Sheet**, **Profit and Loss Statement** (also called **P&L**, **Income Statement**, or **Statement of Operations**), and **Cash Flow**.

Most companies have many variations of financial statements, especially the Profit and Loss Statement. For example, NJW may want to have an overall company P&L as well as a separate P&L for their three revenue centers: hardware, software, and services. In addition, they would like to have an actual versus budget P&L once the budgeting functionality is in place.

As part of your planning, identify the following:

- A list of all financial statements needed.
- A sample of each financial statement, even if it does not exist today. An example in Excel or even sketched out manually is fine.
- A list of users that will need to run financial statements.
- A list of users that will be creating or modifying financial statements. (In many companies, this consists of only one or two people).

Pay particular attention to the variations of P&L's needed and also watch out for multiple control accounts on Balance Sheets. Both of these may cause you to change how you implement Dynamics GP, or lead to some further discussion and possible changes in accounting practices or reporting.

## Multiple control accounts on Balance Sheets

A **control account** is a General Ledger account that holds the summary of a **subledger**. The most common examples of control accounts are Accounts Payable, Accounts Receivable, Inventory, Cash, and Fixed Assets.

Dynamics GP has modules that are subledgers for each of these control accounts. However, **Cash** and **Fixed Assets** are the only two modules that allow for easy reconciliation of the subledger to multiple General Ledger accounts. While it is possible to have multiple **Accounts Payable** (**AP**), **Accounts Receivable** (**AR**), and **Inventory** accounts, the setup, reconciliation, and reporting for these can sometimes get very complicated.

If multiple control accounts for AP, AR, and Inventory are currently used, find out why. If the answer is "that's how we have always done it", then you have a good case for suggesting combining all the control accounts into one. It also may be that previous systems required the use of multiple control accounts to enable separate subledger reporting for them. Dynamics GP can most likely fill that requirement with existing subledger reports, thus eliminating the need for the multiple control accounts in the General Ledger.

For example, AR or AP aging and inventory stock status reports can be filtered by a Class ID assigned to each customer, vendor, or inventory item. So, if the NJW company needs to print separate reports for the hardware versus software inventory, this can all be handled in the Inventory subledger, with only one GL Inventory account. However, it may be that NJW needs to provide a monthly Balance Sheet to their bank, showing the hardware and software inventory as separate items. In that case, the answer may be that multiple control accounts are needed and should stay the way they are on the current financial statements. Make sure you keep this in mind as you continue planning.

## Variations of Profit and Loss Statements

There are two methods of grouping details on P&L's. One is to show separate line items for major groupings. For example, NJW sells hardware, software, and services. Therefore, they may want to see sales and costs on all P&L's broken out into these three categories:

| P&L - NJW | 2012 | 2013 |
|---|---|---|
| **SALES:** | | |
| Hardware | $12,577,910 | $11,486,676 |
| Software | 8,846,376 | 8,465,432 |
| Services | 1,540,528 | 1,532,864 |
| **Total Sales** | **22,964,815** | **21,484,972** |
| **COSTS:** | | |
| Hardware | 9,433,433 | 8,615,007 |
| Software | 6,015,536 | 5,756,494 |
| Services | 308,106 | 383,216 |
| **Total Costs** | **15,757,074** | **14,754,717** |
| **GROSS PROFIT:** | **7,207,741** | **6,730,255** |

The alternative to this is having one summary report:

| P&L - NJW - ALL | 2012 | 2013 |
|---|---|---|
| SALES | $22,964,815 | $21,484,972 |
| COSTS | 15,757,074 | 14,754,717 |
| GROSS PROFIT | **7,207,741** | **6,730,255** |

And then have individual sub-reports for each category:

| P&L - NJW - Hardware | 2012 | 2013 |
|---|---|---|
| SALES | $12,577,910 | $11,486,676 |
| COSTS | 9,433,433 | 8,615,007 |
| PROFIT | **3,144,478** | **2,871,669** |

| P&L - NJW - Software | 2012 | 2013 |
|---|---|---|
| SALES | $ 8,846,376 | $ 8,465,432 |
| COSTS | 6,015,536 | 5,756,494 |
| PROFIT | **2,830,840** | **2,708,938** |

| P&L - NJW - Services | 2012 | 2013 |
|---|---|---|
| SALES | $ 1,540,528 | $ 1,532,864 |
| COSTS | 308,106 | 383,216 |
| PROFIT | **1,232,423** | **1,149,648** |

Understanding all the variations required for reporting will help you plan the implementation, so spend some time talking with the management team to gather these requirements.

# Management reports

Management reports are just about every other report you can think of besides financial statements. Typical examples are Receivables Aging, Payables Aging, Inventory Stock Status, General Ledger Trial Balance, and Monthly Sales Summaries—by customer, salesperson, item, or by item type. Commission reports and lists of open customer orders or open purchase orders are also frequently requested.

These reports vary greatly from company to company and often will be a source of frustration for users. For example, sales commission reports commonly take hours to put together each month. There will also be wish-list reports that have been identified as helpful, but that currently no one knows how to obtain. Identifying these reports will be more challenging than the financial statements. Talk to the Accounting and Operations resources on your team about these and possibly spend some time interviewing end users to ask what reports would help them do their jobs more effectively.

Some management reports will be standard in any accounting package. However, you should not assume that Dynamics GP will have built-in reports that are the same as what your previous system had. We have seen many users coming from other systems be surprised at what is or is not included out-of-the-box in Dynamics GP.

As part of your planning, identify the following:

- A list of all management reports needed.
- An example of each report, even if they do not exist today. An Excel mockup or even something sketched out manually is fine.
- Any logic for these reports. For example, when there are lending relationships with banks, a company may need two different versions of their AR Aging report—one for the bank, aged by invoice date and a different one for internal use aged by due date.

# Business forms

Business forms is a common name for anything a company sends routinely to customers and vendors, and these typically have some more stringent requirements for formatting. Common examples of business forms are invoices, packing lists, picking tickets, customer statements, purchase orders, and payables checks. Some companies may only need a few forms, while others will need many business forms, with some variations of each one.

Companies will usually have a very clear idea of exactly how their business forms should look. Most of these will need to have the company logo; some companies will want everything in a particular font. Often, companies can use the Dynamics GP implementation as a chance to change things they are not entirely happy with on their business forms.

As part of your planning, identify the following:

- A list of all business forms and the variations that are needed.
- A sample or mockup of each report, even if they do not exist today.
- Any logic for these forms. For example, currently NJW has two different invoices, one for hardware and software, and another for services. They make sure to never put both types of items on the same invoice. The service invoices have detailed descriptions of the work performed. The hardware and software invoices have serial numbers and/or agreement numbers when applicable.

# Running two systems concurrently

Should you plan to run Dynamics GP at the same time as your old system for a period of time? The answer can depend on many variables. Some companies will absolutely insist on it and you will not be able to dissuade them. In that case, you really do not have a choice. However, most companies will listen to the advice of the implementer on this and you should be prepared to discuss the pros and cons.

## Pros

Running two systems simultaneously will provide the following benefits:

- Help identify any missing functionality, workflows, and reports that have been left out of the planning.
- Give the opportunity for additional time to address any missing items identified.
- Give the company management a sense of security. Running a new system concurrently with the old one will feel like a more conservative, safer decision to many people.

## Cons

The negative aspects of running two systems at the same time include the following:

- Up to triple the regular amount of work will be required from most users. They will need to:
    - Perform their regular daily work in the old system
    - Re-enter their regular daily work in the new system, making sure everything is entered in the exact same way (or whatever the new equivalent is)
    - Compare the new system to the old system, identify any differences and make adjustments where needed

  Asking most employees to take on this kind of additional work can have a detrimental effect on the overall morale in the company. It can also cause significant inefficiencies, and thus delays, during the time the two systems are run concurrently. In practical experience, I have also seen this cause both systems to end up being incorrect.

- The implementation timeframe becomes much longer. Usually to fully test a new system at the same time as still running the old system will require at least one or two months of running both systems.
- The implementation becomes much more costly. This is really a consequence of the previous two items, but cost is often a critical component of an implementation and deserves to be mentioned separately.

## Recommendation

In my experience, you can accomplish most Dynamics GP implementations without having to run two systems concurrently. At the very least, consider not running everything at the same time. For example, **General Ledger** and **Accounts Payable** are two fairly straightforward modules with high volume and low complexity that can be excluded from concurrent testing.

The following strategies will help implement Dynamics GP without running two systems concurrently:

- **Plan**: Planning is critical—spend more time on the planning and, if needed, testing functionality upfront. Whatever extra time this takes, it will still save many months of work when compared to running two concurrent systems.

- **Phase**: If there are many modules and a lot of functionality to replace, use a phased approach. For example, start with just the General Ledger and Accounts Payable. Next, add in Accounts Receivable and invoicing. You can add any new functionality not currently present in the old system after the existing functionality is replaced.
- **Train**: Spend the time to train the end users so they are comfortable with Dynamics GP and the tasks they will be performing. There is a fine line when deciding how much or how little to show users. Typical training classes always start with the setup and configuration of each module before getting to the transactions, reporting, and inquiries. Consider instead skipping the configuration and setup for most users, as they will not be the ones performing these tasks. For example, an accounts payable clerk will most likely never need to know how to perform setup for the Payables Management module, nor are they likely to even have security access to the setup windows. Also, consider briefly mentioning, but omitting from training, any tasks that are performed on a yearly basis. An example of this is the preparation of 1099s. By the time users actually need to do this, it will likely be many months after the training and they will need a refresher anyway. You can find a more detailed discussion on training methodology and recommendations in *Chapter 10, Training, Tools, and Next Steps*.
- **Support**: Many companies have had prior experience with various implementations where a system was installed, and that was the last that anyone saw of the implementation team. Plan to ensure good post Go Live support by making certain the budget includes this and the users expect it. This can go a long way to addressing the fear of not running two systems simultaneously.

# Populating data

During the planning of a Dynamics GP implementation, decisions should be made about what type of data needs to be populated into the system prior to, or possibly after, Go Live. Data can be grouped into three categories: **master data**, **historical data**, and **open transactions**. Each should be discussed in detail and planned for separately.

# Master data

Master data includes customers, vendors, inventory items, fixed assets, and General Ledger accounts. There is no question that you need to populate this data as part of the implementation. However, there are a few considerations you must plan for, such as where to get the data, how much of it has to be cleaned up or changed, and how to accomplish actually getting it into Dynamics GP.

Implementing a new ERP system is a great opportunity to re-examine the existing master data and do some renumbering or general cleanup. At this stage of the planning, you should put together a list of what master data needs to be populated into Dynamics GP and details about each type of data. Here is a sample list for the NJW company:

| Data Type | Approx. Count | Notes/Considerations/Tasks |
|---|---|---|
| General Ledger accounts | 200 | Overall, NJW is happy with their current Chart of Accounts. However, it may need to be re-examined to determine if anything is missing that would be needed to facilitate the desired financial statements. |
| Vendors | 700 | Many of the existing vendors are no longer used and there are many duplicates. NJW would like to perform significant cleanup of their vendor list prior to entering it into Dynamics GP. They would also like to revise the numbering scheme for vendors; currently, all are numeric only, which NJW feels is counterintuitive for users and the cause for the majority of the duplicates. |
| Customers | 2,000 | NJW has some customers in the current system that they have not worked with for a number of years, so a little cleanup may be required. The customer list is considerably cleaner than the vendor list; however, NJW may want to revise the numbering for customers (currently all numeric). |
| Inventory Items | 5,000 | Many of the current inventory items are obsolete and NJW is not very happy with the numbering scheme, which is all numeric. Significant cleanup will be required for inventory items. |
| Salespeople | 8 | This is a fairly straightforward and short list. However, NJW wants to make sure that salespeople are entered properly to facilitate commission calculations and reporting. |
| Fixed Assets | 300 | NJW is keeping their fixed assets list in Excel right now. Some minor cleanup may be needed, but the current list should be pretty much ready to use for importing into Dynamics GP. |

As part of the data gathering process for master data, you may find it helpful to ask for lists of the existing data. Looking at these will help you determine if there is additional data cleanup needed past what you already know. For example, some software packages keep the entire address for a customer or a vendor in one field. Dynamics GP has separate fields for three address lines plus city, state, zip, and country. If the address needs to be separated into individual fields for 2,000 customers and 700 vendors, that will require some time and effort and you should plan for it accordingly.

Once you have your list of master data and tasks, decide who will perform any cleanup or renumbering needed. Depending on the volume of each type of data, you should also decide how this data will be populated into Dynamics GP. For the sample list we created previously showing NJW's master data, the recommendation would be to import everything except the salespeople, which should be entered manually. Usually, the determination between whether to import or manually enter records depends on the combination of the total number of a particular type of data and how much cleanup is needed. Anything over 100 records may be a good candidate for importing.

Have a plan for how to handle master records that may be added during the implementation. For example, let's say you have the following plan:

- Export the list of vendors from the current system on June 9
- Have someone work on cleaning it up and renumbering it until June 15
- Import a new list of vendors into Dynamics GP on June 15
- Go Live will be on July 1

What happens if a new vendor is added between the export on June 9 and the Go Live on July 1? If a vendor needs to be added prior to the import into Dynamics GP, there may still be time to add them to the import list. If that is not an option or the vendor is added after the import is done, that vendor will need to be manually entered into Dynamics GP. Communicate this plan to the users that may be adding any new master records so they are aware that there will be an additional step needed for any new master records added during the implementation.

# Historical data

Historical data includes any transactions that have already been completed, paid, or settled. This data typically includes the following:

- Prior year General Ledger transactions
- Fully paid Accounts Payable transactions
- Received and invoiced Purchase Order Processing transactions
- Fully paid Accounts Receivable transactions
- Fulfilled and posted Sales Quotes, Orders, and Invoices
- Reconciled cash transactions
- Prior Inventory transactions

While all of this data can be imported into Dynamics GP during (or even after) your implementation, choose wisely when deciding how much historical data to bring in. Importing historical data generally adds a high level of complexity, time, and cost to implementations for what is usually determined to be of very little value as quickly as one or two months after the Go Live. Consider also any renumbering you may be planning as part of the implementation. Anything renumbered will need to be remapped prior to import, adding yet another time and cost component.

When discussing historical data with the implementation team, ask why each particular type of historical data may be needed. The following are the three most common reasons for importing historical data into Dynamics GP with some thoughts about each:

- **Looking up details on individual transactions**: If the historical data is needed for looking up individual transactions, then suggest keeping the old system available for this for a period of time after the Dynamics GP implementation. In my experience, after the first few months, details of individual transactions are very seldom needed, and thus if the old system is available for infrequent lookups, there is no need to import the detailed history into Dynamics GP.
- **Reporting**: The company may require reporting that includes past history either for General Ledger transactions, sales, purchases, or inventory movements. Most of this is only needed on a monthly basis in summary and there are options in most modules of Dynamics GP to enter historical summary data without having to import detailed transactions. Depending on where the existing data is and exactly what type of reporting is needed, creating a report that spans both the old system and Dynamics GP could be an option. Finally, it may be easier to create custom tables in Dynamics GP to store summary historical data for use in reporting.
- **Audits**: No matter how much historical data is imported, most audits for the first year after an ERP implementation will require going back to the old system for data. If any GL accounts, customers, vendors, or inventory numbers are changed during the Dynamics GP implementation, then any historical printed reports may not match up with what is in the new system. After spending a considerable amount of time to map and import the history, there may still be a need to revisit the old system. With that given, consider how much time and effort should be spent to import historical data into Dynamics GP.

The preceding discussion does not mean that you should not import any historical data. There are some situations where it is the right course of action. Certainly for the General Ledger, it is recommended that at least one or two years of summary data be imported to facilitate comparative financial reporting. However, consider all the implications and the effort needed carefully when deciding whether to import historical data and, if so, how much.

# Open transactions

Open transactions include all transactions not completed, paid, or fully applied by the cut-off date and any outstanding bank transactions after the last bank reconciliation. Open transactions also include all GL transactions for the open fiscal year. Cut-off dates should be determined for each module, and as much clean-up as possible should be done in the old system to prepare the data that will be exported and then populated into Dynamics GP.

Open transactions will be entered or imported into Dynamics GP as regular transactions, typically with a description indicating that they have been imported from the previous system. For every different type of transaction that needs to be populated, consider the following five questions:

- What is the process for exporting this data out of the old system? Is it straightforward to export the required data into an electronic file in a format you can use? If not, you need a plan to gather this data. Get samples of the export files for each type of data so that you can address any issues ahead of time and be prepared for any data manipulation that may be needed.
- Are there many old transactions that require cleanup? Consider any transactions over a few years old that are still open. If they need to be written off, perhaps it is better to do this in the old system. This work can start as soon as these items are identified, well ahead of the Dynamics GP implementation.
- Are there unapplied credit memos or payments that can be applied to open invoices? Looking at the sample lists you have gathered, are there invoices and credit memos or payments for the same customers or vendors that can be applied to each other? Plan to do this cleanup prior to exporting the final lists during your implementation.

- Taking all the cleanup into consideration, how many open transactions are left? The answer to this will determine whether to manually enter or import this type of transaction. Typically, anything under 100 transactions may be a good candidate for manual entry, especially for Purchase Order Processing and Sales Order Processing transactions, as they are usually fairly complex to import. Another determining factor should be how much importing experience the implementation team has versus how many resources are available to manually enter transactions. Some companies may also decide to use manual entry of open transactions as a way to complement user training during an implementation.
- What is a reasonable cut-off date? For each type of open transaction, determine when it would be practical to stop entering transactions into the old system and export the list for population into the new system.

Let's go through the typical list of open transactions and some additional considerations for each of the core modules in Dynamics GP and look at a few examples.

# General Ledger

The General Ledger is somewhat of a special case and almost always requires a combination of historical and open year data to be imported to facilitate comparative financial statements as well as ongoing inquiries. This is very straightforward in Dynamics GP, and importing the historical and open year data can be done at the same time.

For example, NJW wants to start using Dynamics GP on July 1, 2013. NJW is on a calendar fiscal year and plans to close June 2013 in their old system. They expect the 2012 fiscal year will have been audited and closed by Go Live. However, June's closing numbers will not be completed until sometime in July. NJW would also like to be able to print comparative financial reports going back to December 2010.

NJW has decided that with the old system available for lookups and audits through the beginning of 2013, there is no reason to spend the time and effort to import detailed 2013 GL transactions into Dynamics GP. Keeping in mind that the GL account numbers may change during the GP implementation, here is the task list for NJW's GL transactions:

- Create the 2010, 2011, 2012, and 2013 fiscal years in Dynamics GP.
- Export the ending 2010 GL account balances from the old system.
- Export the monthly GL account net changes for 2011, 2012, and 2013 (through May) from the old system.

- Once the new General Ledger Chart of Accounts is finalized, create a mapping of the old to new GL accounts.
- Update the exported 2010 ending balances and all the monthly net changes with the new GL account numbers.
- Import the ending balances as of December 31, 2010 and the net changes for each month of 2011, 2012, and 2013 through May 31, 2013 into Dynamics GP prior to Go Live.
- Import the June 2013 net change once the month of June is closed in the old system.
- Post all imported transactions and close the 2010, 2011, and 2012 years to update Retained Earnings and roll forward all the Balance Sheet account balances. This should be done one year at a time so that balances can be checked against previously generated financial statements and fixed if needed before closing each year. Even though some account numbers may change, at the summary level everything should match. For example, total assets on the Balance Sheet should be the same and the monthly net gain or loss should stay the same.

Starting to use Dynamics GP and then importing the General Ledger numbers for the month of June should not cause any problems, although correct financial reports and account balances for 2013 will not be available in Dynamics GP until all data has been imported.

General Ledger balances and net changes are typically straightforward to export out of the previous system. However, this is definitely something to check, as it may require additional work. The minimum data columns needed to enter or import GL transactions into Dynamics GP are:

- **Transaction Date**: If importing monthly net changes, use the last day of the month. If your fiscal periods are not calendar months, use the last day of each fiscal period.
- **Account Number**: Use the new GL account number in Dynamics GP if you are changing account numbers.
- **Amount**: This can either be one column with positive numbers for debits and negatives for credits, or two separate columns, one for debits and another for credits.

# Payables Management

Open transactions for **Payables Management** include all unpaid or not fully applied payables transactions as of the cut-off date.

> The open portion of these transactions is what is still unpaid or unapplied. If an invoice was originally $5,000, but you have already paid $2,500 of it, this invoice should be brought into Dynamics GP as $2,500.

One option that companies may consider is entering summary open balances into Dynamics GP. This method results in one transaction per vendor for the entire balance due to that vendor, whether that is made up of one invoice or fifteen. This is not recommended as it is usually necessary to specify what invoices are being paid on each check to a vendor, which will not be possible with this method. So the time saved by this approach will be used up by constantly referring to the old system for details. Best practice is to import an individual transaction into Dynamics GP for every existing unpaid transaction in the current system.

The following are the minimum data columns needed and some important notes for entering or importing payables transactions into Dynamics GP:

- **Vendor ID**: This will be the new Vendor ID in Dynamics GP. If you have decided to change these, after exporting the data from the current system, you will need to update all the transactions with the new Vendor IDs.
- **Transaction Date**: If you have a number of old transactions that are still open, you may want to consider using the first date of the earliest year you have set up in GP and entering a note with the actual date. For example, if you have a transaction dated May 25, 2008 and the first year set up in Dynamics GP will be 2010, use January 1, 2010 as the date for this transaction. This will avoid any possible issues caused by having transactions in non-existing years. You can add the original date from the old system into a Note or Description field.
- **Transaction Type**: It is recommended to only import Invoices and Credit Memos. If you have unapplied payments, enter them as credit memos. Entering payments will cause unwanted transactions to be created in the Bank Reconciliation module that will have to be cleaned up afterwards.
- **Document Number**: This will typically be the invoice number, but some systems allow you to have transactions without a number or duplicate transaction numbers per vendor. The transaction number is required in Dynamics GP and should be unique per vendor.

> You can keep track of a reference or invoice number from the old system for each transaction in the Description or Note.

- **Amount**: Dynamics GP will not accept a negative transaction amount. The transaction type controls whether you owe the vendor or the vendor owes you. If your current system allows for negative amounts on invoices, you will need to enter these into Dynamics GP as credit memos. Remember that the amount should be the open balance for each transaction and not the original amount.
- **Currency ID**: If using Multicurrency, the currency of the transaction is needed. If not using Multicurrency, this is not required.

## Receivables Management

If you are planning to use the Sales Order Processing module, it may be tempting to import detailed line items for open receivables invoices. This is certainly an option, although most companies do not choose to do this because it will typically lead to a lot of extra and possibly unneeded work. Instead, all open balances are typically brought into the Dynamics GP Receivables Management module without any line item detail. The considerations and options for receivables transactions are very similar to those for payables transactions.

The following is a list of the minimum information required and some additional guidelines for importing or entering receivables transactions into Dynamics GP:

- **Customer ID**: This will be the new Customer ID in Dynamics GP. If you have decided to change these, after exporting the data from the current system, you will need to update all the transactions with the new Customer IDs.
- **Transaction Date**: If you have a number of old transactions that are still open, you may want to consider using the first date of the earliest year you have set up in Dynamics GP. You can add the original date from the old system into a Note or Description field.
- **Transaction Type**: It is recommended to only import Invoices, Debit Memos, Credit Memos, or Returns. Credit memos and returns are almost identical, both indicate a negative receivable. For statistical and reporting purposes, it may be useful to separate them. The same idea applies to invoices and debit memos. Both indicate that the customer owes the company money, but may be useful to separate different types of transactions. If you have unapplied payments, enter them as credit memos. Entering payments will cause unwanted transactions to be created in the Bank Reconciliation module that will have to be cleaned up afterwards.

- **Number**: This will typically be the invoice or credit memo number from the current system. Some systems allow for transactions without a number, especially for debit and credit memos, or they allow for duplicate transaction numbers. Dynamics GP requires transaction numbers and these must be unique per receivables transaction type (not just per customer).

> You can keep track of a reference or invoice number from the old system for each transaction in the Description or Note.

- **Amount**: This has to be a positive number, as Dynamics GP will not accept a negative number. The transaction type will control whether the customer owes you or you owe the customer. If your old system allows for negative amounts on an invoice, this will need to be entered into Dynamics GP as a credit memo or return. Keep in mind that the amount should be the open balance on each transaction and not the original amount.
- **Currency ID**: If using Multicurrency, the currency of the transaction is needed. If not using Multicurrency, this is not required.

## Inventory

Existing inventory quantities will need to be populated into Dynamics GP. In an ideal situation, a physical inventory count would be performed prior to the implementation. However, this is not always possible at the time of the implementation, so use the current system, or whatever inventory tracking methods are available, to export the existing inventory quantities and populate them into Dynamics GP.

It is recommended to enter or import inventory quantities prior to entering any new Sales Order Processing transactions. The following are the required fields for entering or importing inventory quantities into Dynamics GP:

- **Date**: This should be the date of the inventory export or stock count.
- **Item Number**: If inventory item numbering changes as part of your implementation, you will need to update these with the new Item Numbers for Dynamics GP.
- **Unit of Measure**: This may be optional if the default unit of measure for the item is set up in Dynamics GP and that is what is being used for the transaction.
- **Site ID**: This is the warehouse or inventory location in Dynamics GP where the item is located. If only one inventory location will be set up in Dynamics GP, this can defaulted and does not need to be part of the import.

- **Quantity**: Quantity in the unit of measure specified.
- **Unit Cost**: The unit cost per item in the unit of measure specified.

> Changing accounting systems may seem like a good time to change your inventory valuation methods. Before considering anything like this, you will want to check with your auditors and/or tax consultants to make sure this will conform to GAAP and IRS regulations.

# Purchase Order Processing

If purchase orders were used in the old system, there will typically be a number of open (not yet received) purchase orders. Depending on how many open POs there are and how many line items are on them, a decision needs to be made on whether to populate these into the **Purchase Order Processing** (**POP**) module in Dynamics GP and, if so, whether to enter them manually or import them. If open purchase orders are not entered into Dynamics GP, it will still be possible to enter receipts and invoices for these POs as they are received.

If you are bringing in open purchase orders into Dynamics GP, keep in mind that both the vendor and inventory item numbering may have been changed. A decision will also be needed as to whether to enter only line items that were not received yet or all line items. The recommendation is to only enter line items and quantities that have not yet been received. Even though the resulting POs may not accurately reflect the original POs, this will save a lot of time in updating the inventory and PO statuses, and will easily allow for accurate reporting on open PO items only.

There are many details that can be entered or imported for purchase orders. The following are the minimum data columns required for POs in Dynamics GP:

- **PO Number**: Even if you start a new numbering scheme for purchase orders in Dynamics GP, this should be the existing PO number. PO numbers in Dynamics GP must be unique.
- **Vendor ID**: This will be the new Vendor ID in Dynamics GP.
- **PO Date**: The date that was printed on the purchase order.
- **Currency ID**: If using Multicurrency, the currency of the transaction is needed. If not using Multicurrency, this is not required.
- **Item Number**: If item numbering will change as part of your implementation you will need to update these with the new Dynamics GP Item Numbers.
- **Unit of Measure**: This may be optional if the default purchasing unit of measure for the item is set up in Dynamics GP and that is what is on the PO.

- **Site ID**: This is the warehouse or inventory location in Dynamics GP where the item will be received. This can also be defaulted if there is only one location.
- **Quantity**: The recommendation is to enter the remaining (not yet received) quantity only.
- **Unit Cost**: The unit cost per item in the unit of measure specified.

# Sales Order Processing

Any open customer sales orders, back orders, or quotes in the old system can be entered into the **Sales Order Processing** (**SOP**) module in Dynamics GP. Similar to purchase orders, SOP orders, back orders, and quotes are not required to be able to enter sales invoices into Dynamics GP. If bringing in open SOP transactions, decisions will need to be made as to whether to import or enter manually, and what exactly to bring in for partially fulfilled transactions.

It is recommended to enter or import open SOP transactions after inventory quantities have been populated into Dynamics GP so that any back order or inventory availability issues can be avoided. There are many details that can be imported for SOP transactions. The following is the minimum information needed for SOP transactions in Dynamics GP:

- **Customer ID**: This will be the new Customer ID in Dynamics GP if customers' numbers have been changed.
- **Bill To Address ID**: This will default from the customer if not specified. Note this is not the actual address, but an address ID, so the addresses will need to be populated for customers for this to work.
- **Ship To Address ID**: This will default from the customer if not specified. This can be the actual address instead of the address ID; in that case this address will be stored with the transaction only and may or may not exist on the customer record in Dynamics GP.
- **Date**: The date of the transaction.
- **Transaction Type**: Hopefully, it is possible to post all Invoices and Returns in the old system prior to cutover. In that case, only Quotes, Orders, or Back Orders will need to be entered or imported into Dynamics GP.
- **Document Number**: This is required in Dynamics GP and has to be unique per transaction type.
- **Currency ID**: If using Multicurrency, the currency of the transaction is needed. If not using Multicurrency, this is not required.
- **Item Number**: If items are renumbered as part of your implementation this will need to be the new Dynamics GP Item Number.

- **Unit of Measure**: This may be optional if the default selling unit of measure for the item is set up in Dynamics GP and that is what is being used.
- **Site ID**: This is the warehouse or inventory location in Dynamics GP that the item will ship from. This can also be defaulted if there is only one location.
- **Quantity**: For any partially fulfilled orders or back orders, the recommendation is to only enter the remaining quantity to ship.
- **Unit Price**: The unit price per item in the unit of measure specified.

# Bank Reconciliation

Any outstanding or unreconciled bank transactions will need to be populated into the Dynamics GP **Bank Reconciliation** module if it is part of your implementation. In most cases, bank statements are monthly and companies can download statements from the bank on the first of the following month to finish reconciling their cash quickly. If planning to use Bank Reconciliation, it is recommended that you do this from the start. For companies that have a lot of bank accounts and a high volume of transactions, not starting to use Bank Reconciliation from the onset will typically cause a lot of frustration and additional work when the decision is made to start using the module.

Often, we find that bank reconciliations are being done manually (in Excel) with the older accounting systems. This should make it easy to obtain the outstanding transaction list. The following lists the information required for entry or import of bank transactions:

- **Transaction Type**: It is recommended to only use the following:
    - **Check**: Transactions that will show up on the bank statement with a check number.
    - **Withdrawal**: Transactions that will show up as cash coming out of the bank account, but not a check. Typically, this is used for wires, as well as any electronic payments or bank fees that are not entered through payables.
    - **Decrease Adjustments**: Any money coming out of the bank account that might need to be differentiated from checks or withdrawals. This is not used too often.
    - **Increase Adjustments**: For outstanding transactions, use this to record any money coming into the bank account. This will avoid having to go through an additional step of depositing these transactions in Dynamics GP.

- **Transaction Date**: For checks, this should be the date the check was written. For all other transactions, it should be the date the cash was withdrawn from or deposited into the bank account.
- **Checkbook ID**: The Dynamics GP equivalent of a bank account. Every bank account will have a unique Checkbook ID.
- **Number**: For checks this should be the check number, for other transactions this is typically a reference number assigned to the transaction. While Dynamics GP will allow non-unique numbers for bank transactions, I recommend using something that will help quickly identify these transactions during back statement reconciliation. If this is not present in the old system, you can come up with a simple numbering scheme to use. For example, a monthly bank fee on June 30, 2013 can be `130630 BANK FEE`.
- **Paid to/Received from**: An optional field, but highly recommended as it is helpful to have this information available for lookups and searches in Dynamics GP.
- **Amount**: This should be the outstanding amount, although for bank transactions this will most likely be the same as the original transaction amount. All amounts should be positive, as the transaction type determines whether the money is coming in or going out of the bank account.

Have a plan for what to do if an open transaction needs to be added after the cut-off date. This is often needed for payables checks—a check may need to be cut right away and this can happen after the payables open transactions have been exported from the current system and are being prepared for import. Any transaction needed after the cut-off will need to be entered into both the old system and Dynamics GP in the same way. Communicate this to any users that may need to enter transactions and make sure they know to keep detailed records of any transactions like this so they can be entered into Dynamics GP once it is available.

# How to import

After all of the discussion about whether to manually enter or import data, you may be wondering how to actually accomplish importing data into Dynamics GP.

The recommended tool for importing master data, historical data, and open transactions into Dynamics GP during an implementation is **Integration Manager**. Integration Manager is a separately installed application that imports data into Dynamics GP while preserving the same business logic as if you were manually entering that data using the Dynamics GP user interface. Integration Manager does not require any coding and is generally geared towards a technical end user. The limitations of Integration Manager include speed (it may take considerable time to import large sets of data) and a limited number of master data and transaction types that are available for importing.

Any new license of Dynamics GP sold currently includes a 240-day conversions license for Integration Manager. For situations where Dynamics GP was purchased previously and you are either past that initial 240 days after purchase or are performing a reimplementation, Integration Manager can be purchased separately. With the new Perpetual Licensing for Microsoft Dynamics GP 2013 it is part of the **Customization Pack**. Detailed instructions for using Integration Manager to import data into Dynamics GP are provided in *Chapter 9, Populating Initial Data*.

Other options available for importing data into Dynamics GP are:

| Tool/Method | How it is sold | Basic explanation and recommendations |
|---|---|---|
| Tool: eConnect | This is sold as part of the Customization Pack with Dynamics GP 2013 | eConnect is ideal for setting up recurring data imports that are scheduled or triggered by an event (such as new data being available in a specified location or table). eConnect is also better suited for importing large volumes of transactional data and is much faster than Integration Manager. To use eConnect, a fair amount of programming will be required and it is not recommended for one time or infrequent imports. |
| Tool: Table Import | No purchase needed—tool included with any purchase of Dynamics GP | Table Import provides some basic guidelines for importing data into Dynamics GP, so the import is somewhat easier than importing directly into SQL Server tables. However, business logic is not checked and knowledge of the Dynamics GP table structure is required to perform imports. Table Import is only recommended for non-transactional data and when Integration Manager or eConnect are not available. |
| Method: import directly into SQL Server tables | No purchase necessary—use SQL Server Management Studio to import directly into tables | Importing directly into the SQL Server tables is only recommended when there are no other options. Thorough knowledge of Dynamics GP tables is required and extensive testing should be performed. Importing directly into SQL Server tables is only recommended for non-transactional data and when Integration Manager or eConnect are not available. |

There is no reason that a company cannot mix and match importing tools as needed. You may find that Integration Manager is the best tool for the initial implementation and some ongoing imports. For future projects, you may decide to add eConnect as a more automated import tool.

# Training

Training users is a critical component of any ERP system implementation and should be planned for accordingly. Best practices for training include:

- **Plan training close to the Go Live date**: Training users a month before they start using a new system is not very effective. It is also better to train users after Dynamics GP is already installed so they can experiment with the sample company and look at the screens in the system.
- **Plan to retrain**: Having to retrain users does not mean that the initial training was not a success. Repetition helps people learn. Typically, following the Go Live, many of the topics covered in the initial training will need to be revisited. In fact, some companies choose to have the bulk of their training right after the Go Live, so that users can start learning with their own data and real transactions.
- **Don't train everyone on everything**: Most end users of a system do not need to go through any of the setup, maintenance, or troubleshooting training. Separate your training sessions by roles or job activities. Very few users, if any, will need to be part of all the training sessions.
- **Keep the training sessions reasonable**: After a few hours in a training session, most users lose interest and end up not retaining the content. Schedule training sessions for two to three hours at a time.
- **Get a knowledgeable trainer**: If there is no available resource that understands Dynamics GP well, find a trainer for this. This may be a good role for the Dynamics GP resource on your team. If bringing in an external trainer, make sure you give them enough information about the company and your Dynamics GP implementation so they are able to tailor the training accordingly.

Do not skimp on the training—well-trained users are much more productive. For a more detailed discussion on the training topics mentioned previously, please refer to *Chapter 10, Training, Tools, and Next Steps*.

# Implementation timeline

Using what you have learned in this chapter, you should now be able to start putting together a list of implementation tasks with dates. First, the implementation team will need to determine the Go Live date. The best Go Live dates are during the slow season for a company and when there are no vacations planned for the members of the implementation team or the accounting system users. This may mean that January 1 is not a great Go Live date, as there are too many distractions and vacations at that time of the year.

Once you choose a Go Live date, start there and work backwards. Try to keep in mind the amount of work needed for each task and the resources needed. For example, cleaning up and renumbering a list of 2,000 customers or 5,000 inventory items may take some significant time and you should allot more time to that task than cleaning up 200 vendors. In addition, if the same resource needs to perform multiple cleanup tasks, they will not be able to do them at the same time, so you may need to either get creative and split up some of the work or allot more time for it.

If you are comfortable working with Microsoft Office Project or a similar application for your planning, that is certainly a suitable tool. However, I have seen many implementations that simply utilize Excel with great success. Choose a tool or application that you are comfortable with and that will be available to other members of your implementation team.

A sample task list with dates for our NJW sample company is as follows:

| Task | Description | Start Date | Finish By |
|---|---|---|---|
| Chart of Accounts | Clean up, renumber and import General Ledger accounts | May-17-2013 | Jun-01-2013 |
| AP Checks | Order check stock for printing Dynamics GP payables checks | Jun-01-2013 | Jun-01-2013 |
| Vendors | Clean up, renumber and import vendor master records | Jun-09-2013 | Jun-15-2013 |
| Customers | Clean up, renumber and import customer master records | Jun-10-2013 | Jun-16-2013 |
| Inventory Items | Clean up, renumber and import inventory master records | Jun-09-2013 | Jun-17-2013 |
| GL import | Import GL balances through May 2013 | Jun-11-2013 | Jun-18-2013 |
| AP cleanup | In old system, write off any old payables transactions and apply as many unapplied credit memos and payments as possible | Jun-07-2013 | Jun-24-2013 |
| AP open transactions | Import open payables transactions | Jun-25-2013 | Jun-25-2013 |
| Business forms | Create or modify any business forms required | Jun-01-2013 | Jun-27-2013 |
| AR cleanup | In old system, write off any old receivables transactions and apply as many unapplied credit memos and payments as possible | Jun-07-2013 | Jun-27-2013 |
| AR open transactions | Import open receivables transactions | Jun-28-2013 | Jun-28-2013 |
| Open POs | Enter open POs | Jun-29-2013 | Jun-29-2013 |
| Inventory | Import item quantities | Jun-28-2013 | Jun-29-2013 |

| Task | Description | Start Date | Finish By |
|---|---|---|---|
| Open SOP transactions | Enter open customer quotes, orders, or back orders | Jun-29-2013 | Jun-30-2013 |
| Financial statements | Create financial statements | Jun-01-2013 | Jun-30-2013 |
| Go Live | Start using Dynamics GP with the following modules: General Ledger, Payables Management, Receivables Management, Inventory, POP, SOP, and Bank Reconciliation | Jul-01-2013 | Jul-01-2013 |
| Cash open transactions | Import or enter outstanding cash transactions as of June 30, 2013 | Jul-05-2013 | Jul-05-2013 |
| Training | User training | Jun-21-2013 | Jul-09-2013 |
| Post Go Live support | Provide support for users as they start using Dynamics GP | Jul-01-2013 | Jul-09-2013 |
| Management reports | Create or modify any management reports needed | Jun-01-2013 | Jul-23-2013 |
| June GL import | Import or enter June 2013 net change for the General Ledger | Jul-22-2013 | Jul-23-2013 |
| Budgeting | Set up and import budgets | Jul-19-2013 | Aug-02-2013 |
| Budget reporting | Add budgets to financial statements | Aug-03-2013 | Aug-06-2013 |
| Fixed Assets | Setup, import, and start using Fixed Assets | Jul-26-2013 | Aug-20-2013 |
| Remote access | Set up remote access for Dynamics GP users | Aug-09-2013 | Aug-31-2013 |

The preceding list is sorted by **Finish By** date for illustration purposes. You may prefer to sort yours by **Start Date** instead. In addition to the columns shown, you should add columns to your list showing who is responsible for each of the tasks.

# Summary

In this chapter, we have discussed how to put together an implementation team and start planning your Microsoft Dynamics GP implementation. We went over important planning concepts and questions including reporting requirements, training, and the pros and cons of running two systems concurrently. Details of importing different types of data and the various import tools and methods available were outlined. We also introduced a sample company and put together a sample implementation task list.

In the next chapter, we will continue our implementation planning by delving into the details of the Dynamics GP.

# 3

# Planning – Dynamics GP System

Now that you have put together your business requirements, you should plan out the details of your Dynamics GP system. In this chapter, we will go over the second implementation planning phase and focus on the following topics:

- How many companies to set up in Dynamics GP
- Integration with other systems
- General Ledger account framework and account format
- Numbering schemes for master records
- Fiscal year and period setup
- Users and security planning
- Sales and purchase tax setup
- Additional setup considerations including shipping methods, payment terms, credit cards, posting setup, and multicurrency

## Companies in Dynamics GP

A critical decision that is very difficult to change after implementation is whether or not to have multiple companies in Dynamics GP. Sometimes there is no question, as there is only one company or there are clearly separate entities. However, often there are multiple legal entities, branches, or subsidiaries that may not only require separate accounting records and procedures but also share customers or inventory items.

There is no limit on the number of companies you can setup in Dynamics GP. Each company created becomes a separate SQL Server database and behaves autonomously, except for a few shared characteristics global to the entire Dynamics GP installation, such as system users, currency setup, and exchange rate tables.

There are situations when separate companies are clearly recommended in Dynamics GP:

- If accounting records must be kept in different functional currencies to conform to local requirements
- When using Dynamics GP Payroll and there are different Federal ID Numbers
- If there are entities that have different fiscal periods
- Some types of business entities require separate accounting books to be kept to comply with various federal and state regulations

If the requirement is simply to keep separate General Ledger accounts for each separate entity, this is fairly easy to accomplish within one Dynamics GP company/database. In some situations, there is no right or wrong answer as to whether to have one or multiple Dynamics GP companies; the following sections will discuss the benefits of the two approaches in more detail.

# Benefits of having one company in Dynamics GP

The benefits of having one company in Dynamics GP are as follows:

- **Initial company setup is faster**: Even if there are different General Ledger accounts for multiple entities within one company, significant time can be saved by only having one Dynamics GP company to set up.
- **Ongoing maintenance and support are simpler**: Multiple companies add on-going incremental time, and thus cost, to maintenance and support. Even though many maintenance tasks can be automated, monitoring and support is simpler for a single company database. Any changes, service packs, or additional products installed may need to be performed separately for each company. Upgrades will typically take less time for one large company database than multiple smaller ones.

- **Less storage space is needed**: Having multiple databases in SQL Server increases the storage space needed because each separate database will have some duplicated overhead. Also, keep in mind that each additional company will require added capacity for backups. This benefit may not be so important anymore, with storage being much more affordable than it has been in the past, but it is still something to consider.
- **Yearly processing is faster**: Yearly closing for various modules only has to be done once if there is one Dynamics GP company. Other yearly company-specific tasks, such as creating new fiscal years and yearly budgets, will take less time with one company.
- **Reporting is simpler**: Typically, creating reports for one company takes significantly less time. There are no built-in multiple-company reports in Dynamics GP for the core modules discussed in this book.
- **Ability to share vendors, customers, and inventory items**: Dynamics GP does offer an Intercompany module, but it is fairly limited. For example, there is no way in Dynamics GP to sell an inventory item from one company to a customer in another company. There are third-party add-on products that can help mitigate this somewhat, however it is still much more straightforward to have everything in one company if resources need to be shared often.
- **Imports and integrations with other systems may be simpler**: As a general rule, imports and integrations with other systems are easier to set up and maintain with only one Dynamics GP company.
- **Availability of additional products or modules is not limited**: There may be some modules or products that will not support multiple Dynamics GP companies easily. Having one company will obviate any concerns about this.
- **Additional licensing costs**: Dynamics GP licensing is for concurrent users, so one user logged into three different companies at the same time will use three concurrent licenses out of the total available. If users will routinely need to be in multiple companies, this may result in significant additional licensing costs.

# Benefits of having multiple companies in Dynamics GP

The following is a list of the benefits of multiple companies in Dynamics GP:

- **Very clear delineation between companies**: All the records for each entity are clearly separated. Having multiple companies makes it more difficult to enter something in the wrong company.

- **Ability to separate vendors, customers, and inventory items**: This is the flip side to not being able to share vendors, customers, and inventory items and may be a benefit rather than a hindrance, depending on your requirements. For example, if your customers consider your divisions or subsidiaries to be separate companies, they would expect to receive separate statements from each company and pay each separately. Having all the transactions in one Dynamics GP company could make it very difficult to accomplish that separation without a lot of customization.
- **Security**: Additional security options are a direct result of the ability to separate vendors, customers, and inventory items. Consider a situation where you acquire a subsidiary and do not want all of your newly acquired employees to see any of the General Ledger details, customer information, or inventory details from your main company. With only one Dynamics GP company, it is impossible to achieve this without significant customizations, but a separate Dynamics GP company automatically accomplishes this.
- **Ability to perform yearly closing at different times**: This could be a benefit if the accounting and yearly closing procedures and timing vary for the different entities.
- **Different setup options possible for each company**: An example of this may be different receivables aging buckets needed or aging performed a different way for different business entities. The only way to accomplish this within one Dynamics GP company is with custom reporting. However different companies make this a non-issue.

Whether to set up one or multiple companies is a topic that should be carefully considered when planning your Dynamics GP implementation. If you are not sure of the proper approach for your specific situation, carefully go through your business requirements, as well as legal and other governmental regulations, and speak to your Dynamics GP resource in detail to help determine the best course of action.

Once the decision is made, you will need to have a company name and a database name for each company you are planning to set up:

- **Company name**: Maximum of 65 characters. This is what users will see when they log into Dynamics GP and are presented with a list of companies. It will also be what is defaulted at the top of most reports to identify the company, and what shows on every window when using Dynamics GP. Even though 65 characters are possible, it is recommended to keep this shorter, as only 35 characters will typically fit on the login screen. If you are planning to create multiple Dynamics GP companies, make the names different enough so that there is no confusion for users (for example, Not Just Widgets, Incorporated).

- **Database name**: Maximum of five characters. This will be the SQL Server database name. It should be alphanumeric and cannot start with a number or have special characters. While most end users may never see the database name, more technical users and system administrators may use it quite often, and it may be seen on reports and used for some setup steps (for example, NJW).

# Integration with other systems

Are there existing systems in place that your Dynamics GP system will need to integrate with? A good example of this in many companies is a sophisticated web application already in place for customer orders and billing. Other examples may be systems for employee time tracking, fixed assets, or shipping software.

> Excel spreadsheets, no matter how complex, are not usually considered existing systems. Existing systems are typically other database applications or separately purchased software packages to accomplish specific tasks.

If there are existing systems in place, part of the implementation planning will be to decide whether to keep these systems and integrate them with Dynamics GP, or replace the functionality with Dynamics GP. Other approaches may be hybrids of these, keep some existing systems but replace others, or keep existing systems for now and replace their functionality with Dynamics GP in a more phased approach, one at a time, after the implementation.

To help decide on the best approach, ask the following questions, keeping in mind that the goal, whenever possible, should be a single data entry point:

- **How well does the existing system fulfill the current requirements?** If the system is not meeting today's business needs, maybe because the requirements have changed significantly in the ten years since it was implemented, then it is a good candidate for replacement. However, if the existing system is accomplishing what is needed, even if a few small tweaks are needed, it may be more prudent to keep it.
- **How easy would it be to integrate the current system with Dynamics GP?** There are three parts to this question:
    - Would it be fairly straightforward to import data from the current system into Dynamics GP? Or would considerable work be needed?
    - Does the data flow need to go one way only (from existing system to Dynamics GP), or does it need to be bidirectional? If bidirectional, what is the process of importing data into the existing system?

    - How timely does the integration have to be? Should new data be imported into or out of Dynamics GP monthly, weekly, daily, or real-time?

  If the data import is fairly straightforward and one of the existing Dynamics GP import tools can be used, that would make a decision to keep an existing system in place more viable. If creating the integration would require considerable work and real-time integration is needed, it may be a good candidate for replacement. This is especially true if the existing system is not meeting all the current requirements.

- **What would be the cost of replacing the functionality with Dynamics GP?** While the existing system may be sufficient, it may also be fairly easy to duplicate its functionality with Dynamics GP. If that is the case, the decision should be based on the comparison of the cost of duplicating the functionality in Dynamics GP (which may involve an additional module purchase or customization), and creating and maintaining the integration. In this situation, even if the cost of moving the functionality to Dynamics GP is slightly higher upfront, it is better to not keep the existing system. Having only one system to maintain will pay for itself in the long run and will also result in increased end user satisfaction.
- **Will keeping the existing system prevent any planned upgrades?** The current system may be performing perfectly and meeting all the business needs. However, it may be a custom application that is no longer supported or one that has a very costly upgrade path to move to new operating systems, versions of SQL Server, or some other planned technology upgrade. This may make it a good candidate for replacement with a phased approach, after the Dynamics GP implementation.

Once these questions are answered, compare the cost and time of keeping the current systems, and creating integrations, with the cost and time of replacing them. Keep in mind that there are many third-party (also called Independent Software Vendor or ISV) add-ons available for Dynamics GP, even if the functionality needed is not available in Dynamics GP out-of-the-box.

# General Ledger Chart of Accounts

The key building block of the Dynamics GP system is the General Ledger account. Prior to installing Dynamics GP, you will need to determine your **Account framework** and **Account format**.

# Account framework

The account framework sets the maximums and sorting options that will be available for all your Dynamics GP companies.

Dynamics GP allows the following maximums for the account framework:

- Up to 10 account segments.
- Up to 66 characters, not including separators between segments.
- Maximum of 82 bytes. Bytes are calculated as the length of each segment plus 1 for each segment with an odd number of characters, or plus 2 for each segment with an even number of characters. For example, an account framework with 7 segments of 6 characters and 3 segments of 8 characters will have 86 bytes: ((6+2) * 7) + ((8+2) * 3) and thus will not be allowed.

In the past, there may have been space considerations that would justify limiting the account framework chosen when installing Dynamics GP. This is usually not the case anymore and even if a 10 segment General Ledger account will never be needed, a typical account framework is the following: maximum of 66 characters and 10 segments of six characters each.

> Even though this only adds up to 60 characters, this is fine, as 66 is simply the maximum. Having a standard account framework simplifies setting up development environments and moving installations in the future.

The main reason to think about the account framework at this stage is if you foresee needing account segments longer than six characters. You will need to make sure that the account framework selected when you install Dynamics GP encompasses the maximum General Ledger account length you will need. Changing the account framework after the Dynamics GP installation is possible, but not trivial and would require an additional tool or service to be purchased.

# Account format

The General Ledger account format can be different for each Dynamics GP company, as long as it is within the account framework defined during the Dynamics GP installation.

General Ledger accounts can be alphanumeric and Dynamics GP will add a separator character of your choosing in-between the segments. While the separator can be different for each company, the most commonly used separator is a dash (-).

Even though Dynamics GP will allow for a very long GL account number and it may be tempting to track many details in the General Ledger, this is not recommended. Most Dynamics GP windows will only display approximately 25 characters without having to scroll to see the entire account. Best practice is to keep the account number to three or four segments and a total of not more than 15 or 20 characters, including the separators.

Here are examples of some common account formats:

| Account | Segment details |
|---|---|
| 4000-100-10 | Natural account - Division (or Cost center) - Location |
| 01-5050-250-00 | Company (Entity) - Natural account - Subaccount - Department |
| 03-62100-000 | Location - Natural account - Subaccount |
| 5100-60-05-10110 | Natural account - Department - Region - Cost center |

At this stage of your implementation planning, you should decide on the account format for each Dynamics GP company planned and start putting together your General Ledger Chart of Accounts. If you are planning on multiple Dynamics GP companies and will need consolidated financial reports or other multi-company reports based on GL account numbers, it is highly recommended that all the companies have the same account format and that the Chart of Accounts be as similar as possible.

Additional notes for General Ledger Chart of Accounts in Dynamics GP:

- You do not need to create roll-up accounts in Dynamics GP. You can accomplish any roll-ups needed when you set up the financial statements. With the **Account Rollup** functionality in Dynamics GP you can create roll-ups for inquiries without having to define separate accounts for them. For example, if there are four individual accounts for travel expenses (Airline, Lodging, Car, and Other Travel), there is no need to create a fifth account called Travel.
- All General Ledger accounts should be predefined ahead of time. It is not enough to create a list of all natural accounts and a list of all possible values for each of your other segments. Although you can create accounts on the fly, this is not recommended because most users are typically not given the security to create GL accounts and there is a high potential for errors and inconsistencies when this is done.
- It is not recommended to have spaces in your GL account numbers. Spaces will make using the account numbers difficult for users and may also cause reporting issues, as reporting tools may interpret spaces differently. Instead of spaces, use zeros.

- The General Ledger account name can have a maximum length of up to 50 characters and you can change it at any time.

When creating the Chart of Accounts, keep in mind the reporting requirements you have identified during your business requirements planning. Try to keep accounts that will be in the same groupings on the Balance Sheet and Profit and Loss Statements together, leaving enough room for inserting accounts in the future.

The following table lists the minimum data required for General Ledger account setup:

| Data | Details | Example |
|---|---|---|
| Account Number | This should be the entire account number, including separators. | 4000-100-10 |
| Account Name | String with a maximum of 50 characters. It is recommended to make the account name (referred to as Account Description in Dynamics GP) as complete as possible to help users find the appropriate account during transaction entry. | Sales - Hardware - US |
| Category | Dynamics GP has a preset list of categories available - you can modify or add to these if needed. Categories can be helpful when setting up your financial statements and are required when creating General Ledger accounts. A list of default Dynamics GP categories can be found in *Appendix A*. | Sales |
| Posting Type | Balance Sheet or Profit and Loss. This option is important for Dynamics GP, as it determines whether the account balance needs to be brought forward to the next year during the year-end close process or closed into Retained Earnings. | Profit and Loss |
| Typical Balance | Debit or Credit. This is not too critical, however it is a required field when setting up a new GL account. This setting sometimes helps to default data during General Ledger transaction entry. | Credit |

# Master record IDs and names

Dynamics GP has an **ID** and a **name** for each master record. Both are strings and all IDs within the same type of record must be unique, while names can be duplicated. IDs in Dynamics GP will typically be in all capitals. Special characters (anything other than letters or numbers) are allowed in IDs and while spaces or dashes are fine to use, other special characters should be discouraged. There is a much higher potential for application errors if special characters have not been properly excluded or coded around. It is also sometimes difficult to differentiate between some special characters when looking at an ID on the screen.

Some companies prefer to have IDs that are numeric only and use the next number available for any new record. Others decide to use IDs that are more descriptive and use mostly alpha characters. Both of these approaches are fine, however it is recommended that the numbering scheme for each type of record is consistent for all records created. The following are two important points to keep in mind when deciding on numbering schemes:

- Dynamics GP does not have functionality to automatically suggest the next number available when using numeric IDs, at least for the modules covered in this book. The user creating the new record will have to determine what the next ID number should be.
- Just about every transaction entered and lookup used in Dynamics GP will require one or more ID to be entered by the user. While autocomplete and lookups help with this, it is typically more user friendly to use IDs that will be easily recognizable by the users.

There are many possible numbering schemes. Consider some typical examples for a vendor called American Express:

| Vendor ID | Explanation and notes |
|---|---|
| AMEX | What the vendor is typically called, this is easy to use and remember, however not all vendors will lend themselves easily to this type of ID. |
| 10001 | A numerical ID, regardless of the vendor's name. This method ensures that all the IDs are of the same length which is usually nicer to see on reports. On the other hand, it is typically more difficult for users, because it can add an extra step to the process of entering an ID for every transaction or lookup window. One advantage this numbering scheme provides is that if the vendor changes their name, the ID is independent of the name and can stay the same. |
| AMERICANEXPRESS | This ID may make it easier for users to find the vendor, however it is a lot to type and not all vendors will easily lend themselves to this type of ID. |
| AMEEXP<br>or<br>AME001 | First three letters of each of the first and second word of the vendor name, or first three letters of the first word and a sequential number. Again, this makes all the IDs have the same length and it also provides a bit of structure to the numbering scheme that is straightforward for users to follow. |
| AMERICAN EXPRES | As much as will fit of the vendor name, including spaces. This makes it easier for users to find, but may look strange for some vendors when cut off, like in this example. |

I have seen all of these numbering schemes implemented; probably, the hardest for users to work with is the method of using only numbers in IDs.

To illustrate the use of these numbering schemes, the following screenshot shows an example of what users would see if they start typing `AM` in the **Vendor ID** field on a payables transaction when using the autocomplete feature:

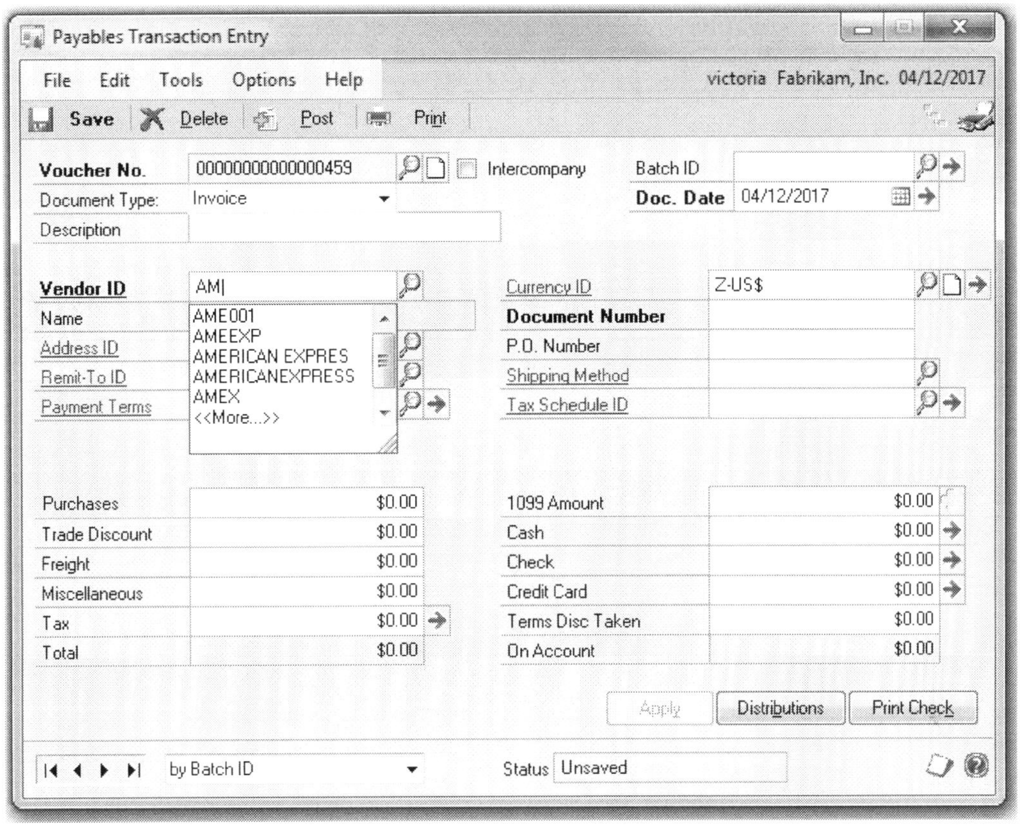

All the IDs suggested previously will show in the autocomplete choices, except the numeric one. In addition, using a numbering scheme like AME001 may result in many others, such as AME002, AME003, and so on, for company names starting with American. On a list such as this, it would be impossible to tell what those IDs represented without memorizing them. So, the user would have to either click on the **<<More...>>** option or the **Lookup** button to open the **Vendors** lookup window and see additional choices:

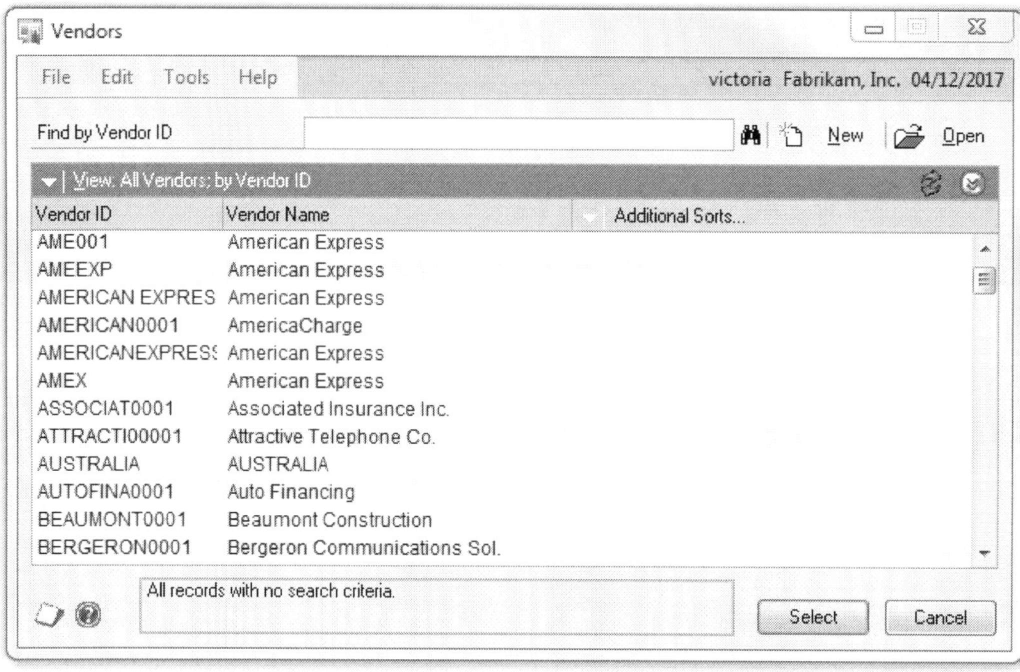


As you can see in the preceding screenshot taken from the Dynamics GP sample company (Fabrikam), many of the Vendor IDs are the first eight letters of the name and a four-digit number. In most companies, the likelihood of having ten thousand vendors having the same first eight letters is remote, so this is not a commonly seen numbering scheme for implementations I have worked with.

Whether you have decided to renumber and rename your vendors, customers, inventory items, or fixed assets, or just clean up the existing data, make sure that what you are planning will work with Dynamics GP. The following are maximum field lengths for the most common Dynamics GP master record IDs and names:

| Master record | ID length | Name length | Notes |
|---|---|---|---|
| Vendor | 15 | 64 | Some built-in reports or windows may not show all 64 characters of the vendor name. On the **Vendors** lookup window (shown in the preceding screenshot) only the first 35 to 40 characters will be shown. |
| Customer | 15 | 64 | Some built-in reports or windows may not show all 64 characters of the name. On the **Customers** lookup window (often used to select customers during transaction entry), only the first 35 to 40 characters will be shown. |
| Inventory Item | 30 | 100 | Many built-in reports may only show 50 characters of the item name, as this was the original length of this field before it was increased several versions ago. Getting all 100 characters to show on Dynamics GP reports may be a challenge, as strings in Report Writer are limited to 80 characters. |
| Inventory Site | 10 | 30 | Typically, all 30 characters of the name will show on lookups. |
| Fixed Asset | 15 | 40 | An additional Extended Description field of another 40 characters is also available for assets. |
| Checkbook | 15 | 30 | Typically, all 30 characters of the name will show on lookups. |
| Salesperson | 15 | 15 + 15 + 20 | First Name (15 characters), Middle Name (15 characters), and Last Name (20 characters) are available for Salesperson. |
| Sales Territory | 15 | 30 | Typically, all 30 characters of the name will show on lookups. |

Once created, master records IDs are not editable in the out-of-the-box Dynamics GP. The **Professional Services Tools Library** (**PSTL**), now available for free from Microsoft, contains many useful tools, including ones allowing modification of all the master record IDs listed previously, as well as General Ledger accounts. There are also tools available in the PSTL to combine the following: Vendor IDs, Customer IDs, General Ledger accounts, Inventory Item IDs, Inventory Site IDs, and Sales Territories. More information about the PSTL is provided in *Chapter 10, Training, Tools, and Next Steps*.

Knowing tools are available to make changes in the future may take some of the pressure off the numbering scheme decisions upfront. However, they are still important decisions that should be well thought out, as making changes after the implementation can be time consuming and costly if consulting help is required. Typically, I do not see companies having the need to modify master records for at least the first year or two after their initial Dynamics GP implementation, unless there is a significant change in the business.

# Fiscal periods and years

Dynamics GP allows an unlimited number of historical and open fiscal years. The following are important guidelines for fiscal years and periods in Dynamics GP:

- Each fiscal year can have up to 367 fiscal periods.
- Fiscal years cannot overlap.
- Each fiscal period within a fiscal year can have a different length.
- Fiscal year IDs can only be a four-digit number.
- Up to three periods can have the same starting date. This is sometimes, although rarely, used for adjustment periods and is typically not recommended. Best practice is to not have overlapping fiscal periods. If you feel that this will help with your requirements, discuss this with your Dynamics GP resource to determine if this is right for you.
- You can make changes to fiscal periods after they have been set up.
- You can only post transactions to the last historical (closed) fiscal year. For example, if 2011 and 2012 are closed and 2013 is the first open year, you can still post to 2012, but you cannot post to 2011 anymore.

Most companies have fiscal years that are calendar years and choose to have 12 periods (one for each month), so the fiscal period setup would look like the following screenshot:

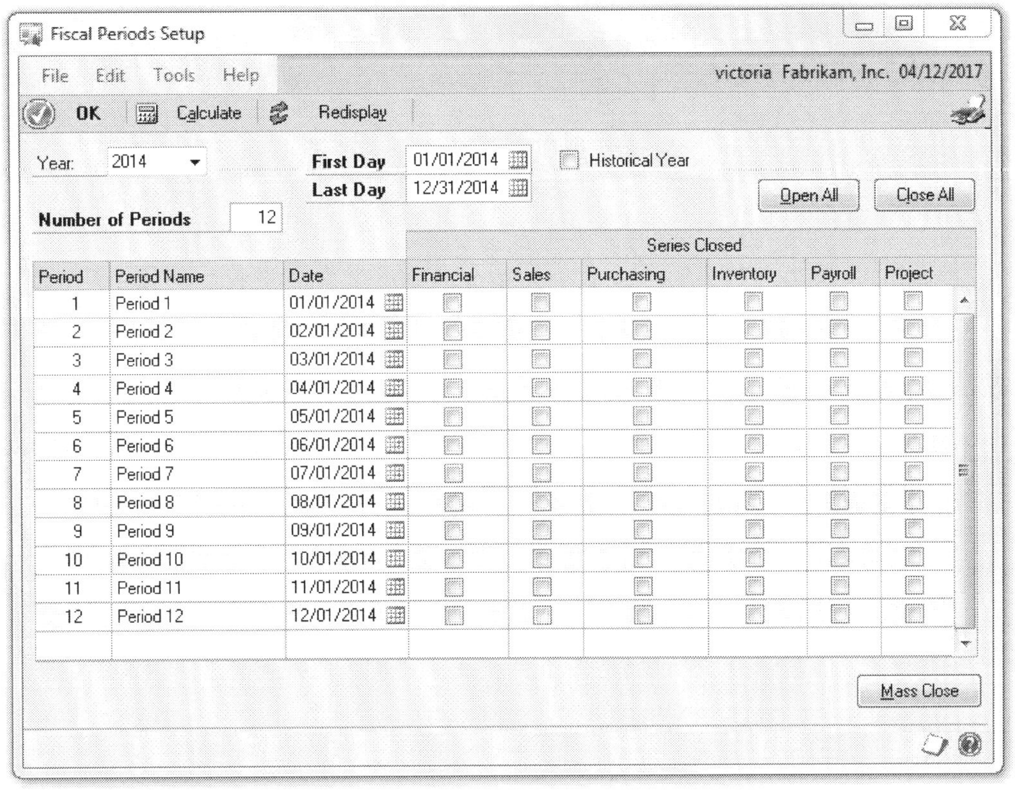


If your company fiscal year is not the calendar year, most likely the year is referred to by the date it ends. For example, if the fiscal year is from July 1, 2012 to June 30, 2013, it will typically be referred to as fiscal year 2013. This is more of an accepted convention and Dynamics GP will not enforce the naming of your years. If you think that there is a possibility you will want to change your fiscal year to a calendar year sometime in the near future, consider renaming the years during your Dynamics GP implementation to use the number of the beginning year, for example:

| Fiscal year | Start date | End date |
|---|---|---|
| 2011 | July 1, 2011 | June 30, 2012 |
| 2012 | July 1, 2012 | June 30, 2013 |
| 2013 | July 1, 2013 | June 30, 2014 |

This approach will allow you to seamlessly add a short year whenever you are ready to switch to a calendar year:

| Fiscal year | Start date | End date |
|---|---|---|
| 2014 | July 1, 2014 | December 31, 2014 |
| 2015 | January 1, 2015 | December 31, 2015 |

The alternative to this would be to keep the fiscal year numbering you currently have and if the change to a calendar year is made, use the **Fiscal Period Modifier** tool from the PSTL which will allow you to rename your existing years.

When choosing how many years to set up, consider what you have decided about importing historical General Ledger balances. In our example, in *Chapter 2, Planning – Business Requirements*, we detailed NJW's decision to import ending balances for 2010 and monthly balances for 2011, 2012, and 2013, so they will need to create fiscal years starting with 2010.

# Users and security

Prior to implementing Dynamics GP, it is helpful to plan out all the system users and the security needs for them. If you have implemented Dynamics GP for versions prior to 10.0 and have not worked with the new Dynamics GP security yet, you may want to forget everything you have learned about Dynamics GP security in the past, as it has been completely overhauled.

Starting with Dynamics GP 10.0, the security model is pessimistic. Considered long overdue by many consultants and system administrators, this means newly created users will not have permissions to anything and will need to be explicitly granted any and all permissions.

The components of Dynamics GP security are:

- **Operations**: These are the lowest level security building blocks. Operations include access to windows, reports, tables, tools, posting permissions, and SmartList objects.
- **Tasks**: Groupings of operations. Tasks typically group operations across common fairly low-level functions, such as creating customers or entering sales transactions. Tasks can cross Dynamics GP products and modules. Multiple tasks can have the same operations.
- **Roles**: Groupings of tasks. Multiple roles can have the same tasks. When setting up user security, Dynamics GP users get assigned one or more roles.

Many operations, a large number of tasks, and some roles are predefined in Dynamics GP. You can change existing tasks and roles and create new ones as needed. Any user can be assigned one or more roles.

A **DEFAULTUSER** task is available containing the basic system operations required by just about every user. When a new role is created, the DEFAULTUSER task is automatically added to it. Some third-party products will also add basic permissions required by their products to the DEFAULTUSER task.

A **POWERUSER** role is available for any system administrators that should have access to all functionality in Dynamics GP. This is similar to the sa user in SQL Server, which bypasses security completely. Any user with the POWERUSER role assigned does not need any other role assigned to them, unless there are additional permissions required by a third-party product.

To start planning for security setup in Dynamics GP:

- Identify all the users that will need access to Dynamics GP. Make sure to get the correct full name of the user, as this is helpful to fill in when creating users in Dynamics GP.
- Decide on the user ID naming convention. Even though Dynamics GP does not use Windows Authentication, the recommendation is to make the user IDs the same as the Windows user IDs to minimize user confusion.

> Unlike Windows user IDs, Dynamics GP user IDs are case sensitive.

- Determine the Dynamics GP functions each user will be performing. This is sometimes easier to start as a simple list of the tasks and then refine with additional detail as an iterative process.
    - It may be just as important to decide what a user should not be able to do. For example, some users may only be allowed to create transactions and should not have the ability to post them.
    - If you are planning on multiple Dynamics GP companies, determine what users should be granted access to each company. While not common, if needed, users can have different security settings in each company.
    - Evaluate the preset tasks and roles in Dynamics GP and compare these against the requirements for all users. This may become a daunting task and may be another good place to involve your Dynamics GP resource if you have not had much experience with the security in Dynamics GP.

Following the example set by Dynamics GP, best practice is to take a pessimistic approach to setting user security. Start by granting users only roles and tasks that they need to perform their work. It is easier to grant someone additional access when needed, rather than take away something a user already had or, even worse, having to fix issues caused by a user inadvertently changing a setting they should not have had access to in the first place.

# Sales and purchase taxes

As part of the planning for your Dynamics GP setup, determine whether sales and purchase taxes should be calculated and tracked by the system. Even though the concept is the same, sales and purchase taxes must be set up separately, because a tax in Dynamics GP can only be one or the other. Many small and mid-size companies in the US choose not to track purchase taxes separately. However, any business selling goods or services will often need to collect and remit sales taxes to each state they do business in and have detailed records of taxable transactions for state reporting purposes.

Setting up taxes in Dynamics GP involves the creation of **Tax Details** and **Tax Schedules**. Tax Details are the lowest level of taxes a company wants to track; Tax Schedules are a combination of one or more Tax Details that are used together to calculate the total tax for a transaction. The same Tax Detail can be used on multiple Tax Schedules. Tax Schedules are assigned to customers, vendors, items, and transactions that need to be taxed.

Here is a typical example:

<table>
<tr><th>Tax Schedule</th><th>Tax Details included</th><th>Tax percent</th><th>Explanation</th></tr>
<tr><td>New Jersey Sales Tax</td><td>NJ State Sales Tax</td><td>7.00 %</td><td>With very few exceptions, New Jersey only has one tax rate across the entire state. In this case, there is one Tax Detail in the Tax Schedule.</td></tr>
<tr><td rowspan="2">New York City Sales Tax</td><td>NY State Sales Tax</td><td>4.375 %</td><td rowspan="4">In New York State, there is typically a state and a county or local tax. Setting up separate details for the state and each county or locality offers the following benefits:<br>Reporting on each individual tax can be easily accomplished (this is a requirement in some states).<br>If one of the details changes, it is easy to change all the Tax Schedules related to it in one step. For example, if the state tax goes to 4.75%, simply changing the NY State Sales Tax Detail will update all the related Tax Schedules automatically.</td></tr>
<tr><td>New York City Sales Tax</td><td>4.50 %</td></tr>
<tr><td rowspan="2">Washington County, NY Sales Tax</td><td>NY State Sales Tax</td><td>4.375 %</td></tr>
<tr><td>Washington County Sales Tax</td><td>3.00 %</td></tr>
</table>

The followings screenshot shows a typical Tax Detail setup window:

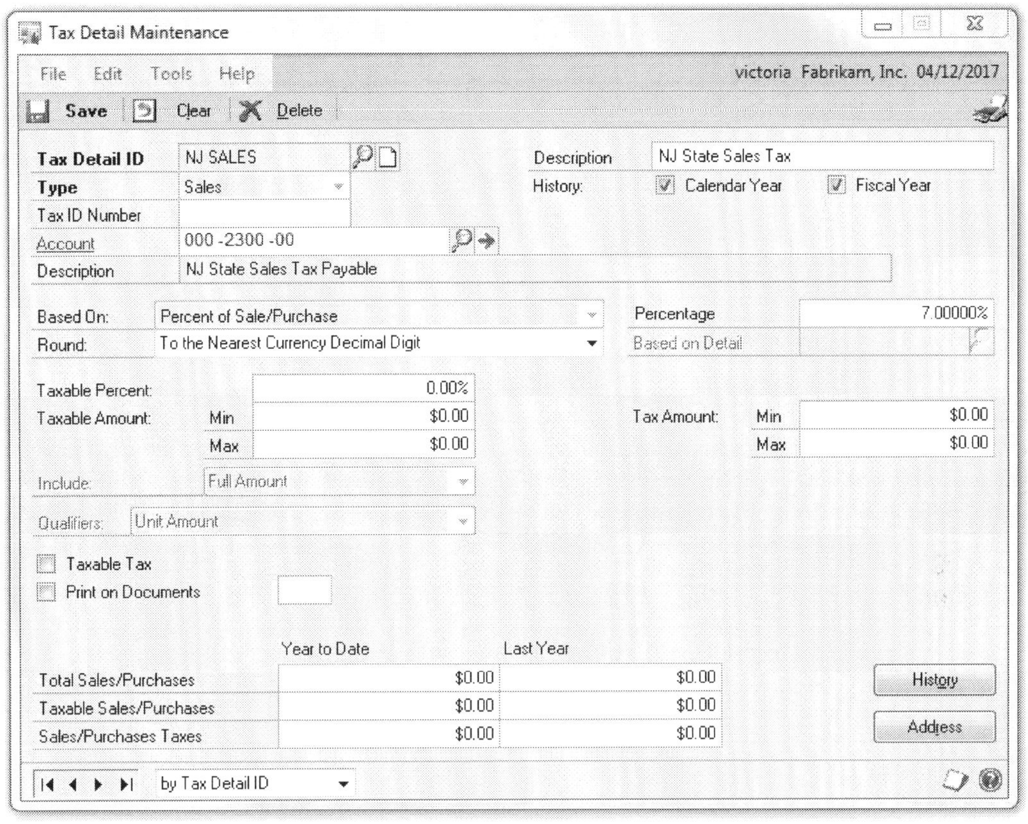


If planning to set up taxes, gather the following information for each Tax Detail you want to set up:

| Data | Explanation |
|---|---|
| Tax Detail ID | This may be another place you want to decide on some consistent numbering, especially if there are many taxes to be set up. Always putting the state abbreviation in front will allow for better sorting and selection of ranges during reporting. Maximum length is 15 characters. |
| Description | Optional, but very helpful when looking at a long list of Tax Details during the setup of Tax Schedules or reporting. Maximum length is 30 characters. |
| Tax Type | Sales or Purchases. If the same Tax Detail is needed for both sales and purchase taxes, it will need to be set up with 2 separate IDs. In this case, consider adding something to the ID to indicate this, maybe a "-S" for sales and "-P" for purchases at the end of the ID. |

| Data | Explanation |
|---|---|
| Tax ID Number | The company's tax ID number with the taxing authority – this is optional for the setup, but can be helpful if you need to look up this information in the future. |
| GL Account | The General Ledger account number where the tax liability is accumulated. Typically, this is a Payables account. |
| Tax Based On | How the tax is calculated. Options are:<br>• Flat Amount per Unit<br>• Percent of Another Tax Detail<br>• Percent of Cost<br>• Percent of Sale/Purchase<br>• Percent of Sale/Purchase plus Taxable Taxes<br>• Tax Included with Item Price<br>The most common of these is Percent of Sale/Purchase. If one of the other methods are chosen there may be some additional options needed for setup. |
| Percentage | You can enter up to 5 decimal places for the tax percentage. |
| Round | Rounding options for the tax calculation. Available options include nearest up, nearest down, to the nearest decimal place, or whole digit. The recommendation is to round to the nearest decimal place, as this is the most commonly expected calculation method. |

# Additional setup considerations

In addition to the setup categories we have discussed so far, there are a few more topics that are sometimes not looked at until after installation but that you may want to consider prior to starting your implementation.

## Shipping methods

Shipping methods are company specific and are used to define all the possible shipping options a company uses to deliver goods to customers or receive goods from vendors. During the Dynamics GP installation, a default list of shipping methods can be populated.

The two major functions of shipping methods are to communicate the shipping information to employees, customers, and vendors on transactions and documents, and to determine what taxes Dynamics GP calculates automatically. For example, if the shipping method on a customer invoice has a type of "Delivery", then the customer's shipping address will determine the tax. If the shipping method has a type of "Pickup", then your company's warehouse location will determine the tax.

# Payment terms

Payment terms are company specific and define the terms offered to customers and available from vendors for payment of invoices. During the Dynamics GP installation, you can load default payment terms and change or add to them, as needed.

If your company has a large list of available payment terms, you may want to identify them ahead of time so that you can create them during the implementation. Payment terms, when set up for customers and vendors, will default on all transactions and automatically calculate due dates and discounts, making transaction entry faster and more accurate.

# Credit cards

Credit cards can be set up in Dynamics GP to be used for payment to vendors and to be accepted as payment from customers.

## Credit cards accepted from customers

There are two options for credit cards accepted as payment from customers:

- **Bank Card/Checkbook ID**: This will associate a credit card with a bank account (also called Checkbook) in Dynamics GP. When a customer payment is entered using this type of credit card, the payment amount will automatically go to the bank account specified. This setup option is typically used when the full amount of the credit card charge is deposited into the company's bank account by the credit card processor, and the credit card processing fees are taken out separately on a monthly basis.
- **Charge Card/Account Number**: This will link the credit card to a General Ledger account. When a customer payment is entered using this type of credit card, the payment amount will be posted as a debit to the GL account specified, and will require a separate entry to move the payment out of this GL account into the bank account. This type of credit card setup is useful when the credit card processor takes their discount or fees out of every transaction. For example, a customer pays $500 with a credit card, but only $487.50 is deposited into the bank account with a $12.50 fee deducted right away.

## Credit cards used to pay vendors

There are also two options for setting up credit cards used to pay vendors in Dynamics GP:

- **Credit Card/Vendor ID**: This will associate a credit card with a vendor in Dynamics GP. When a vendor payment is entered using this type of credit card, the payment amount will automatically create an invoice payable to the credit card vendor specified. This setup option should be used for traditional credit card accounts that send a monthly statement to be paid separately. A detailed discussion of this approach can be found in this blog post: `http://victoriayudin.com/2009/01/04/using-credit-cards-to-pay-vendors-in-dynamics-gp/`.
- **Check Card/Checkbook ID**: This option will link the credit card to a bank account (Checkbook) in Dynamics GP. When a vendor payment is entered using this type of credit card, the amount will be posted as a cash withdrawal from the Checkbook specified. This credit card option setup is used for what is commonly called Debit Cards, where each purchase is deducted from the bank account right away.

Credit card setup is company specific in Dynamics GP. Different companies cannot share credit cards.

# Posting setup

Each type of transaction posted in Dynamics GP can be set up to behave differently. Posting settings are company specific, so the same type of transaction can have different settings in each Dynamics GP company. All of the posting settings can be changed at any time, but there are a few important settings that may require additional discussion or planning ahead of time: **Post Through General Ledger Files**, **Create a Journal Entry Per**, **Posting Date From**, and **Require Batch Approval**.

The following screenshot is an example of what the posting settings may look like for transactions originating on the **Payables Transaction Entry** window in Dynamics GP:

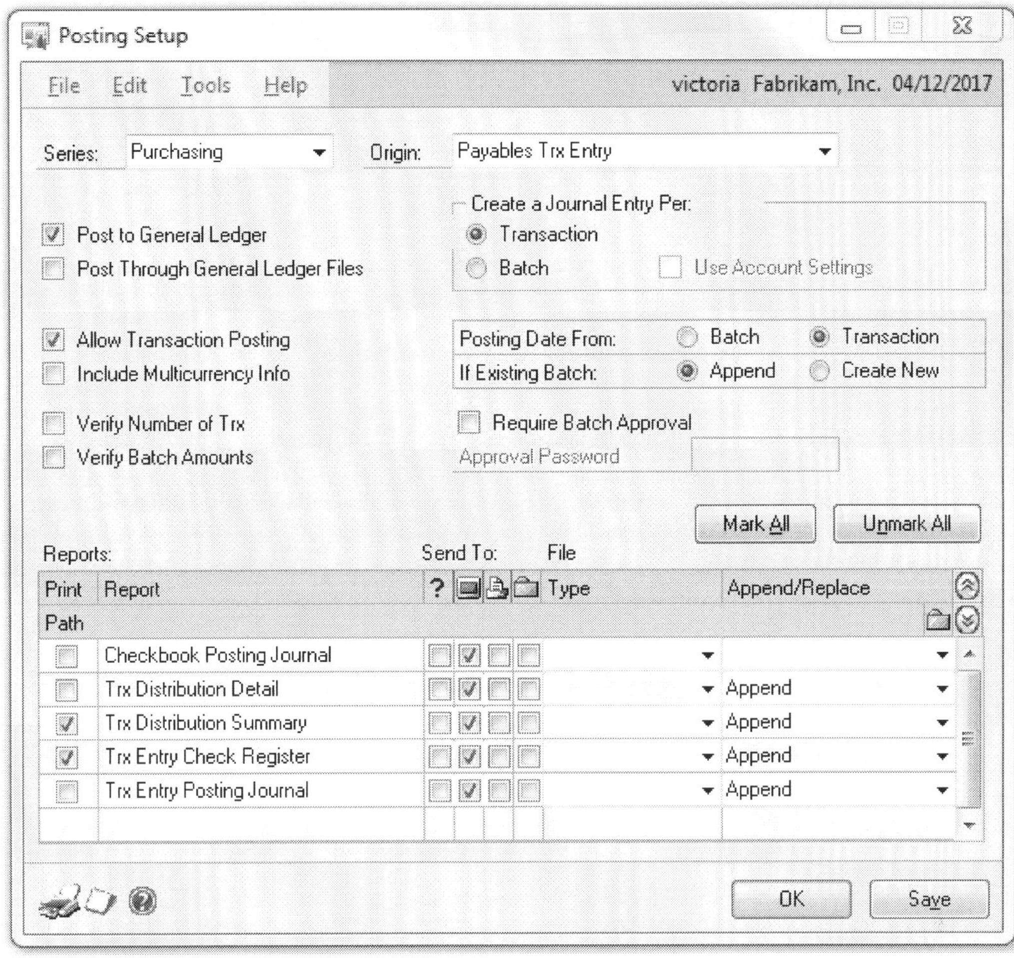


## Post Through General Ledger Files

With very few exceptions, all transactions in every subledger will be set to **Post to General Ledger**. This will create GL entries after the subledger posting is completed. Choosing the **Post Through General Ledger Files** setting will automatically post the resulting GL entries right after the subledger posting is completed. If this setting is not chosen, a user will manually need to post the GL entries that have been created from subledger postings as a separate step.

Many companies, when first starting to use Dynamics GP, decide not to have transactions automatically posted through to the GL. This gives them the chance to examine the General Ledger entries created and make sure they understand how the system is behaving with regard to dates and account numbers defaulted. However, as it takes less time and work to have transactions automatically posted through to the GL, eventually many transaction types are changed to use the **Post Through General Ledger Files** option.

## Create a Journal Entry Per

When posting a subledger batch with multiple transactions, the **Create a Journal Entry Per** setting determines whether a General Ledger entry is created for each individual subledger transaction, or whether one GL entry is created summarizing the entire subledger batch.

Choosing to create one GL entry per subledger **Transaction** allows for greater drill-back capability. When looking at a particular General Ledger entry it is possible to drill back to the originating transaction in the subledger. The benefit of choosing to create one GL entry per subledger **Batch** is that the GL does not get as cluttered up with individual transactions.

Consider a company that has 500 sales invoices a day. If each of these creates a GL entry, in a 260 workday year it will result in 130,000 GL entries, just from the sales invoices. Many sales invoices will have numerous GL distributions, so with an average of 8 GL distributions per invoice, that will become 1,040,000 lines in the General Ledger per year from sales invoices alone. Typically, this much detail is not needed, as no one will be looking through it at this detail level given this volume of transactions. In this scenario, if those 500 invoices are split into five batches per day, then only five GL entries are created each day, resulting in 1,300 GL entries per year for sales invoices instead of 130,000.

To determine the right approach, consider the volume expected for each type of transaction. If there is any question, the recommendation is to err on the side of having more detail and creating a GL entry per transaction. It is much easier to summarize detailed data with reports than to recreate detail from subledger records. You can always change this setting in the future if your transaction volume increases.

## Posting Date From

Every subledger transaction in Dynamics GP will have two dates: a subledger date and a General Ledger date. The subledger date is typically the actual date on an invoice received from a vendor or sent to a customer. The General Ledger date is the date a transaction is posted to the GL and will show up on financial statements.

Dynamics GP easily allows these two dates to be different and keeps track of all the dates throughout the accounting process. Reports that are printed will usually have an option for selecting transactions using the subledger date (also referred to as Document Date) or the GL date (also referred to as the posting date or GL posting date). For example, a company may need to print two different Receivables Historical Aged Trial Balance reports: one using the subledger dates, which are actual invoice dates, to see the true aging of customer accounts, and another using the GL dates to reconcile the Receivables subledger to the General Ledger.

The two choices for the **Posting Date From** setting are **Batch** and **Transaction**. Choosing **Batch** means that all transactions entered in the same batch will be posted with the same GL date, set at the batch level. Choosing **Transaction** will allow each transaction within a batch to have its own GL date. If **Create a Journal Entry per Batch** is selected, this option will be grayed out and automatically set to **Batch**.

As dates are critical to keeping accounting records accurate, this setting should be considered carefully and may need to be different for different types of transactions, depending on how they are entered or imported into Dynamics GP. The more commonly seen recommendation is to set the **Posting Date From** option to **Transaction** to allow for greater control of the dates during transaction entry.

> To decide what is better for your company, consider how transactions are entered. For example, do you typically have payables invoices being entered at the same time that may belong to more than one fiscal period? If so, it may be better to set the GL posting dates at the transaction level for payables transactions, so that users can have one batch with transactions in multiple periods.
>
> Now think about your sales transactions; do you typically bill at the beginning of the month for sales in the prior month? If so, it may be better to set the GL posting date for sales transactions at the batch level, so transactions entered over a few days will all go into a batch with the end of the last month as the GL posting date.

## Require Batch Approval

For certain types of transactions it may be helpful to prevent users from posting their transaction batches until someone else has reviewed and approved them. In many companies, this is accomplished with training and there is no need to have Dynamics GP enforce this behavior. However, if desired, the **Require Batch Approval** setting in Dynamics GP will ensure that a batch cannot be posted without an **Approval Password**.

# Multicurrency

If you have decided to use the Multicurrency module, currencies and exchange rate tables should be planned out.

## Currencies

Determine all the currencies that will be used and what the ID for each currency should be. Additional considerations for currencies are the symbols to use, the number of decimal places to keep, what separators to use for decimals and thousands, and what company in Dynamics GP will have access to each currency. The following screenshot is an example of a typical **Currency Setup** window:

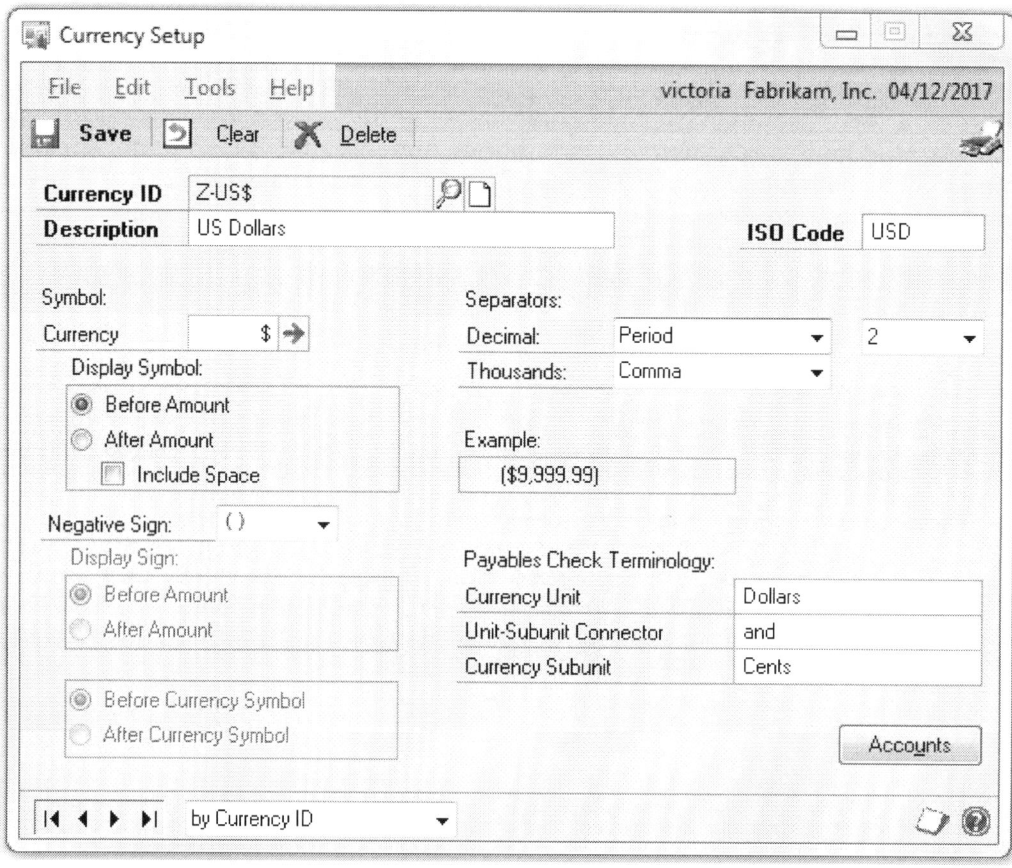


One suggestion for Currency IDs is to use the ISO codes. You can see additional information about ISO codes and download a link of all the ISO codes at the following URL: `http://www.iso.org/iso/home/standards/currency_codes.html`.

# Exchange Rate Tables

If using Multicurrency, decide what the source for your exchange rates will be and whether to use one or more rate types. Dynamics GP allows for SELL, BUY and AVERAGE rates, however there is no requirement to use all of them. Many companies use only a single AVERAGE rate. Another decision is how often the exchange rate table should be updated. The following screenshot is an example of the **Multicurrency Exchange Rate Table Setup** and **Multicurrency Exchange Rate Maintenance** windows:

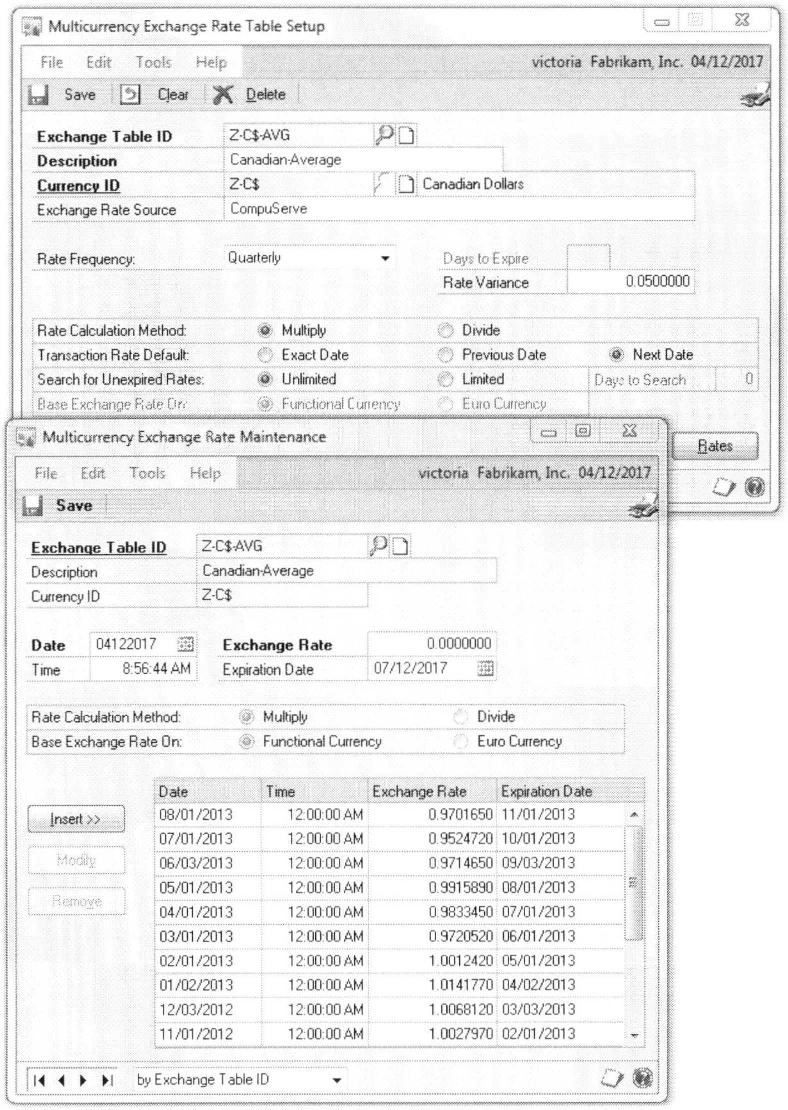

# Summary

In this chapter, we have focused on planning for your Dynamics GP system setup. We went over the important factors in choosing how many companies to have in Dynamics GP and what to consider when deciding whether to integrate with existing systems or replace them. General Ledger account frameworks and account formats were examined and master record numbering schemes were discussed. We talked about fiscal periods, fiscal years, and recommendations for non-calendar fiscal years. Dynamics GP user and security planning and tax setup were reviewed. Additional setup considerations were also outlined.

In the next chapter we will discuss planning the infrastructure for your Microsoft Dynamics GP implementation.

# 4

# Planning – Infrastructure

Having completed the business requirements and Dynamics GP system planning phases, the next step is to plan out the infrastructure required for your Microsoft Dynamics GP implementation.

In this chapter, we will cover the following topics:

- General concepts for infrastructure planning
- Minimum requirements and recommendations for the Dynamics GP client, server, and Remote Desktop Services
- Dynamics GP 2013 Web Client
- Additional considerations for configuration and infrastructure planning, including virtual environments and printers
- What "officially supported" means and why this is important
- The Remote Desktop Services only and Web Client only approaches for client installations
- Network requirements for Dynamics GP
- Options for setting up a test environment
- Considerations for add-on products
- Alternatives for the placement of shared files
- Data backups

# Scope of vision

Planning infrastructure for Dynamics GP cannot be done in a vacuum. Existing systems, as well as future plans and projects, should be considered to determine whether the current infrastructure needs to be augmented to support your Dynamics GP implementation. While your role may be strictly to implement Dynamics GP, together with the IT resource on your implementation team, encourage the company to take a slightly broader approach to planning the infrastructure. Thinking about the shorter term (the next one to three years), as well as the longer term (three to five years ahead), consider the following questions:

- Are there plans to hire more employees or consultants? If so, what applications will these users need access to?
- Are there plans to implement additional systems after Dynamics GP?
- Will there be any integration between Dynamics GP and existing or new systems?
- Are there upgrades already planned for any hardware or software?
- Is there a need for remote users for Dynamics GP, as well as other systems currently in place or planned for the future?
- How old is the current infrastructure? Are both the hardware and software being used today under maintenance and supported?

For most companies, it is reasonable to assume that a server will be replaced after about three years, so the initial planning should include plans for at least the next three years. For our Not Just Widgets example company, the plan is to start with 10 concurrent Dynamics GP users. NJW anticipates increasing the user count to 15 or 20 within the next three years, so they will want to plan their infrastructure for 20 users.

Budgets will often play a role in infrastructure planning. However easy it may be to decide that getting a less powerful server saves money today and upgrades can be done later, consider the following:

- A slower server means less productive users. This is a quantifiable loss of revenue every day. I have seen more than one company save $500 on a server by getting slower hard drives, only to be constantly plagued by slow performance.
- A slower server means less happy users. While this is harder to translate into a financial equivalent, morale is often a critical component of productivity.

- Less capacity means a server may need to be replaced much sooner if more users are added, or the volume of data is higher than expected. So instead of spending slightly more upfront for a more powerful server, the overall expenditure over a few years is potentially doubled, because the server has to be replaced sooner. Also take into account the effort to move a Dynamics GP system from one server to another. It will involve system downtime and possibly additional consulting expense.

A nice middle ground is sometimes found by ensuring that the server configured upfront can be easily upgraded with more RAM, disks, or additional processors. While this may be a good solution for companies that have easy access to resources that can quickly and easily perform these upgrades or when setting up a virtual environment, this is not always the case for all companies. When contemplating this approach, carefully consider whether the savings today justify the cost of potential downtime and resources further down the line when these upgrades are needed.

There is no one answer to what the infrastructure should be and every environment is different. However, in my experience, planning for the future and erring on the side of more robust hardware usually results in a much more successful implementation.

# Dynamics GP system requirements

Microsoft maintains an updated system requirements page for every Dynamics GP version. The following URL is specific to Dynamics GP 2013 and requires access to either PartnerSource or CustomerSource:

`https://mbs.microsoft.com/customersource/documentation/systemrequirements/mdgp2013_system_requirements.htm`

All of this information is updated as new versions and service packs of products are released and tested, so it is important to refer to the current documentation online when planning your implementation.

The system requirements are broken out into several categories: client requirements, server requirements and recommendations, terminal server requirements, and additional notes. The following sections will discuss each one in more detail.

# Client requirements

The client requirements published by Microsoft are typically the minimums needed to install and run Dynamics GP, and should sometimes be taken with a grain of salt. If you have experience with previous versions of Dynamics GP, keep in mind that Dynamics GP 2013 may require more resources than the previous versions.

The following are the published requirements for a client computer running Dynamics GP 2013:

| Item | Requirement Published | Notes |
|---|---|---|
| Operating System | • Microsoft Windows 7 (Professional or Ultimate)<br>• Microsoft Windows 8 (Professional or Ultimate) | Both 32-bit and 64-bit systems are supported.<br>Ultimate does not actually appear to be a valid edition name for Windows 8; my belief is that this is meant to be the Enterprise Edition. For Windows 7, the Enterprise Edition is not mentioned; however, it is supported, as it includes everything in the Professional Edition plus some additional features.<br>2013 is the first version of Dynamics GP that is not supported on Windows XP, so if you are upgrading from an older Dynamics GP version and have existing Windows XP computers, this may require some significant upgrades or an alternative, like Remote Desktop Services or Web Client. |
| Processor | One Dual Core or Single Core Processor 2.6 GHz or higher | This requirement rules out many older computers. If buying a new computer, consider this a minimum. |
| Available Hard Disk Space | 2 GB or more on the system root | Consider upgrading or freeing up additional space on any hard drive that does not have at least 10 percent of its total capacity free. |
| Minimum Available RAM | 2 GB or more | Note that this requirement is labeled "minimum available RAM". The recommendation is for a 64-bit system with 8 GB of RAM for heavy Dynamics GP users or users that typically have many applications open simultaneously and at least 4 GB for all other Dynamics GP users. |
| Microsoft Office | • Microsoft Office 2010<br>• Microsoft Office 2013 | The primary Office components needed for Dynamics GP users are Excel, Outlook, and Word. Note that with Dynamics GP 2013 both 32-bit and 64-bit versions of Office are now compatible. (Some of the features in Dynamics GP 2010 were not supported with Office 2010 64-bit). |
| Network Card | 1 GB Ethernet | This is standard for most computers sold today. |

| Item | Requirement Published | Notes |
|---|---|---|
| Internet Explorer | • Internet Explorer 8.0<br>• Internet Explorer 9.0<br>• Internet Explorer 10.0 (Desktop Mode Only) | This requirement is not critical if not using any of the functionality integrating with Internet Explorer. |
| Adobe Acrobat | • Adobe X | The full version of Adobe Acrobat (either Standard or Professional) is needed to use some optional functionality in Dynamics GP; however, this is not a requirement. |

# Server requirements and recommendations

As mentioned in *Chapter 1, Application Structure and Licensing*, there is no application server needed for Dynamics GP. While most companies choose to install the Dynamics GP application on the server to assist with setup, testing, and troubleshooting, any discussion about the Dynamics GP server in this book is referring to the server that will run the Microsoft SQL Server used by Dynamics GP.

On the Microsoft System Requirements for Dynamics GP 2013 web page: `https://mbs.microsoft.com/customersource/documentation/systemrequirements/mdgp2013_system_requirements.htm` (requires access to either PartnerSource or CustomerSource), there are four customer profiles illustrated to help determine the best server recommendations to follow. Even though you may clearly fall into one of the profiles, take a look at the recommendations for the profiles following yours to see what upgrades may be needed as the organization grows and more users or features are added to Dynamics GP. If you feel that you are between the profiles, it is recommended that you go up to the higher profile.

The following are the minimum system requirements and supported versions for the Dynamics GP server:

| Item | Requirement Published | Notes |
|---|---|---|
| Operating System | • Windows Server 2008 Standard or Enterprise—SP 2 or later<br>• Windows Server 2008 R2 Standard or Enterprise—SP 1 or later<br>• Windows Server 2012 Essentials, Standard, or Datacenter<br>• Windows Small Business Server 2008 Premium—SP 2 or later<br>• Windows Small Business Server 2011 Standard with Premium Add-on | For all the server operating systems listed, both 64-bit and 32-bit (where available) are supported. |
| SQL Server | • MS SQL Server 2008 SP 3 or later—Express, Standard, Workgroup, or Enterprise<br>• MS SQL Server 2008 R2 SP 1 or later—Express, Standard, Workgroup, or Enterprise<br>• MS SQL Server 2012—Express, Standard, or Enterprise | Both 32-bit and 64-bit versions of Microsoft SQL Server are supported. Note that SQL Server 2012 is the only version of SQL Server supported on Windows Server 2012. |
| Processor | One dual core or two single core processors | This should be the minimum considered for processors and should go up based on the number of users and complexity of the implementation. |
| Minimum Available RAM | 2 GB or more | Note again the wording "minimum available"—even for the simplest Dynamics GP implementation it is recommended to have at least 4 GB of RAM on the server. |

| Item | Requirement Published | Notes |
| --- | --- | --- |
| Network Card | 1 GB Ethernet | This is standard for most servers sold today. |
| Disk Configuration | While there is no minimum disk configuration required, this should be considered carefully to optimize performance and reliability of Dynamics GP. | The disk configuration can vary greatly depending on the details of the implementation. Follow general SQL Server guidelines for sizing the number of disks and arrays used. |

The following are additional considerations and recommendations for configuring the Dynamics GP server:

- For any implementations planning on 10 or more concurrent users, it is recommended to have a dedicated Dynamics GP server. Often the recommendations for configuring a server running Microsoft SQL Server are different from a server running other applications. For a small number of users or small transactional volume, a server not optimized for SQL Server may not result in a noticeable performance difference; however in larger, more complex environments, the loss of performance due to a less than optimal server configuration can be a critical concern.
- If a dedicated server is not possible, a dedicated SQL Server instance is recommended for any Dynamics GP implementation, because the SQL Server instance used by Dynamics GP may need to be configured differently from other SQL Server instances. In addition, having a separate SQL Server instance can allow better allocation of server resources and easier maintenance and support of the different applications using SQL Server.
- While Dynamics GP is supported on the SQL Server Express edition for all SQL Server versions listed, this is not recommended for any Dynamics GP production environment. Using SQL Server Express will limit functionality available to set up and monitor SQL jobs for backups and routine maintenance and may also limit the performance of SQL Server. There are also restrictions on database size for SQL Server Express.
- As a general rule, SQL Server performance will improve with the number of disks and RAIDs. The minimum typically recommended is a RAID 5 for all files, preferably with four drives. The next step would be RAID 1 for the operating system, application files, and SQL Server log files and RAID 5 for SQL Server data. For larger implementations, multiple RAIDs are recommended for optimal performance. Please note that this discussion assumes hardware RAID, software RAID is not supported.

- When determining the disk storage size required for Dynamics GP, consider that there may be a number of database and transaction log backups kept locally on the server. Backup retention times may vary from company-to-company, but it is not unusual to keep a week or more of backups locally for quicker access. In addition, the server should have enough hard drive space for at least two or three years of data growth. Taking whatever storage size you think will be needed and doubling it is one common way of calculating hard drive capacity.
- In general, it is better to oversize rather than undersize a server.

Configuring your Dynamics GP server is a very important decision. If you are unsure of the best approach, consult with your IT resource, your Dynamics GP resource, and maybe even a SQL Server expert.

# Remote Desktop Services requirements

Remote access to Dynamics GP is only supported using **Remote Desktop Services** (formerly called **Terminal Services**). Connecting remotely using only a VPN connection is not supported, nor recommended. An excellent explanation for this can be found on the Developing for Dynamics GP blog: `http://blogs.msdn.com/b/developingfordynamicsgp/archive/2010/07/28/why-cant-i-run-microsoft-dynamics-gp-via-odbc-over-a-wan.aspx`. The following are the requirements for a Dynamics GP Remote Desktop Services server:

| Item | Requirement Published | Notes |
|---|---|---|
| Operating System | • Windows Server 2008 Standard or Enterprise—SP 2 or later<br>• Windows Server 2008 R2 Standard or Enterprise—SP 1 or later<br>• Windows Server 2012 Standard or Datacenter | Both 32-bit and 64-bit systems are supported. |
| Citrix (optional) | • Citrix XenApp | Citrix is only recommended for larger environments and when there is a knowledgeable Citrix resource available for setup and ongoing maintenance or support. |
| Processor | Two dual core or four single core processors | This requirement will greatly depend on how many users will be accessing the server and what other applications will be used on it. |

| Item | Requirement Published | Notes |
|---|---|---|
| Disk Configuration | RAID 1 for operating system and applications (two disks) | There will typically be very limited data stored on the Remote Desktop Services server, so storage should not be an issue. |
| Minimum Available RAM | 4 GB or more | RAM should depend on the number of Dynamics GP and other application users planned, and may need to increase as the number of users and applications increase. |
| Network Card | 1 GB Ethernet | This is standard for most servers sold today. |
| Users | 15-20 users per server | This will depend on the specifications of the server, how many users are connected to it concurrently, and what other applications are being used. |

Notes on planning for a Remote Desktop Services server:

- This should be a dedicated server. While it can certainly be used for other applications that need to be accessed remotely, it should not be the Microsoft SQL Server or any other critical server in the organization, for both performance and security reasons.
- If planning on using the TS RemoteApp functionality with Windows Server 2008 or Windows Server 2008 R2, refer to the following URL for more information on a hotfix required for Dynamics GP: `https://mbs.microsoft.com/customersource/support/selfsupport/hottopics/MDGP_RemoteAppIssue` (requires access to either CustomerSource or PartnerSource).

# Web Client

Starting with Microsoft Dynamics GP 2013, a **Web Client** has been introduced for Dynamics GP. This means that users can now access the Dynamics GP application inside a web browser. While this has been much anticipated and a great deal of attention and praise has been lavished on this functionality, when it comes to deploying the Web Client for your organization, it is recommended to be cautious and to do a lot of planning and testing first.

Not all of the existing Dynamics GP functionality has been released for the Web Client yet and there are some significant limitations on support for modifications, customizations, and third-party add-ons. In addition, a successful implementation of the Web Client may require additional investments in infrastructure. Even if you think the Web Client will be helpful to your organization, most likely you will need a combination of Web Client and **Desktop Client**—the name for the traditional method of installing Dynamics GP on either a client workstation or a server running Remote Desktop Services.

Implementing the Dynamics GP 2013 Web Client can encompass a book of its own, so we will not be covering it in this book. Below are links for additional resources if you are looking to learn about or deploy the Dynamics GP Web Client:

- Dynamics GP 2013 Web Client system requirements: `https://mbs.microsoft.com/customersource/documentation/systemrequirements/MDGP2013_system_requirements_webclient` (PartnerSource or CustomerSource access required). As with the other system requirements, it is best to check online for the latest news and updates.
- Dynamics GP 2013 Web Client Hot Topics on PartnerSource: `https://mbs.microsoft.com/partnersource/support/selfsupport/hottopics/hottopic_mdgp2013_webclient.htm`
- Dynamics GP 2013 Web Client Hot Topics on CustomerSource: `https://mbs.microsoft.com/customersource/support/selfsupport/hottopics/hottopic_mdgp2013_webclient.htm`
- Web Client Deployment Guide for Microsoft Dynamics GP 2013 post on the Developing for Dynamics GP blog: `http://blogs.msdn.com/b/developingfordynamicsgp/archive/2013/04/25/web-client-deployment-guide-for-microsoft-dynamics-gp-2013.aspx`
- Microsoft Dynamics GP 2013 Web Client Video Series post on the Developing for Dynamics GP blog: `http://blogs.msdn.com/b/developingfordynamicsgp/archive/2013/01/30/microsoft-dynamics-gp-2013-web-client-video-series.aspx`
- Additional blogs that post frequently about the Dynamics GP Web Client:
    - **The Dynamics GP Blogster** written by fellow Dynamics GP MVP Mariano Gomez: `http://dynamicsgpblogster.blogspot.com/`
    - **Azurecurve** written by Ian Grieve: `https://twitter.com/azurecurve`

# Additional notes and considerations

There are a number of additional factors to consider in your infrastructure planning, including web applications, virtual environments, and printers.

## Web applications

Microsoft publishes separate requirements and recommendations for **web applications**, which include Business Portal, Workflow, Web Services, and SQL Reporting Services: `https://mbs.microsoft.com/customersource/documentation/systemrequirements/MDGP2013_system_requirements_web_apps.htm`. These recommendations work together with different profiles in the Dynamics GP server recommendations. If you are planning on deploying any of these applications, this is an important topic to discuss with your IT and Dynamics GP resources to make sure your planned infrastructure has the appropriate resources to support these applications.

## Virtual environments

Virtual environments have been officially supported with Microsoft Dynamics GP since version 10.0, but they have become much more relied upon in the last few years. I have seen many companies move their existing Dynamics GP implementations to virtual environments or switch to virtual servers during an upgrade. The two major factors to consider with virtual environment are the support and configuration.

### Support for virtual environments

The following virtual environments are listed as supported for Dynamics GP 2013:

- Hardware virtualization
  - Windows Server 2012 Hyper-V
  - Windows Server 2008 R2 Hyper-V
  - Windows Server 2008 Hyper-V
- Software virtualization
  - Microsoft Application Virtualization (App-V) 5.0
  - Microsoft Application Virtualization (App-V) 4.6

Of course, the environments listed above are all from Microsoft. If you would like to use a non-Microsoft virtual environment, you will want to make sure that your virtualization product is listed in the catalog of supported products under the Server Virtualization Validation Program. More details and a link to this product catalog can be found on the Windows Server Catalog website: `http://www.windowsservercatalog.com/svvp.aspx?svvppage=svvpwizard.htm`.

If you already have a virtual environment and want to implement Dynamics GP, even if it is listed as supported when you go through this wizard, make sure you read the fine print. If there is an issue that requires support, often the burden of proof will be on you. To establish that there is really an issue, you will need to reproduce the problem in a non-virtual environment. This may not be a deal breaker and may be a very unlikely scenario given the proliferation of virtual environments, but should be acknowledged and accepted as a potential risk for your implementation by the decision makers in the organization.

Microsoft Support article 897615 details the support policy for non-Microsoft virtualization: `http://support.microsoft.com/default.aspx?scid=kb;en-us;897615`.

## Virtual environment configuration

While the specific resources and configuration of the virtual environment for Dynamics GP will vary greatly depending on your implementation, I have seen one prevalent theme in working with clients' virtual environments over the last few years. If the specifications you have put together will work on a physical environment, they will often not be enough for a virtual environment and you will likely experience performance issues.

Whatever you're planning for, make sure that you are easily able to increase the resources available for the virtual environment. The following is an article with five great tips for SQL Server virtualization from Michael Otey, technical director for Windows IT Pro and SQL Server Pro: `http://sqlmag.com/sql-server/5-sql-server-virtualization-tips`.

# Printers

Prior to mid 2009, each version of Microsoft Dynamics GP had a published printer compatibility list. There were some inherent problems with these lists, because it is virtually impossible to test every printer, and printer models change so quickly that by the time printers were tested and the list was released, most of the printer models on it were already retired by the manufacturers.

An update was published by Microsoft in 2009 that printer compatibility lists would no longer be published as *most printers should be compatible with Microsoft Dynamics GP*. This notice as well as some additional printer resources and links can be found at the following URL: `https://mbs.microsoft.com/customersource/documentation/systemrequirements/MDGP2010_Printer_Compatibility` (requires access to either PartnerSource or CustomerSource). While this references Dynamics GP 2010, at the current time there is no comparable article available specifically for Dynamics GP 2013. However, this is fairly generic and should apply to all Dynamics GP versions going forward.

In my experience not all printers, and more specifically not all printer drivers, will work correctly with Dynamics GP. Possibly the only printer brand we have consistently not seen any issues with is Hewlett-Packard. That is not to say that other printers should not be considered, and if there are already existing printers in the organization, you can easily test them once Dynamics GP is installed to determine if there are any compatibility issues. If planning to purchase new printers, you may want to ask your Dynamics GP partner or Dynamics GP resource for recommendations or experiences with the specific printers you are considering.

Additional considerations for printers with Dynamics GP:

- If planning large or frequent batches of payables checks, many companies find it convenient to set up a dedicated printer for printing checks. This allows the users printing checks to not have to compete with other print jobs, and saves on check stock ruined by others mistakenly printing on it. It also addresses potential issues with lining up checks properly on different printers.
- Depending on the size of reports or check runs planned for Dynamics GP, older printers with limited memory may have issues printing the entire check run or report. For example, a batch of 200 payables checks will first create a file of approximately 7 to 8 MB and then send the entire file to the printer. Newer printer models, even small personal printers, typically have enough memory to handle this, but some older printer models that may only have 4 MB of memory will not be able to handle a check run of this size.
- Top load printers are not very common anymore, but may also present a problem when printing checks or using other preprinted forms, because they tend to feed more unevenly than side or front load printers. Top load printers also have a higher tendency to feed more than one page at a time. For most reports, this may not present an issue, but when printing checks both of these are considerable problems.
- There is a considerably large Dynamics GP online community. If you have a question about a specific printer, you can post a question on the Microsoft Dynamics GP Community Forum (`https://community.dynamics.com/gp/f/32.aspx`) asking if anyone out there is already using this printer.

# Officially supported – what it means to you

Many of the preceding sections, as well as information you may see in various other places, use terminology such as, "supported by Microsoft" or "officially supported". It is important to understand the distinction made between what is officially supported by Microsoft versus what will technically work.

There are many configurations that will fail on a pre-installation compatibility check or return an error during installation. This is the easier scenario to deal with, because you have no choice at that point. However, many configurations may be technically possible, but not supported by Microsoft or may fail in the future. For example, if you had Dynamics GP 9.0 and upgraded to SQL Server 2008, everything kept working fine. However, if you tried to create a new company or went to upgrade to a newer Dynamics GP version, you would get an error that you were on a non-compatible SQL Server version.

Configurations that are not officially supported may simply be things that Microsoft has not tested yet or does not plan on testing, such as new service packs to older operating systems or SQL Server versions. While these may be acceptable for limited testing or some development uses, it is strongly recommended to employ only officially supported configurations for your Dynamics GP production environment. Even though the possibility of an issue may be remote, installing an operation critical application such as Dynamics GP in an unsupported environment is not a risk that many companies are willing to accept. If, for business reasons, the decision is made to use an unsupported environment, make sure that your entire implementation team, including the Champion/Executive, signs off on this.

# Network requirements

To install Dynamics GP on a network, the following are required:

- **Domain**: Domain is listed as a requirement in the Dynamics GP 2013 installation manual, and Peer to Peer environments, previously supported with Dynamics GP, are no longer anywhere in the documentation. This requirement means that all client workstations and servers (including the SQL Server, Remote Desktop Services server, and Web server) must belong to a domain.
- **Network Protocol**: TCP/IP is the only required and supported protocol for Dynamics GP. While Named Pipes can sometimes be used successfully, it is not required and may not be supported.

- **Name resolution**: Name resolution needs to be used so that each computer is identified by a unique host name. Internally handled name resolution is recommended for the most reliable Dynamics GP performance.

# The Remote Desktop Services-only approach

With the proliferation of Remote Desktop Services (previously called Terminal Services) and advances in available functionality, many organizations have been implementing Dynamics GP on a server running Remote Desktop Services, foregoing installations on client workstations completely. Whether this approach is right for your company may depend on a number of factors. Let's take a look at some of the pros and cons.

## Pros of a Remote Desktop Services-only implementation

Following are the benefits of a Remote Desktop Services-only implementation:

- **No need to upgrade any workstations**: This may be a great approach for companies where many client computers do not meet the requirements for Dynamics GP and there are no other reasons to upgrade.
- **Installation, updates, maintenance, and support are all simplified tremendously**: For environments where there are limited IT resources, it is a great deal easier, not to mention less expensive, to install, maintain, and support the Dynamics GP client application on one server as opposed to multiple client workstations. For implementations that have already planned on Remote Desktop Services for remote users, it may add only a small incremental amount of work and cost to set up the rest of the users on the same server.

## Cons of a Remote Desktop Services only implementation

Following are the negatives of a Remote Desktop Services only implementation:

- **Server specifications may need to be more robust**: As there will be more users, the server used for this may need to be significantly more robust, and thus more expensive, than if it were just being used for a limited number of remote users.

- **More licensing costs may be incurred**: Additional Remote Desktop Services users may necessitate the purchase of additional licensing that may not have been planned for otherwise. For example, additional Microsoft Windows user CALs or Office licensing may be needed.
- **Single point of failure**: If all Dynamics GP users are accessing the same Remote Desktop Services server, if that server is down then no users can access Dynamics GP. This can be mitigated by routine maintenance and possibly an additional or standby server.

As you can see from the preceding lists of pros and cons, the Remote Desktop Services-only approach may save time and money on ongoing IT resources, but may cost more in hardware and licensing. As with any infrastructure decision, contemplate this with all the other infrastructure considerations we have discussed to determine the best course of action for your organization.

# The Web Client-only approach

After reading the preceding section about the Remote Desktop Services-only approach, you may be tempted to consider a Web Client-only approach. I believe that this approach is not yet realistic for any except a very small and simple Dynamics GP implementation. And typically the companies that will have a small and simple Dynamics GP implementation will not have the infrastructure in place to support a Web Client installation.

Of course, this may change as more functionality is released for the Web Client and better support is added for customization and add-ons. However, to reiterate my earlier advice, this will need to be thoroughly tested and planned to make sure an approach like this will work for your organization.

# Test/development environment

At different stages of your Dynamics GP implementation, as well as for ongoing development and support, a test or development environment may be required for Dynamics GP.

By this stage of your implementation planning, you will have a good idea of the major components of your Dynamics GP environment and how complicated it will be. A simple environment will include the Dynamics GP application and modules, Management Reporter, and possibly an add-on product. A complex Dynamics GP environment will consist of the Dynamics GP application, Management Reporter, integrations with other systems, and multiple add-on products or customizations.

For a simple Dynamics GP environment, a test environment can be as straightforward as setting up a new company. Dynamics GP has a sample company available, but it will most likely have a different setup, and certainly different data, than your live Dynamics GP companies. To have a more realistic test environment, you can create a new Dynamics GP company and restore a backup of your live company to it. This can provide a much more practical test area for users to train and test functionality. It can also be used by support and development users for their needs; however, this must be done carefully as any system-wide settings changed will impact the production environment. A KnowledgeBase article is available with the steps to create a copy of an existing company: `https://mbs.microsoft.com/knowledgebase/KBDisplay.aspx?scid=kb;en-us;871973` (requires access to PartnerSource or CustomerSource).

For complex Dynamics GP environments, it is recommended to set up a separate server for testing and development. The hardware does not have to be the same, but otherwise the development environment should be as close as possible to your production environment. Your Dynamics GP license allows a development server to be set up for internal use with no additional license needed for the Dynamics GP software (you may still need additional licensing for Windows and SQL Server). The Microsoft Dynamics GP End User License Agreement for Dynamics GP 2013 can be found here: `http://download.microsoft.com/download/C/1/7/C17D132F-6370-45B0-B877-00A4B87F8FF1/Microsoft_Dynamics_GP_2013_and_Microsoft_Dynamics_NAV_2013_End_User_License_Agreement_English.pdf`.

Even with a separate development server, you may decide to create a test company on the production server to facilitate end user training and testing.

# Add-on products

If you are planning on any add-on or third-party products for Dynamics GP, verify the system requirements and recommendations for them. Most add-on products will have the same requirements as Dynamics GP, but some may not yet be supported on newer operating systems or service packs. Some may also require different Dynamics GP service pack levels than what you may be planning.

If the add-on product you're planning on collects large volumes of data, talk to the product manufacturer about expected database growth so that you can plan your storage capacity accordingly.

# Shared files

Most Dynamics GP implementations will have a number of files that may need to be shared by all or some Dynamics GP users. These files could include modified reports and forms dictionaries, OLE notes, and Integration Manager files. I have seen many Dynamics GP implementations share all of these files. This is not a recommended approach as it creates unnecessary network activity and impacts Dynamics GP performance for very little gain. Most of these files are static until there is a service pack or upgrade, and having them local to the Dynamics GP client installation greatly improves stability and performance.

The recommendation is to only share files that are modified or custom for your implementation.

# Modified dictionary files

Recall from *Chapter 1, Application Structure and Licensing* that any modified reports or windows are stored in dictionary (`.dic`) files. Most Dynamics GP implementations will require at least a few report modifications for common reports such as payables checks. The two most typical methods of storing these files are in a shared network location, or locally on each computer running Dynamics GP.

## Shared network location

Using a shared network location is the more common and recommended approach, and most companies already have a file share in place that can be used for this. Having modified dictionary files in one shared network location allows easier maintenance, backup, and updates of these files, as any changes only need to be made in one place. The drawback to this approach is that all users must be out of Dynamics GP before any changes or additional modifications can be made, otherwise it is easy for the dictionary files to get corrupted. This approach can also cause slower performance, although on most networks this is not an issue.

## Locally on each Dynamics GP client

Storing modified dictionaries locally on each client may be a good approach when only a few Dynamics GP users need modified reports, or for situations where performance may be an issue. The major drawback to this is that any change made will have to be propagated to all users that need it. Also, if users are modifying their own dictionaries, backups are needed for all these local files.

If all users are utilizing the same modified dictionaries, there is a technique for automating the distribution of changes described on the Developing for Dynamics GP blog: `http://blogs.msdn.com/developingfordynamicsgp/archive/2008/08/26/automating-distribution-of-customisations-part-2.aspx`.

Keep in mind that this technique may not be easy to set up in all environments, as it relies on all users logging in to Windows daily and having the Dynamics GP installation in the same exact location on each computer, which may not be the case for many companies.

## OLE notes

Just about every screen, transaction, and master record in Dynamics GP has the ability to store associated notes. Notes can be text only, in which case they are stored directly in SQL Server tables, or they can be file attachments. Attachments are stored in an OLE (**Object Linking and Embedding)** container in a predefined location.

The OLE notes location is set individually for each Dynamics GP client. If it is not the same for all installations, users across your Dynamics GP implementation will not be able to see each other's attachments. The recommendation is to have this location on a network share.

## Integration Manager files

If Integration Manager will be used for the Dynamics GP implementation, a database containing all the integration setup files (typically called `IM.imd`) can be shared by all Integration Manager users. Sometimes this is useful, other times it is better to have the integration database stored locally for each installation because the integrations differ by user.

One final consideration for all the shared files we have discussed is that all Dynamics GP users will require full control of these files.

# Data backups

Most organizations implementing Dynamics GP will already have a backup solution and schedule in place. If there is no existing backup solution, it is highly recommended to implement one prior to the Dynamics GP implementation. For new or existing backup solutions, you should verify that there is adequate room to add the additional data generated by Dynamics GP.

For backup solutions with a lot of available space, companies may choose to backup an entire server. At the very least, plan to back up the following:

| What to back up | How often | Notes |
|---|---|---|
| SQL Server databases:<br>• master<br>• GP system database<br>• All GP company databases | Full backups: daily<br><br>Transaction logs: several times a day | After the initial installation and configuration of Dynamics GP, the `master` database does not get updated very often in most environments. However, it is also typically not very large and is very useful to have if a complete system restore is ever required. |
| Modified dictionary files | Daily and before changes are made | Whether these files are local (and different) on each workstation or shared on a network, these should be backed up regularly, as they can easily get corrupted. |
| Integration Manager database | Daily | Local copies or on a network share. |
| OLE Notes directory | Daily | Local copies or on a network share. |

Depending on the components of your Dynamics GP implementation, you may need to add to the list of what data you back up. Backup frequencies and retention policies may differ by organization, but if there is any question, it is always better to err on the side of having more backups available. No one ever got in trouble for having too many backups.

Something that few companies do is test their backups. Once Dynamics GP is in place, consider testing your backups periodically to make sure they can be used to restore your data successfully.

# Additions to the implementation timeline

At this point, you should be able to augment your implementation task list with dates that include equipment purchases, upgrades, installation, and configuration. Using Not Just Widgets as an example, the following is a sample list of infrastructure-specific tasks:

| Task | Description / Notes | Start | Finish By |
|---|---|---|---|
| Order/receive new server for Dynamics GP | NJW will be getting a new dedicated server for Dynamics GP. | April-20-2013 | May-15-2013 |

| | | | |
|---|---|---|---|
| Order and receive new desktops or upgrades | Several desktops are old and were planned to be replaced soon anyway. A few other desktops are fine, but will be upgraded with more RAM. | May-14-2013 | Jun-16-2013 |
| Configure new server and install SQL Server | Includes installation and configuration of Windows Server 2012 and SQL Server 2012 and all the latest service packs for both. | May-16-2013 | May-28-2013 |
| Network share for Dynamics GP | Set up a network location for all shared files for Dynamics GP. Make sure to add this share to backups. | May-28-2013 | May-29-2013 |
| Install Dynamics GP and IM on server | Installation of Dynamics GP 2013, Integration Manager 12.0, and latest service packs for all. | May-30-2013 | May-31-2013 |
| Test printers and buy new ones as needed | Once Dynamics GP is installed, test it with existing printers; order new printers if needed. At the very least one new printer for check printing is planned. | May-31-2013 | Jun-25-2013 |
| Start the configuration of Dynamics GP | This will be an ongoing process, but at this stage at least the NJW company needs to be created and enough setup completed to allow importing of General Ledger data (planned to start Jun-11-2013). | Jun-01-2013 | Jun-10-2013 |
| Configure SQL Server maintenance and backups | Create SQL Server weekly maintenance plans for Dynamics GP databases and set up full database and transaction log backups, also test backups. | Jun-10-2013 | Jun-10-2013 |
| Install Dynamics GP and IM on desktops | End user training starts on Jun-21-2013, so all desktops should have the software installed by then. Not all users will be getting IM. | Jun-16-2013 | Jun-18-2013 |
| Determine what is needed for remote access | NJW would like to start using Dynamics GP first before making the final decision on remote access, so a decision will be made a few weeks after going live. | Jul-16-2013 | Jul-20-2013 |

# Summary

In this chapter, we have focused on the infrastructure planning phase of your Dynamics GP implementation. We discussed general concepts and scope of infrastructure planning, as well as minimum requirements and recommendations for client, server, and Remote Desktop Services. Additional configuration considerations and requirements for networks were detailed. The meaning of official support by Microsoft, and Remote Desktop Services-only and Web Client-only implementations were introduced. Test or development environments, add-on products, and placement of shared files were discussed. Details of data backups were talked about and we put together a sample list of additional implementation tasks.

Now that the planning phases are completed, in the next chapter we will start our installation of Microsoft SQL Server, Dynamics GP, and Integration Manager.

# 5

# Installation of SQL Server, Dynamics GP, and Integration Manager

Now that you have completed the planning for your Dynamics GP implementation, it is time to perform the installation.

This chapter will cover the following topics:

- Pre-installation checklist
- Why installation as the local administrator is important
- Installing Microsoft SQL Server 2012 for Dynamics GP
- Installing the Dynamics GP 2013 application
- Creating an ODBC data source
- Completing the Dynamics GP installation by running Dynamics GP Utilities
- Loading the sample company and creating your new company
- Installing Integration Manager
- Post-installation SQL Server and database settings
- Creating SQL Server maintenance jobs

> Please note that the installation steps and recommendations in this book are based on a US installation. If you are installing Dynamics GP in a different country, please consult with your Dynamics GP resource for anything that may need to be different for your installation.

# Pre-installation checklist

Prior to starting your Microsoft SQL Server and Dynamics GP installation, check your server for requirements and additional recommendations. To ensure no delays, verify that you have all the necessary media, service packs, and license keys that you will need.

It is also a good idea to check for any last-minute updates or known issues added to the Dynamics GP system requirements: `https://mbs.microsoft.com/customersource/documentation/systemrequirements/mdgp2013_system_requirements.html` (requires access to CustomerSource or PartnerSource).

# Checking your server

Check your server for the SQL Server and Dynamics GP prerequisites and requirements, and verify the recommended server settings for Dynamics GP.

## Dynamics GP requirements

In *Chapter 4, Planning – Infrastructure* we went through the requirements and recommendations for Dynamics GP in great detail. Before you start your installation on any computer, confirm that the required service packs have been installed and all other prerequisites are in place.

## SQL Server requirements

Depending on your SQL Server edition and Windows server operating system, some additional components may be required to install SQL Server. For a full list of these, you can refer to the Hardware and Software Requirements for Installing SQL Server:

- For SQL Server 2012: `http://msdn.microsoft.com/en-us/library/ms143506(v=sql.110).aspx`
- For SQL Server 2008 R2: `http://msdn.microsoft.com/en-us/library/ms143506(v=sql.105).aspx`
- For SQL Server 2008: `http://msdn.microsoft.com/en-us/library/ms143506(v=sql.100).aspx`

## Additional recommendations

For the Dynamics GP server where you will be installing SQL Server, the following recommendations can help optimize performance:

- Turn off any unused or unnecessary services.
- Change the virtual memory paging file size to one and a half times the RAM on the server. Microsoft provides documentation about this at the following URL: `http://msdn.microsoft.com/en-us/library/ms187877.aspx`.

> If your server has a large amount of RAM, this recommendation may not be optimal. Additional information is available at the following URL: `http://support.microsoft.com/kb/889654`.

- Set the processor scheduling for background services.

> Please note that if you are not using a dedicated server for Dynamics GP, some of these settings may cause issues for other existing applications and you may need to check with your IT resource on this.

## Ensuring you have all media and license keys

Before starting your installation, gather all your media, service packs, and license or registration keys in one place. Some of the downloads can be quite large and you may want to start them prior to the installation, so that you are not stalled while waiting for them to finish. Common practice is to create an installation directory on a file share or the Dynamics GP server where all the needed installation media will reside, as you will likely need it again for other installations.

> Once a Dynamics GP version is no longer supported by Microsoft, it is often very difficult to find downloads for it. Consider storing all the media for your current versions on your network in case it is needed again.

The following is a typical list of the media and keys you will need:

| Item | Component | Notes/Download links |
|---|---|---|
| Microsoft SQL Server | Media | Download or disks. |
| | Service Pack | A list of the available SQL Server Service Packs and build numbers, along with links for the downloads, is available on my blog: `http://victoriayudin.com/2008/10/05/what-version-of-sql-server-am-i-running/`. |
| | License key | This is often part of the media for SQL Server and gets populated automatically during the installation. |
| Dynamics GP 2013 | Media | Microsoft no longer sends out media for new Dynamics GP versions. You can find the Dynamics GP media downloads at the following URL: `https://mbs.microsoft.com/customersource/downloads/servicepacks/MDGP2013_Release_Download` (requires login). Often there will be a media download available together with the latest service pack to save your time during installation. |
| | Service Pack | Dynamics GP 2013 service packs and hotfixes will be published on the following website: `https://mbs.microsoft.com/customersource/downloads/servicepacks/mdgp2013_patchreleases.htm` (requires login). |
| | License/ Registration keys | You can get your registration (or license) keys on CustomerSource if you are a Dynamics GP customer: `https://mbs.microsoft.com/customersource/` (requires login) or on PartnerSource if you are a partner: `https://mbs.microsoft.com/partnersource/` (requires login).<br>Your Dynamics GP Partner can also help you obtain your registration keys. These will also include Management Reporter and Integration Manager registration keys. |
| Add-ons | Media and registration keys | If you are installing any Dynamics GP add-ons, gather the media and registration keys for each one. Your Dynamics GP Partner can help with this, if needed. |

A few things to remember during your installation:

- Don't be afraid to ask questions—it is a lot easier to pause the installation and get an answer than to have to uninstall and start over.
- Make sure your IT resource is available in case you need passwords or access to systems.
- Make sure your Dynamics GP resource is available in case you have Dynamics GP-specific questions during the installation.

# Installing as the local administrator

Having performed thousands of various software installations and helped troubleshoot many others, one critical recommendation is to always install software while logged into Windows as the **local administrator**. This is true for server, as well as desktop operating systems, and for all the software being discussed in this book.

The local administrator may sometimes be called or identified differently on various operating systems, and on some computers the local administrator may have been renamed; however it will be the account listed as the *Built-in account for administering the computer/domain*. It is important to note that this is not the same as the domain administrator or a user who is in the local administrator's group.

Performing installations as the local administrator ensures that all necessary components get installed and registered properly, and helps avoid various issues in the future. While installing as the local administrator is typically the norm on servers, this is not often the case for desktop operating systems. Many system administrators believe that installing as any local administrator or a domain administrator is adequate. Often installations are not performed as the local administrator because the password is not known. Take the time to either find out or reset the local administrator passwords for all computers that will be part of your Dynamics GP implementation. The time spent on this should be minimal and will pay for itself with the first installation that does not have to be fixed or reinstalled.

I often get push-back on this from IT departments and companies. To them I say - yes, it is possible that you can perform installations while logged in as a user other than the local administrator and the installations may turn out absolutely fine. However, you might encounter problems or issues, if not during the initial installation, then afterwards. Why take the chance? Logging in as the local administrator for all installations will ensure that all of your installations go smoothly the first time.

# Installing Microsoft SQL Server for Dynamics GP

The first step in your installation will be to install Microsoft SQL Server. Installations may vary slightly, depending on the SQL Server version, what components are already installed on the server, and what options you choose to install.

Whether the Dynamics GP SQL Server will reside on a new dedicated server or another existing server, it is typically recommended that a new SQL Server instance be installed for Dynamics GP. This will allow for the settings needed by Dynamics GP to not interfere with settings that may be different for other applications using SQL Server. It will also allow for better control and easier maintenance. With a separate SQL Server instance if the SQL Server services need to be restarted for Dynamics GP, other applications on the server will not be affected.

# Installation steps

The following are steps for a typical installation of SQL Server 2012 Standard with SP 1 on Windows Server 2012:

1. Start the Microsoft SQL Server installation by running `setup.exe`, or having the `autorun` start when you insert the SQL Server installation disk into the server.
2. If the installation detects that you are missing any prerequisites, you will see a notification asking you to install them. Depending on what prerequisites are missing, the message may differ.
3. On the **SQL Server Installation Center** window, select **Installation** on the left-hand side, then select **New SQL Server stand-alone installation or add features to an existing installation**:

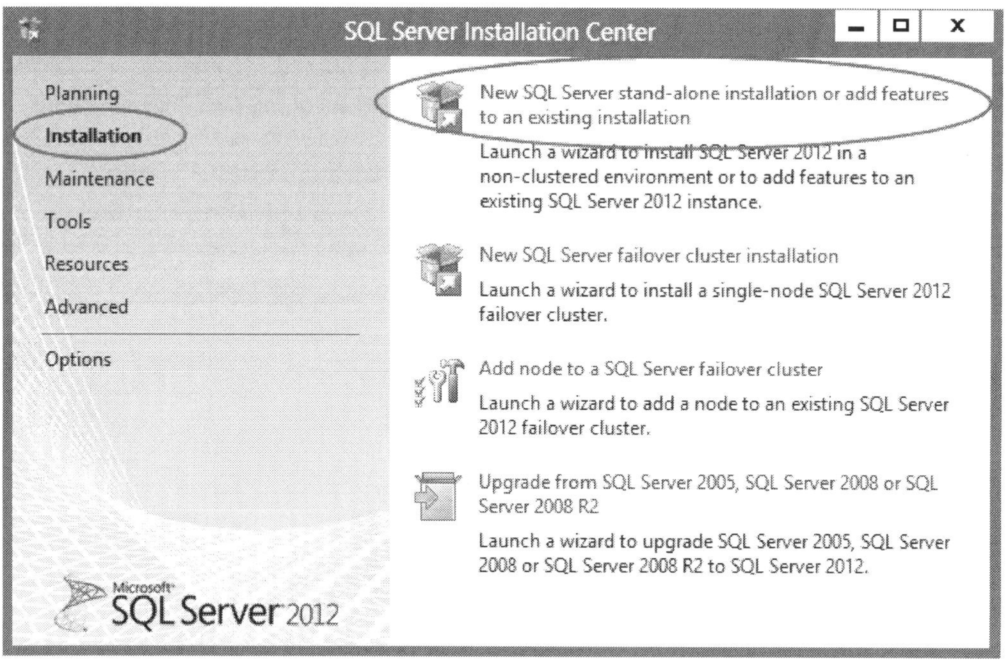

4. The **Setup Support Rules** window will open with details on any issues that SQL Server may encounter during installation. You can see additional details by clicking on the **Show details** button. Clicking on the **Status** hyperlinks will give more details for each rule. Once all the rules show a status of **Passed**, you can continue the installation by clicking on **OK**.
5. The **Product Key** window will typically have your product key already filled in, if not, enter your product key and click on **Next**.
6. On the **License Terms** window, read the license terms and if you agree, then select the **I accept these license terms** checkbox and click on **Next**.
7. The **Product Updates** page will suggest any available updates to be included in the installation. While this is up to you, I prefer to only install major service pack releases for SQL Server. That way it is easy to duplicate an environment and also to determine what service pack you are on at any time. If your media, like mine, already includes the latest Service Pack for SQL Server 2012, you can uncheck the **Include SQL Server product updates** option and click on **Next**:

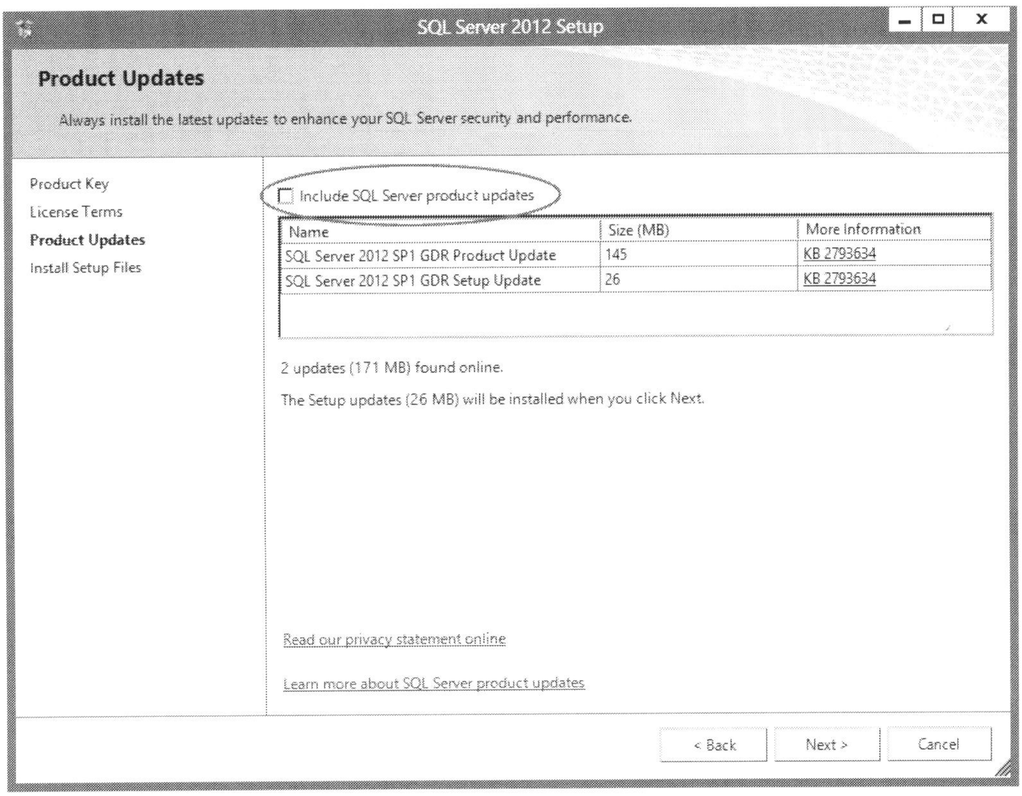

8. The **Setup Support Rules** window will open again showing any issues that were encountered. If the details are collapsed, you can click on **Show details** and then click on the **Status** hyperlink to see details for any of the rules. The following is an example of the warning for the **Windows Firewall** rule:

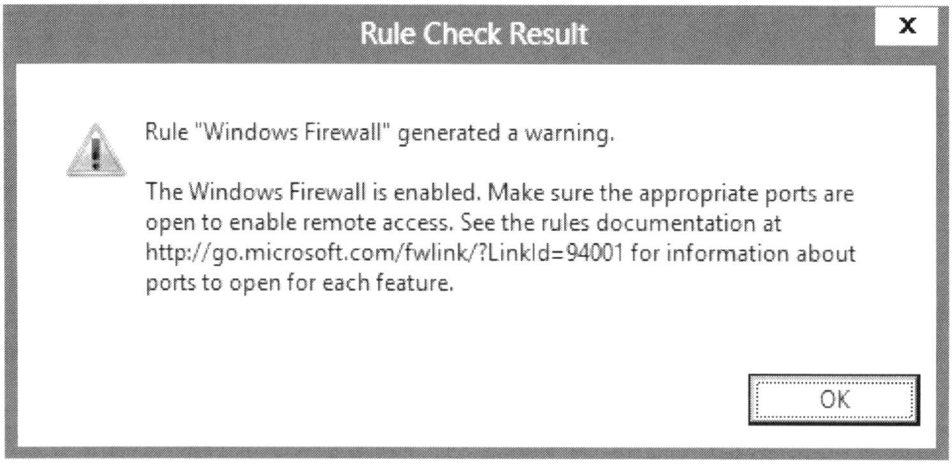


   Click on **Next** on the **Setup Support Rules** window to continue the installation.

9. On the **Setup Role** window you can select **SQL Server Feature Installation** to go to the next window where you will select the features you want to install or **All Features With Defaults** to have all the fetaures installed for you automatically. You can see more details about the defaults by clicking on the **Help** button on this window.

10. If you selected **SQL Server Feature Installation** in the previous step, choose the components you would like to install. The minimum features required for Dynamics GP are **Database Engine Services** and **Client Tools Connectivity**. **Management Tools**, while not required, is also recommended. Whether you have the option for **Basic** or **Complete** will depend on the SQL Server version you are installing. If you have the **Complete** option, that is recommended.

    If you are not going to be using SQL Server Reporting Services or Analysis Services, do not install them, they can be added later if needed. However, if you already have plans for them in the future, it may be simpler to install them now. To get more details about all the features available, click on **Help** or refer to the following URL: `http://technet.microsoft.com/en-us/library/ms143786.aspx`. The following is a typical feature selection:

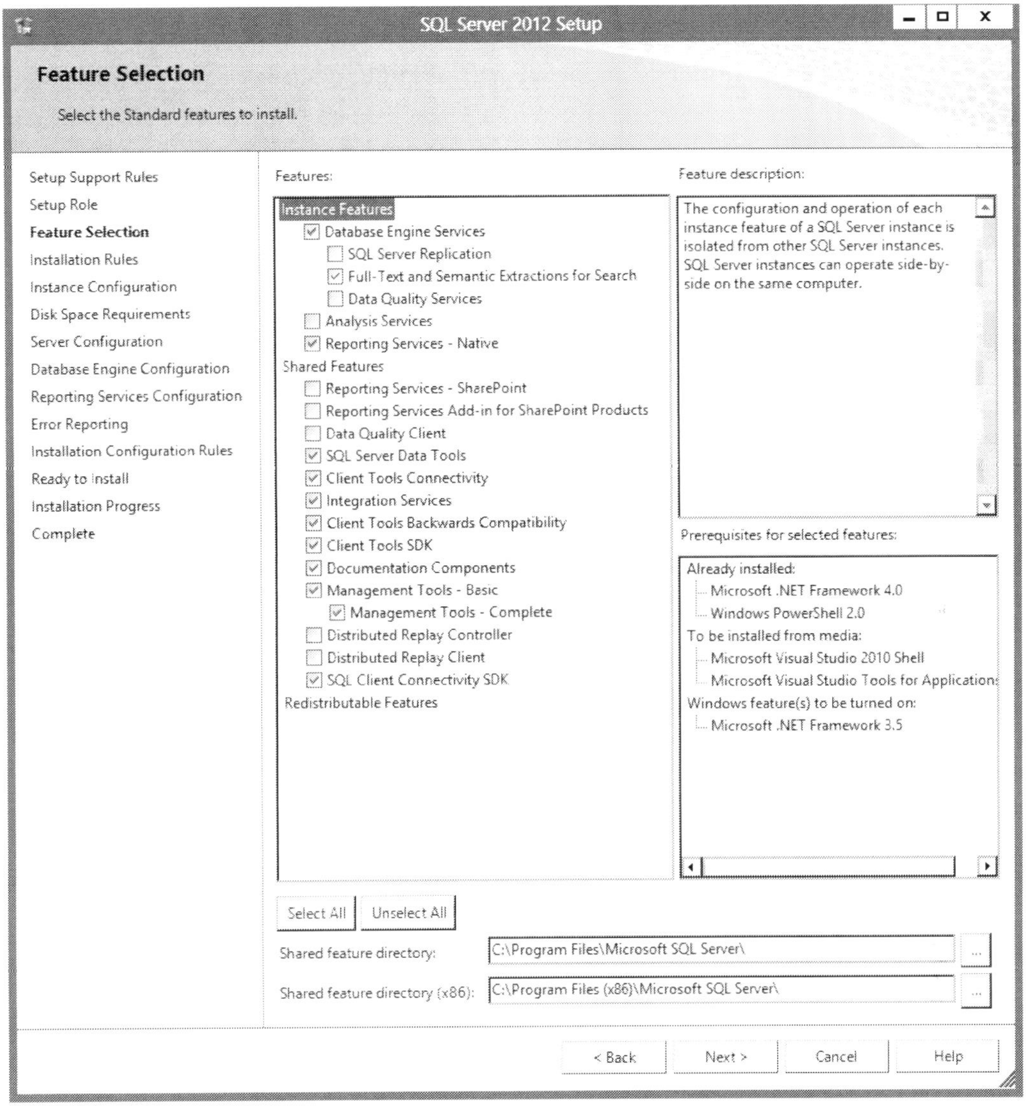


The shared feature directories can be changed if you would like to put them somewhere other than the default locations. Click on **Next** to continue.

11. The **Installation Rules** window will alert you about anything found that would interfere with the installation, click on **Next** to continue.

12. On the **Instance Configuration** window, the typical recommendation is to select **Named instance** and choose a name for your SQL Server instance. Even if there is no default SQL Server instance on this computer, it is recommended to use a named instance, not the default one, and to call it something simple, such as GP. This will help to quickly and easily identify the Dynamics GP SQL Server in the future, when connecting to it from other computers on the network or looking through a long list of SQL Server instances.

    > While it may be tempting to use the Dynamics GP version number in the instance name, consider that you may upgrade Dynamics GP versions and stay on the same SQL Server version and instance. Renaming the SQL Server instance is not a simple endeavor, so it may be best to keep the version number out of the name.

    Changing the **Named instance** on this screen will automatically fill in the same for the **Instance ID**. It is recommended to leave this and not rename the Instance ID. SQL Server instance names:

    - Are not case sensitive
    - Can be a maximum of 16 characters
    - Must start with a letter
    - Cannot contain spaces or special characters except for the dollar sign ($) and underscore (_)
    - Cannot start or end with an underscore (_)
    - Cannot contain reserved words

    On this window you can also change the installation path for SQL Server if you do not want it installed in the default location. The following screenshot shows a typical selection for the **Instance Configuration** window:

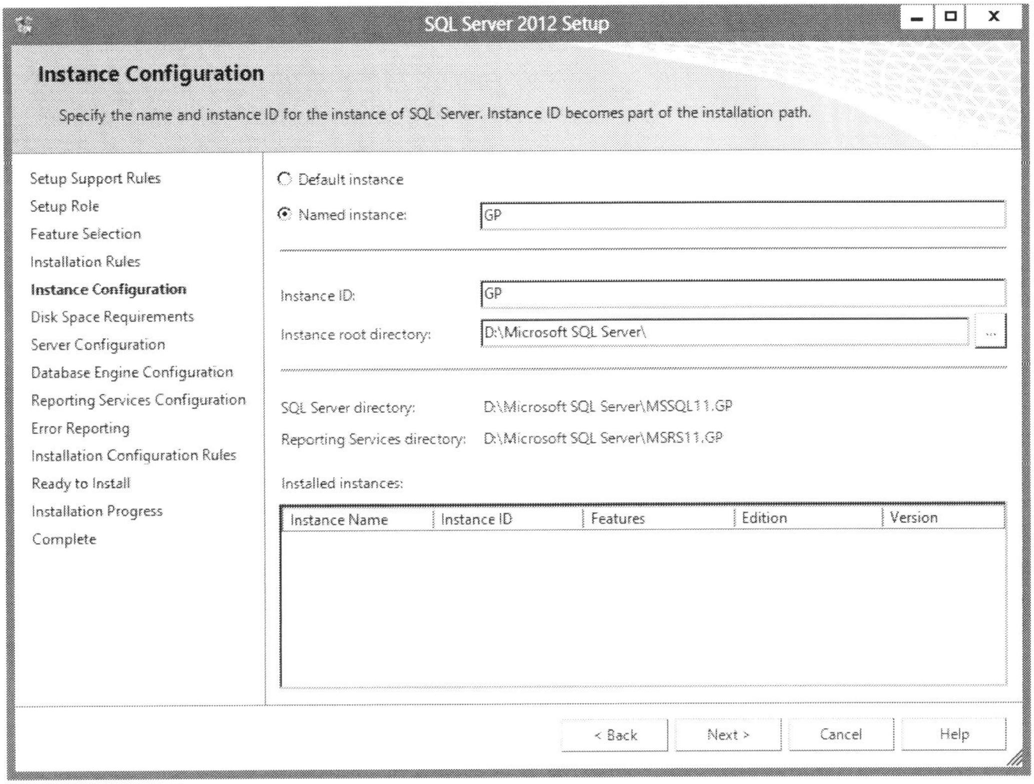


Click on **Next** to continue your installation.

13. The **Disk Space Requirements** window will show you the required and available space for your installation. Make sure there is plenty of space and click on **Next** to continue.
14. On the **Server Configuration** window you can specify the startup type for each SQL Server service, the accounts to use for these services, and the SQL Server Collation.

The defaults on the **Service Accounts** tab should be fine. However if you want to maximize security, you should consult with a SQL Server DBA. Change the services to start automatically under **Startup Type**. Note that you will not be able to change the **Startup Type** or **Account Name** for some of the services.

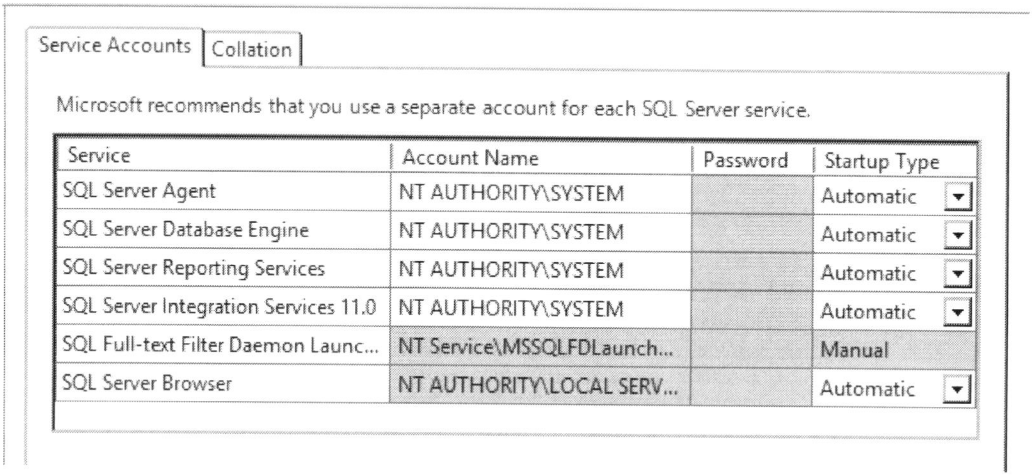


On the **Collation** tab, verify the collation setting for your SQL Server. For US installations of Dynamics GP, use collation with a code page of 1252. Dynamics GP only supports the following two sort orders:

- **DOCI (dictionary order, case-insensitive)**: Sort order 52
- **Binary**: Sort order 50

The corresponding choices for these with a US installation are:

- **DOCI**: **SQL_Latin1_General_CP1_CI_AS**
- **Binary**: **Latin1_General**

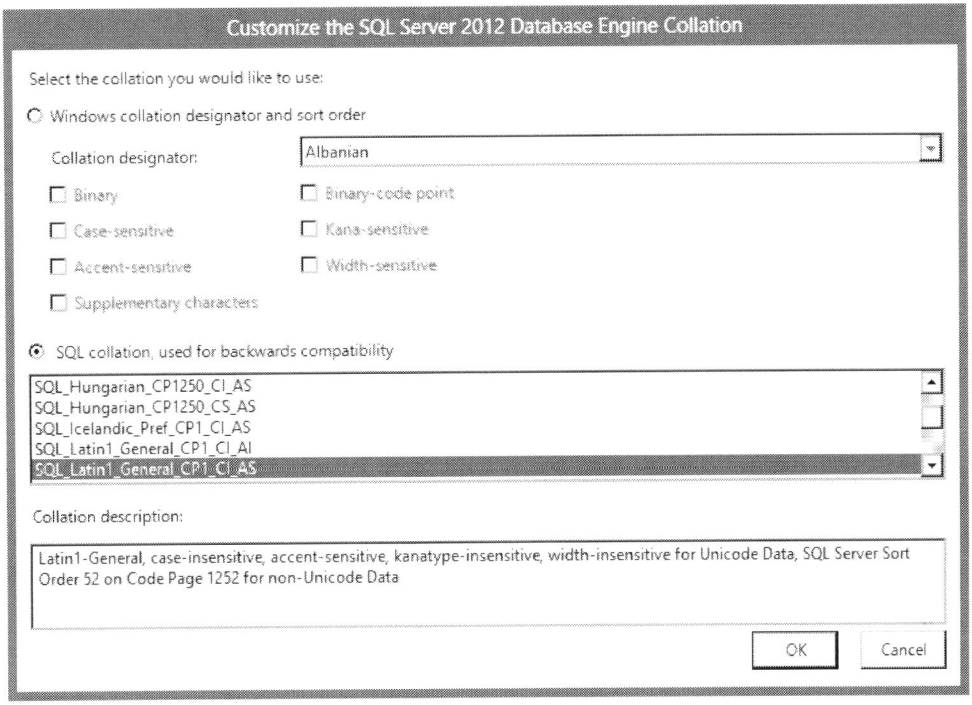
Customize the SQL Server 2012 Database Engine Collation
Select the collation you would like to use:
Windows collation designator and sort order
Collation designator:
Albanian
Binary
Binary-code point
Case-sensitive
Kana-sensitive
Accent-sensitive
Width-sensitive
Supplementary characters
SQL collation, used for backwards compatibility
SQL_Hungarian_CP1250_CI_AS
SQL_Hungarian_CP1250_CS_AS
SQL_Icelandic_Pref_CP1_CI_AS
SQL_Latin1_General_CP1_CI_AI
SQL_Latin1_General_CP1_CI_AS
Collation description:
Latin1-General, case-insensitive, accent-sensitive, kanatype-insensitive, width-insensitive for Unicode Data, SQL Server Sort Order 52 on Code Page 1252 for non-Unicode Data
OK
Cancel

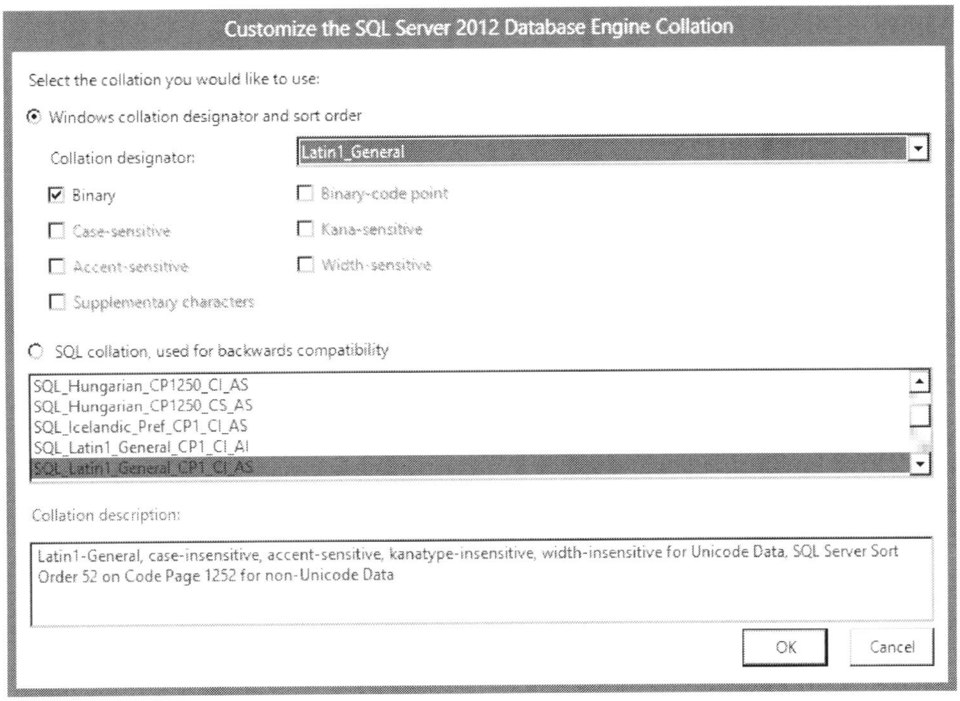
Customize the SQL Server 2012 Database Engine Collation
Select the collation you would like to use:
Windows collation designator and sort order
Collation designator:
Latin1_General
Binary
Binary-code point
Case-sensitive
Kana-sensitive
Accent-sensitive
Width-sensitive
Supplementary characters
SQL collation, used for backwards compatibility
SQL_Hungarian_CP1250_CI_AS
SQL_Hungarian_CP1250_CS_AS
SQL_Icelandic_Pref_CP1_CI_AS
SQL_Latin1_General_CP1_CI_AI
SQL_Latin1_General_CP1_CI_AS
Collation description:
Latin1-General, case-insensitive, accent-sensitive, kanatype-insensitive, width-insensitive for Unicode Data, SQL Server Sort Order 52 on Code Page 1252 for non-Unicode Data
OK
Cancel

For most Dynamics GP installations it is strongly recommended to use the DOCI sort order. This will provide a more consistent user experience, as most applications in use today do not perform case sensitive sorting. It will also allow for greater integration and extension options, as various modules and third-party products you may decide to implement in the future may not be compatible with a binary sort order.

During your SQL Server installation, the collation will typically default to **SQL_Latin1_General_CP1_CI_AS**. However, it is important to verify this. Click on **Next** to continue.

15. On the **Database Engine Configuration** window make sure to change the setting on the **Server Configuration** tab to **Mixed Mode**. Dynamics GP requires SQL Server authentication, so this is not optional. Enter and confirm a password for the SQL sa account.

    If desired, you can use the buttons at the bottom of the window to add Windows users or groups as SQL Server administrators. This is optional and can also be done at a later time. The following screenshot shows an example of having added the local administrator on the server using the **Add Current User** button:

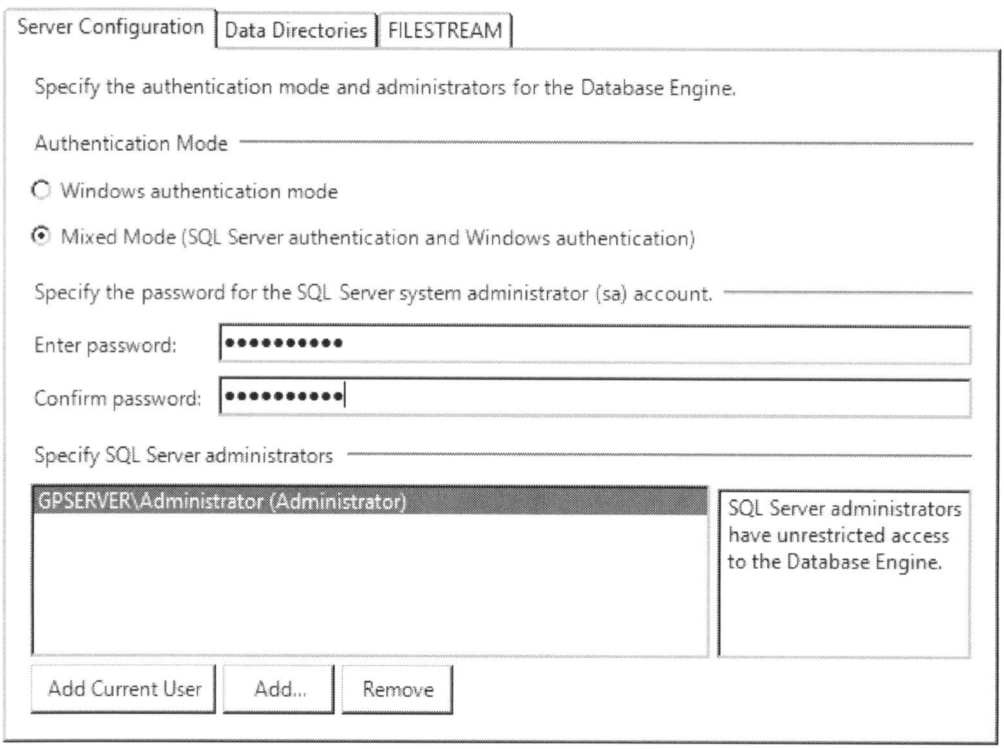

16. If you would like to change the default locations for the SQL Server databases or backups, switch to the **Data Directories** tab to set these. Click on **Next** to continue.
17. If you selected **Reporting Services** during the **Feature Selection**, the **Reporting Services Configuration** window will come up. Here you can decide whether you want to only install Reporting Services or configure them as well. Click on **Next** to continue.
18. On the **Error Reporting** window, decide if you would like to automatically send error reports to Microsoft and click on **Next** to continue.
19. Another test will be performed to verify that no installation processes will be blocked. You can view details and more information on the **Installation Configuration Rules** window. Click on **Next** to continue if there are no failures showing.
20. The **Ready to Install** window will list all of the settings you have chosen so that you can confirm everything is correct. If you need to change anything, use the **Back** button, otherwise click on **Install**.
21. Once the installation is completed, the **Installation Progress** window will show all the components that have been installed. Click on **Next** to continue.
22. The **Complete** window will give you additional information about your installation and show you the location of the installation log file.

After the installation of SQL Server, if your installation did not already include it, it is recommended to install the latest service pack, as long as that service pack is supported for Dynamics GP. For the latest updates on compatibility, check the **Microsoft System Requirements for Dynamics GP 2013** web page: `https://mbs.microsoft.com/customersource/documentation/systemrequirements/mdgp2013_system_requirements.htm` (requires access to either PartnerSource or CustomerSource). A list of SQL Server build numbers and what service packs they correspond to is available at the following URL: `http://victoriayudin.com/2008/10/05/what-version-of-sql-server-am-i-running/`.

For both SQL Server 2008 and 2012 you can see the build number next to the SQL Server instance name at the top of the **Object Explorer** pane in SQL Server Management Studio. You can also execute the following query in SQL Server Management Studio to get the version number and edition of SQL Server installed:

```
select @@version
```

# Installing the Dynamics GP 2013 application

It is usually recommended to install the Dynamics GP application on the SQL server to help with administrative, maintenance, and troubleshooting tasks. However, this is not a requirement, as there is no application server needed for Dynamics GP. If you have chosen not to install the Dynamics GP application on the same server as SQL Server, you can perform the first Dynamics GP installation on any computer on your network.

The steps for installing the Dynamics GP application are the same for server and client installations. If you are used to installing prior Dynamics GP versions, you will notice that there is no longer a choice for client or server installations as we go through the installation steps.

The following steps and screenshots detail the steps for installing Microsoft Dynamics GP 2013 on Windows Server 2012. The media used for this installation is for Dynamics GP 2013 with Service Pack 1, which can be downloaded from PartnerSource or CustomerSource.

1. Start the Dynamics GP installation by running `setup.exe` from the media.
2. If the installation detects any missing components, the **Microsoft Dynamics GP 2013 Bootstrapper Setup** window will open, showing what components are missing:

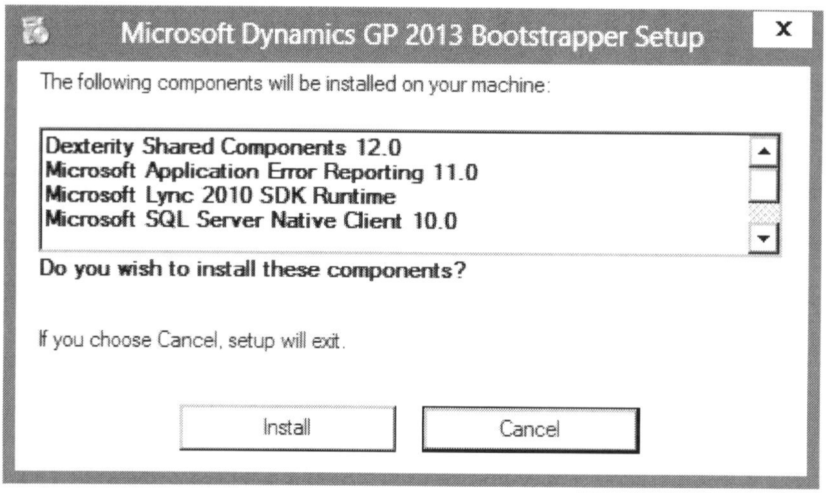


3. Select **Install** to install all the needed components. Click on **Close** after all the components have been installed. This will typically not require a restart.

4. Select **Microsoft Dynamics GP** under the **Install** section:

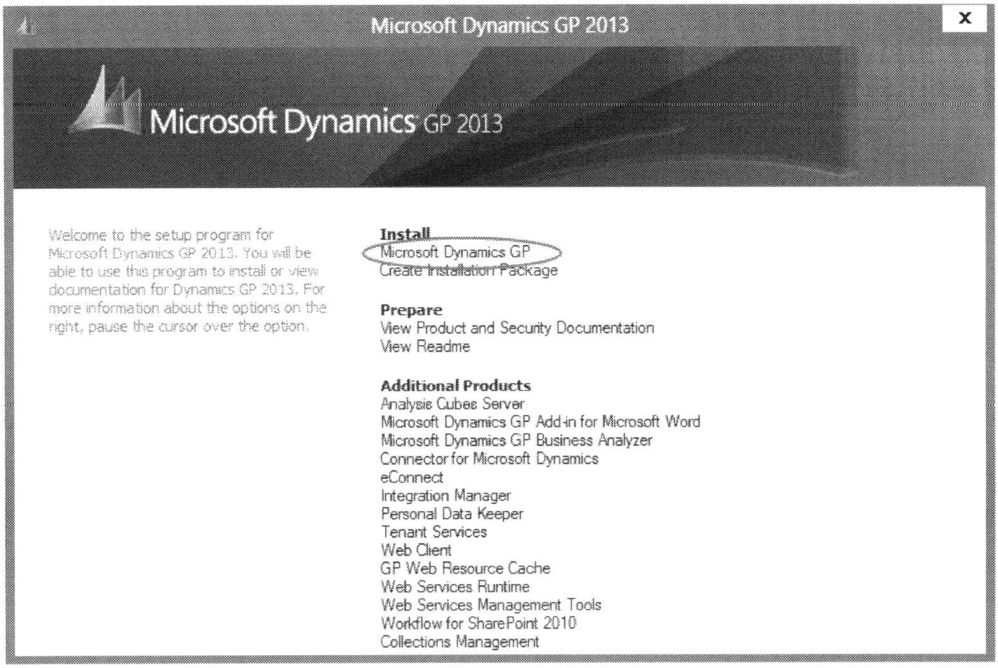


5. On the **Country/Region Selection** window select the appropriate option and click on **Next**:

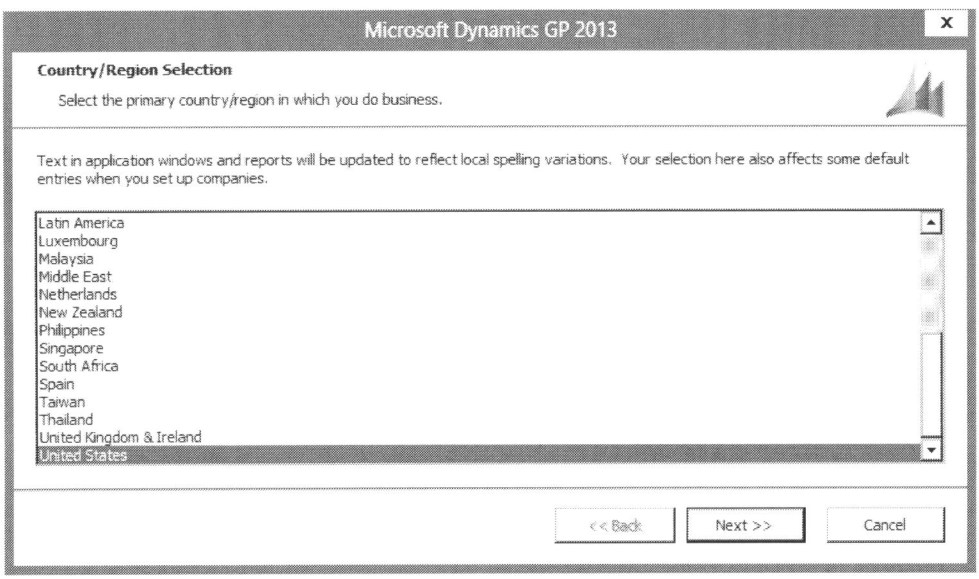

6. On the **License Agreement** window, review the license terms and, if you agree, select the **I accept the terms in the License Agreement** radio button, then click on **Next**.
7. The **Select Features** window will present you with features available to install. While it may be tempting to select all the features to be installed, I strongly recommend that you do not do this. Installing features you do not own, or will not use, will complicate maintenance and upgrade of your Dynamics GP, will cause startup and some functionality of the application to be slower for users, and may actually interfere with functionality that you do want and need. All of the components can be added later if needed, so stick to installing only what you need. If you are not certain about some of the options, consult your Dynamics GP resource.

   One feature that I would recommend for everyone to install is the **Professional Services Tools Library** (PSTL). This is a collection of helpful tools that are now offered free from Microsoft and it is useful to have this installed on all computers where you are using Dynamics GP.

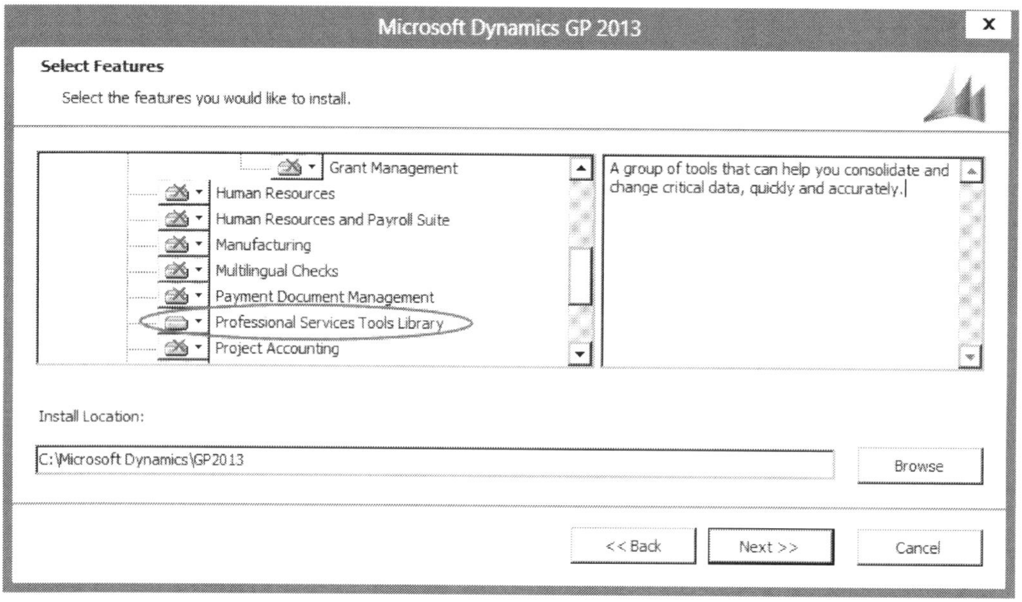


8. For the **Install Location**, consider making this the same location on all your computers and also putting it outside of the **Program Files** directory. While this is not a requirement, it may help mitigate issues with permissions in the future. I have installed Dynamics GP successfully both inside and outside of the **Program Files** directory. If you choose to change the **Install Location**, it does not have to already exist, it will be created as needed. Click on **Next** to continue.

9. The **SQL Server** window will offer to create the **ODBC** (Open Database Connectivity) data source for you. I prefer not to have the installation create the data source because you do not get an option to change the name. If you want to determine your own data source name, select the **Do not create a data source** checkbox. If you do decide to have this created for you, enter the **SQL Server Name** in the format `Server\SQL Server Instance`. The data source created will be called `Dynamics GP`.
10. New to Dynamics GP 2013 is the ability to choose the name of the system database. As we talked about in *Chapter 1, Application Standard and Licensing*, this database holds all the system-wide settings that are shared globally by all Dynamics GP companies. Prior to Dynamics GP 2013 this was forced to be called DYNAMICS. Unless you have a good reason to name this something different, it may be easier to keep this as DYNAMICS for your installation. It will still be referred to as DYNAMICS for many years to come and there may be some customizations, modifications or third-party products that still use the `DYNAMICS` database name.

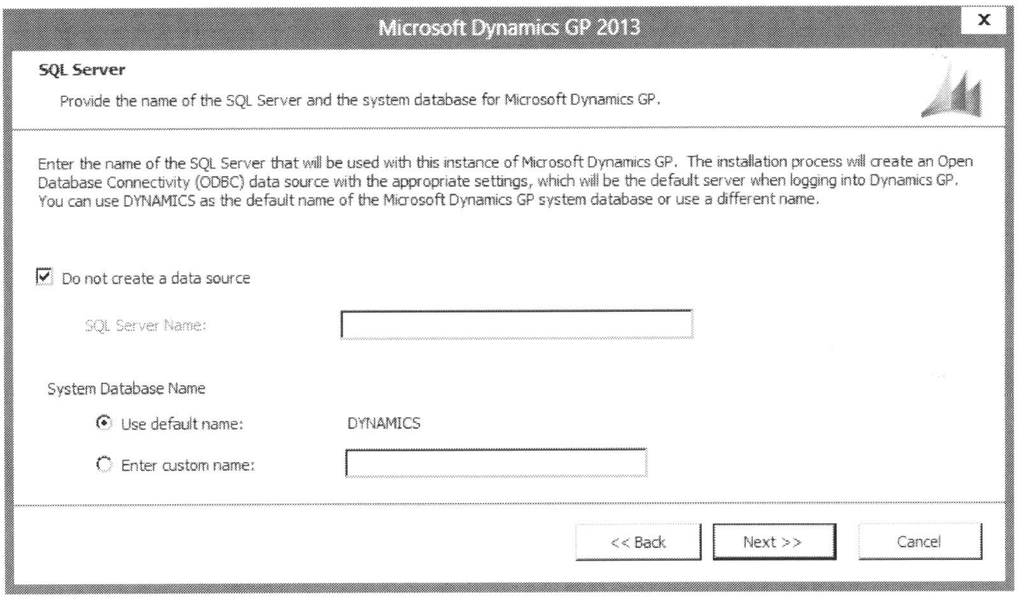

> Changing the name of the system database will allow you to have multiple Dynamics GP installations on the same SQL Server instance. For example, you could have a prior version of Dynamics GP running alongside Dynamics GP 2013 without needing a separate SQL Server instance.

Click on **Next** to continue.

11. The **Install Program** window gives you a final chance to go back and make changes. Click on **Install** to start the installation.
12. The **Installation Progress** window will open during the installation. Once it has finished, it will say **Installation Complete**. Click on **Exit**.
13. If you did not use installation media with the latest service pack, install the latest service pack for Dynamics GP 2013. Service pack information and downloads can be found at the following URL: `https://mbs.microsoft.com/customersource/downloads/servicepacks/mdgp2013_patchreleases.html` (requires login).

> Dynamics GP will check the build number of the client application against the Dynamics GP SQL Server database on every login, and will not allow logging into the application if the versions are not the same. So, for example, if the database has been upgraded to service pack 4, but the client computer only has service pack 3 installed on it, Dynamics GP will not allow the login from that client computer.
>
> Even if this was not checked automatically by the application, it is critical to keep all installations of Dynamics GP on the same exact build number, as there are often database and code changes in new builds.

# Creating an ODBC data source

Every computer that will be running the Dynamics GP application will need to have an ODBC data source pointing to the SQL Server. This is true for all servers and workstations, including the server where SQL Server is installed if you are installing the Dynamics GP application there.

Even though Dynamics GP is supported on 64-bit operating systems, it is a 32-bit application and requires a 32-bit ODBC data source. To create a 32-bit ODBC data source on a 64-bit operating system, run the `Odbcad32.exe` file, found in the `C:\Windows\SysWOW64\` directory instead of following Step 1 as shown in the following section, then follow the steps starting with Step 2.

# Steps to create the ODBC data source

The following are steps to create the ODBC data source for Dynamics GP:

1. Go to **Start** | **Control Panel** | **Administrative Tools** | **Data Sources (ODBC)**.
2. Click on the **System DSN** tab.
3. Click **Add** and choose one of the following drivers:
    - **SQL Server Native Client 10.0** (for SQL Server 2008 or 2008 R2)
    - **SQL Server Native Client 11.0** (for SQL Server 2012)
4. Click **Finish**.
5. On the **Create a New Data Source to SQL Server** window enter the **Name**, **Description**, and **Server**:

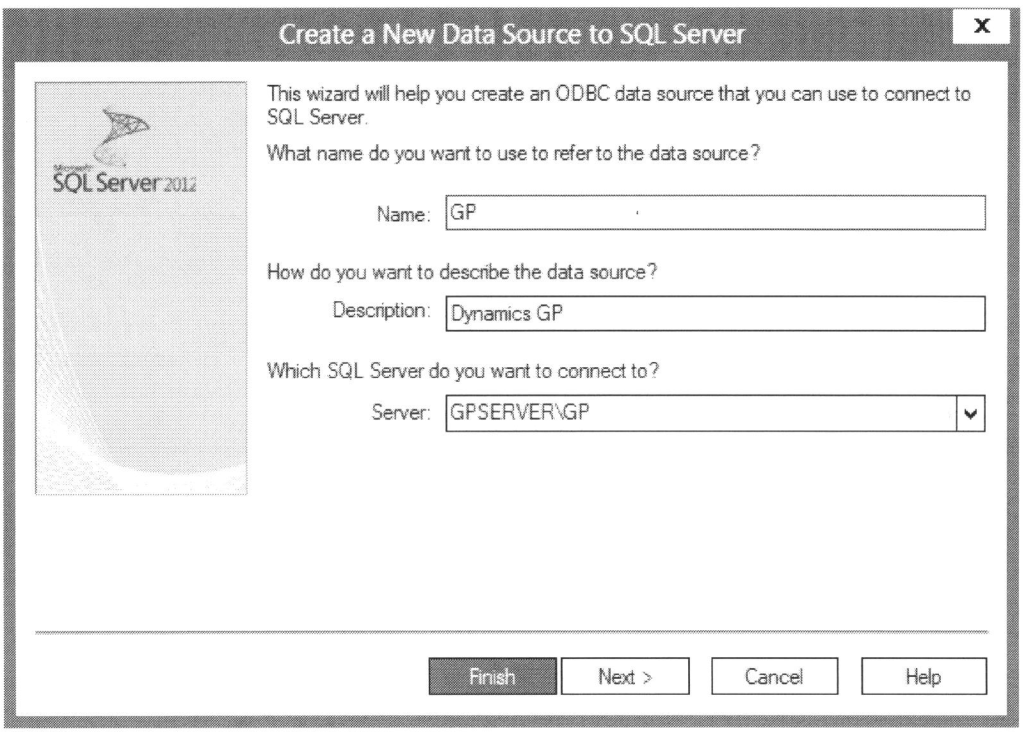

While the **Name** can have spaces and numbers, it is recommended to keep it as simple as possible. This will be what users see as the **Server** when they log into Dynamics GP. The **Description** is optional and can be anything you like. The **Server** is the name of your SQL Server instance, which will be in the format `Server\SQL Server Instance`. For a default instance of SQL Server, it will be `Server`. If you know it, it is usually faster to type this in, otherwise you can click on the drop-down arrow to have the system search for available SQL Servers and select it from the list. Click on **Next** to continue.

6. Select the **With SQL Server authentication using a login ID and password entered by user** radio button and enter the sa **Login ID** and **Password**.

> The sa password will not be stored with the ODBC data source, it is only needed for this initial step of connecting to the server.

Click on **Next** to continue.

7. Uncheck all the options on the next window:

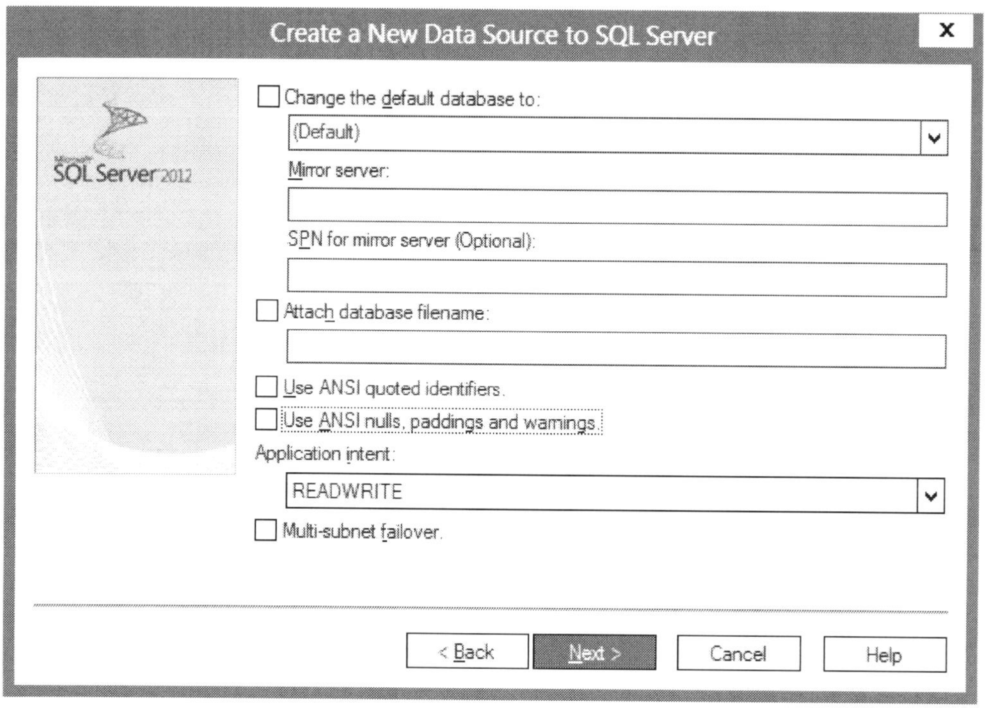

In particular, unchecking the two **ANSI** options is important, because these are not supported by Dexterity, Dynamics GP's development environment. If you would like to change the default database, this will not cause any issues (nor will it be used) for Dynamics GP. Click on **Next**.

8. Again, uncheck all the options on the next window:

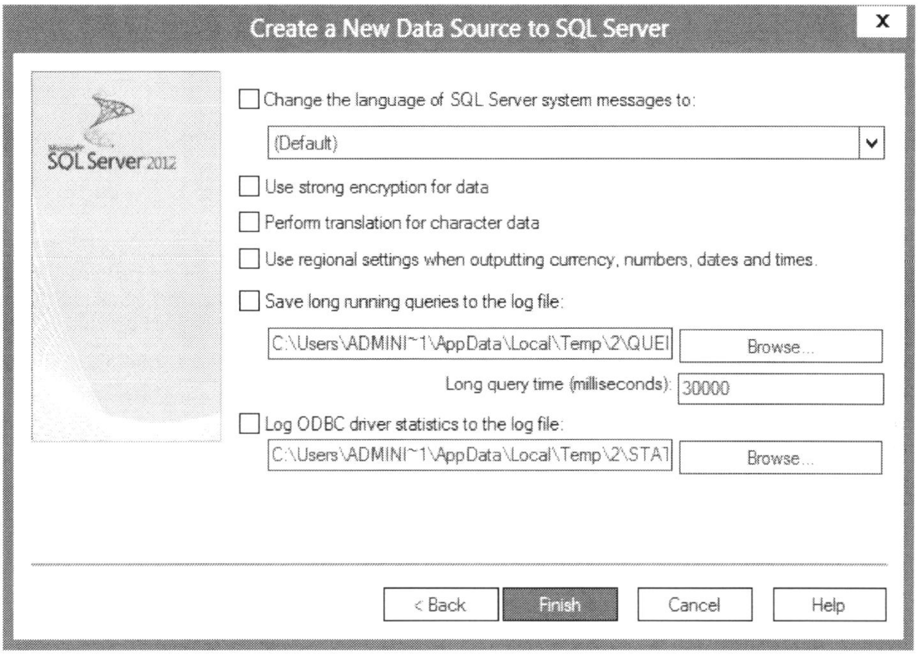


Of particular importance for Dynamics GP are the **Perform translation for character data** and **Use regional settings when outputting currency, numbers, dates and times** options. If left checked, these options could cause the SQL Server to return data to the Dynamics GP application in a format that is different from what the application is expecting. Click on **Finish** to continue.

9. Click on the **Test Data Source...** button, and you should get a message saying **TESTS COMPLETED SUCCESSFULLY!** Click on the **OK** button three times to close all the ODBC windows.

This ODBC data source can now be used to connect the Dynamics GP application to your SQL Server.

> It is critical to create all your ODBC data sources with the same name and options selected to avoid issues with logging into Dynamics GP.

# Dynamics GP Utilities

Dynamics GP Utilities are used to perform global administrative tasks such as:

- Completing the Dynamics GP installation, which consists of:
    - **Creation of the Dynamics GP system SQL Server database**: While you specified the name for the system database during your Dynamics GP installation, it is not actually created until you run Dynamics GP Utilities for the first time.
    - **Creation of the DYNSA user**: DYNSA is a SQL Server login created by Dynamics GP and set to be the database owner of all the Dynamics GP databases.
    - **Creation of the DYNGRP and DYNWORKFLOWGRP SQL Server database roles**: Security for the Dynamics GP application is set inside the application itself, not in SQL Server. Typically, no SQL Server permissions are needed for the individual Dynamics GP users. All permissions are granted to the DYNGRP role and Dynamics GP users are added to the DYNGRP role when they are created by the application and granted access to companies.
    - Defining the account framework.
    - Setting passwords for DYNSA, Dynamics GP system, and Lesson Users.
- Creating new companies.
- Performing upgrades.
- Loading and reloading the sample Dynamics GP company data.
- Turning off the SOP and/or Invoicing module warning message.
- Synchronizing the Dynamics GP application to the system database.

In the following sections, we will go over the steps needed to complete the Dynamics GP installation, load the sample company, and create a new company.

# Completing the Dynamics GP installation

The next step in the Dynamics GP installation is to run Dynamics GP Utilities to create the account framework and the necessary SQL Server components. Follow these steps to continue your Dynamics GP installation:

1. Launch Dynamics GP Utilities by navigating to **Start** | **All Programs** | **Microsoft Dynamics** | **GP 2013** | **GP Utilities**.
2. If you installed a Service Pack separately from the initial installation of Dynamics GP, you will be prompted to include **New Code**, select **Yes**.
3. Choose your ODBC Data Source Name (DSN) under **Server** (it will default if it is the only one that exists on the computer), enter `sa` for the **User ID** and type in the sa **Password**. Click on **OK**.

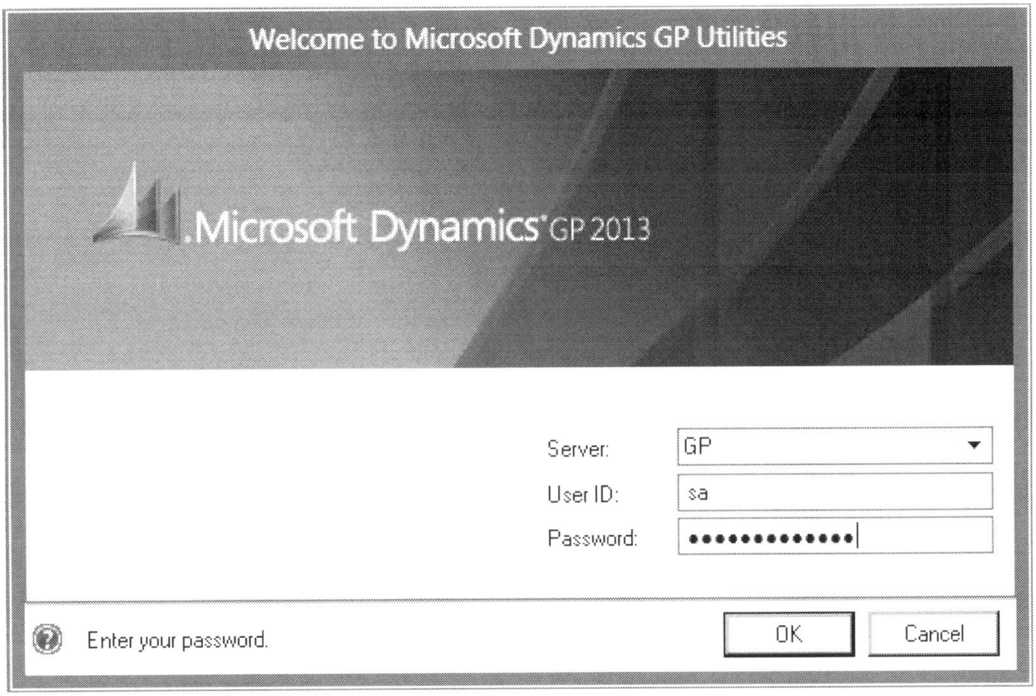


4. On the next **Welcome to Microsoft Dynamics GP Utilities** window, click on **Next**.

5. The **Installation Options** window will let you know that the Microsoft Dynamics GP system database has not been created yet and ask you to choose an installation option:

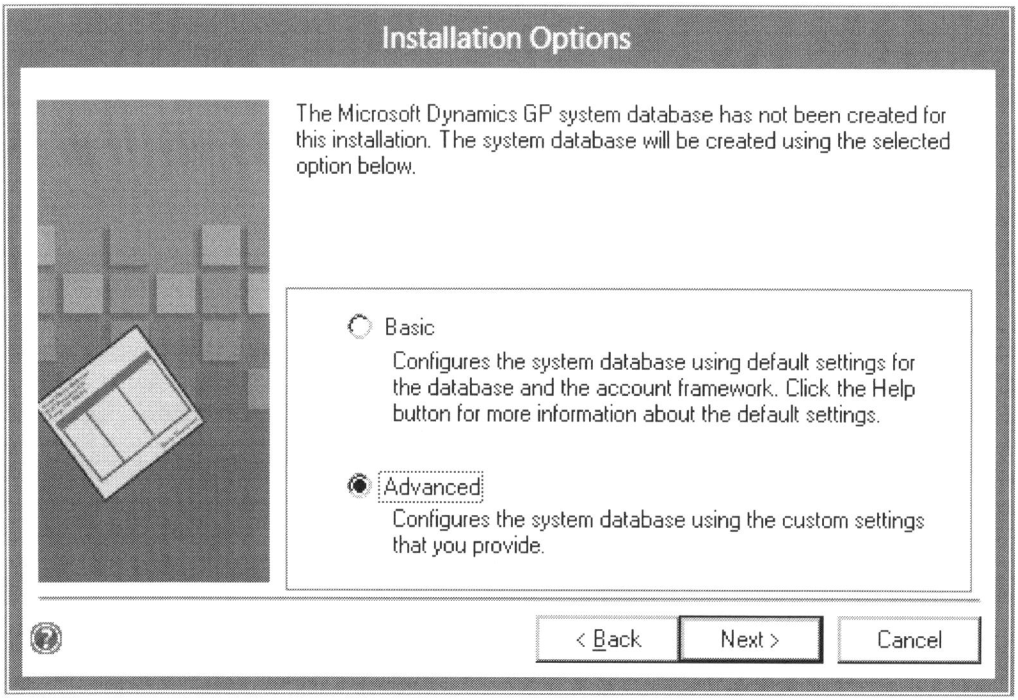


Using the **Basic** option is not recommended. One of the key disadvantages of the Basic option is that it will not let you select your own account framework. For the Basic installation option, the account framework will have five maximum segments of nine characters each and no sorting options. The Basic option will also not allow changes to the locations of the database files and will leave the Dynamics GP system password blank.

Select **Advanced** and click on **Next**.

6. On the **Database Setup** window you can change the location of the SQL Server database files:

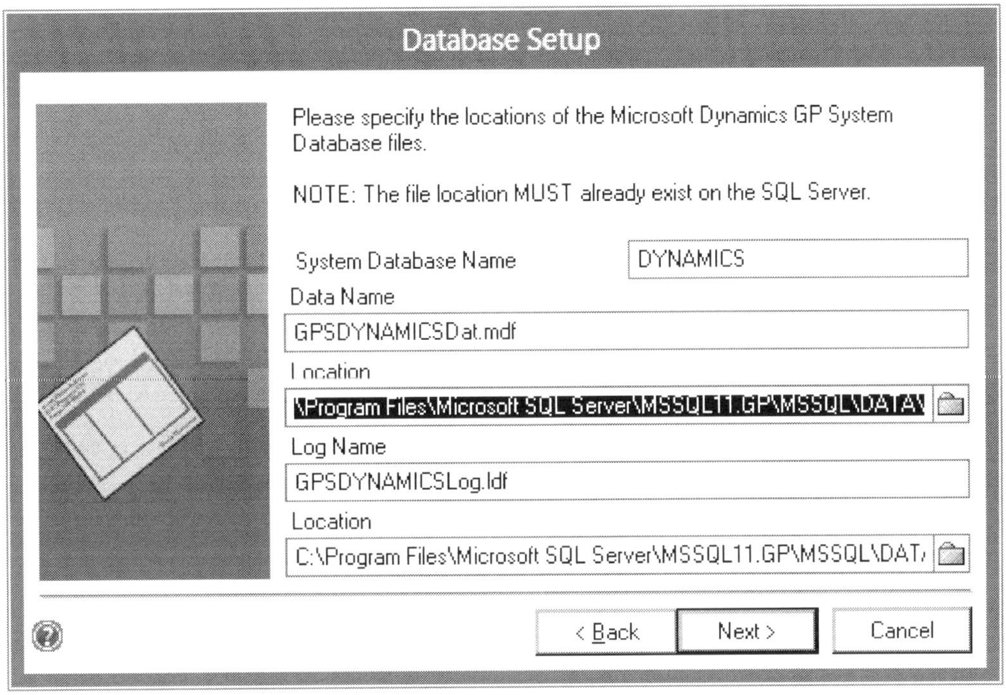


Note that you can see, but not change the **System Database Name** you selected during installation. You also cannot change the **Data** and **Log** file names for the system database. The file locations will default to the setting of your SQL Server. If you decide to change the locations of the files, the locations have to already exist. After making any desired changes, click on **Next**.

7. On the **Set Up Account Framework** window, enter what you have decided to use for the General Ledger account framework. For more details on this, please refer back to the account framework section in *Chapter 3, Planning – Dynamics GP System*.

   These will be the maximum values allowed for General Ledger accounts in any Dynamics GP company you create in the future. These are also not possible to change easily without purchasing additional tools or services, so if you are not sure about this, consult with your Dynamics GP resource.

   The following illustrates the typical settings for the account framework:

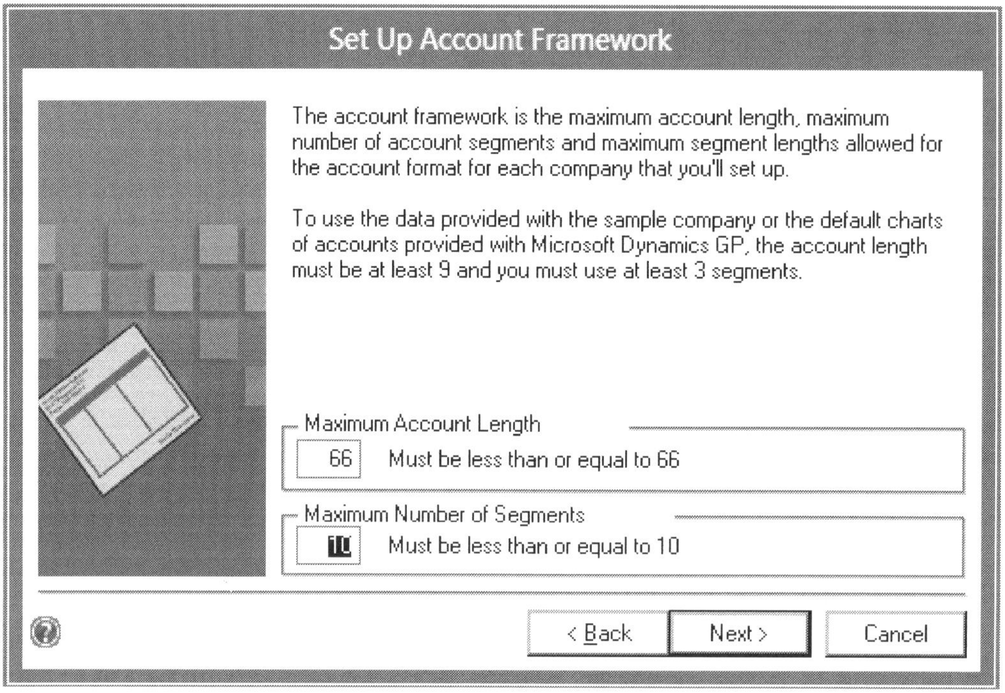


   Click on **Next** to continue.

8. Having selected 66 and 10 for the maximums on the previous window will result in 10 segments each with a maximum length of 6 on the **Set Up Account Segment Lengths** window:

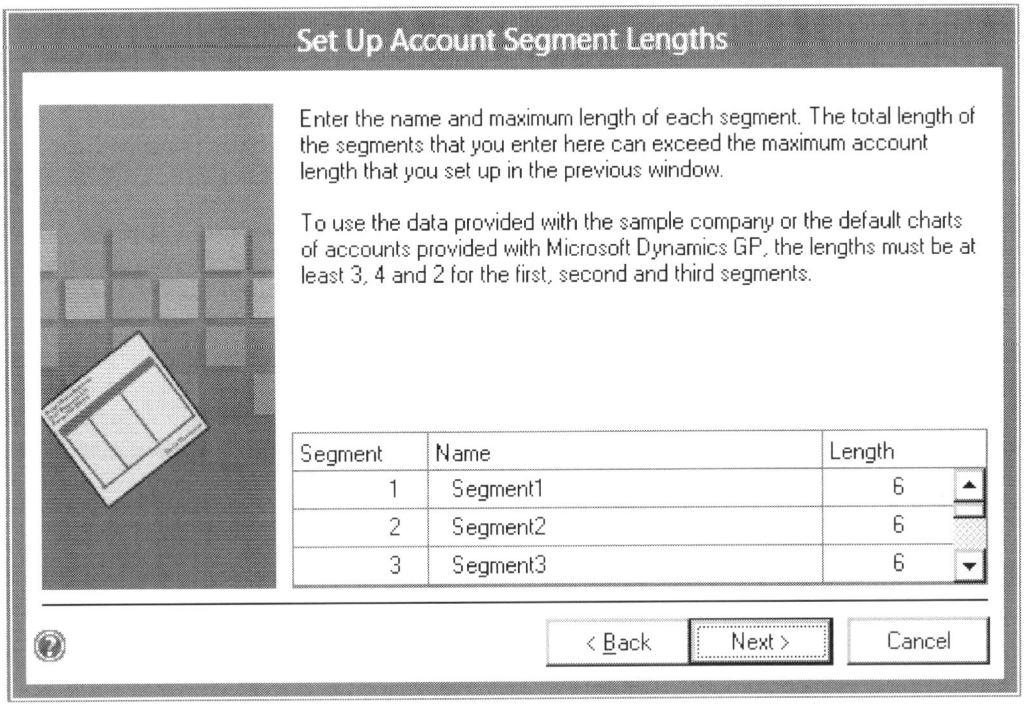


Scroll through the list and make any changes desired, then click on **Next**.

9. Additional sorting options allow users in Dynamics GP to sort, create reports, individually display, and search by each account segment for which a sorting option exists. It is recommended to create a sorting option for each account segment in your account framework.

   On the **Define Additional Sorting Options?** window select **Yes** and then click on **Next**:

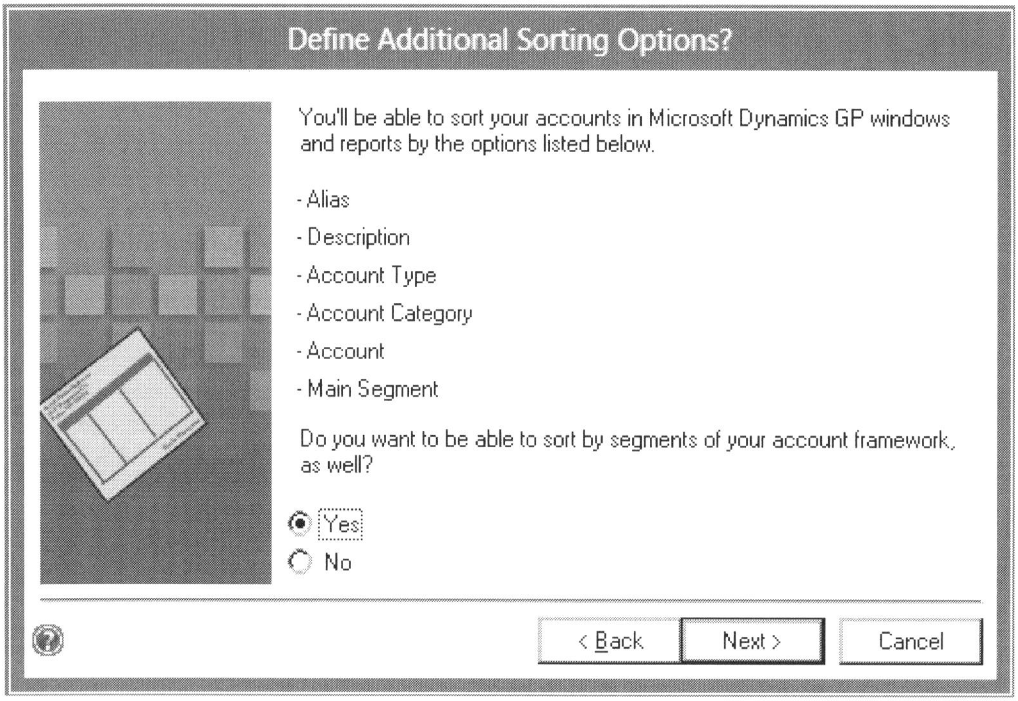

10. On the **Set Up Additional Sorting Options** window, add each segment from the **Available Segments** list on the left to the **Selected Sorting Options** list on the right. When you are done, it will look similar to the following screenshot:

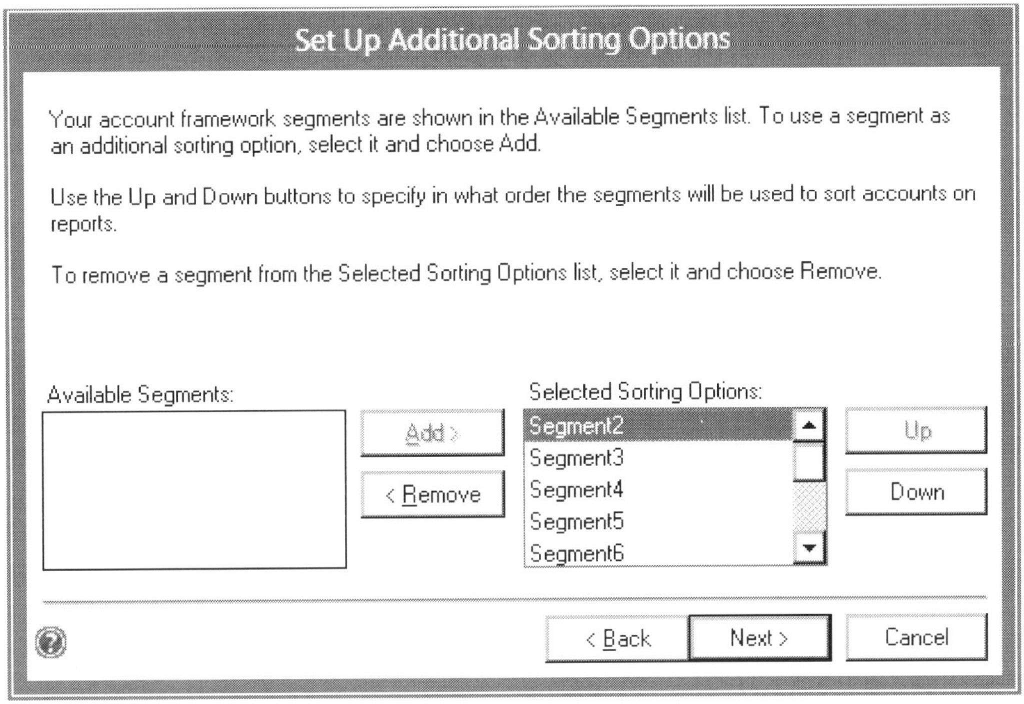


The sorting options are not something that can be changed later, so it is important to set them correctly during the installation. Click on **Next** to continue to the **Verify Account Framework** window. This will recap what you have entered on the previous windows. If everything is correct, click on **Next**.

11. On the **Enter DYNSA User Password** window, enter and confirm a password for the DYNSA user. A password for DYNSA is required. DYNSA can be used to manage users in the Dynamics GP application and is important because it must be the owner of the Dynamics GP SQL databases for various operations including updates and upgrades. Often this password is set to be the same as the sa, as the same user would typically be using them both. This password can be changed later in the Dynamics GP application.

12. On the **Enter System Password** window, enter and confirm a system password for Dynamics GP. This password will be used inside the Dynamics GP application to restrict access to all system windows. While a blank password is allowed here, it is highly discouraged as it will leave your Dynamics GP system settings open to all Dynamics GP users that may have permissions to them. Some notes and recommendations for the Dynamics GP system password are as follows:
    - Do not make the system password the same as your sa or DYNSA password. There may be times when you want users to have one of these passwords, but not the others. As it is sometimes confusing to users which password they are being asked for, they may inadvertently know a password they should not and gain access to areas they should not see if these passwords are the same.
    - The system password can be changed at any time from the Dynamics GP user interface (entering the current password is required).
    - Consider leaving the system password blank while setting up the system prior to allowing users in. This is typically when you will need to enter the system setup windows often, so you can save yourself some time by doing this. If you do this, make sure to set the system password prior to having users log in to Dynamics GP.

    Click on **Next** to continue.

13. The settings you have chosen will be listed on the **Confirmation** window. You can use *Ctrl+A* to select all the settings shown, *Ctrl+C* to copy them, and *Ctrl+V* to paste them somewhere else if you would like to print or save these for the future. Click on **Back** if you need to change anything else, or click on **Finish** to continue.
14. The **Server Installation Progress** window will list all the steps in the creation of the system database and show you the progress.
15. After the system database is created, the **Business Intelligence Reports Setup** window will give you the option of deploying SSRS and/or Excel reports. If you know you're planning on using these, you can set them up now, otherwise you can do this at a later time.

    Note that with this step you are simply entering the default locations to be used when you create a new company in Dynamics GP. At that point, these settings will default in, but can be changed as needed.

    Click on **Next**. If you have not selected to set up SSRS or Excel reports, skip to step 18.

16. On the **SQL Server Reporting Services Reports Setup** window, enter the **Report Server Mode**, **Reports Server URL** and **Report Manager URL** for your SSRS Server. Using the installation settings shown in this example, the setup would look like the following:

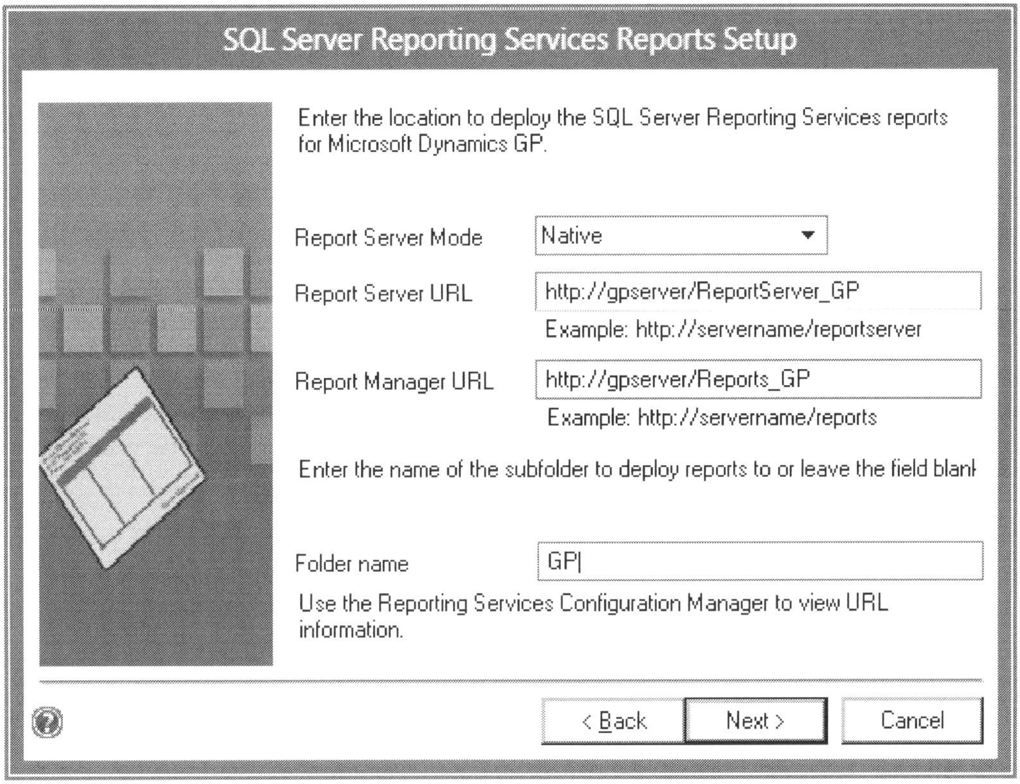


The **Folder name** is optional and might only be needed if you have non-Dynamics GP reports in SSRS as well. Click on **Next**.

17. If you have chosen to include Excel reports, choose the location for these on the **Excel Reports Setup** window:

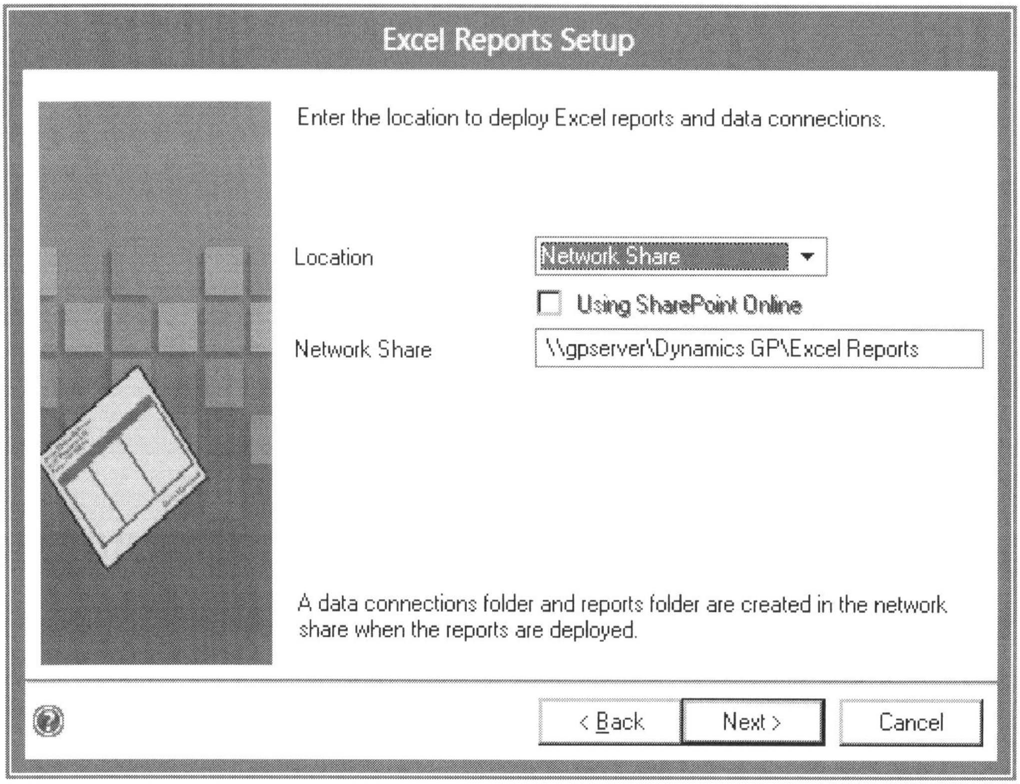


Note that the **Network Share** location should already exist. Click on **Next**.

18. The **Additional Tasks** window will open with options for creating a company, loading the sample company data, and other settings.

Once the Dynamics GP system database is in place, you can load the sample company and create your own Dynamics GP companies.

# Loading sample company data

The sample Dynamics GP company, Fabrikam, can be used for testing as well as training. The following steps will go through adding the sample company to your Dynamics GP installation:

1. Select **Add sample company data** from the drop-down list on the Dynamics GP Utilities **Additional Tasks** window and click on **Process**.

2. A new option in Dynamics GP 2013, the **Database Setup** window will let you change the **database name** of the sample company (previous versions forced it to be `TWO`). Note that while the field will let you type in up to ten characters, only the first five will be used. So, in the example illustrated in the following screenshot, even though `SAMPLE` is selected as the database name, the database that is created will be called SAMPL:

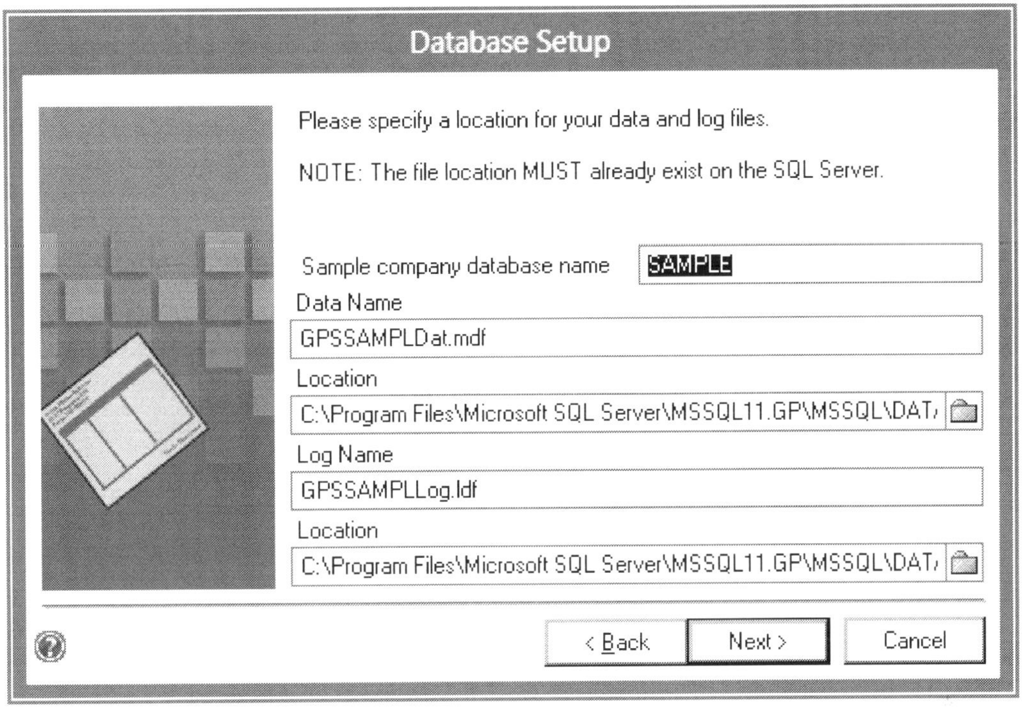


The **Data** and **Log** file names will not be editable, and will default from the database name you have selected. The **Locations** of the files will default to settings in SQL Server, but can be changed if you would like.

Click on **Next** to start the creation of the sample company. This will create the new SQL Server database as specified and populate it with sample data.

3. Once the database is created, the **Business Intelligence Reports Setup** window will let you determine if you would like to deploy SSRS and/or Excel reports for the sample company:

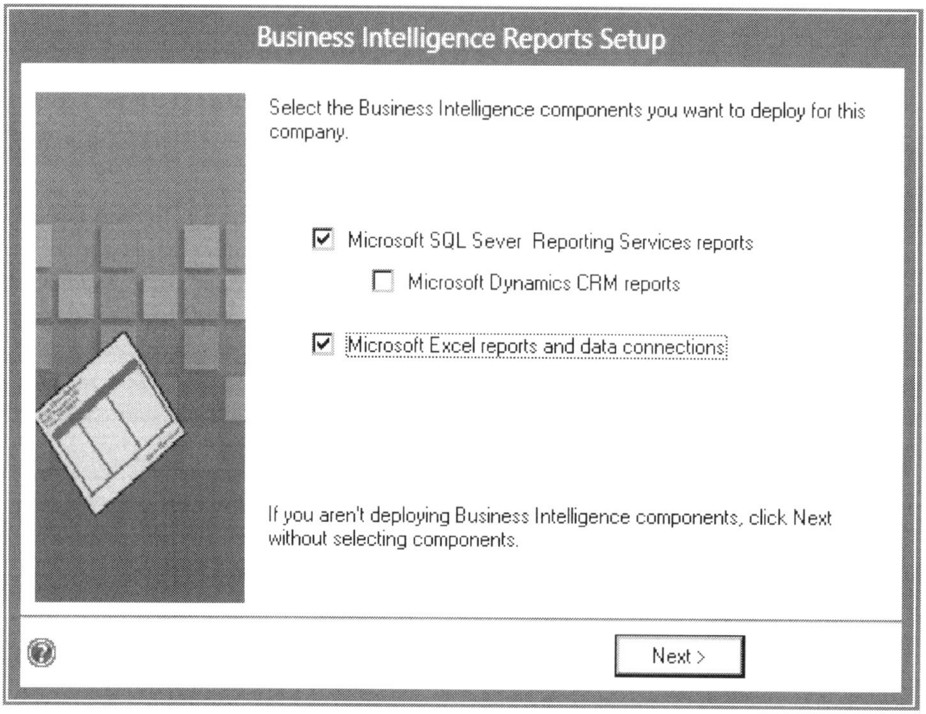


Important: If you are setting up SSRS reports, before continuing, add the `maxRequestLength` setting to your SSRS `web.config` file by following the instructions on the Mariano Gomez's blog at the following URL: `http://dynamicsgpblogster.blogspot.com/2011/07/ssrs-deployment-has-exceeded-maximum.html`. These were originally written for Dynamics GP 2010, but will work for Dynamics GP 2013, as well.

Click on **Next** to continue. If you have not selected any options on this window, you can skip to step 8.

4. The **SQL Server Reporting Services Reports Setup** window will bring up the default settings (if any) that you selected when first creating the system database. At this point you can change them as needed. It may be tempting to put the company name into the **Folder name** field. This will not break anything, but is typically not needed, as the system will automatically create additional folders for each company to segregate the reports that are company specific. Click on **Next**.

5. Similarly, the **Excel Reports Setup** window will populate with the default settings if you selected them and allow you to change them as needed. Reports for each Dynamics GP company will be added to a separate folder automatically, no need to specify the company name in the path of the **Network Share**. Click on **Next**.
6. The **Verify SQL Server** window will list all the settings you have chosen and give you the opportunity to go back and make changes. Click on **Finish** to deploy the reports you have selected.
7. The **Business Intelligence Deployment Progress** window will show you the progress.
8. Once done, you will be brought back to the **Additional Tasks** window.

At this point, the Dynamics GP sample company (Fabrikam) is populated with sample data and is ready to use for training and testing.

# Creating a new Dynamics GP company

To create your own Dynamics GP company, follow these steps:

1. Click on the drop-down arrow on the **Additional Tasks** window, select **Create a company**, and click on **Process**:

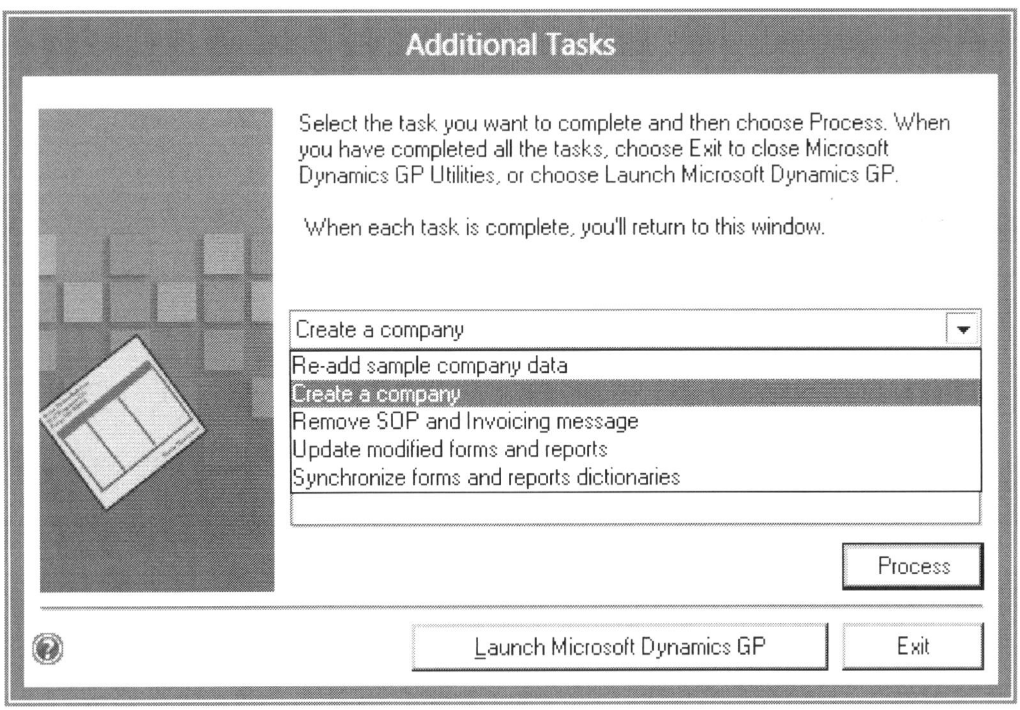

2. On the **Create Company** window you are presented with a number of options:

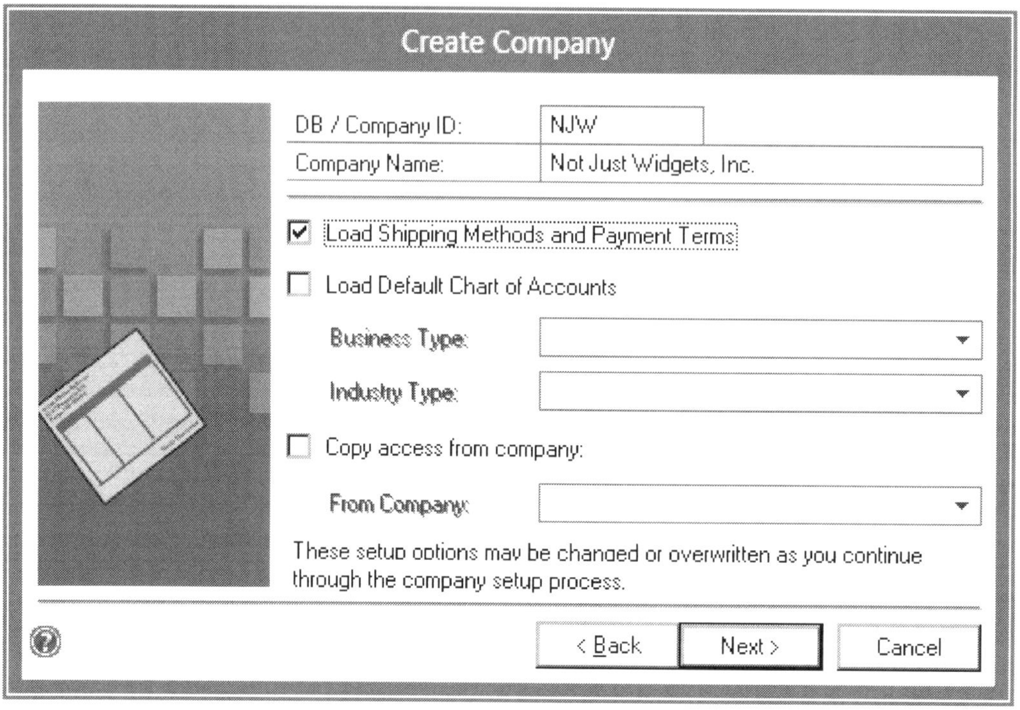


   - The **DB/Company ID** is the SQL database name and must adhere to the following guidelines:
     - Have a maximum of five characters
     - Can have numbers or letters
     - No special characters (the underscore is an exception to this, but it is not recommended)
     - Must start with a letter (so A1 is ok, but 1A is not)
     - All capital letters should be used (this will be forced as you type in the ID)

Most end users will rarely use or see the Company ID unless they are working with Intercompany transactions. However, anyone involved with support, administration, or reporting for Dynamics GP will use it extensively. If you are planning on setting up multiple companies in Dynamics GP, try to make the Company IDs distinctive so that it is easy to differentiate between companies when looking at a list of databases. The Company ID cannot be changed once created.

- The **Company Name** is what will show up on every window in Dynamics GP and on the list of available companies when users log into Dynamics GP. As with the Company ID, if there are multiple companies being setup, try to make them easy for users to differentiate between. If the company name is very long, consider using a shorter version or an abbreviation. The company name can be changed at any time after the company is created.
- Choosing **Load Shipping Methods and Payment Terms** will populate your company with a short list of predefined payment terms and shipping methods. They can always be deleted from the Dynamics GP user interface later if not needed and may provide a good starting point.
- The **Load Default Chart of Accounts** option will automatically create a General Ledger Chart of Accounts in the new company. As the Chart of Accounts is one of the critical building blocks of the Dynamics GP system, using a default is not recommended.
- **Copy access from company** may be useful for companies created in the future to copy security access from an existing company to a new one. As there is no security set up yet, this option will result in an empty drop-down list.

Once you have decided on the options, click on **Next** to continue.

3. On the **Database Setup** window, choose the file names and locations for the SQL Server database. Even though you can change the physical file names for your company databases, it is recommended that you leave them as defaulted, so that all the Dynamics GP databases have consistent naming.

   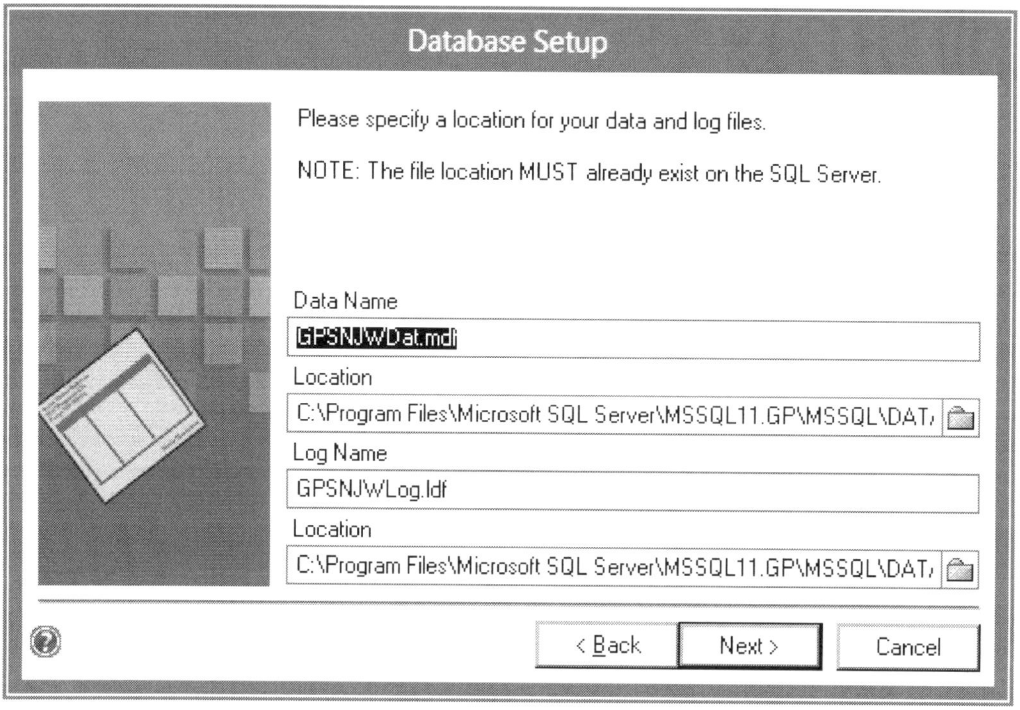
   

   Click on **Next** to continue.

4. After the new company database is created, you will see the now familiar **Business Intelligence Reports Setup** window with the option of deploying SSRS and/or Excel reports for the new company. You may note that the defaults selected here will be what you selected when you were creating these for your sample company (if you changed them from the defaults originally entered). You can change these as needed. Click on **Next** to continue. If you have not selected any of the options on this window, please skip to step 8.

> Important: If you are setting up SSRS reports and have not done so already, before continuing, add the `maxRequestLength` setting to your SSRS `web.config` file by following the instructions on the Mariano Gomez's blog at the following URL: `http://dynamicsgpblogster.blogspot.com/2011/07/ssrs-deployment-has-exceeded-maximum.html`. These instructions were originally written for Dynamics GP 2010, but will work for Dynamics GP 2013 as well.

5. The **Excel Reports Setup** window will populate with the default settings if you selected them (or the last settings you used if you changed them) and again, allow you to change them as needed. Reports for each Dynamics GP company will be added to a separate folder automatically, no need to specify the company name in the path for **Network Share**. Click on **Next**.
6. The **Verify SQL Server** window will list all the settings you have chosen and give you the opportunity to go back and make changes. Click on **Finish** to deploy the reports you have selected.
7. The **Business Intelligence Deployment Progress** window will show you the progress.
8. Once done, you will see the **Company Setup Options** window. If your Dynamics GP resource has recommended that you use RapidStart Services, please confer with them on the next steps. To follow along with the rest of this book, leave the defaulted **Set up the company later** option and click on **Next**.

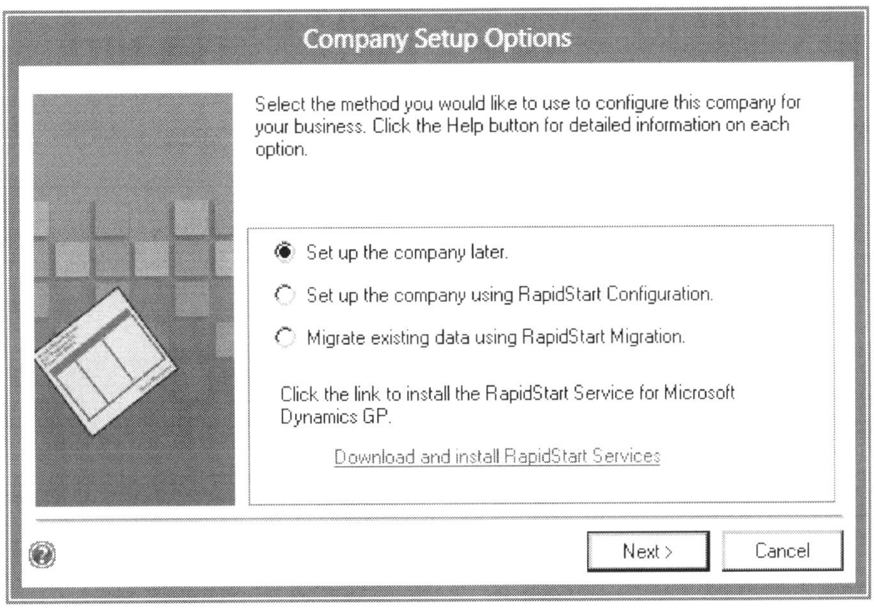

Your new company is now created and the Dynamics GP Utilities **Additional Tasks** window will open again.

# Additional steps

There are a few additional steps to complete the Dynamics GP installation: removing the SOP and Invoicing message, changing paths for reports dictionaries, forms and OLE Notes, installing any additional products, logging into Dynamics GP for the first time and verifying versions.

## Removing the SOP and Invoicing message

Both the SOP and Invoicing modules are installed with the core Dynamics GP installation. The Invoicing module is very rarely used, as SOP offers the same functionality, but also includes some additional features, and there is no longer an additional price for the SOP module with any currently sold Dynamics GP licensing models.

However, the Invoicing module remains in the system for some companies that may still be using it, and you will want to prevent users from inadvertently using both Invoicing and SOP, as the transactions from these modules will be placed in different sets of tables and will make reporting and inquiries quite difficult.

One way to prevent use of the Invoicing module is to not grant user access to any Invoicing windows using Dynamics GP security. That may work for most users, but will not work for anyone with a POWERUSER role, as they have access to everything. To help address this issue, the default behavior in Dynamics GP is to warn users when they open a window for either the SOP or Invoicing transactions. This is helpful, but may also get tedious for users that constantly have to acknowledge the warning and may generate unnecessary support questions.

A better way to handle this is to set the warning message to only appear in the Invoicing module, the one you do not want to use. Here are the steps to do this:

1. On the **Additional Tasks** window in Dynamics GP Utilities, select **Remove SOP and Invoicing message** from the drop-down list. Click on **Process**.
2. Uncheck **Warn in Sales Order Processing**, leaving only **Warn in Invoicing** checked:

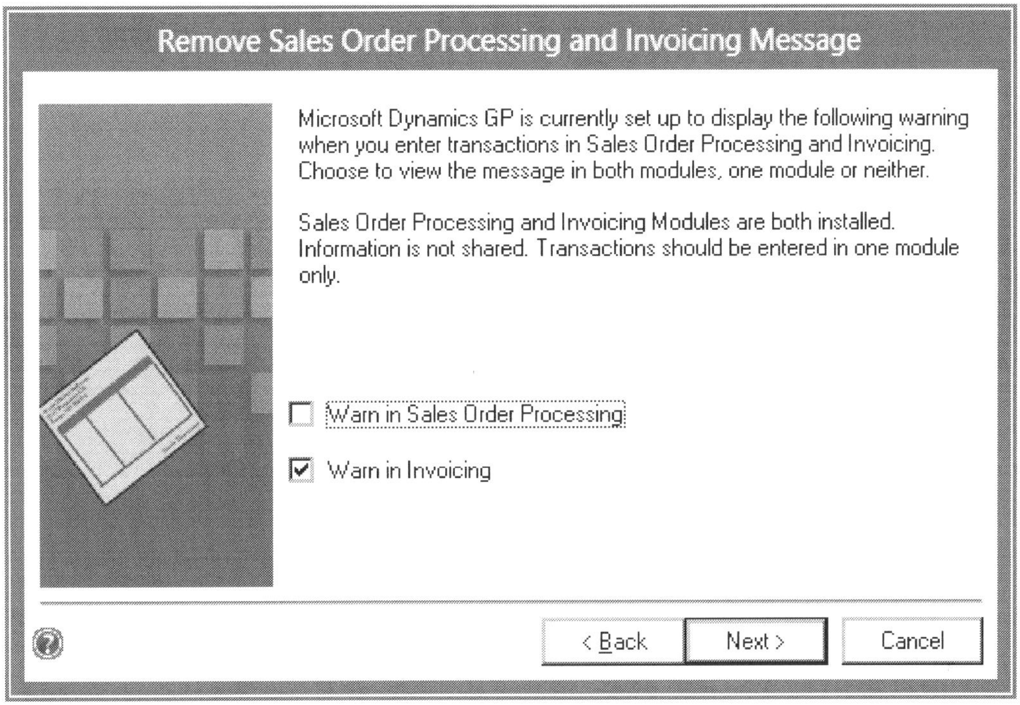


3. Click on **Next** to return to the **Additional Tasks** window.

At this point, you are done with Dynamics GP Utilities and can click on **Exit** to close the window.

# Changing paths for modified reports and forms dictionaries

If you are planning on any modifications to the Dynamics GP reports or forms (windows) and have decided to use the most common method of storing these on a network share, you will need to point the Dynamics GP application to your network share. The typical way of doing this is to change the `DYNAMICS.SET` file:

1. Navigate to the folder where Dynamics GP was installed and find the `DYNAMICS.SET` file.
2. Right-click on `DYNAMICS.SET` and choose **Open With** then select **Notepad**. `DYNAMICS.SET` is also called the launch file and holds information about every product installed for Dynamics GP. Recall from *Chapter 1, Application Structure and Licensing* that a product is typically a module, with the exception of the Microsoft Dynamics GP product, which holds most of the core Dynamics GP modules together. Each product has a name, number, and three dictionary files associated with it: the product dictionary, forms dictionary, and reports dictionary.

   The number at the top of the `DYNAMICS.SET` file will show the total number of products you have installed, the list below that total number will have two lines per product with the product number, then name. Below the last product name will be the line **Windows** and underneath that will be three lines for each product, showing the paths for the product dictionary, forms dictionary, and reports dictionary (in that order).

   If you are planning on changing the payables check layout or some of the other reports in the core Dynamics GP product, those will all be in the `REPORTS.DIC` file, the path for it will be on the third line of the `DYNAMICS.SET` file after the **Windows** line. Change this path to point to the location of your `REPORTS.DIC` on the network share, as in the following example:

```
Windows
:C:Microsoft Dynamics/GP2013/Dynamics.dic
:C:Microsoft Dynamics/GP2013/Data/FORMS.DIC
//server/fileshare/DynamicsGP/REPORTS.DIC
```

A UNC path is recommended, however a mapped drive will work as well. The `REPORTS.DIC` file does not have to exist at the shared location yet; it will be created as needed once Report Writer is opened or a modified report is imported. This setting is specific to the computer where each `DYNAMICS.SET` file is located. Note the use of forward slashes in the preceding example. While that is the default syntax in the `DYNAMICS.SET` file, either forward or backslashes will be accepted when specifying paths in this file.

3. Once done, save and close the `DYNAMICS.SET` file.

## Changing the path for OLE Notes

OLE Notes are used to store file attachments in Dynamics GP. To allow sharing of these file attachments by users across your Dynamics GP implementation, all the Dynamics GP installations need to point to the same location for OLE Notes.

The location of the OLE Notes for each Dynamics GP installation is stored in the `Dex.ini` file, found in the `DATA` directory inside the Dynamics GP installation folder. The `Dex.ini` file contains the defaults for each installation of Dynamics GP. To change the location of the OLE Notes:

1. Open the `Dex.ini` file.
2. Locate the `OLEPath=` line inside the file. It is typically about halfway down the list for a default installation. (If it is not there, you can add a line for it at the bottom).

3. Change the path to your shared location. UNC is preferable, but this can also be a mapped drive. Note that there should be a backslash at the end of the path:

When using a UNC path, make sure that the folder you are pointing to exists and contains a folder for each Dynamics GP Company ID with an `OLENotes` folder inside each company folder. In our example, with two databases called `SAMPL` and `NJW`, and a folder called `Notes` inside the `DynamicsGP` file share, the line in the `Dex.ini` file will be: `OLEPath=\\server\fileshare\DynamicsGP\Notes\` and the `Notes` folder will need to have two folders in it, each with an `OLENotes` folder inside:

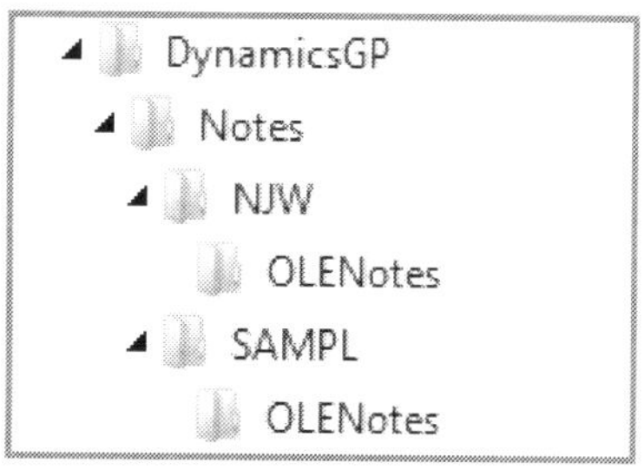

> In a default installation, you may notice that right below the `OLEPath` line in the `Dex.ini` file are two lines holding paths for the reports and forms dictionaries. These are defaults for products that will be installed in the future and are not the same thing that we changed in the preceding section.
>
> However, starting with Dynamics GP 2013, this is automatically updated when the `DYNAMICS.SET` is changed. It is recommended to leave these defaults pointing locally, so you may actually want to change this back to the defaulted local path (in our example, `C:\Microsoft Dynamics\GP2013\Data\`). Similar to the `DYNAMICS.SET` file, either forward slashes or backslashes will work for these.

4. Save and close the `Dex.ini` file.

As with the `DYNAMICS.SET` file, the settings in the `Dex.ini` file are specific to the computer where the `Dex.ini` file is located. Unlike the `DYNAMICS.SET` file, changes to the OLE Notes path in the `Dex.ini` file take effect right away, even if the application is open. However, to be safe, it is better to close the Dynamics GP application when making settings changes.

# Installing additional products

If you are installing any additional products for Dynamics GP, you can either do this now or wait until after you log into Dynamics GP for the first time. Typically, every product will have detailed installation instructions; it is important to follow these instructions, especially for the first installation which often invloves creation of SQL Server objects.

## Logging into Dynamics GP for the first time

Follow these steps to log into Dynamics GP for the first time:

1. Navigate to **Start** | **All Programs** | **Microsoft Dynamics** | **GP 2013** | **GP**. On the **Welcome to Microsoft Dynamics GP** window make sure that the Server is pointing to your ODBC DSN (in our example it was `GP`).

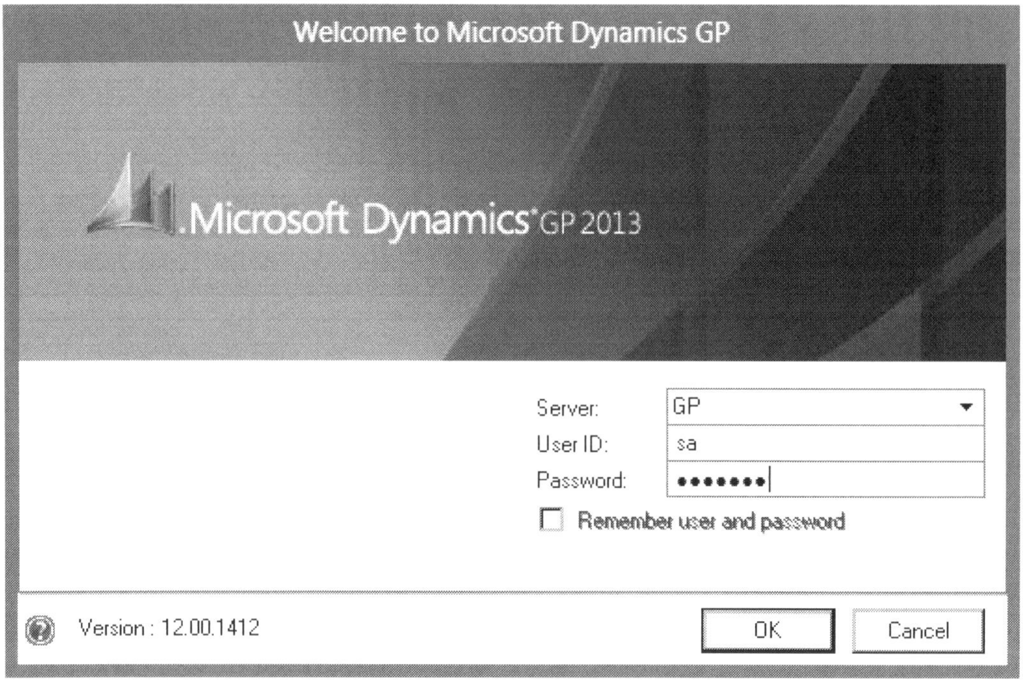


   Note that the currently installed Dynamics GP build number will be listed in the lower left corner.

2. As we have not created any users yet, log in as `sa` or `DYNSA`. The first time you run the Dynamics GP application on a computer it will take some time, as the application updates SQL messages from the server to the local computer.
3. On the **Company Login** window select either the sample company (**Fabrikam**) or your new company from the **Company** drop-down list.
4. If you have selected the sample company, you will see a pop-up message letting you know that you are logging into the sample company and that the user date for it has been set to April 12, 2017. Click on **OK** to continue.

5. The **Select Home Page** window will come up asking you to select an **Industry** and **role**. These are used for pre-populating the Dynamics GP **Home Page** with links and options, and these choices can be changed at any time. The **Home Page** settings in Dynamics GP are user specific, so whatever you choose will be set for the user you are logged in as. Pick an **industry** and **role** (IT Operations Manager is a good role to pick for sa) and click on **OK**.
6. The **Reminders** window will pop up, and you can click on **Close** or minimize it.

> If you are on a computer that has Microsoft Outlook installed, but not opened or configured, you may get the Outlook profile or setup wizard pop-ups (typically at least two). Cancel or close those, as they are not needed at this time.

You are now able to navigate inside the Dynamics GP company you have logged into.

# Checking versions

It is important to make sure that all your Microsoft Dynamics GP installations have the same build numbers for each product installed. This will help avoid errors and possible data corruption that can be caused by version mismatches. While Dynamics GP will check the major versions for the core products installed automatically, it may not always check specific build numbers for each product you have installed.

Every product installed with Dynamics GP will have its own build number. There will also be a build number for Dexterity, even though it is not listed as a separate product. If you have installed a service pack or additional products, it is important to verify that everything was installed with the expected versions before continuing on to other client installations.

For a list of the Dynamics GP build numbers for the three major products (Dynamics GP, Dexterity and SmartList), you can refer to this URL: `http://victoriayudin.com/2010/09/11/dynamics-gp-version-numbers-and-service-packs/`. That web page will also provide links to resources for additional details on build numbers and downloads.

To check the builds of the three major products on your computer, you can click on the **Help** icon (question mark) in the upper right corner of the main Dynamics GP window and choose **About Microsoft Dynamics GP...**. Other products installed will typically specify a path to check the build number in the installation or setup instructions.

If you find that you are not on the expected build number for any of the products you have installed, you can reapply the latest service pack. Once you are satisfied that all your versions are correct, you can move on to installing the Dynamics GP application on other computers.

# Installing Integration Manager

Integration Manager is often used to load initial data into Dynamics GP and can also be used for ongoing imports of data. Integration Manager only needs to be installed on the computers (servers or desktops) that will be used to launch an import. To run Integration Manager on a computer, the Dynamics GP application must also be installed on the same computer.

## Installation steps

Following are the steps to install Integration Manager 12.0 for Dynamics GP 2013:

1. Run `setup.exe` from the Dynamics GP 2013 media.
2. Click on **Integration Manager** under **Additional Products** and choose **Install**:

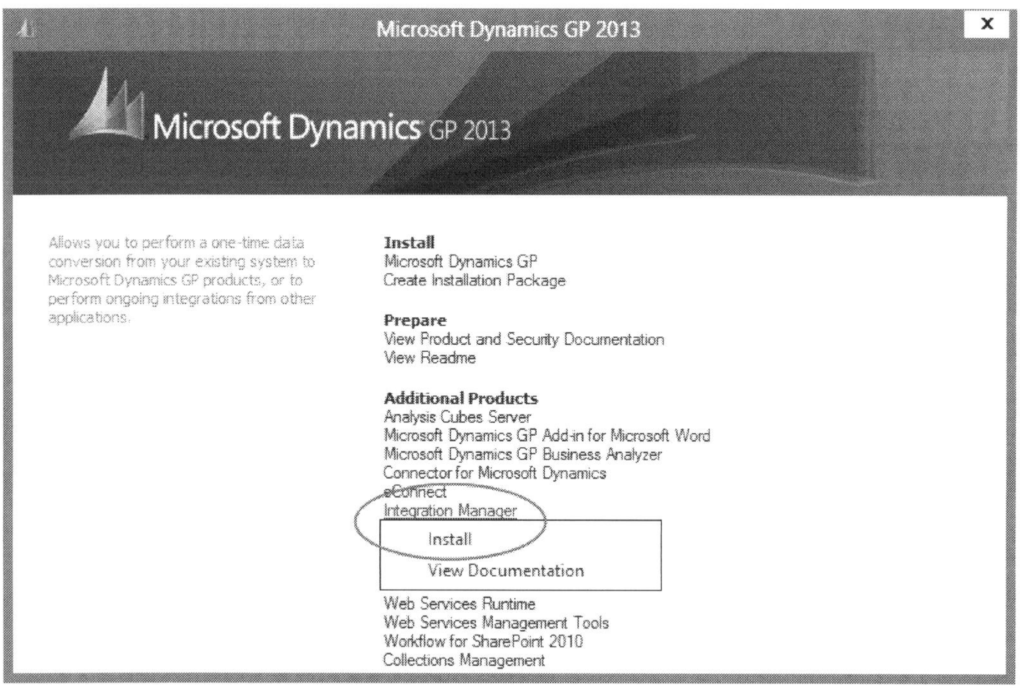

3. On the **License Agreement** window, review the license terms and, if you agree, select the **I accept the terms in the License Agreement** radio button, then click on **Next**.
4. On the **Select Features** window you can choose what adapters to install – these determine what options are available to use with Integration Manager. The examples covered in this book show how to use the **Dynamics GP Destination Adapters**.

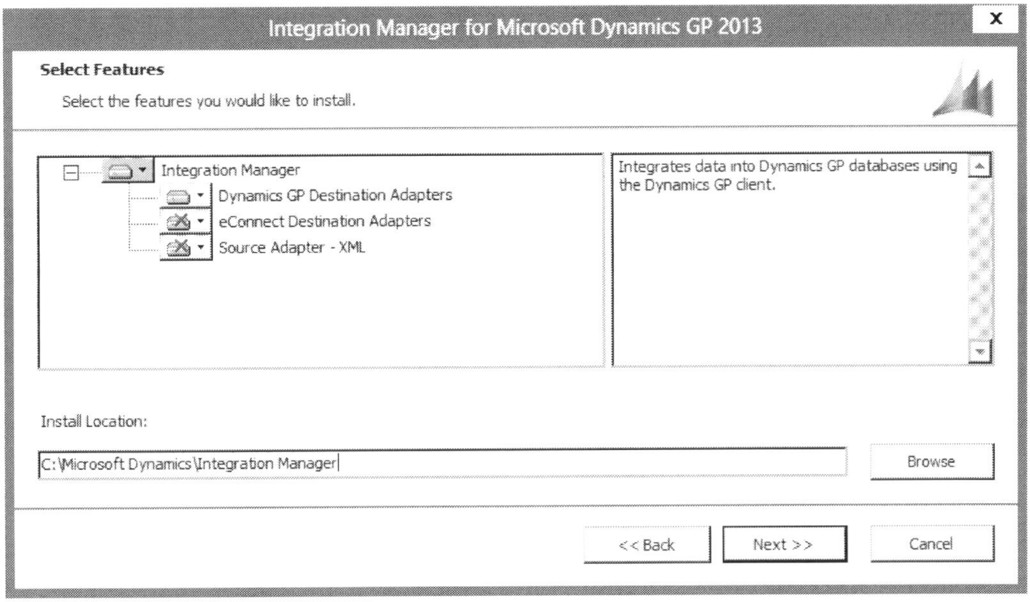


If you decide you need other adapters, they can be installed at a later date. You can also change the **Install Location** if you wish. It is recommended, though not required, to install Integration Manager in the same location where the Dynamics GP application is installed. Click on **Next** to continue.

> Dynamics GP supports installation of multiple versions and multiple instances of the same version on the same computer. However, Integration Manager can only be installed once on a computer. If you have an older version of Integration Manager, it needs to be uninstalled before you can install a new version.

5. The **Ready to Install** window will open. Click on **Install** to start the Integration Manager installation.

6. Once the window shows **Installation Complete**, click on **Exit** to close the window. The main **Microsoft Dynamics GP 2013** installation menu will still be open, so you can choose to install additional components or close it at this time.

> Note that Collections Management is now separately listed under Additional Products - it was previously an option on the core installation of Dynamics GP. This is because Collections Management is transitioning back to its original developer, Professional Advantage. You can read more about this on the Inside Microsoft Dynamics GP blog: `http://bit.ly/18ETB1p`.

Integration Manager is now installed, however it may not be ready to use until you perform the additional steps outlined in the next section.

# Additional steps

A few additional steps are needed after installing Integration Manager: entering registration keys, checking the installed version, applying service packs and changing the Integration Manager database path to a shared location.

## Entering registration keys

To enter registration keys for Integration Manager:

1. Launch Integration Manager by navigating to **Start** | **All Programs** | **Microsoft Dynamics** | **Integration Manager 12** | **Integration Manager**.
2. A pop-up window will ask if you want to register Integration Manager.
3. Choose **Register Now** and enter your Integration Manager registration keys. These can be found under your account on CustomerSource or your Dynamics GP partner can help you get your registration keys.

Choosing **Register Later** may result in limited functionality in Integration Manager. To get to the **Registration** window from the main window, navigate to **Tools** | **Registration**.

## Checking the version and applying service packs

To find the version or build installed for Integration Manager, navigate to **Help | About Integration Manager** from the main Integration Manager window.

A list of Integration Manager build numbers and corresponding service packs can be found here: `http://victoriayudin.com/2009/01/28/dynamics-gp-integration-manager-versions/`. For previous versions of Dynamics GP, service packs were provided for Integration Manager separately from the main Dynamics GP product. Starting with Dynamics GP 2013, Integration Manager installations are part of the main Dynamics GP installation media. If that changes in the future and there are separate service packs available for Integration Manager, they will be listed on the Microsoft Dynamics GP 2013 downloads page: `https://mbs.microsoft.com/customersource/downloads/servicepacks/mdgp2013_release_download.htm` (CustomerSource or PartnerSource access required).

## Changing the Integration Manager database path

If multiple users will be using Integration Manager and you would like them to share a common Integration Manager database, you can place this in a shared directory on the network.

To create a new Integration Manager database, navigate to **Tools | Create Database**. Enter the **Database Name**, select the shared location on your network, and click on **Create**. Once the database is created, go to **Tools | Options**, change the **Default Integration Manager Database** to the one you just created and click on **OK**. You will need to restart Integration Manager for this change to take effect.

If you would like to copy any of the sample integrations into your new database, navigate to **File | Import Integrations**.

For all subsequent installations of Integration Manager navigate to **Tools | Options** and change the **Default Integration Manager Database**.

# Post-installation SQL Server and database settings

A number of SQL Server settings may need to be checked or changed after installing Dynamics GP and creating companies. These include SQL Server settings and the individual database settings for the Dynamics GP databases.

## SQL Server settings

There are a few settings to verify or change for the entire SQL Server instance that Dynamics GP will be using. These include the maximum memory, cursor threshold, and processor settings. All of these settings are found on the **Server Properties** window for your SQL Server. To open this window, right-click on the SQL Server instance name in **SQL Server Management Studio** and choose **Properties**.

### Maximum memory

Most documentation recommends letting SQL Server manage memory on its own. This is generally fine, however a good practice is to set a limit on the maximum amount of memory SQL Server will use and leave at least 512 MB RAM free for the operating system and any other services running on the server. This will ensure that SQL Server is not competing with the operating system for resources. If your server is not a dedicated Dynamics GP SQL Server, the amount of memory left free may need to be higher, depending on what else is running on the server.

To change the memory settings, choose **Memory** from the list of pages on the **Server Properties** window. Enter the **Maximum server memory (in MB)** and click on **OK**. As an example, for a dedicated Dynamics GP SQL Server with 4 GB of RAM, set the **Maximum server memory** to `3584` MB.

### Cursor Threshold

The Cursor Threshold setting specifies the number of rows in the cursor set at which cursor keysets are generated asynchronously. The default setting is **-1**, meaning all keysets are generated synchronously. This is a requirement for Dynamics GP transactions to post correctly.

To check the Cursor Threshold setting, select the **Advanced** page on the **Server Properties** window:

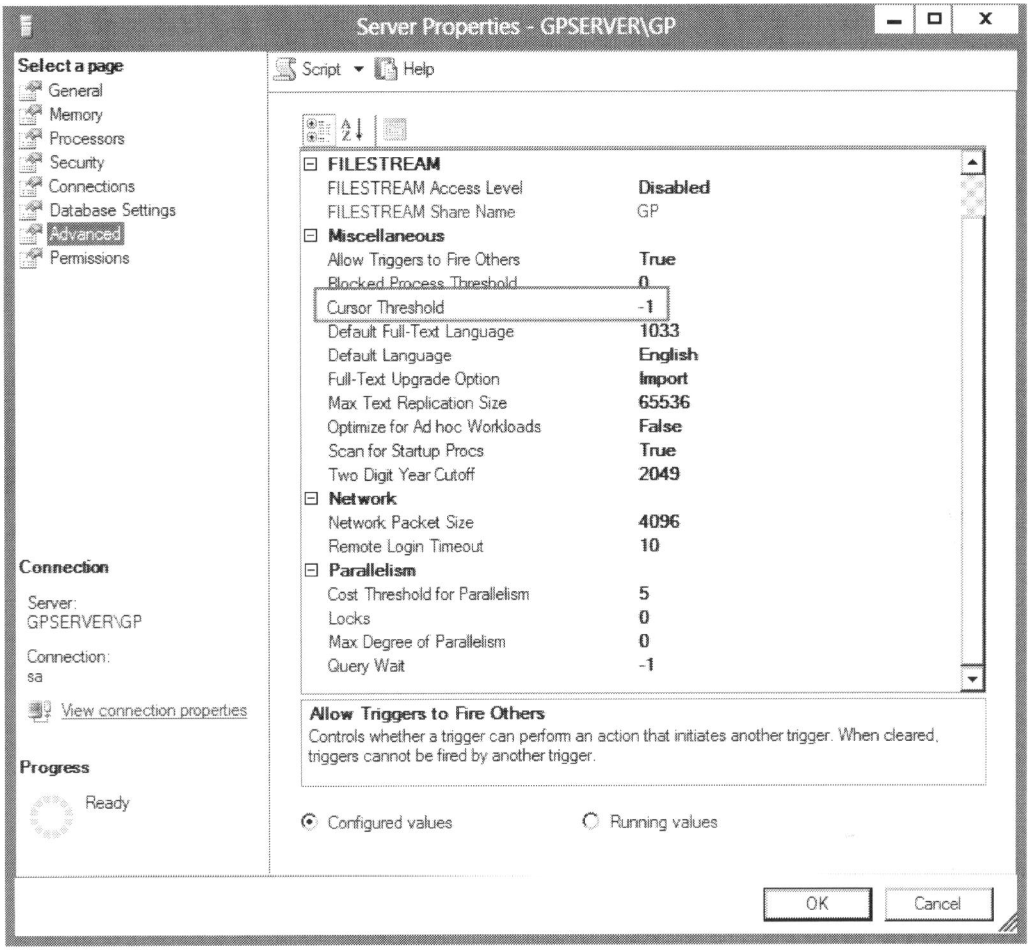


# Processor

On the **Processors** page for the **Server Properties**, verify that the following two settings are unchecked:

- **Boost SQL Server priority**
- **Use Windows fibers**

You can find more information on both of these settings in Microsoft's KB Article 319942 called *How to determine proper SQL Server configuration settings*: `http://support.microsoft.com/kb/319942`.

# Database settings

Once the system database, the sample company, and your Dynamics GP company are created using Dynamics GP Utilities, **Microsoft SQL Server Management Studio** will list them all in the **Object Explorer** section for your SQL Server instance:

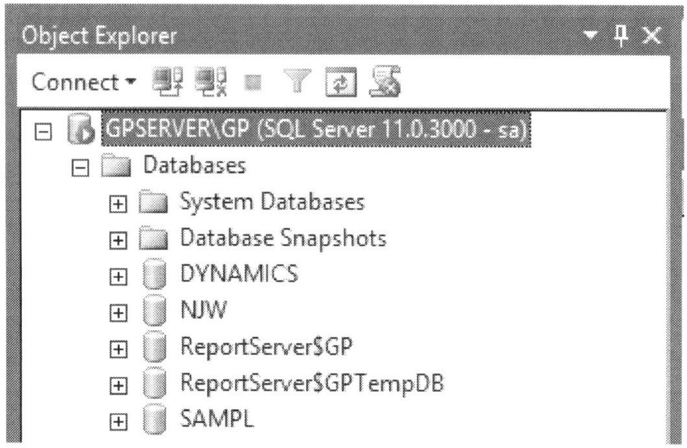


Right-click on a database and choose **Properties** to open the **Database Properties** window. The following sections detail the pages that are important to check for each database.

## General

The **General** page will list details about the database. A critical item to check on this page is the **Database Owner**, which should be **DYNSA** for all Dynamics GP databases. While Dynamics GP will typically operate with no issues if DYNSA is not the database owner, installing additional modules or products and applying service packs or upgrades will often fail. To change the database owner, run the following query against the database:

```
sp_changedbowner 'DYNSA'
```

## Files

The **Files** page lists details about the files for the database including their locations, sizes, and **Autogrowth** settings. Microsoft KB article 315512, `http://support.microsoft.com/default.aspx/kb/315512`, goes over the considerations and performance implications for SQL Server autogrowth.

There is no single recommendation for the autogrowth settings, as the best approach will vary based on the details and usage of the Dynamics GP system. Often I see these changed to Megabytes instead of percentages to allow more control over the file size growth.

> If you are planning to import a large volume of data upfront, consider manually increasing the database files to maximize performance during the import.

Part of the routine maintenance for the Dynamics GP system should be to check the sizes and autogrowth settings of all the Dynamics GP databases, to make sure they still make sense and there are no issues.

Keep in mind that different Dynamics GP databases will grow at different rates and should be evaluated individually. For example, the system database may add a large amount of data upfront, as system users are created and security settings for them are applied. However, after this initial period, the system database typically will not grow very quickly. On the other hand, your company database is expected to keep growing at a fairly steady rate as daily transaction processing occurs.

# Options

The **Options** page contains two important sections: the **Recovery model** and **Other options** for each SQL Server database.

## Recovery model

The recovery model for a SQL Server database will determine what options are available to you for disaster recovery planning. Briefly, the three options are:

- **Simple**: No transaction log backups are available and point in time recovery is not an option. Offers best performance and eliminates the need to back up and check the size of the SQL Server transaction logs.
- **Full**: All transactions are logged, allowing for point in time recovery. Transaction log backups are required to keep the transactions log growth in check.
- **Bulk-logged**: Not all operations are logged in the transaction log and thus no point in time recovery is possible in most cases. This offers better recovery options than the Simple recovery model, and better performance than the Full recovery model. This recovery model is seldom seen in practice.

For an application such as Dynamics GP, storing mission critical data for an organization, the Full recovery model is highly recommended for all production databases, including all live company databases and the system database. This will allow restoring your data back to a specific date and time, so if you can identify when an issue occurred, you can go back to right before it happened. For the sample database or any test databases you may create in the future, the Simple recovery model is typically sufficient.

## Other options

There are quite a number of settings under the **Other options** section. The recommendation is to leave most of them as defaulted. The specific options with recommendations for Dynamics GP are:

- **Auto Close**: **False**

  Setting **Auto Close** to **False** will help optimize SQL Server performance for Dynamics GP by not incurring the overhead to close and reopen the database frequently.

- **Auto Create Statistics**: **True**

  Statistics will help optimize SQL Server by improving query performance.

- **Auto Shrink**: **False**

  Automatically shrinking the database can cause significant performance issues and is typically not recommended for most SQL Server applications.

- **Auto Update Statistics**: **True**

  Statistics help optimize SQL Server performance. This setting will allow statistics to be updated as needed.

- All **ANSI** options: **False**

  ANSI settings can cause problems with Dynamics GP data, all **ANSI** options should be set to **False**.

- **Quoted Identifiers Enabled**: **False**

  Similar to the ANSI settings, quoted identifiers can cause problems with Dynamics GP data.

- **Recursive Triggers Enabled**: **False**

  Dynamics GP does not use recursive triggers.

- **Page Verify**: **CHECKSUM**

  The **Page Verify** setting determines the option used for incomplete I/O transactions caused by disk I/O errors. The recommendation for this setting is **CHECKSUM**.

All of the settings discussed in the preceding section are database specific and should be checked individually for each of your Dynamics GP databases.

# SQL Server maintenance jobs

To optimize Dynamics GP performance, it is recommended to set up a SQL Server **Maintenance Plan** to perform a number of maintenance and optimization tasks. The following are the steps to create a typical SQL Server maintenance plan for Dynamics GP. The specific steps for your plan may vary, depending on your needs and setup.

1. In **SQL Server Management Studio**, expand your SQL Server instance in the **Object Explorer** and then expand the **Management** folder. Right-click on **Maintenance Plans** and select **Maintenance Plan Wizard**:

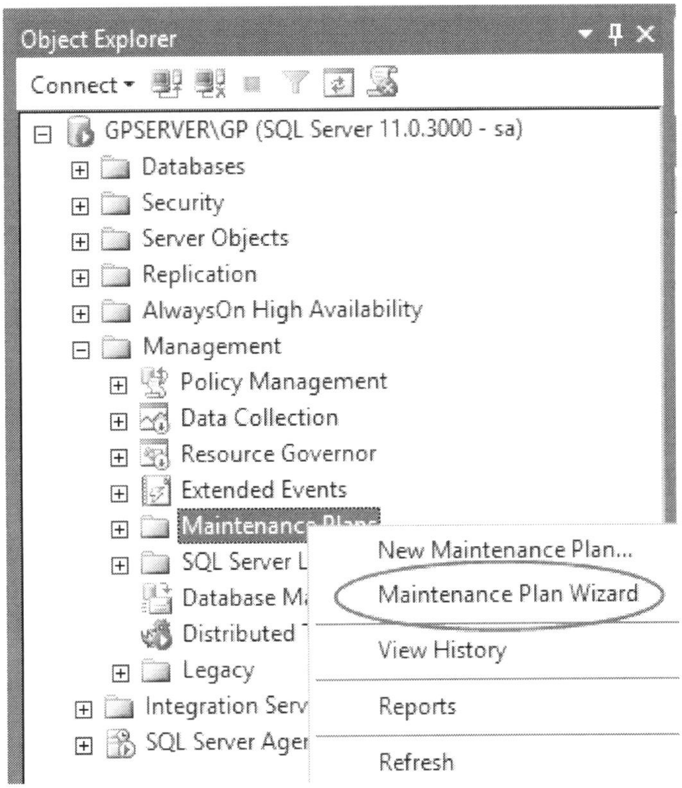

2. Click on **Next** on the **Maintenance Plan Wizard** window.
3. Give your maintenance plan a **Name** and (optionally) a **Description**. Select the **Separate schedule for each task** radio button and click on **Next**.
4. On the **Select Maintenance Tasks** window choose all the tasks selected in the following screenshot:

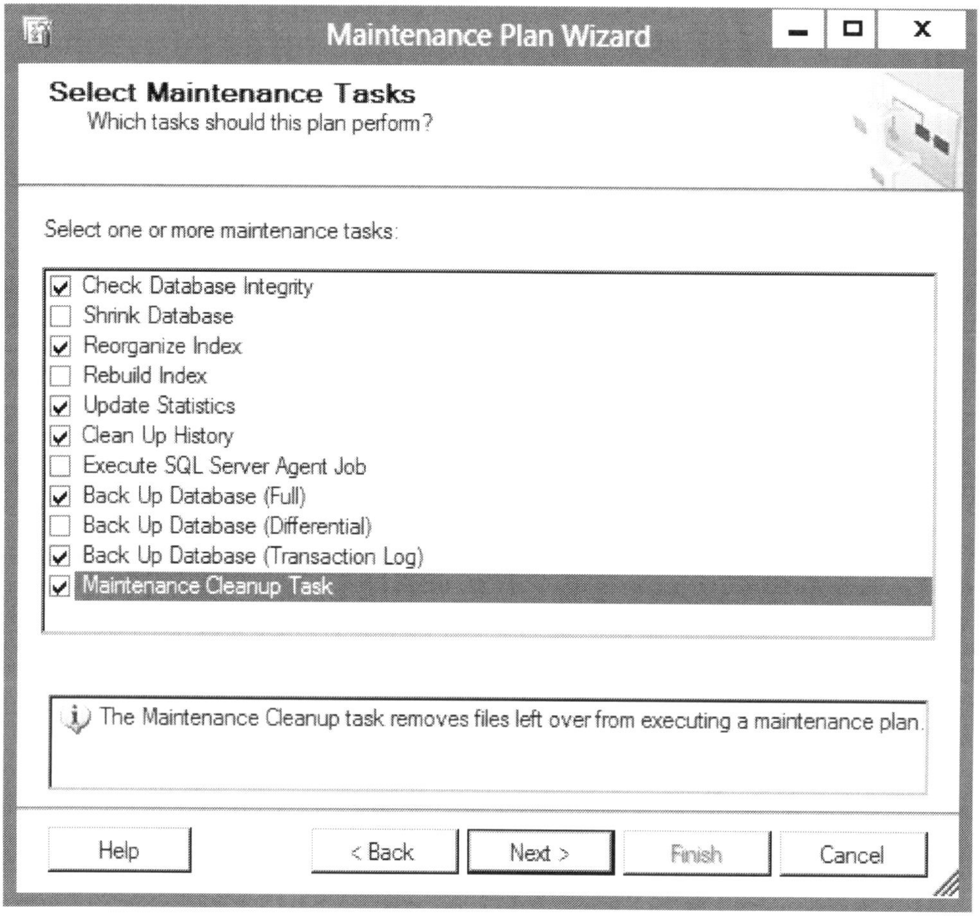


5. Click on **Next** and **Next** again on the **Select Maintenance Task Order** window. (Since you selected to set up a separate schedule for each task, the **Select Maintenance Task Order** options are disabled).

6. On the **Define Database Check Integrity Task** window:
    - Click on the drop-down next to **Database(s)** and select either **All user databases** (this will capture all databases created in the future and may be the better choice if you are planning on creating additional Dynamics GP companies) or **These databases**, then manually select the desired databases.
    - Click on **OK** and then click on the **Change** button next to **Schedule**. Pick the day of the week and time that you want this part of the maintenance plan to run. It is recommended to perform the weekly maintenance during off hours. A typical schedule may look like the following:

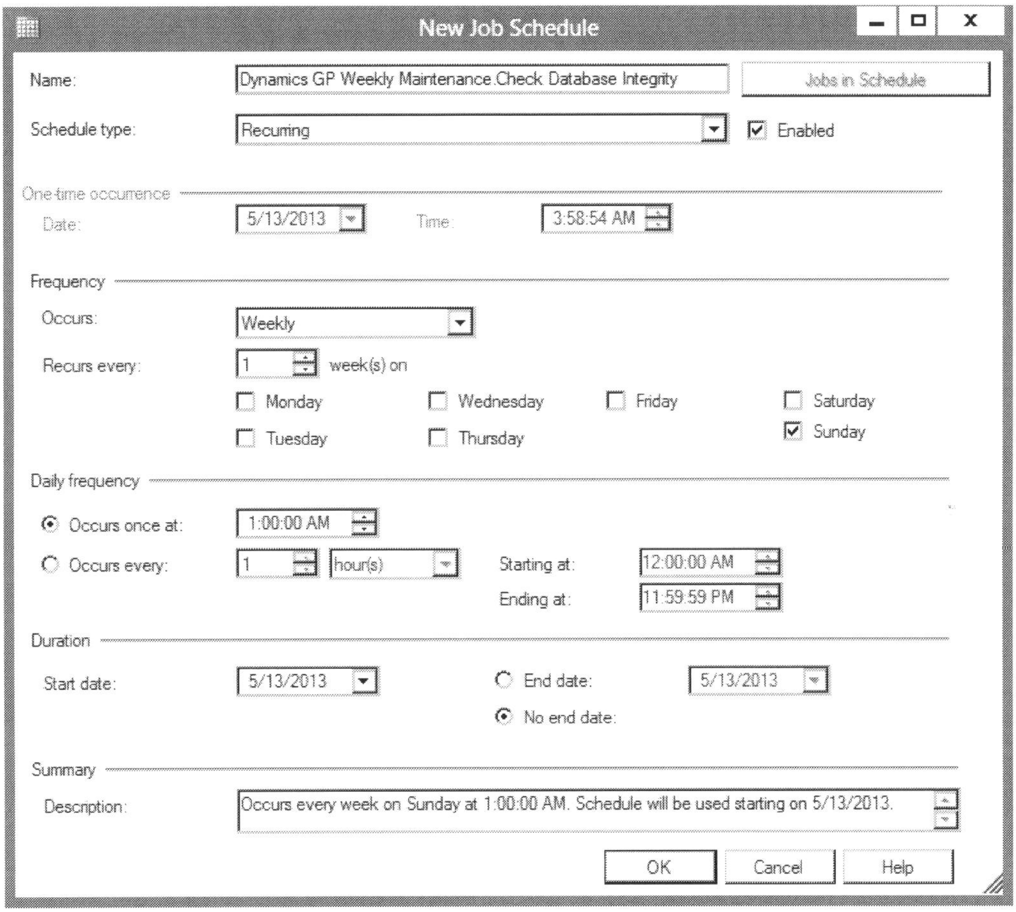


    - Click on **OK** to close the schedule window and **Next** to move on to the next task.

7. On the **Define Reorganize Index Task** window:
    - Choose your **Database(s)**.
    - Click on **Change** to set the schedule for this task. It is recommended to leave time between the tasks so that they do not overlap. How much time to leave will depend on the number and size of your databases, as well as available resource. However, a gap of 30 minutes between tasks is usually sufficient. This should be set as a weekly task.
    - Click on **Next**.
8. On the **Define Update Statistics Task** window:
    - Select your **Database(s)**.
    - Change the **Schedule** to make this a weekly task.
    - Click on **Next**.
9. Historical logs for **Backup and restore activity**, **SQL Server Agent job history**, and **Maintenance plan history** are all helpful for troubleshooting and maintenance. However, old logs are typically not very helpful for current problems and it is a good idea to delete them periodically, so that you do not keep filling your hard drive up with unneeded data. If these logs are deemed important, they can be part of the backup routine to be kept for the standard retention policy of the company. On the **Define History Cleanup Task** window:
    - Select all the options.
    - Choose a time frame to remove historical data. A typical setting is somewhere between one month and six months. What you decide may depend on the plan for database maintenance in your organization. For example, if there is a plan to have someone check the SQL Server, logs, and jobs on a weekly basis, then keeping one or two months of historical data should be enough.
    - Set a **Schedule**. Performing this task weekly is typically adequate.
    - Click on **Next** to continue.

10. Backups are critical for your Microsoft Dynamics GP and you may already have software performing backups of your SQL Server data. In case you do not, or if you want to have additional local backups directly on the server for easy access, on the **Define Back Up Database (Full) Task** window:
    - Select your **Database(s)** and consider adding the `master` and `msdb` databases to the full backups—they are handy to have if you need to restore. If you have installed and set up SSRS, you may also want to include those databases.
    - Choose to **Create a backup file for every database**.
    - Check **Create a subdirectory for each database**. This is an easy way to have SQL Server automatically create a separate folder for each of your databases. The folder names will be the names of the databases, and SQL Server will put both the full backups and the transaction log backups for each database (which we will configure in the next step) into the appropriate folder.
    - Choose a destination **Folder** for the backups.
    - Select **Verify backup integrity**.
    - Click on **Change** to set a **Schedule**, then click on **Next**.

> Note in the following example that even though the previous tasks were set on weekly schedules, the full database backup is a daily task. This is a typical and recommended schedule for full SQL Server backups of the Dynamics GP data. However, if your backup process or disaster recovery plan requires something different, set this to your desired frequency. While there is no issue with taking a SQL Server database backup when users are in the system, it is recommended to schedule backups off-hours, especially for larger databases, to minimize impact on performance. Also, consider having the full backup start before other tasks, so that a database backup is performed before any other maintenance tasks run.

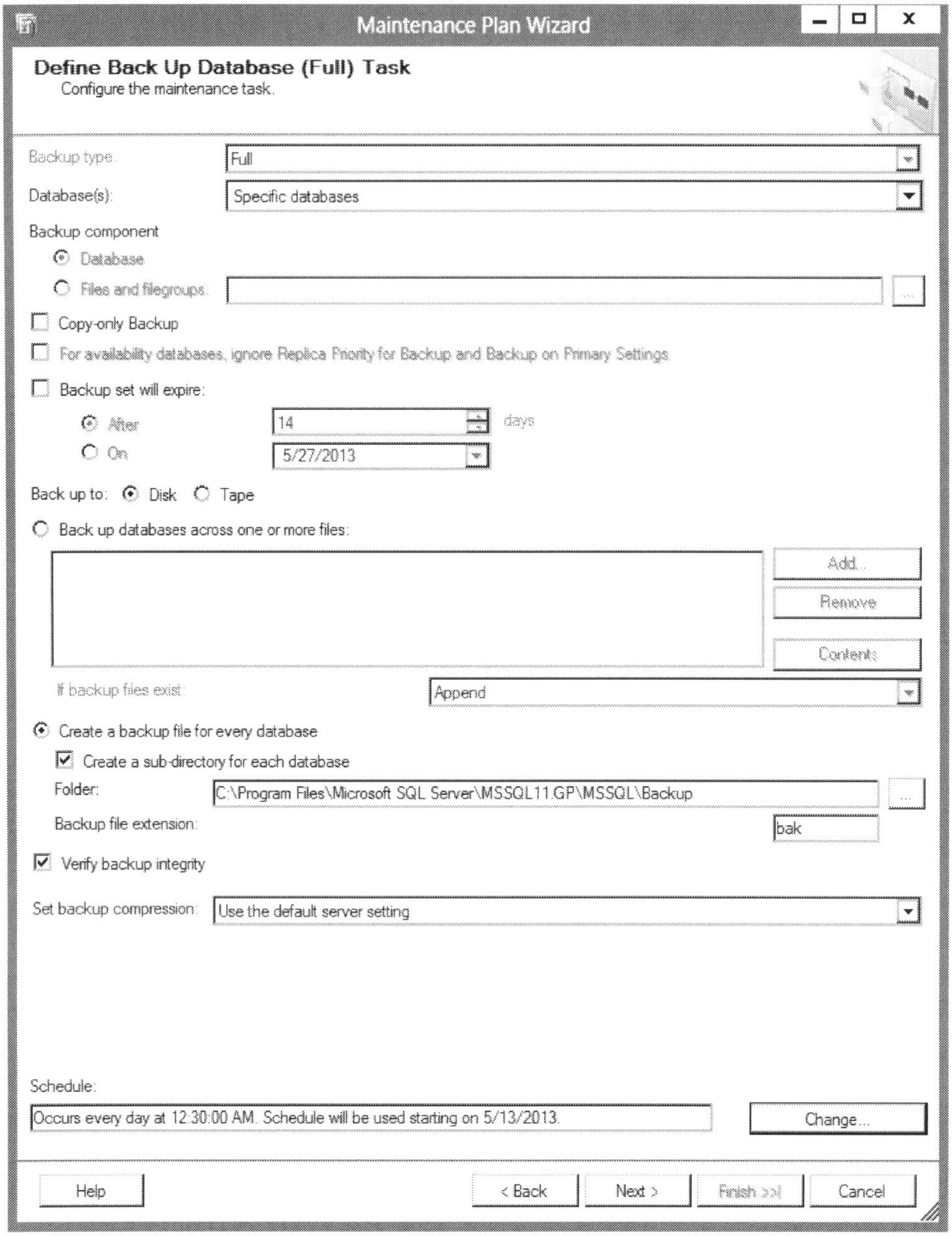


11. On to the **Define Back Up Database (Transaction Log) Task** window:
    - Select your **Database(s)**. Databases with the Simple recovery model should not be chosen for transaction log backups and they will automatically be excluded.

- Choose to **Create a backup file for every database**.
- Select **Create a subdirectory for each database**. This will put the transaction logs for each database into the same directory as the full backups if the same destination folder is selected in the next step.
- Choose a destination **Folder** for the backups.
- Select **Verify backup integrity**.
- Set a **Schedule** and click on **Next** to continue.

> A common schedule for transaction log backups is every 4 hours. However, since many things are often scheduled on the hour, consider being a little more creative with the schedule, as in the following example.

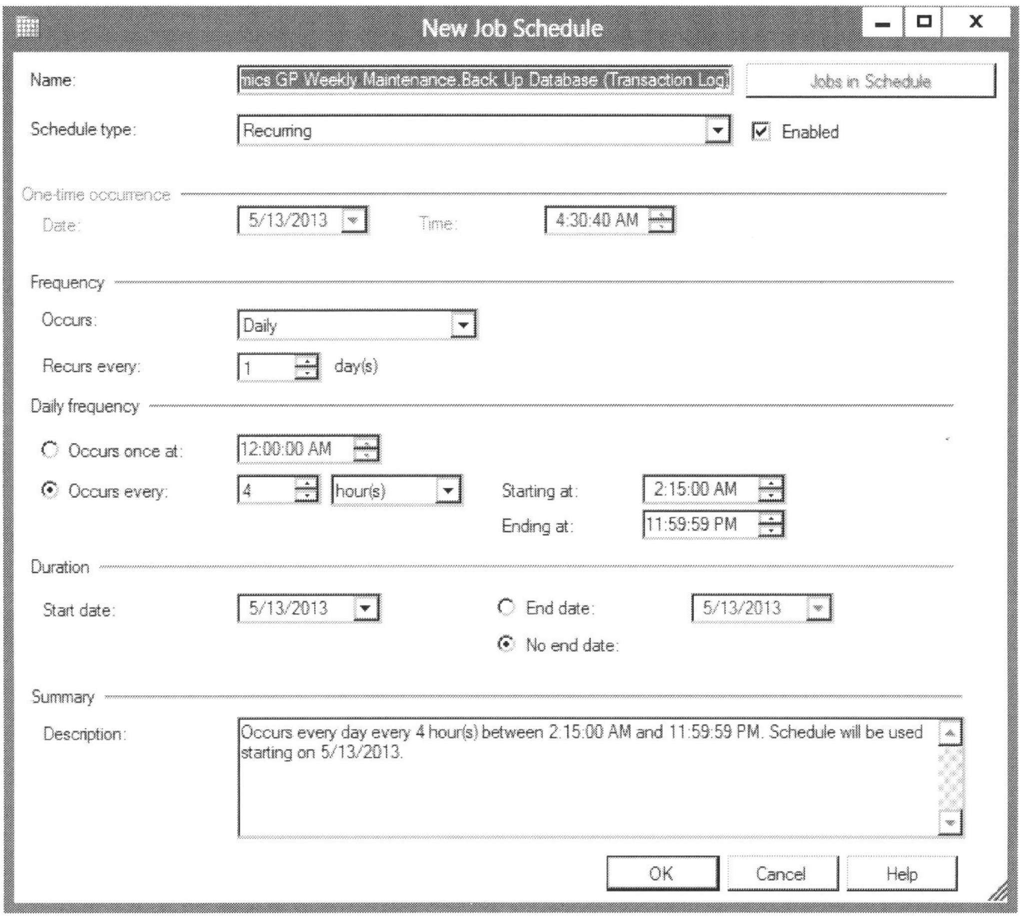

12. On the **Define Maintenance Cleanup Task** window:
    - Select **Backup files** and **Search folder and delete files based on extension**.
    - Select the **Folder** you specified for your backups on the **Define Back Up Database (Full) Task** window. You can use the **Back** button to go back and copy/paste the folder location.
    - Enter `bak` for the file extension. Note that this will create the cleanup task for the full database backup files, but not the transaction logs. A separate step will be required after completing the Maintenance Plan Wizard to add a cleanup task for the transaction log backups.
    - Check **Include first-level subfolders**.
    - Select how long to keep the full backup files under **File age**. Depending on space available and other considerations, many companies usually limit this to one or two weeks.
    - Set the **Schedule** for this task. This should be a daily task if databases are backed up daily.
    - Click on **Next**.
13. On the **Select Report Options** window select the **Folder** location for the maintenance plan report and click on **Next**.
14. On the **Complete the Wizard** window verify all your settings are correct. If you need to change something, use the **Back** button, otherwise click on **Finish**.
15. The **Maintenance Plan Wizard Progress** will open, showing you the progress while the SQL Server jobs for your maintenance plan are created. Each task you defined will create an individual job. Once done, click on **Close**.
16. Add an additional task to delete old transaction log backups:
    - In the **SQL Server Management Studio Object Explorer** expand the **Management** folder, then the **Maintenance Plans** folder.
    - Right-click on the maintenance plan you created using the preceding steps and select **Modify**.
    - In the list of **Subplans** on the right side, click on the last one. It will show up in the pane underneath the list.
    - Select **View** from the top menu and choose **Toolbox**. This will open a new **Toolbox** object on the left side of the window.
    - From the **Toolbox** select **Maintenance Cleanup Task** and drag it over to the window on the right, next to the **Maintenance Cleanup Task**.

- Click on **Maintenance Cleanup Task** and drag the green arrow from it to the new **Maintenance Cleanup Task 1** to connect the two objects:

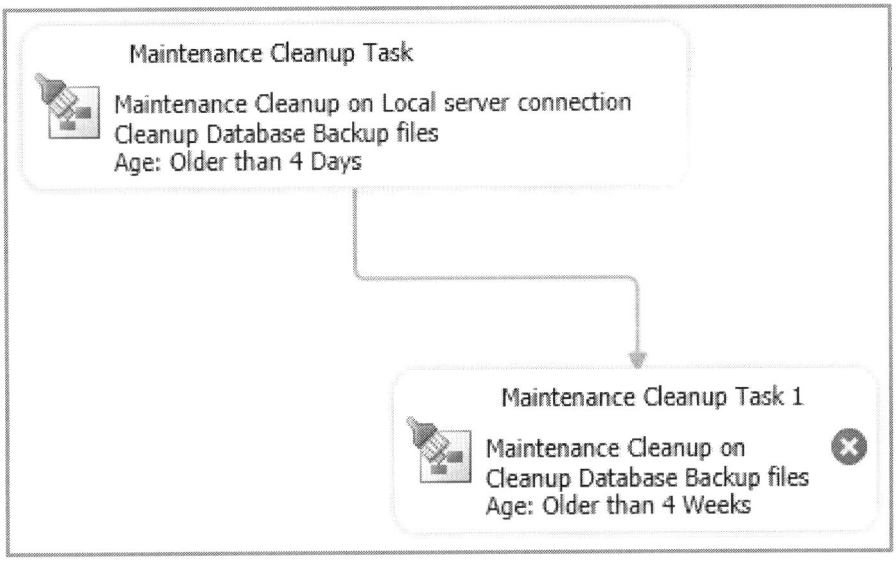


- Double-click on the new **Maintenance Cleanup Task 1** object to open it.
- Select **Backup files** and **Search folder and delete files based on an extension**.
- Select the **Folder** you specified for your transaction log backups.
- Enter `trn` for the **File extension**.
- Check **Include first-level subfolders**.
- Select how long you want to keep the transaction log backups under **File age**. Depending on space available and other considerations, many companies usually limit this to one or two weeks. Click on **OK**.
- Click on **Save** on the toolbar at the top (or *Ctrl+S*) to save the changes to your maintenance plan.

17. As an optional step, consider renaming the subplans in your maintenance plan to make them more user-friendly. To do this, double click on each step in the list (where they are listed **Subplan_1**, **Sublplan_2**, and so on) to open the **Subplan Properties** window and change the **Name** at the top. You can see what each subplan is at the top of the object that opens behind the **Subplan Properties** window. For example, the subplan that is open in the following screenshot is **Clean Up History**:

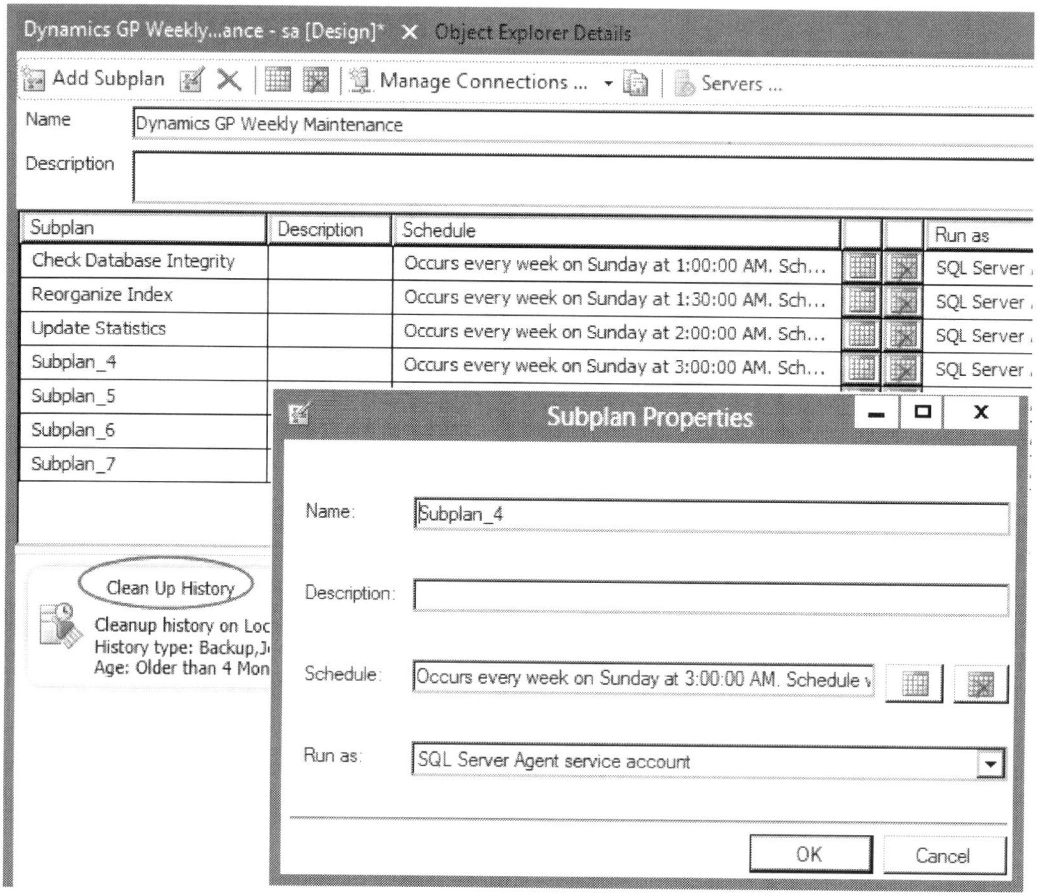

Once you are done renaming the subtasks, save the maintenance plan again.

You can see all the SQL Server jobs created for your maintenance plan by expanding the **SQL Server Agent** folder in SQL Server Studio Management and double-clicking the **Job Activity Monitor**:

Agent Job Activity:

| Name | Enabled | Status | Last Run ... | Last Run | Next Run | Category | Runnable |
|---|---|---|---|---|---|---|---|
| Dynamics GP Weekly Maintenance.Check Database Integrity | yes | Idle | Unknown | never | 5/19/2013 1:00:00 AM | Databa... | yes |
| Dynamics GP Weekly Maintenance.Clean Up History | yes | Idle | Unknown | never | 5/19/2013 3:00:00 AM | Databa... | yes |
| Dynamics GP Weekly Maintenance.Daily Full Database Backup | yes | Idle | Unknown | never | 5/14/2013 12:30:00 AM | Databa... | yes |
| Dynamics GP Weekly Maintenance.Maintenance Cleanup Task | yes | Idle | Unknown | never | 5/14/2013 4:00:00 AM | Databa... | yes |
| Dynamics GP Weekly Maintenance.Reorganize Index | yes | Idle | Unknown | never | 5/19/2013 1:30:00 AM | Databa... | yes |
| Dynamics GP Weekly Maintenance.Transaction Log Backup | yes | Idle | Unknown | never | 5/13/2013 6:15:00 AM | Databa... | yes |
| Dynamics GP Weekly Maintenance.Update Statistics | yes | Idle | Unknown | never | 5/19/2013 2:00:00 AM | Databa... | yes |

Once these steps are completed, your Dynamics GP databases will be backed up and maintained by SQL Server. Part of the ongoing maintenance for Dynamics GP should include checking these jobs to make sure they are running and that there are no errors.

# Backing up data

In *Chapter 4, Planning – Infrastructure* we discussed details for the data that you will want to plan on backing up and some suggested frequencies for these backups. A quick recap of the items:

- SQL Server databases
- Modified dictionary files
- Integration Manager database
- OLE Notes directory

Now that everything is installed, it is important to make sure that all your Dynamics GP data is added to your regular backups so that you can confidently start working on the Dynamics GP system setup.

# Summary

In this chapter, we have gone over the steps for a typical installation of SQL Server 2012, Dynamics GP 2013, and Integration Manager 12. Creating a 32-bit ODBC data source for use with Dynamics GP was illustrated. We covered both pre and post-installation steps, including setting up a SQL Server maintenance plan and SQL Server optimization settings. We also discussed important installation concepts, such as performing installations as the local administrator and making sure your Dynamics GP data is included in regular backups.

In the next chapter, we will start setting up your Dynamics GP system and company.

# 6

# System and Company Setup

Once SQL Server and Dynamics GP are installed, you are ready to start the system and company setup. This chapter will cover logging into Microsoft Dynamics GP for the first time and the steps for setting up your Dynamics GP system and company.

## Logging into Dynamics GP

After installation and creation of the system database, the sample company, and your new company using Dynamics GP Utilities, you can perform the Dynamics GP application installation on any computer where it will be used. The rest of the setup steps, whether for the system or a company, can be performed on any computer where Dynamics GP is installed.

When you launch Dynamics GP for the first time on a new computer, you will be prompted for a **Server**, **User ID**, and **Password**:

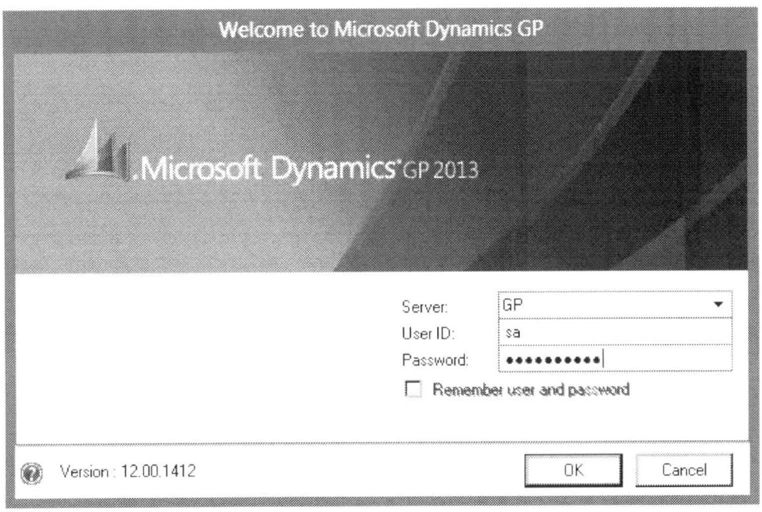

For the **Server**, choose the ODBC data source pointing to your SQL Server (remember from *Chapter 5, Installation of SQL Server, Dynamics GP, and Integration Manager*, that this will need to be created identically on each computer).

The first time you log in, use `sa` for the **User ID**. Dynamics GP will detect that this is a new installation and will prompt you to run Dynamics GP Utilities. Select **Yes**, log into Dynamics GP Utilities as `sa`, and follow the prompts. Your local Dynamics GP application will be initialized and synchronized to the settings on the server. Once done, click on the **Launch Microsoft Dynamics GP** button at the bottom of the **Additional Tasks** window.

Log into Dynamics GP again as `sa` and you will see the **Company Login** window with a drop-down selection for the companies that you have created in Dynamics GP. For performing system setup steps, you can choose any company on the list. To perform company setup, you will need to choose the specific company you will be setting up.

> If you need help with basic terminology and navigation for Microsoft Dynamics GP, please consult *Chapter 2* and *Chapter 3* of the *Microsoft Dynamics GP System User's Guide*. To open this guide, navigate to the **Help** icon in the upper right corner of the main Dynamics GP window and choose **Printable Manuals**—it will be under the **System** section.

# System setup

System setup for Dynamics GP includes settings that are global to your entire Dynamics GP installation such as the system password, registration, creating users, setting up user security, currency settings, exchange rates, and some additional system-wide settings.

A very useful feature in Dynamics GP is the **Setup Checklist**, which lists all of the setup steps with a brief description of each and provides automatic links to the related setup windows. The setup checklist also gives you the ability to assign tasks to others and change the status of the various installation tasks as you go through them to allow you to easily see the setup progress. In the following sections, the navigation paths for each setup window will be detailed using the Dynamics GP menus. However you may find that bringing up the setup checklist can save you time during the setup. The setup checklist is found by navigating to **Microsoft Dynamics GP | Tools | Setup | Setup Checklist**.

Before starting the setup, there are two recommended changes: showing required fields and setting the system password, described in more detail in the following sections.

# Show required fields

To help with system setup you may want to have Dynamics GP highlight the required fields on windows for you. This option is turned off by default, to turn it on:

1. Click on the **Help** icon in the upper-right corner of the main Dynamics GP window and click on **Show Required Fields**. This setting is a toggle, once selected it will display a checkmark next to it to show it is activated.
2. Navigate to **Microsoft Dynamics GP | User Preferences**. On the **User Preferences** window, click on **Display** to open the **User Display Preferences** window. Change the settings under **Required Fields** to be something other than the default settings (which are **Black** and **Regular**). You can click on **Apply** to preview your changes and click on **OK** to close the window.

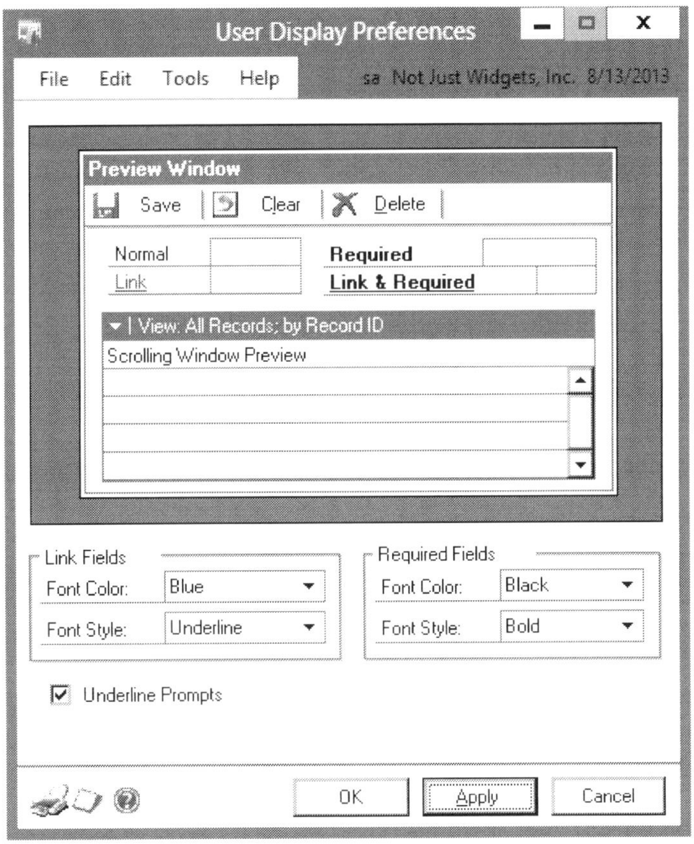


Changes to the display preferences are specific to the Dynamics GP user. Once set, they will be used on any computer where the same user logs into Dynamics GP.

# System password

All system setup windows will require the Dynamics GP system password that is typically set during the initial Dynamics GP installation. You can set this password to be blank while performing the system setup, so that you are not constantly prompted for it. To change the system password, navigate to **Microsoft Dynamics GP | Tools | Setup | System | System Password.** It is strongly recommended to assign a system password once you are done with the system setup.

The following sections can be reached by following the links on the **Setup Checklist** or by navigating the Dynamics GP menus using the paths shown.

# Dynamics GP registration

The Dynamics GP application will install without asking for registration keys, however, you should enter your registration keys prior to continuing with the system setup to ensure that the system is set up with the modules you are registered for. Registration keys can be obtained either from your Dynamics GP partner or from Microsoft.

To enter your registration keys, navigate to **Microsoft Dynamics GP | Tools | Setup | System | Registration**. On the **Registration** window enter your **Site Name** and **Registration Keys**. The **Site Name** is listed under **License Holder** on your licensing information and must appear the exact same way, with the same punctuation, spelling, and spacing. Even though there are five **Registration Keys** possible, you may have less. The keys listed as—**No key**—on the licensing information should be left blank on the **Registration** window.

Click on the **Validate** button and the **Modules** list will populate with the Dynamics GP modules you have purchased. It is recommended to uncheck any modules that you are not planning to use to inactivate them. Leaving all the modules activated may cause some functionality not to work as expected and to require setup for those modules prior to entering transactions for other modules. There are also some modules that may conflict with others you are planning to use. Any module can be activated at a later time, if needed, however deactivating modules may be more difficult if they were activated and set up. Some of the modules may not sound familiar, but may be core or internal modules needed for other functionality you are using. If you are unsure about some of the modules on the list, consult with your Dynamics GP resource.

# Creating Dynamics GP users

Dynamics GP is licensed for concurrent users, so you can create as many named users as you would like. (Please refer to the *Dynamics GP licensing* section in *Chapter 1, Application Structure and Licensing* for more detail on this.) It is recommended to create a user for each individual that will be using Dynamics GP. Try to stay away from creating generic users like "PAYABLES" or "TEMP", as these do not allow for accountability in the system. The following are the steps to create new Dynamics GP users:

1. Log into Dynamics GP as either **sa**, **DYNSA**, or a user that has been set up in SQL Server with the sysadmin server role.
2. Navigate to **Microsoft Dynamics GP** | **Tools** | **Setup** | **System** | **User**.
3. Enter a **User ID**. Unlike most user IDs, the Dynamics GP user IDs are case sensitive. Consider making user IDs the same as the users' Windows logins. Even though Dynamics GP uses SQL Server authentication, it may be easier to administer users when all the IDs follow the same pattern.
4. Enter the **User Name**. While not required, it is helpful to enter the full name of the user, so this information is available when looking through a list of users in the future.
5. Enter and confirm the **Password**. Dynamics GP passwords are case sensitive. If you leave the password blank, the user will be required to create a password the first time they log into Dynamics GP. While that sounds like a handy feature, this can be a security risk because while the password is blank anyone can log in with just the user ID. This is not a concern if the user will be logging in immediately, however if users may log in for the first time days, or even weeks later, this is not very secure. Users can change their own passwords in Dynamics GP at any time, so create a unique password for each user and ask them to change it as soon as they log in the first time.
6. **Class ID** is an optional setting that may be useful for grouping users in the future. With the changes to the Dynamics GP security model starting with version 10.0, user classes are not widely used anymore and are not needed for security setup. The **Class ID** for any user can be changed at any time.
7. Setting the **Home Page Role** is also optional. If set while creating the user, this will save the user from having to pick their home page role when they first log into Dynamics GP.
8. Select if this will be a **Full** or **Limited** user under **User Type**. For a refresher on this, please refer to the *Dynamics GP licensing* section in *Chapter 1, Application Structure and Licensing*.

9. Set the **Advanced SQL Server** options. These options allow using your Active Directory domain password policies with Dynamics GP. This is a feature that sometimes proves cumbersome to use. There are many limitations and workarounds for this, detailed in Microsoft KB article 922456, Frequently asked questions about the advanced SQL Server options in the User Setup window in Microsoft Dynamics GP: `https://mbs.microsoft.com/knowledgebase/KBDisplay.aspx?scid=kb;en-us;922456` (requires login). A common recommendation is to uncheck the **Advanced SQL Server** options when creating new Dynamics GP users.
10. The **Status** will default to **Active** when you are creating a new user. As needed, you can change this to **Inactive** or **Lesson User**. If a user is **Inactive**, they are not able to log into Dynamics GP. A **Lesson User** can only log into the sample company.

> Lesson Users also do not take up a concurrent user in Dynamics GP. So any number of Lesson Users can be logged into the sample Dynamics GP company without taking away from your total number of concurrent user licenses available.

11. You can click on the **Summary** button to see a list of all your users and licenses.
12. If you already have other users set up, clicking on **Copy Access** will allow you to copy all security settings from another user to the one you have selected.

A typical **User Setup** window is as follows:

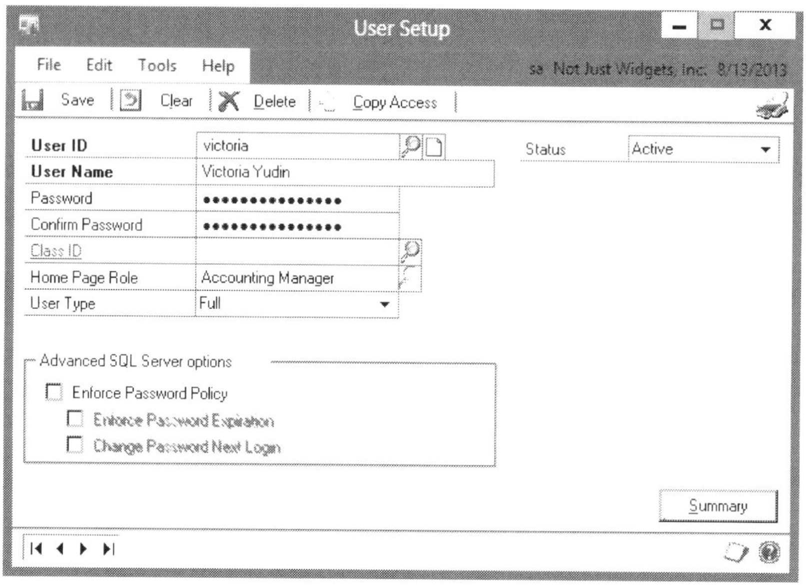

> When a user is created in Dynamics GP, a corresponding SQL Server login is created with the DYNGRP role. The user password is encrypted by Dynamics GP so that this login cannot be used outside of the Dynamics GP application.

# User security and company access

Once Dynamics GP users are created, they need to be granted access to the Dynamics GP companies they can log into and security needs to be set up for them.

## Access to companies

To give a user access to Dynamics GP companies, navigate to **Microsoft Dynamics GP | Tools | Setup | System | User Access**. Select the user in the **Users** list on the left and check the **Access** checkboxes for the companies listed on the right.

> When a user is given access to a company in Dynamics GP, the SQL Server login for that user is added to the corresponding SQL Server database.

## User security

*Chapter 3, Planning – Dynamics GP System* detailed the concepts for planning your Dynamics GP user security. Refer to the decisions you made during your implementation planning for the security you will be setting up for your users. The following is a refresher on the Dynamics GP security components and the navigations paths for them:

| Component | Description | Navigation path |
|---|---|---|
| Operation | The lowest level security building block. Operations include access to windows, reports, tables, tools, posting permissions, and SmartList objects. Operations are already part of the system, so there is no setup for them. | n/a |
| Task | A grouping of operations. Tasks typically group operations across common fairly low-level functions, such as creating customers or entering sales transactions. Tasks can cross Dynamics GP products and modules. Multiple tasks can have the same operations. | **Microsoft Dynamics GP \| Tools \| Setup \| System \| Security Tasks** |

| Component | Description | Navigation path |
|---|---|---|
| Role | A grouping of tasks. Multiple roles can have the same tasks. When setting up user security in Dynamics GP, users get assigned one or more roles. | **Microsoft Dynamics GP \| Tools \| Setup \| System \| Security Roles** |

You can assign roles to your Dynamics GP users on the **User Security Setup** window (**Microsoft Dynamics GP** | **Tools** | **Setup** | **System** | **User Security**).

As security can differ by Dynamics GP company, select a **User ID** and **Company**, then select the **Roles** for that user and company. Multiple roles can be assigned to each user, even if those roles contain overlapping tasks. A user with no roles assigned will be able to log into Dynamics GP, but will not have access to anything in the system.

Before modified forms or reports are set up in Dynamics GP, there will only be one option, called **DEFAULTUSER**, available in the **Alternate/Modified Forms and Reports ID** drop-down list. Even though there might only be one choice, this is a required field, so you must select an option for the **Alternate/Modified Forms and Reports ID**.

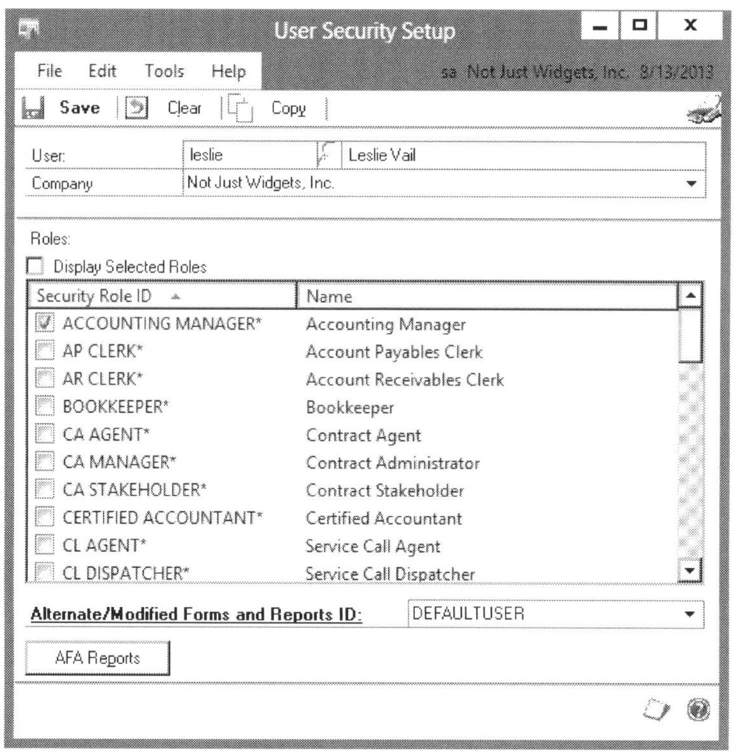

The **AFA Reports** button will bring up an additional window to set up security for **Advanced Financial Analysis** (**AFA**) reports. If AFA will not be used, no setup is needed for AFA. You may recall from the *Financial reporting section* in *Chapter 1, Application Structure and Licensing*, that AFA is a financial reporting tool within Dynamics GP that is not used by most companies anymore, and typically Management Reporter or FRx are used instead.

Clicking on the **Print** icon in the upper-right corner of the **User Security Setup** window will print a report showing all the roles assigned and the tasks included in each role for the selected user and company. The **Copy** button will allow you to copy the selected user and company settings to any other company for the same user. Once you have users set up and have granted them access to companies and security roles, you can copy all their permissions on the **User Setup** window (**Microsoft Dynamics GP** | **Tools** | **Setup** | **System** | **User**) by selecting the user to copy to and clicking on the **Copy Access** button.

It is recommended to create a new user for the person performing the Dynamics GP setup and assign them the **POWERUSER** role, rather than using the **sa** login for everything.

# Multicurrency setup

Multicurrency setup is global to your entire Dynamics GP installation, so currencies and exchange rates are set up once and shared by all the companies in the system. There are three steps for setting up the system-wide multicurrency: currency setup, exchange tables, and multicurrency access. If you do not plan on using Dynamics GP's multicurrency functionality, you can skip the exchange table setup, but you will still need to go through the other steps in the following sections for the currency you will be using.

## Currency setup

Dynamics GP is installed with a number of predefined currencies. If desired, these can be used as they are with no additional setup needed. To see the existing currencies in the system or to create new ones, navigate to **Microsoft Dynamics GP** | **Tools** | **Setup** | **System** | **Currency**.

Before a new currency can be used in Dynamics GP, it must be set up on the **Currency Setup** window. Make sure the **Currency Symbol**, **Negative Sign**, **Decimal** places, and **Separators** are correct for each currency you plan to use. These settings will control the display of the currency amounts on all windows and reports throughout Dynamics GP. Verify the **Payables Check Terminology**, as this will determine how amounts in words appear on your payables checks.

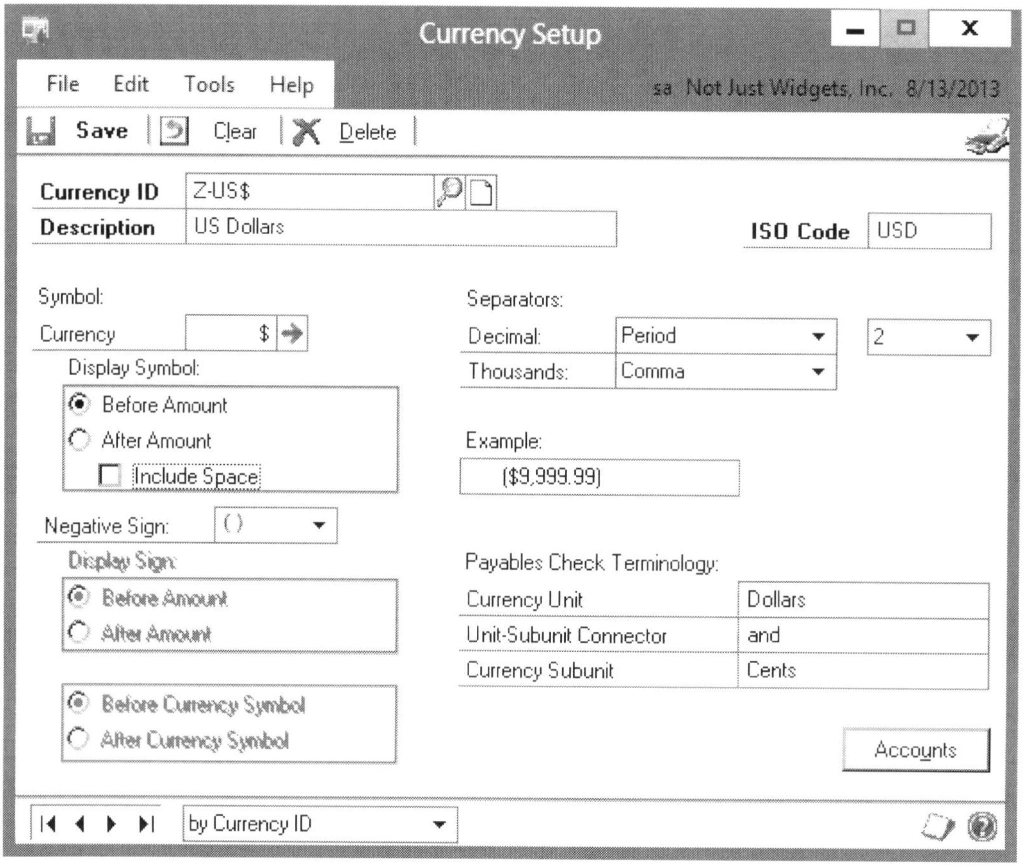


For US companies not planning on using multiple currencies, the default **Z-US$** already set up for the US Dollar is often used, or you can set up your own currency for this if you prefer to call it something else. There is no issue with setting up multiple currencies in Dynamics GP for the same actual currency. However, you must be consistent with the **Currency ID** selected on other setup windows, such as **Vendor Maintenance Options**, **Customer Maintenance Options**, and so on.

# Exchange rate tables

Exchange rate tables must be created for each currency you plan to use that is not your functional currency. Each exchange rate table will define the relationship between the functional currency chosen for a company and the currency of the exchange rate table. There is no built-in method in Dynamics GP to automatically update exchange rates, so typically companies choose to update exchange rates manually on a monthly or quarterly schedule. Often the frequency of the updates will depend on the volatility of the exchange rates.

To create or change an exchange rate table, navigate to **Microsoft Dynamics GP | Tools | Setup | System | Exchange Table**. The following are examples of a typical exchange rate setup and rate table:

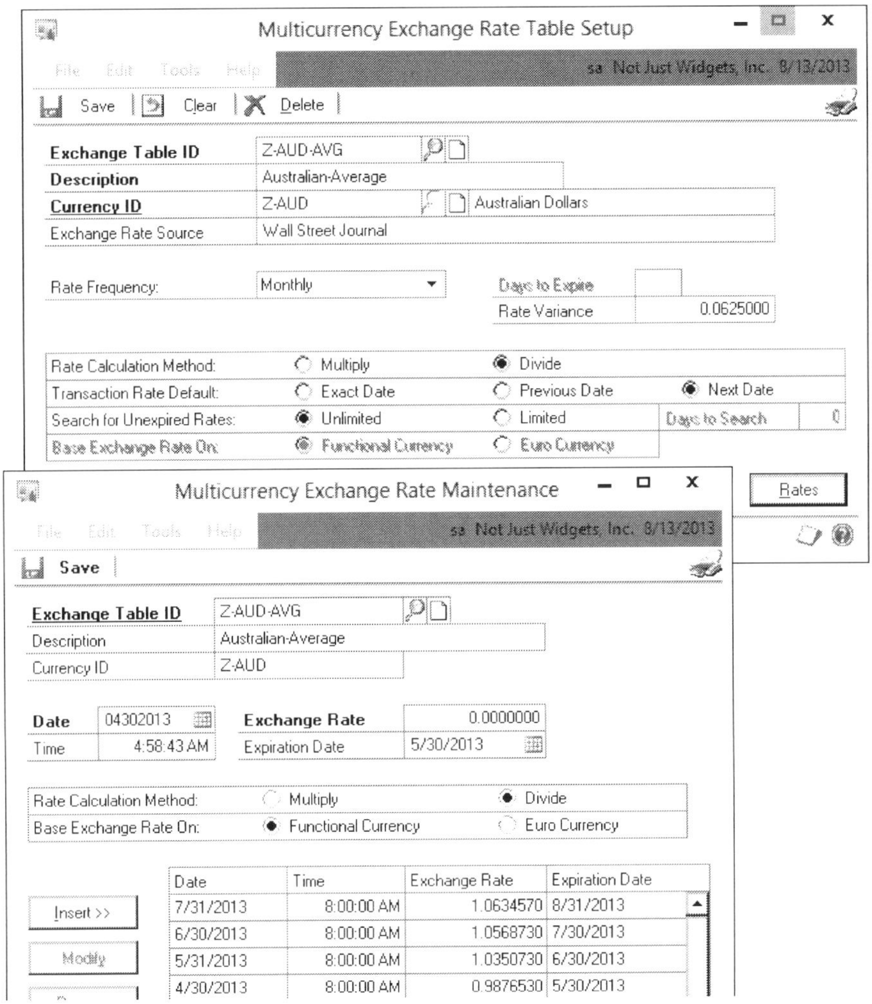

The illustrated settings will cause a transaction entered in Australian dollars to divide the Australian dollar amount by 0.987653 in April and 1.035073 in May to calculate the functional amount for that transaction. With this example, AUD $1 would be US $ 1.0125014 in April and US $ 0.9661154 in May.

The following are explanations of the settings on the **Multicurrency Exchange Rate Table Setup** window:

- **Rate Frequency** can be changed at any time and determines the default **Expiration Date** for new exchange rates entered. If you are not sure how often new exchange rates will be entered you can select **None**, so no expiration date is defaulted. It is important to always have a valid exchange rate, otherwise users may get error messages during transaction entry. This can, however, be mitigated by the **Transaction Rate Default** setting described further in this section.
- **Rate Variance** is a limit on the difference that will be allowed between a new exchange rate entered and the previous rate. This variance limitation will also apply for any rates entered *on-the-fly* during transaction entry, if that is allowed. A rate variance of zero means there is no limit. This setting can be changed at any time and is useful for preventing mistakes when typing in exchange rates. For very volatile exchange rates, consider making the rate variance something large or zero.
- **Rate Calculation Method** determines whether the specified currency gets multiplied or divided by the exchange rate entered to arrive at the functional currency. This setting cannot be changed once exchange rates and transactions have been entered.
- **Transaction Rate Default** determines how the system chooses what exchange rate to use:
    - **Exact Date**: A valid exchange rate must exist for the exact date of the transaction. With this option and the exchange rate table shown previously, a transaction dated September 2, 2013 would cause an error, because there is no valid exchange rate for that date. This setting should only be used if you plan on entering daily exchange rates.
    - **Previous Date**: If there is no valid exchange rate for the transaction date, the exchange rate with the closest date prior to the transaction date will be used. If no previous exchange rate exists, the exchange rate with the closest date following the transaction date will be used. With this option and the exchange rate table shown previously, a transaction dated September 2, 2013 will give an error, as there is no unexpired rate with either a previous or future date. This is the typical setting most companies use, in my experience.

- ◦ **Next Date**: If there is no valid exchange rate for the transaction date, the exchange rate with the closest future date to the transaction date will be used. If no future exchange rate exists, the exchange rate with the closest date prior to the transaction date will be used. With this option and the exchange rate table shown previously, a transaction dated August 2, 2013 will use the 1.063457 exchange rate, as there is no future exchange rate to use.

- **Search for Unexpired Rates** is only available if **Previous Date** or **Next Date** is chosen for the **Transaction Rate Default**. This setting allows you to limit the number of days the system will look backward or forward for an exchange rate. For example, if this were set to 20 on the previous example, a transaction dated August 25, 2013 would not have a valid exchange rate, as the latest expiration date is 25 days prior. This setting can be used to allow a bit of a grace period for entering new rates.

The **Multicurrency Exchange Rate Maintenance** window is opened by clicking on **Rates** on the **Multicurrency Exchange Rate Table Setup** window or navigating to **Cards | System | Exchange Table**. The **Date**, **Time**, and **Expiration Date** will be automatically filled in, but you can change them as needed. Enter the **Exchange Rate** and select **Insert** to add an exchange rate. Click on an exchange rate in the table and select **Remove** to delete the rate. To change an exchange rate previously entered, click on it in the table, change the **Date**, **Time**, **Exchange Rate**, or **Expiration Date**, then select **Modify**.

> Changing previously entered exchange rates will not update any existing transactions, it will only affect transactions entered after the change is made.

## Multicurrency access

Before a Dynamics GP company can use a currency or an exchange rate table, you need to allow that company access to the currency and exchange rate table. This is done on the **Multicurrency Access Setup** window (**Microsoft Dynamics GP | Tools | Setup | System | Multicurrency Access**), which will only be available when no other users are logged into Dynamics GP.

On the **Currencies** list, select one currency at a time and then check the **Access** checkboxes for the companies that can use this currency. If you will be using multiple currencies, select the **Exchange Tables IDs** one at a time and check the **Access** checkboxes for the companies that can use the exchange tables:

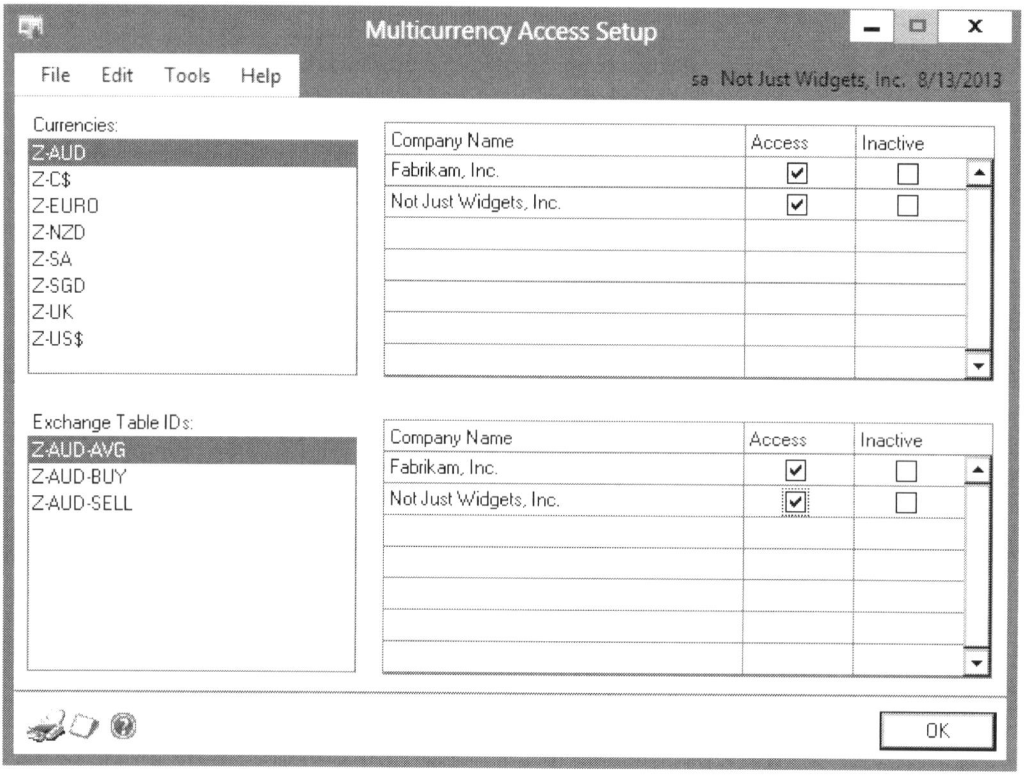


# Additional system-wide setup

There are a few additional system-wide settings that you may want to go through before moving on to your company setup. These are optional and include system preferences, reporting tools setup, and SmartList options.

## System preferences

You can set overall system preferences for Dynamics GP by navigating to **Microsoft Dynamics GP** | **Tools** | **Setup** | **System** | **System Preferences**. All of these settings are optional.

- The **SharePoint URL** is used to enable searching Dynamics GP data from SharePoint.

- The **Email Preferences** section allows you to set options for emailing from Dynamics GP. Selecting **Exchange** for the **Server Type** requires Exchange 2007 SP 1 or greater with Exchange Web Services and will mean that users are prompted for an Exchange login every time they want to email from Dynamics GP. This is not recommended for most implementations and I typically see **MAPI** selected for the **Server Type**. The option to add a **Password** to `.docx` attachments is not typically something we see used, if you do decide to use this, make sure to test it to ensure that it will work with your business workflow.

> If Outlook 64-bit will be used for e-mailing documents from Dynamics GP, the **Server Type** must be **Exchange**. If Outlook 32-bit will be used, either **Server Type** can be selected.

- Under **Home Page Defaults** the **Load To Do: Reminders** option controls whether reminders are loaded on each new user's home page by default.
- **Remember User** is a feature that was added in Dynamics GP 2010. This activates the **Remember user and password** and **Remember this company** checkboxes on the Dynamics GP login windows. Unfortunately, there is no way to separate these two options, which is something I have seen requested many times. While many companies may feel that remembering the company is a nice option for users, remembering the User ID and password may be against security policies in some organizations.

> If you are worried about the safety of allowing the user ID and password to be saved, here is a blog article by Mariano Gomez addressing this: `http://bit.ly/11qWjGm`.

## Reporting tools setup

If you have already deployed SQL Server Reporting Services and Excel reports for your Dynamics GP companies, you can skip this step. However, if you did not deploy these yet, have installed a new component after deploying them, or want to look at the current settings and deployment status, you can do that now by navigating to **Microsoft Dynamics GP | Tools | Setup | System | Reporting Tools Setup**.

# SmartList options

SmartList options allow you to predefine default settings for SmartLists. This may be something you need to come back to after your users have started entering data into Dynamics GP; however, since these changes do not affect any existing SmartList Favorites, it might be helpful if some of these are changed upfront. For example, all SmartLists will default to show only the first 1,000 records found. If you already know that you have 2,000 customers or 5,000 inventory items, you may want to change the related SmartLists to have a higher number of records shown by default.

To open the **SmartList Options** window, navigate to **Microsoft Dynamics GP** | **Tools** | **Setup** | **System** | **SmartList Options**. Choose the **SmartList Category** and change the settings as desired. In addition to changing the **Maximum Records** shown by default, you can also change the **Default Go To** action (this is what happens when users double click on a record in SmartList) and the columns shown in the default SmartList along with their order. The **Search Defaults** options may be useful if you are using a binary sort order, otherwise it is recommended to leave them as defaulted.

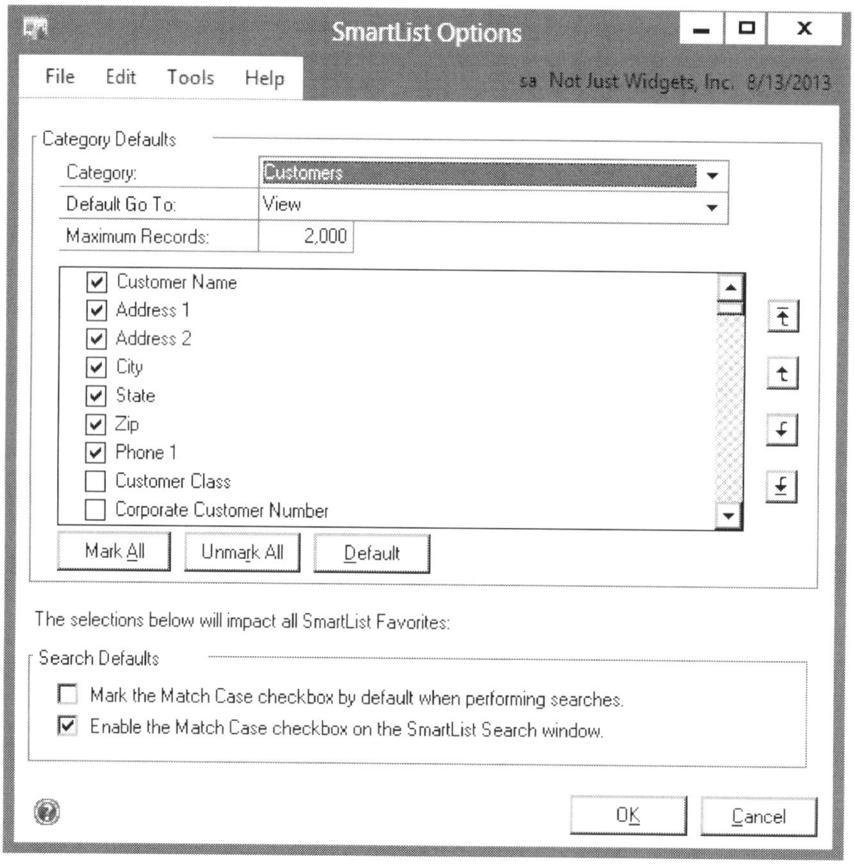

A common pet peeve of many Dynamics GP users is that the **Credit Amount** is shown before the **Debit Amount** on the **Account Transactions** SmartList. This is a great example where changing this during setup will help your users avoid having to change it every time they search for General Ledger transactions in SmartList.

> If you had set the system password to blank during the system setup, you may want to change it now by navigating to **Microsoft Dynamics GP** | **Tools** | **Setup** | **System** | **System Password**.

# Company setup

Once system-wide settings are in place, you will be ready to set up your Dynamics GP company. Any company-specific setup must be done while logged in to that company. Dynamics GP company setup includes the following:

- Account format
- Account setup
- Multicurrency
- Tax Details and Tax Schedules
- Company setup
- Fiscal Periods
- Shipping Methods
- Payment Terms
- Credit Cards
- Posting setup
- E-mail setup

The following sections will go through each of these topics in detail.

> You can still use the **Setup Checklist** to navigate to the setup windows described in the following section; however, they will not go in order, so navigation to each window using the main Dynamics GP menus will also be included.

# Account format

The account format can be different for each Dynamics GP company, as long as it conforms to the maximums of the account framework you selected during your initial Dynamics GP installation. To define the account format for your company, navigate to **Microsoft Dynamics GP | Tools | Setup | Company | Account Format**. No other users can be logged into the Dynamics GP company when you are making changes to the account format for the company.

The NJW company decided on account format XXXX-XX-XXX, representing Natural Account—Subaccount—Division. So their total account length is nine (separators are not counted) and their total number of segments is three.

On the **Account Format Setup** window change the number of **Segments** first, then the **Account Length**. This will automatically change the scrolling list under **Segment** to show the same number of lines as segments. Change the **Name** and **Length** of each **Segment** and identify the **Main Segment ID**. The **Main Segment ID** is important for sorting and searching options on various Dynamics GP windows, and is critical for Management Reporter or FRx to interact with the Dynamics GP General Ledger accounts correctly.

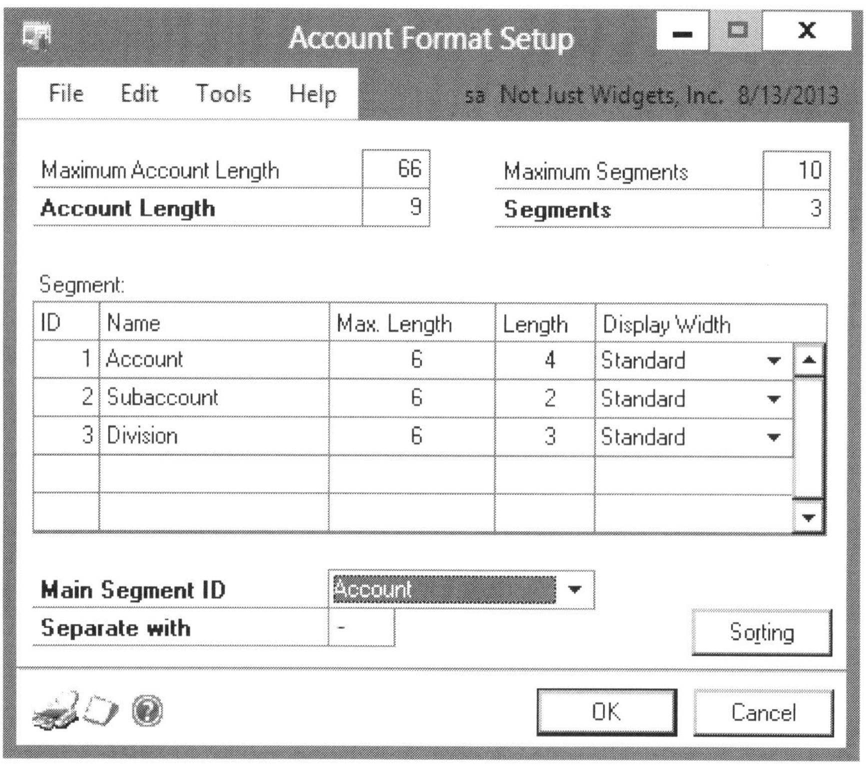

The default for **Separate with** is a dash (-), and while it is possible to change the separator, I have never seen a single company do this.

If you are planning to enter letters instead of numbers for any of your segments, you can change the **Display Width** of that segment. This will resize the width of that segment on every window where it is displayed. There are three possible widths, depending on what letters will be used. For example, the letter W takes up a lot more real estate than the letter I. This setting can be changed at any time, so you may want to see how your account numbers display before making any changes.

# Account setup

General Ledger accounts are needed to perform many other setup steps and should be created as the next step. Even if you have decided to import your chart of accounts, it is helpful to know how to set up new accounts for any that you may want to create manually.

There are four types of General Ledger accounts in Dynamics GP:

| Account Type | Description | Navigation Path |
|---|---|---|
| **Posting Account** | Posting accounts are the typical financial accounts that comprise a company's Chart of Accounts and keep track of financial data. Posting accounts are often simply referred to as '**Accounts**'. | **Cards \| Financial \| Account** |
| **Unit Account** | Unit accounts are used to track non-financial data, for example head count or square footage in a department. Unit accounts can be used for calculations on reports and for allocation calculations. One-sided transactions can be entered for unit accounts. | **Cards \| Financial \| Unit Account** |
| **Fixed Allocation Account** | Fixed allocation accounts allow transaction amounts to automatically be allocated to multiple posting accounts based on hard coded percentages. These allocations occur during posting, so the fixed allocation accounts never have a balance. | **Cards \| Financial \| Fixed Allocation** |
| **Variable Allocation Account** | Variable allocation accounts allow transaction amounts to automatically be allocated to multiple posting accounts based on other account balances (either posting accounts or unit accounts). These allocations occur during posting, so the variable allocation accounts never have a balance. | **Cards \| Financial \| Variable Allocation** |

To create a new posting account, navigate to **Cards** | **Financial** | **Account**. Type in the **Account** number. As you start typing you will receive the following pop-up message:

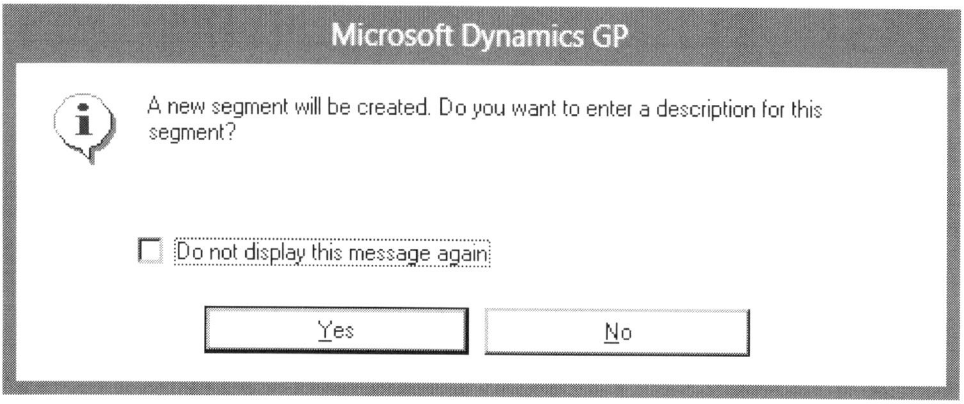


Dynamics GP attempts to get the name for each unique segment of your GL accounts, so that it can suggest names for new accounts created in the future. Most companies find this distracting and not very helpful. To turn off these reminders, check the **Do not display this message again** checkbox and click on **No** to close the window.

The following are explanations for the fields on the **Account Maintenance** window:

| Field | Explanation |
|---|---|
| **Account** | The General Ledger account number—separators will automatically be added, so you can just type the numbers or letters. |
| **Description** | Account name with a maximum of 50 characters. |
| **Inactive** | Used to inactivate accounts no longer used. This is unchecked by default. |
| **Alias** | Optional field that can be used for speeding up data entry for long GL accounts. Most companies do not use aliases, especially with relatively short account numbers. |
| **Allow Account Entry** | Checked by default, this controls whether users will be able to manually type this account number on transactions. Some companies choose to uncheck this for control accounts, such as Cash, Inventory, Accounts Payable, and Accounts Receivable, to prevent errors and reconciliation issues. This can be changed at any time by users with security access to the **Account Maintenance** window. |
| **Category** | A required field that helps group GL accounts. *Appendix, General Ledger Account Categories* contains a list of the default account categories in Dynamics GP. |

<table>
<tr><th>Field</th><th colspan="2">Explanation</th></tr>
<tr><td>Posting Type</td><td colspan="2">Balance Sheet or Profit and Loss—this is a critical setting that controls behavior of account balances during the year-end close process. Balance Sheet account balances are brought forward to the following year, Profit and Loss balances are closed out into Retained Earnings.</td></tr>
<tr><td>Typical Balance</td><td colspan="2">Either Debit or Credit—select whatever the typical entry for this account would be. This is not critical, but is sometimes helpful when manually entering General Ledger transactions or creating reports.</td></tr>
<tr><td>Level of Posting from Series</td><td colspan="2">Available for Sales, Inventory, Purchasing, and Payroll modules, this works together with the company's posting setup to determine whether posting from subledgers creates summary or detail entries in the General Ledger. It is typically not recommended to control the posting detail at the GL account level, as it gets cumbersome to maintain and confusing for users. These will all be defaulted to Detail, which is the recommended setting.</td></tr>
<tr><td>Include in Lookup</td><td colspan="2">This setting determines whether the account will be shown in a default lookup (or search) from a transaction for each module listed. By default all the series are selected, and this is typically the recommended setting.</td></tr>
<tr><td>User Defined</td><td colspan="2">Four additional fields are available to hold information for each account. When migrating from other systems these are sometimes used to store the corresponding account numbers from the old system. The labels for these fields can be changed on the General Ledger Setup window which will be discussed in Chapter 7, Module Setup - General Ledger, Bank Reconciliation, Payables, and Receivables.</td></tr>
<tr><td rowspan="5">Buttons at the bottom</td><td>Summary</td><td>Opens a window showing the summary of the period balances for the selected account for open years.</td></tr>
<tr><td>History</td><td>Opens a window showing the summary of the period balances for the selected account for historical years.</td></tr>
<tr><td>Budget</td><td>Opens the Budget Maintenance window to allow entry or changes of budgets (the budget must already exist).</td></tr>
<tr><td>Analysis</td><td>Opens the Account Analysis Defaults window of the Multidimensional Analysis (MDA) module.</td></tr>
<tr><td>Currency</td><td>Allows multicurrency setup for the account—this will not be available until the currency settings for the company are completed and is typically easier done on a more global scale, rather than one account at a time.</td></tr>
</table>

The following is a typical General Ledger account:

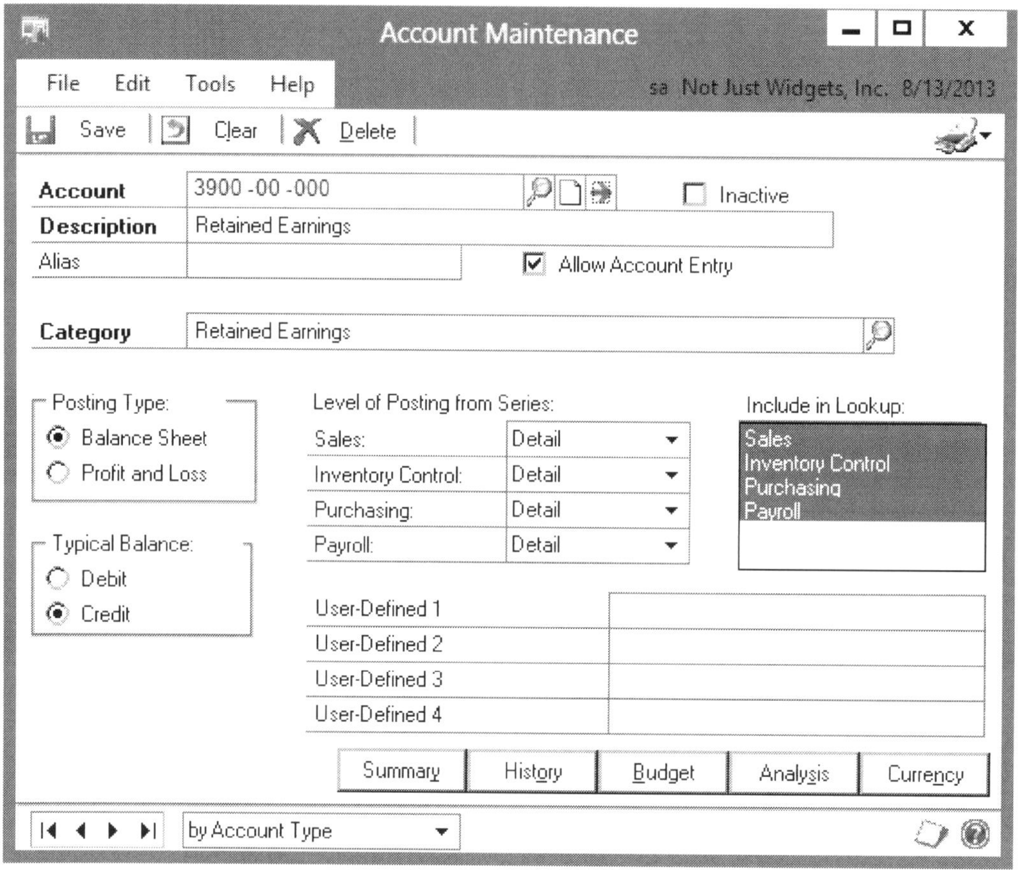


# Multicurrency

If you are following the **Setup Checklist** in Dynamics GP, **Multicurrency** setup is listed under the **Financial** series, however it is important to complete this before some of the other setup steps. Even if you are not planning on using the Multicurrency functionality, you will need to define the functional currency for your Dynamics GP company.

Navigate to **Microsoft Dynamics GP | Tools | Setup | Financial | Multicurrency** to open the **Multicurrency Setup** window. The **Functional Currency** is the currency your financial records will be kept in and is not possible to change once you start entering transactions into Dynamics GP. The **Reporting Currency** may often be the same as your **Functional Currency**. If you are setting up a subsidiary with a different functional currency than your main company, the reporting currency will typically be the functional currency of your main company. The **Default Transaction Rate Types** are the defaults, but can be changed as needed during transaction entry.

The **Currency Translation Default Exchange Table IDs** section is fairly new to Dynamics GP and allows for reporting on your General Ledger accounts in a currency that is not the functional or originating currency of each transaction. This can get very complicated quickly and it is best to consult with your Dynamics GP resource if you have a need for this.

If you will be using Multicurrency, decide whether to allow any of the **Exchange Rate Options** and (optionally) enter **Passwords** for the selections:

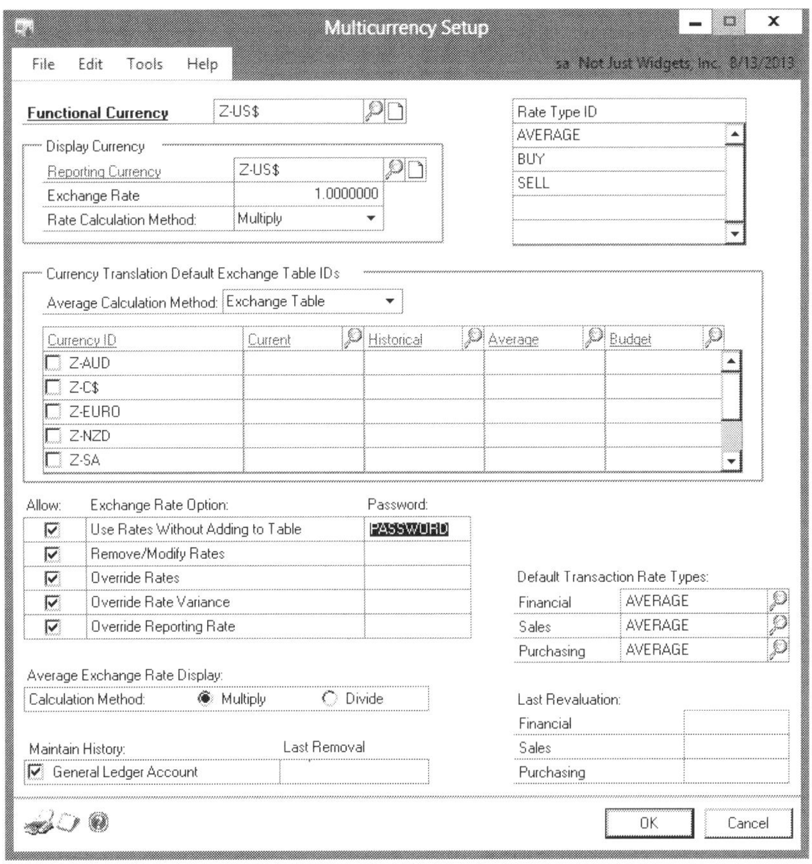

Note that the passwords are not masked, so anyone with access to this window will be able to see and change them. When the settings on this window are changed, you will receive the following pop-up message:

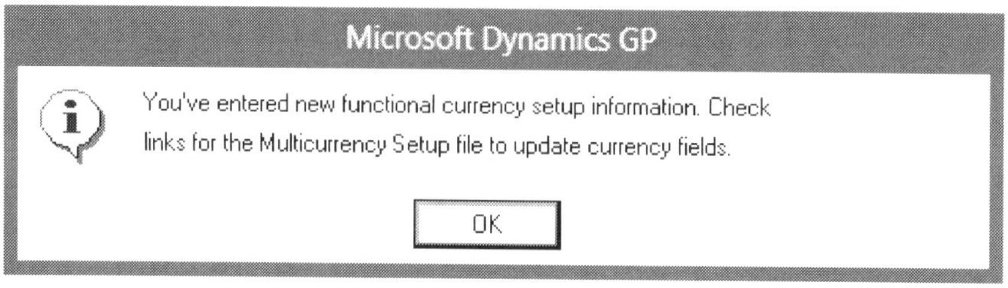


**Check Links** is a process that checks for consistency between related Dynamics GP tables, restores missing or damaged data, and clears out orphaned records. Best practice is to make a backup of your system and company databases prior to running this process.

Check links is found under **Microsoft Dynamics GP | Maintenance | Check Links**. Select **Financial** under **Series**, select **Multicurrency Setup** in the list of **Logical Tables**, and click on **Insert** to move your selection to the **Selected Tables** list.

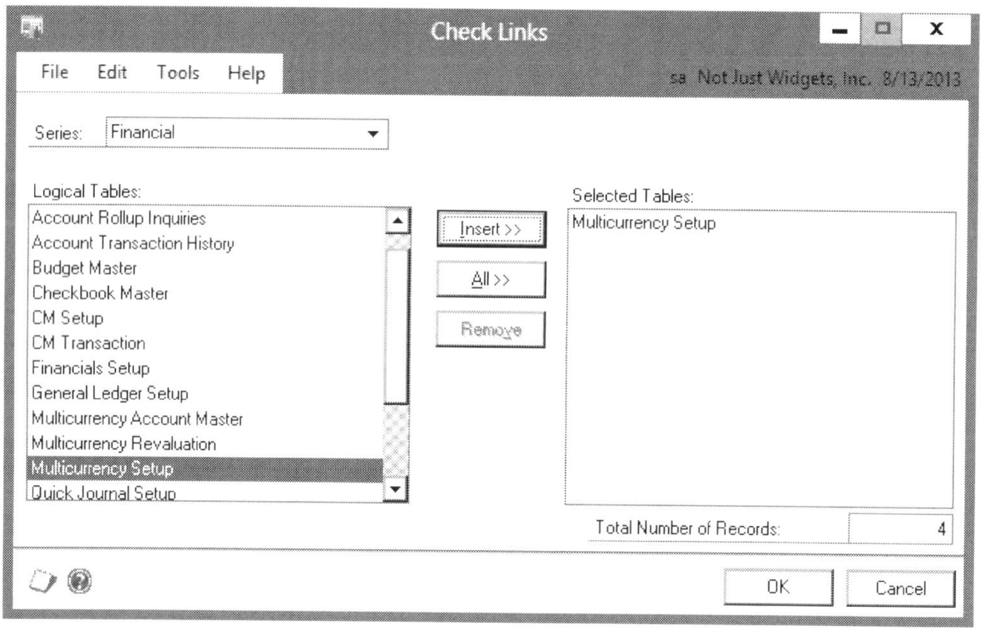


When you click on **OK** you will be asked for a **Report Destination**, select **Screen**. This process should run fairly quickly and return with a **No errors found** message on the report. If your report shows any errors, consult with your Dynamics GP resource.

If you are planning on using multiple currencies and have already set up exchange rate tables during the system setup in the preceding sections, you can complete the Multicurrency setup for your Dynamics GP company by navigating to **Microsoft Dynamics GP | Tools | Setup | Financial | Rate Types**. One at a time, select the **Exchange Table IDs** that you plan to use with this company and the **Rate Types** to be used with each. The **Accounts** button will open the **Multicurrency Posting Account Setup by Rate Type** window where you can select realized gain/loss and rounding accounts for this particular exchange rate table and type. If you will be using different GL accounts for different exchange rates and types, fill in the accounts on this window. Otherwise, if these accounts will be the same for all exchange rates and types, leave this blank. You will have an opportunity to define these accounts on a company-wide basis further on in the setup process.

# Taxes

If you will be tracking sales or purchase taxes in Dynamics GP, you will first need to set up **Tax Details** and **Tax Schedules**. Recall from the *Sales and purchase taxes* section of *Chapter 3, Planning - Dynamics GP System* that tax details are the lowest level of taxes that need to be tracked or reported on and tax schedules are groupings of one or more tax details. Tax schedules are assigned to customers, vendors, items, and transactions in Dynamics GP.

## Tax Details

To start setting up taxes, navigate to **Microsoft Dynamics GP | Tools | Setup | Company | Tax Details**. To create a tax detail:

1. Type in a **Tax Detail ID**—this cannot be changed later.
2. Type in a **Description**—the description will help you identify this tax detail on reports and it can be changed at any time.
3. Select **Sales** or **Purchases** for the **Type**. This cannot be changed later.
4. The **History** checkboxes will be checked by default. It is recommended to track all history in Dynamics GP, so leave these checked.
5. Optionally, enter the **Tax ID Number**. This ID is informational only, but may be a handy place to store this information.
6. Fill in the GL **Account** number for the tax. This account will be credited for sales taxes and debited for purchase taxes.
7. Select what the tax should be calculated on under **Based On**. The most common option for this is **Percent of Sale/Purchase**. Two other common options are **Tax Included with Item Price**, which backs out the tax from a sale amount, and **Percent of Sale/Purchase plus Taxable Taxes**, which is used when setting up taxable taxes.

8. Select a rounding method under **Round**. The most common method is **To the Nearest Currency Decimal Digit** which should help you get as close as possible to the tax calculations if you were doing them manually. Note that this is not the default rounding method on this window. No matter which rounding method you choose, it is important to have the same rounding method for all your tax details.
9. Enter the tax **Percentage**.
10. If applicable, enter the **Taxable Percent** and **Min** and **Max** values for **Taxable Amount**. These are used when either a portion of the sales gets taxed or there are minimums or maximums for an item to be taxable. When a **Min** value is entered, the **Include** option gets enabled and you can choose if the tax is based on the **Full Amount** up to the maximum or the **Amount Within Range**, using the difference between the **Min** and **Max** values. If a **Max** value is entered, the **Qualifiers** option is enabled so you can choose how the tax is calculated.
11. If you are setting up a tax that another tax is calculated on, select the **Taxable Tax** checkbox.

While there are a lot of options on the **Tax Detail Maintenance** window, a typical tax setup is fairly simple and looks like the following example:

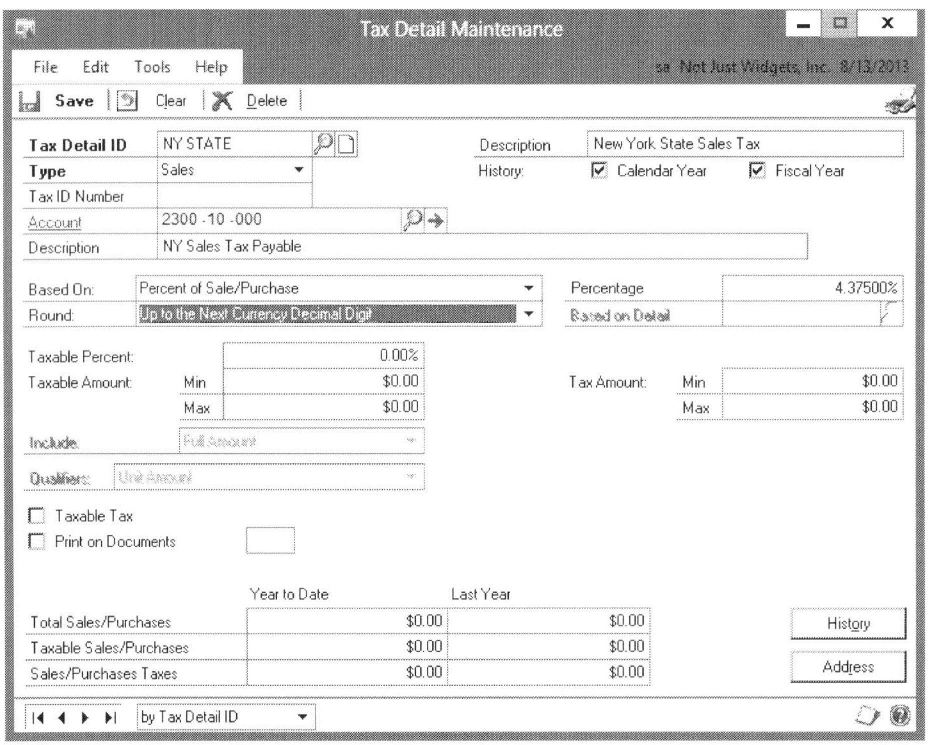

## Tax Schedules

Once all your tax details are created, you can set up tax schedules by navigating to **Microsoft Dynamics GP | Tools | Setup | Company | Tax Schedules**. On the **Tax Schedule Maintenance** window type in a **Tax Schedule ID** (this cannot be changed once saved) and **Description**. Select one tax detail at a time from the list of the **Available Tax Detail IDs** on the left and click on **Insert**. The selected tax detail will be added to the list of **Selected Tax Detail IDs** on the right.

In the following example, the **NYC SALES** tax schedule includes the **NY STATE** and **NYC** tax details:

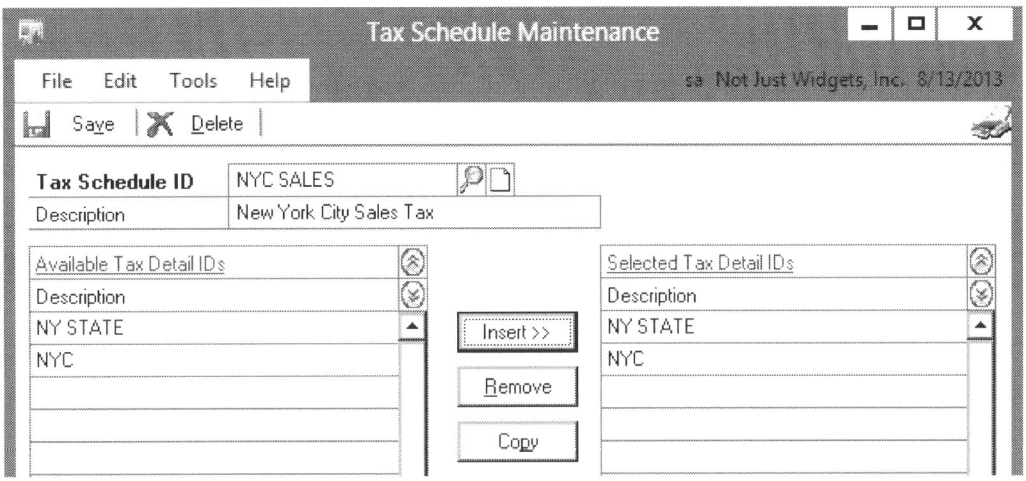


There is no limit on how many tax details and tax schedules can be set up and the same tax detail can be part of any number of tax schedules. Changing the percentage on a tax detail will cause all the tax schedules using that tax detail to calculate with the new percentage for future transactions. No existing transactions, whether they are already posted or not, will change when changes are made to a tax detail or tax schedule.

# Company

There are a number of company settings, such as addresses, tax registration, internet user defined field labels, and additional setup options, that are grouped together on the **Company Setup** window in Dynamics GP. To open the **Company Setup** window, navigate to **Microsoft Dynamics GP | Tools | Setup | Company | Company**.

## Company Setup window

The name you entered for your company when you were creating it in Dynamics GP Utilities will show at the top under **Company Name**. You can change the **Company Name** at any time, and this is what controls the name that shows in the drop-down list of companies available when you log into Dynamics GP. It is also what shows at the top of every window in Dynamics GP. For example, NJW has decided there is no reason to have the `Inc.` shown here, so they have changed the **Company Name** to `Not Just Widgets`. As soon as **OK** is clicked on the **Company Setup** window this change will be propagated throughout Dynamics GP.

When creating a test company, you can add `<TEST>` to the end of the **Company Name**. This will cause a message to pop up every time a user logs into that company, letting them know this is a test company and should not be used for live data. If you are using the Payroll module, this will also cause employees created in the test company to not be counted against the purchased registered employee count.

> The letters TEST must be in all capitals for this feature to work.

You can see the SQL database name for this company under **Company ID**—this is informational only and cannot be changed.

Because a company could have multiple addresses, each address needs to be assigned an **Address ID**. These are alphanumeric and can be up to 15 characters long. The recommendation for company **Address IDs** is to pick something simple and meaningful to users. So if a company has two offices and three warehouses, one option for their **Address IDs** may be: NJ OFFICE, NY OFFICE, NJ WAREHOUSE, NY WAREHOUSE, and PA WAREHOUSE.

On the **Company Setup** window, enter the **Address ID** for the main company location. The **Name** field under the **Address ID** is where the full company name should be entered and this is what will be printed on reports. Enter the **Contact**, **Address**, **Phone**, and **Fax** details for the main location. Additional addresses can be entered by clicking on the **Address** button, which will open the **Company Addresses Setup** window.

There are two **User Defined** and two **Tax Exempt** fields that can hold additional information that may need to be added to various reports or just stored. The **Tax Registration** field should be filled in with the company's tax ID (EIN), this will be what populates on the 1099 forms printed by Dynamics GP. If you prefer not to put the tax registration number here, the EIN can be filled in manually every time you print 1099s. Defaults for the **Sales** and **Purchases Tax Schedules** for the company can optionally be filled in.

The **Security** checkbox will be checked by default—it is strongly recommended to leave this checked. Unchecking **Security** will disable all the security settings in Dynamics GP. The following is an example of the NJW **Company Setup** window after having changed the **Company Name** and filled in the details:

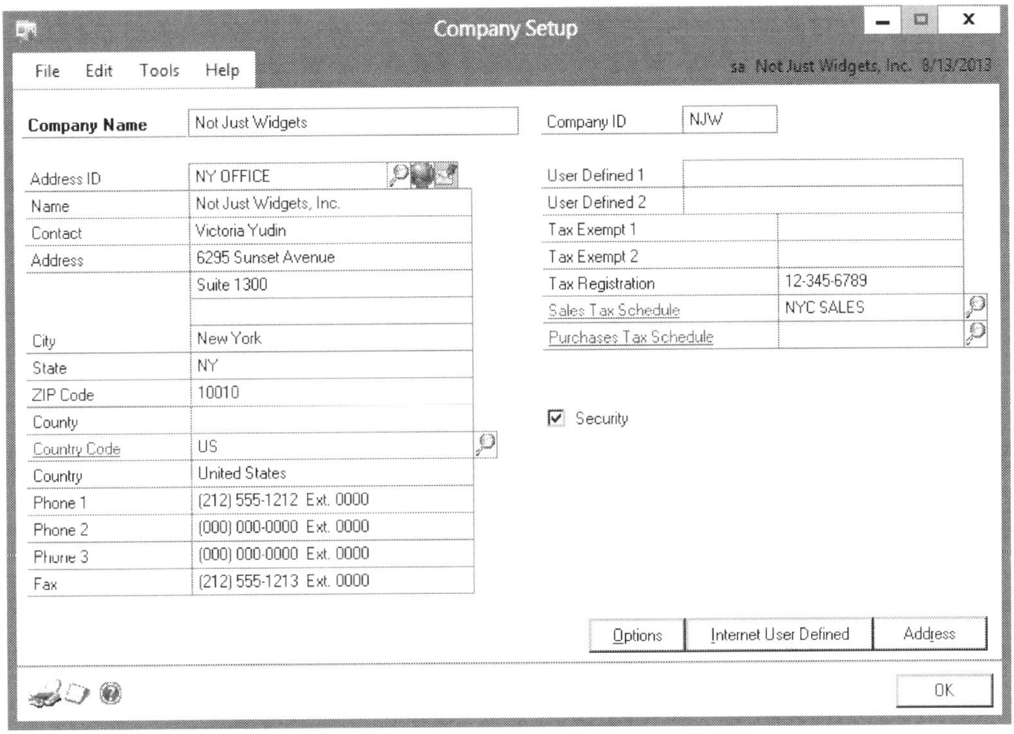

# Internet user defined

Clicking on the **Internet User Defined** button on the **Company Setup** window will open the **Internet User Defined Setup** window. There are eight labels that can be changed for the internet information stored for a Dynamics GP company. These labels are shared by vendors, customers, inventory items, salespeople, and company addresses, so if you decide to change them, try to use labels that will be generic across all those objects.

The **Internet User Defined Labels** can be changed at any time, however, if they are changed after data is already entered, additional data manipulation may be required to move the data into appropriate fields.

The following is an example of the **Internet User Defined Setup** window with a few changes from the defaults. As the last two fields (corresponding to **Label 7** and **Label 8**) have browse buttons next to them, NJW has decided to make them file locations for customer or vendor contracts and proposals:

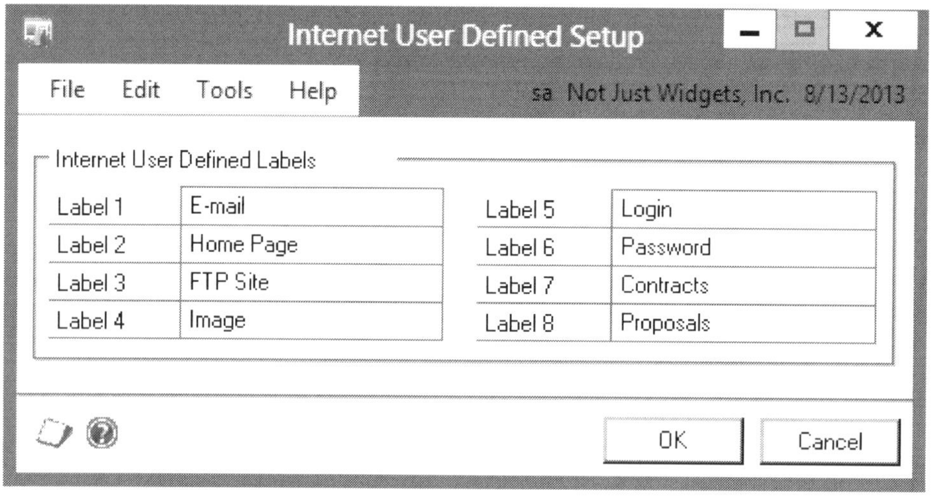


As soon as the changes are made, these labels will now be used on the **Internet Information** window (accessed by clicking on the **Internet** icon to the right of the **Address ID** field):

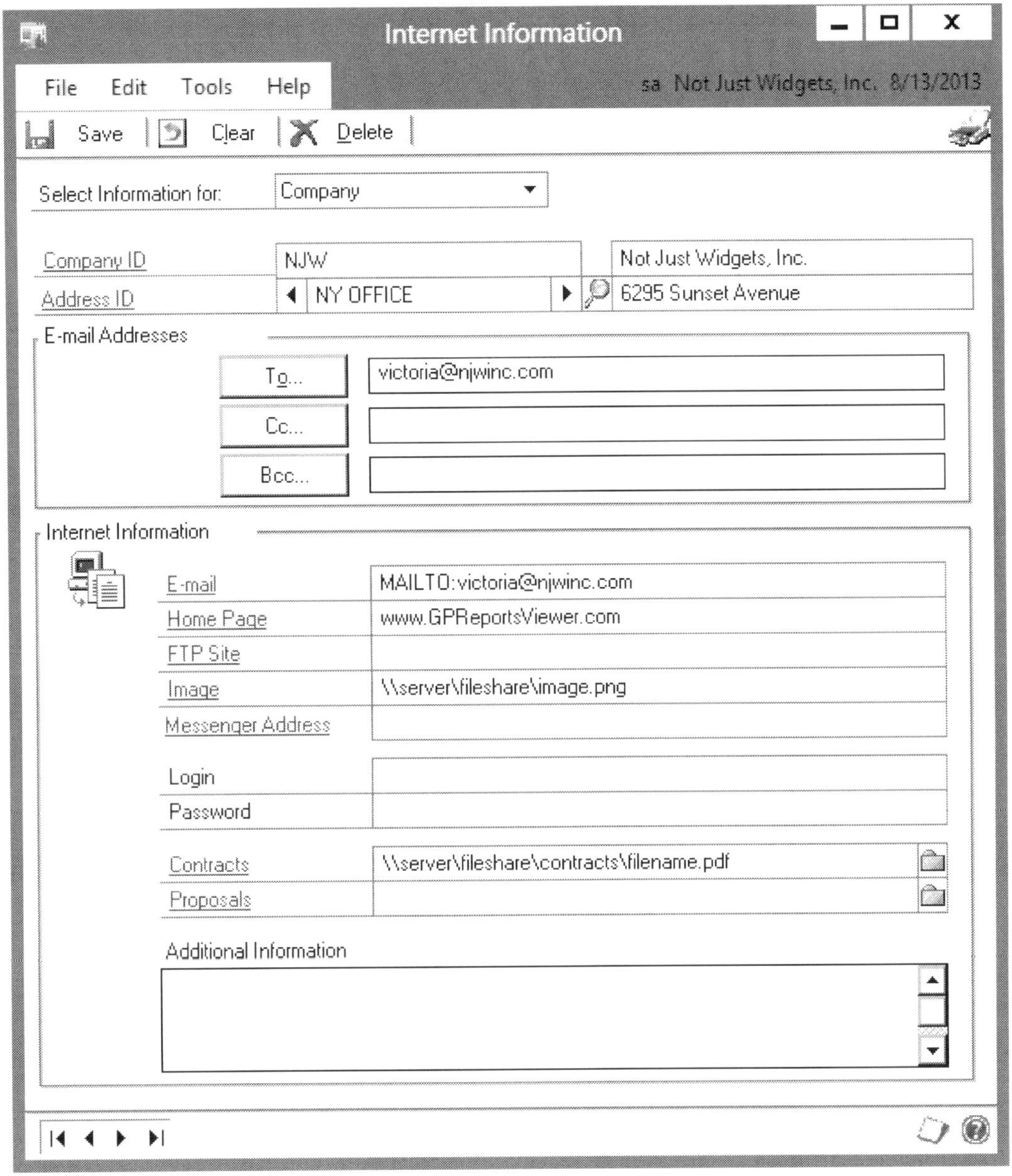


The **E-mail Addresses** section on the **Internet Information** window is used if you are sending e-mail documents from Dynamics GP to your customers and vendors. These should be in the regular e-mail address format and you can enter multiple e-mail addresses separated by a semicolon (;) in each of the fields.

In the **Internet Information** section any e-mail addresses must be prefaced with a `MAILTO:` to work. URLs and file locations can be in the regular format, as shown in the previous example.

## Company options

Clicking on the **Options** button on the **Company Setup** window opens the **Company Setup Options** window. Here you will find a lengthy list of options that can be turned on or off as needed for various functionality inside Dynamics GP. A detailed explanation of each option can be found by clicking on the **Help** icon or **F1** on your keyboard and selecting **Fields**.

Most of these options are either only applicable to particular countries or rarely used, and only two are checked by default:

- **Use Shipping Method when Selecting Default Tax Schedule**: Typical Dynamics GP functionality is to determine what tax schedule to use for purchasing and sales transactions based on the type of shipment method selected. For example, on a sales invoice, if the shipment is being delivered to the customer, then the customer's tax schedule is used. If the customer is picking up the shipment at your location, then your company's tax schedule is used. Unchecking this option would cause Dynamics GP not to take the shipment method into consideration and would always use the tax schedule for the customer or vendor on transactions.
- **Allow Summary-Level Tax Edits**: This option allows tax summary values to be edited, which may be useful for some reports. Changing summary values does not change any transactional data or calculations. Most companies do not use summary values, however it does not hurt anything to leave this option enabled.

For most Dynamics GP implementations the preceding two options are the only ones that need to be selected.

> If you need to track use taxes, take a look at this method described on the Dynamics University blog: `shar.es/J9kjH` which make use of the **Enable Reverse Charge Taxes** option on the **Company Setup Options** window.

# Fiscal Periods

**Fiscal Periods** define the structure of your accounting periods and years in Dynamics GP. Each company set up in Dynamics GP has a completely independent fiscal period setup. During installation, Dynamics GP will create a default fiscal year based on the calendar year of the installation date. Prior to entering any transactions into Dynamics GP, be sure to go through the fiscal period setup, especially if your fiscal year is not a calendar year with twelve standard months.

To open the **Fiscal Periods Setup** window navigate to **Microsoft Dynamics GP | Tools | Setup | Company | Fiscal Periods**. Depending on how much historical data you have decided to enter or import, you may need to set up multiple fiscal years. For example, NJW uses a calendar fiscal year and has decided to import ending balances for 2010, and then monthly balances for 2011, 2012, and 2013. The following are the steps to create years 2010 through 2013 for NJW:

1. Type `2010` in the **Year** field and press **Tab**.
2. Change the **First Day** to `01/01/2010` and the **Last Day** to `12/31/2010`.
3. Confirm that the **Number of Periods** is `12`. (This should be the default.)
4. Click on **Calculate**. This will fill in the grid with twelve lines, one for each month.
5. Confirm that the **Date** column has the correct beginning date for each period/month. If your fiscal periods are not calendar months, you will need to manually type in the beginning date for each period in the **Date** column.
6. Optionally, change the **Period Name** for each **Period** to the name of the month. This is not required, and certainly for a calendar fiscal year, it is easy to understand that Period 5 is May. However, the **Period Name** is what will show on all Dynamics GP reports and inquiry windows and it is much easier for users to see the month names here. For a non-calendar fiscal year this is even more important. To speed up progress on this window, once you finish typing in a month name, press the down arrow on the keyboard to go to the next month.

> If you are setting up multiple years or multiple companies, it may be faster to use the script provided in this blog post to change the period names: `http://bit.ly/10JBhy2`.

7. Once done with 2010, repeat steps 1 through 6 for years 2011 through 2013. For the year already created during installation, you only need to repeat steps 5 and 6.

When done, your **Year** drop-down should look like the following example:

The **Fiscal Periods Setup** window for the year 2013 should look similar to the following:

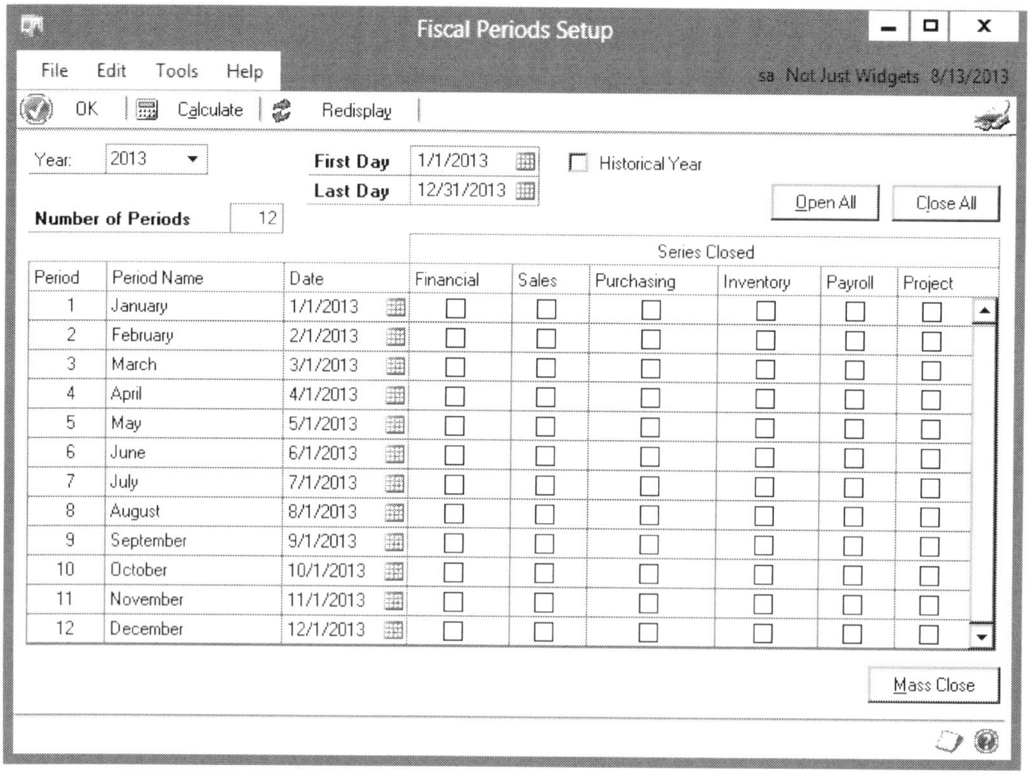


Note that there is no **Save** button on the **Fiscal Periods Setup** window. All changes on this window are applied as soon as they are made. If you are looking to test or experiment with changes on this window, switch to the Fabrikam sample company instead of testing in your live company.

# Shipping Methods

**Shipping Methods** in Dynamics GP perform two functions:

- They can be used to determine the tax schedule used for a particular transaction.
- They can store information to be used internally and communicated to customers or vendors about the method of shipment for a transaction.

To create or modify shipping methods, navigate to **Microsoft Dynamics GP** | **Tools** | **Setup** | **Company** | **Shipping Methods**. If you selected **Load Shipping Methods and Payment Terms** when you were creating your company in Dynamics GP Utilities, you will already have a number of shipping methods available.

To create a new shipping method only a **Shipping Method ID** and the **Shipping Type** are required—all other fields are optional and can be left blank. As most reports and windows in Dynamics GP will only show the **Shipping Method ID** (and not the **Description**), consider making the ID something descriptive enough and appropriate for users, customers, and vendors to see. The following is an example of a typical **Shipping Method Setup** window:

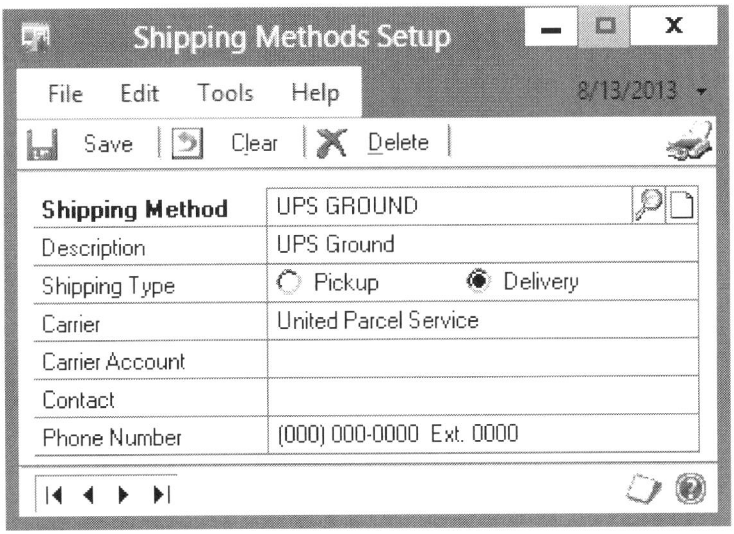


If you are planning on storing the **Carrier**, **Contact**, and **Phone Number** and want to make this available to the Dynamics GP users, make sure that the users needing this data have security access to the **Shipments Methods Setup** window or the **Shipping Methods** report under **Reports** | **Company** | **Setup**.

# Payment Terms

**Payment Terms** in Dynamics GP help communicate the terms for each transaction to vendors and customers. More importantly, in most cases, they automatically calculate due dates which can save time and effort during transaction entry.

To create or modify payment terms navigate to **Microsoft Dynamics GP | Tools | Setup | Company | Payment Terms**. If you chose **Load Shipping Methods and Payment Terms** when you were creating your company in Dynamics GP Utilities, you will already have a number of payment terms available.

To create new payment terms only the **Payment Terms ID** is required. Entering the **Payment Terms ID** only will allow the payment terms to be used for informational purposes, but will default the due date of a transaction using these payment terms to the transaction date.

The following are explanations of the fields available for payment terms setup:

| Field / Options | | Explanation |
|---|---|---|
| **Payment Terms** | | The **Payment Terms ID** is what will be shown on all transactions, reports, and windows in Dynamics GP. Try to make this something that will be clear to Dynamics GP users, vendors, and customers. |
| **Due** | **Net Days** | Enter the number of days to add to the invoice date to determine the due date. |
| | **Date** | Enter the date a payment is due. For example, if the payment is always due on the 20th of the month, enter 20. This will make the due date the 20th of the same month for any transactions entered through and including the 19th of that month, and the 20th of the following month for any transactions entered on the 20th or after. |
| | **EOM** | This selection will make the due date be the last date of the month of the transaction. |
| | **None** | Choosing **None** will make the due date the same as the transaction date. |
| | **Next Month** | Enter the date of the next month when the payment will be due. |
| **Discount** | **Days** | Enter the number of days after the invoice date that a discount will be available for. |
| | **Date** | Enter the date until which a discount will be available. |
| | **EOM** | This option will allow a discount until the end of the month of the transaction date. |
| | **None** | Use this option for no discount available. |

| Field / Options | Explanation |
|---|---|
| **Discount Type** | Either a **Percent** or **Amount** is possible for the **Discount Type**. |
| **Calculate Discount On** | Select all the components of the total that a discount will be calculated on. |
| **Use Customer/ Vendor Grace Periods for Date/ EOM Payment Terms** | This option is only available when selecting **Date**, **EOM**, or **Next Month** under **Due**, and will add the days entered during the customer or vendor setup to the due date specified for the payment terms. For example, for terms of EOM 65, you can enter `Date` and `4` under **Due** and `60` for the **Due Date Grace Period** for the vendor or customer with these terms. With this setup, a transaction dated May 5th will calculate the due date as August 4th. This might not always be exact, but it is very close and does not require customization or manual intervention during transaction entry. |

The following is an example of how the setup would look for payment terms of 2% 10 days/Net 30 days:

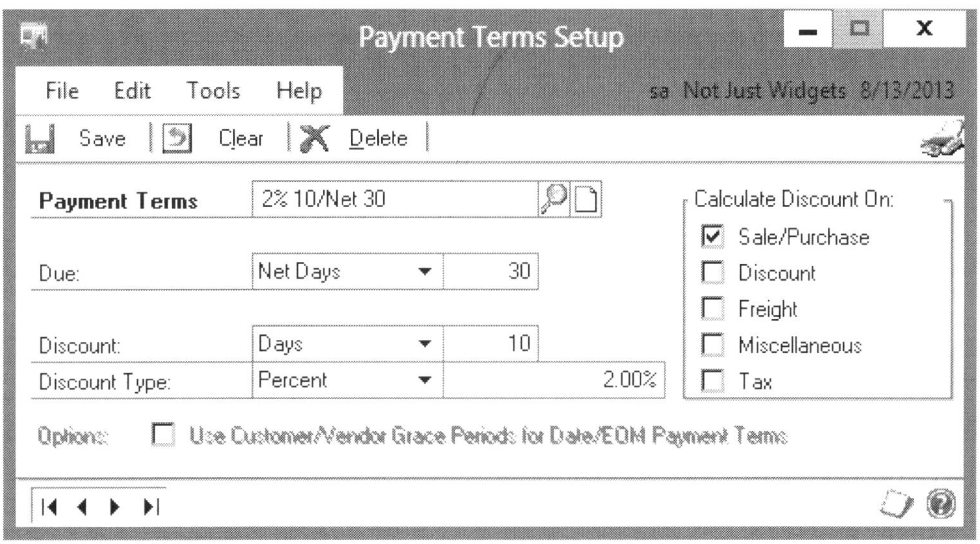


Note that this example only has the **Sale/Purchase** option checked for the discount calculation, so only the subtotal of the transaction using these payment terms will be used to calculate the discount.

# Credit Cards

**Credit Cards** in Dynamics GP can be used to record payments to vendors and payments from customers. Please refer to the detailed discussion in *Chapter 3, Planning – Dynamics GP System* to see which credit card setup options will work best for your company. Often a combination of various options will be needed.

To open the **Credit Card Setup** window navigate to **Microsoft Dynamics GP | Tools | Setup | Company | Credit Cards**. Both credit cards accepted from customers and ones used as payment by the company are set up on this window, and one credit card can be setup as both, as illustrated in the screenshot below. In this example **PAYPAL** is accepted as payment from customers and will go into a General Ledger account. **PAYPAL** is also a vendor of the company and is used to pay other vendors:

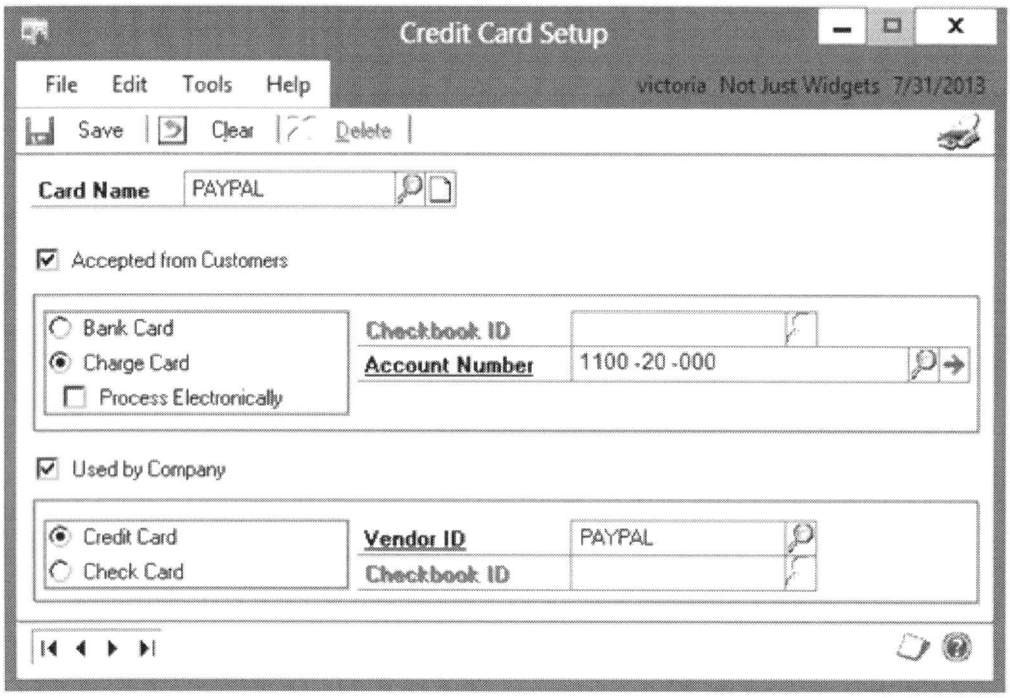


It is recommended to keep the **Card Name** short, but as descriptive as possible, so that Dynamics GP users can easily pick the correct credit card from a list of choices when entering transactions. While it is not possible to change **Card Names** afterwards, you can create as many additional credit cards as needed and there is no issue with multiple credit cards pointing to the same **Vendor ID**, **Checkbook ID**, or **Account Number**.

> If vendors, checkbooks, or GL accounts are not setup yet, you may want to mark this as a setup task that you need to return to after these other components are in place.

# Posting setup

The two windows that control posting behavior in Dynamics GP are **Posting Setup** and **Posting Accounts Setup**.

## Posting

Options chosen on the **Posting Setup** window determine the behavior of each type of transaction that is posted in Dynamics GP. To open the **Posting Setup** window, navigate to **Microsoft Dynamics GP** | **Tools** | **Setup** | **Posting** | **Posting**. Transactions on the **Posting Setup** window are grouped by **Series**, for example Payables Management and Purchase Order Processing transactions will be under the Purchasing Series. Once you select a **Series**, the available transactions for the series will populate the **Origin** drop-down:

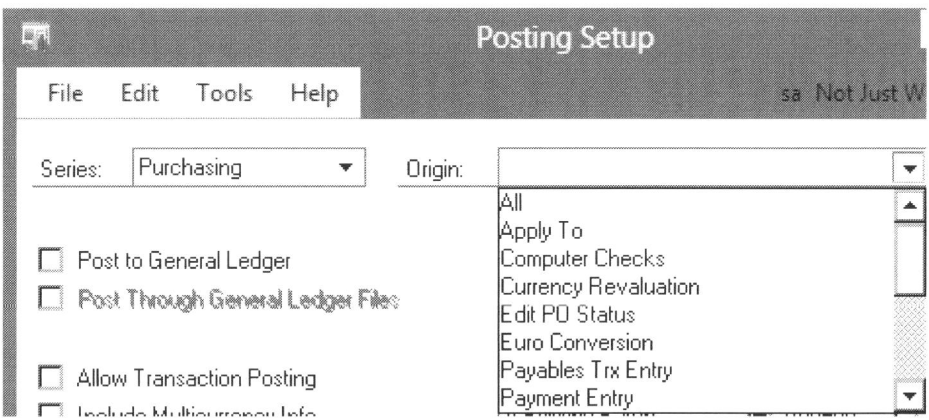


Any changes made when the **Origin** is set to **All** will propagate to all the transactions for the selected **Series** when the **Save** button is clicked. As only changes will propagate, if the **All** selection already shows the desired setting, it does not necessarily follow that each transaction within the **Series** has that same setting. So while it may be more time consuming to go through each individual transaction **Origin**, you are safer doing that than making changes using the **All** selection.

*Chapter 3, Planning – Dynamics GP System*, covered quite a bit of detail and theory on the available posting setup options. The following is a list of the posting settings and recommendations for them:

- **Post to General Ledger**: This should be checked for every transaction type.
- **Post Through General Ledger Files**: For companies just starting to use Dynamics GP it may be advantageous to leave this option unchecked, so that users have an opportunity to examine the GL transactions that get created as a result of subledger transaction postings. However, eventually I typically see most companies select this setting to automatically post subledger postings through to the General Ledger, as that saves time.
- **Allow Transaction Posting**: This is typically left checked, allowing users to post a transaction without having to save it in a batch first. If you want to ensure users put all transactions in batches, you can uncheck this option.
- **Include Multicurrency Info**: If Multicurrency is being used, this should be checked, otherwise it should not.
- **Verify Number of Trx** and **Verify Batch Amounts**: These options are available to help catch mistakes during data entry. If a batch of 20 cash receipts is being entered and the total of the cash receipts is $25,000, these totals can be entered during the creation of the cash receipt batch as control totals. As each cash receipt is saved, the actual totals will be incremented by Dynamics GP. Once transaction entry is done, if the actual totals for the batch do not match the control totals, Dynamics GP will prevent the batch from being posted. Most companies do not choose to use these options, as they can slow down transaction entry.
- **Create a Journal Entry Per**: The most commonly used setting for this is **Transaction**, which will allow for the most detailed level of records kept. Companies with very large volumes of certain types of transactions may decide to change this.
- **Posting Date From**: The more common setting for this is **Transaction**, although this can greatly depend on the accounting habits and practices within each company.
- **If Existing Batch**: **Append** is recommended so that your system does not end up with a very large number of batches quickly.

- **Require Batch Approval**: Most companies do not use this option, however this is another setting that may depend greatly on your accounting practices and the desired controls. With this, one user can enter transactions, but will not be able to post a batch until someone approves it by typing in a password. The password can be different for each transaction type.
- **Reports**: There are a number of posting reports that print for every transaction posted in Dynamics GP. If you choose a transaction type under **Origin** you will see all the reports for that particular transaction type listed at the bottom. When you choose **All** for **Origin** you will see every report possible for the **Series** you have selected.

  By default, all the reports are set to print to the printer and many companies find this to be a big waste of paper. Some reports are quite useful, so it may not be practical to turn all the reports off (which sometimes becomes tempting when five reports come out after posting each transaction). An alternate option may be to change all reports globally to automatically print to the screen, so the users can look at each report and decide whether they want to print that particular report to the printer. You can change all the posting reports to print to the screen by running the following SQL script against your company database in SQL Server Management Studio:

  ```
  UPDATE SY02200

  SET PRNTJRNL = 1, ASECTMNT = 0, PRTOPRNT = 0, PRTOSCNT = 1,
  PRTOFLNT = 0, EXPTTYPE = 0, APNDRPLC = 0
  ```

The **OK** button on the **Posting Setup** window will close the window. The **Save** button will apply your selections and clear all the options, but keep the window open.

> All changes on the **Posting Setup** window, except those made using the **All** origin, are applied right away. If users are posting transactions in Dynamics GP or unposted batches for a particular type of transaction exist, making changes to the posting settings can have unpredictable results.

The following is an example of the **Sales Transaction Entry** posting settings using the previous recommendations:

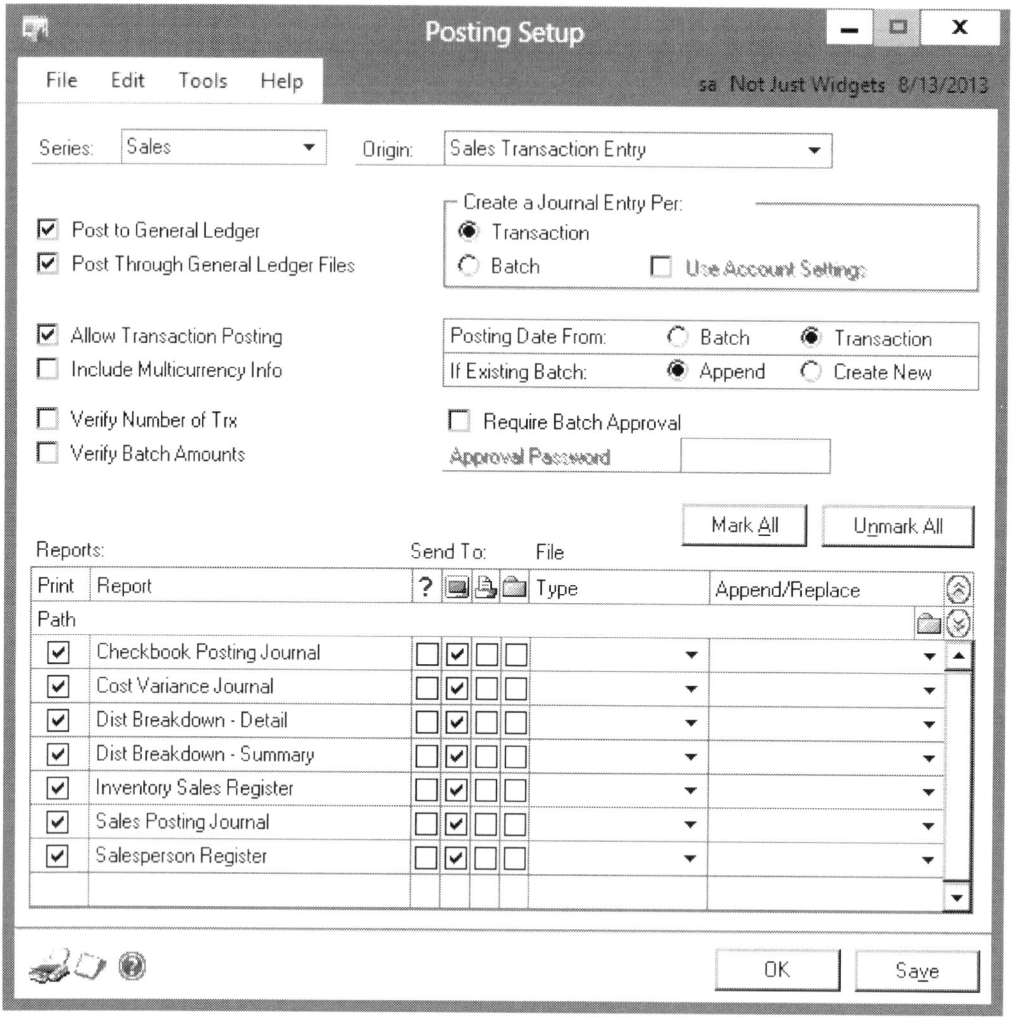


Note that this transaction type has seven posting reports associated with it. Typically, companies will decide to turn off at least three or four of these reports, depending on the details of their sales transactions, but it is recommended to have the users take a look at the reports first to see if they are deemed useful.

# Posting Accounts

**Posting Accounts** are company-wide defaults used by Dynamics GP to determine what General Ledger accounts to use for various transaction components. Setting up posting accounts can reduce the amount of time and effort it takes to enter transactions into Dynamics GP, and can also help avoid errors caused by users choosing incorrect accounts during transaction entry.

The company-wide posting accounts will be superseded by the accounts set up on individual objects, such as vendors, customers, inventory items, and multicurrency rate types. Also, during transaction entry, almost every transaction in Dynamics GP allows the user to override defaulted accounts prior to posting the transaction. If there is only one Accounts Receivable or Accounts Payable GL account, consider specifying these globally for the entire company. This will eliminate the need of setting them up for each customer or vendor, or having the users type the account numbers in every time a transaction is entered.

To set up posting accounts, navigate to **Microsoft Dynamics GP | Tools | Setup | Posting | Posting Accounts**. The **Posting Accounts Setup** window will list all available **Posting Accounts** that can be set up in Dynamics GP. You may find it easier to navigate around this window and find accounts if you choose a series under the **Display** drop-down first.

There is no requirement to fill in every **Posting Account**, as many companies may not ever enter transactions that will use all the possible accounts listed. Only fill in what is needed and what is global to the entire company. If you have not yet created your entire Chart of Accounts in Dynamics GP, you may want to mark this as a setup task to return to once the GL account numbers are created.

> Any changes to posting accounts will only affect future transactions. No existing transactions will be updated when changes are made on the **Posting Accounts Setup** window.

# E-mail setup

Starting with Dynamics GP 2010, functionality was added to e-mail certain types of reports directly out of Dynamics GP to your customers and vendors. Each module that allows e-mailing functionality will have some additional setup steps, however the company e-mail setup must be completed first.

## Company e-mail setup

To set up the company-wide options for e-mail, navigate to **Microsoft Dynamics GP | Tools | Setup | Company | E-mail Settings**. On the **Company E-mail Setup** window, select whether to allow the option to **Embed Documents in Message Body** on an e-mail, **Send Documents as Attachments**, or both. If **Send Documents as Attachments** is selected, choose the **File Formats Allowed**:

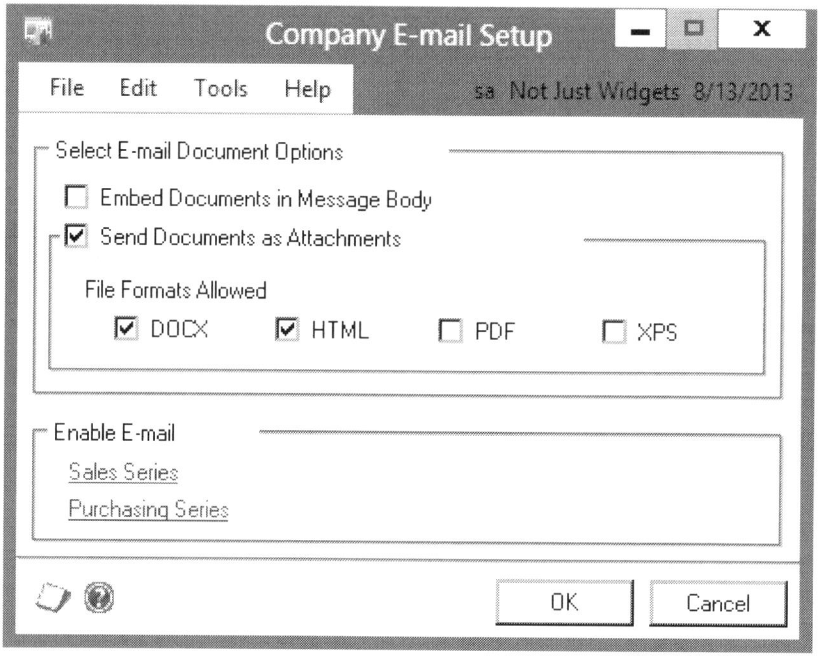


We will address the **Enable E-mail** settings for the **Sales Series** and **Purchasing Series** when we talk about those modules in more detail in *Chapter 7, Module Setup General Ledger, Bank Reconciliation, Payables, and Receivables*.

# Summary

In this chapter, we went over logging into Microsoft Dynamics GP for the first time and the basic steps of setting up the Dynamics GP system, including creating users and setting up security. Company setup steps were detailed and illustrated with examples.

In the next chapter, we will move on to setting up core Dynamics GP modules.

# 7

# Module Setup – General Ledger, Bank Reconciliation, Payables, and Receivables

Now that you have completed the system and company setup for Dynamics GP, you are ready to move on to module setup. You do not need to set up any modules you will not be using with the exception of the General Ledger. Even if you are not planning to use the General Ledger, it is recommended to set it up because all the other modules are dependent on it.

In this chapter, we will cover setup for the following modules:

- General Ledger
- Bank Reconciliation
- Payables Management
- Receivables Management

Detailed navigation will be provided for each setup window, or you can keep using the setup checklist (**Microsoft Dynamics GP** | **Tools** | **Setup** | **Setup Checklist**).

> To perform the module setup, you can be logged in as any Dynamics GP user with appropriate permissions. Usually, the user performing the setup should be given the POWERUSER security role.

Typically, each module will have an overall setup window, where global settings and options are chosen, and a few additional windows where the basic settings or templates for the module are chosen.

All module settings are company specific. If you have multiple companies in Dynamics GP, you will need to set up each module in each company separately. This is often advantageous, as different companies may require different settings. However, for situations where you want to have an identical setup for multiple companies, the *Microsoft Dynamics GP KnowledgeBase* article 872709 describes how to copy setup tables from one Dynamics GP company to another: `https://mbs.microsoft.com/knowledgebase/KBDisplay.aspx?scid=kb;en-us;872709` (CustomerSource or PartnerSource login required). There is also a Company Copy tool available as part of the Professional Services Tools Library—you can read more about this in *Chapter 10, Training, Tools, and Next Steps*.

> If you are planning on creating a large number of companies on an ongoing basis, consider creating a template company with all the desired settings and no transactions so that it can be copied to new companies as they are created.

# General Ledger

The **General Ledger** (**GL**) module is part of the Financial series in Dynamics GP and the menu choices for it will start with **Financial**. The SQL Server tables for the General Ledger module will begin with `GL`. There are three setup steps for the GL module:

- General Ledger Setup
- Categories
- Segments

Creating General Ledger accounts is typically considered part of the GL module setup; however, we went over creating GL accounts as part of the company setup in *Chapter 6, System and Company Setup*. There is also an optional step of setting up account currencies if you are using the Multicurrency module.

# General Ledger Setup

To open the **General Ledger Setup** window, navigate to **Microsoft Dynamics GP | Tools | Setup | Financial | General Ledger**. This window controls the next journal entry number, the Retained Earnings account used for closing the General Ledger, history settings, and options allowed for GL transactions. These settings can be changed at any time; however, as most users should not have access to setup windows, it is best to choose settings and defaults that will be most helpful to the majority of the Dynamics GP users. The following is an explanation of the settings on the **General Ledger Setup** window:

- **Next Journal Entry**: The system default is to start with 1 and auto increment as journal entries are posted. This can be changed to any other number you prefer.
- **Next Budget Journal Entry**: The ability to enter budget transactions was added in Dynamics GP 2010, allowing updates to budgets while keeping track of the changes. This setting determines the next budget journal entry number.
- **Next Reconciliation**: New in Dynamics GP 2013 is the ability to number subledger to General Ledger Reconciliations. This will set the next reconciliation number.
- **Display**: This controls the default display on any General Ledger inquiry window that offers a choice between **Net Change** and **Period Balances**. The display can always be changed on each individual inquiry window, so this setting is not critical.
- **Retained Earnings**: There are two options in Dynamics GP—close all Profit & Loss accounts to one Retained Earnings account or close to multiple Retained Earnings accounts, one per division. The latter is not very common and will require you to select a segment of your GL account number to identify your divisions. You will need to have a Retained Earnings account set up for each possible division if choosing this option.
- **Maintain History**: It is recommended to keep all transaction history, so select all three history options. You can always delete transaction history if you do not want it, but you cannot get it back if you never had it.
- **Allow**:
    - **Posting to History**: This box must be checked prior to posting transactions to the last historical year. To prevent mistakes, it is recommended to keep this unchecked and change it only when needed.

    - **Deletion of Saved Transactions**: It is recommended to uncheck this option to prevent users from inadvertently deleting saved GL transactions. A more detailed discussion and explanation of the need for this can be found in the following blog post: `http://victoriayudin.com/2009/04/11/where-did-my-transaction-go/`.
    - **Voiding/Correcting of Subsidiary Transactions**: This setting prevents users from voiding or correcting GL transactions that originated in a subledger. The scope of this is fairly limited, as a user will still be able to enter a manual GL entry to re-class a subledger transaction. However, this may help somewhat mitigate subledger reconciliation issues.
    - **Back Out of Intercompany Transactions**: If the Intercompany module is used to allow posting from one Dynamics GP company to another, this setting can prevent users from backing out any intercompany GL transactions. Backing out an intercompany transaction in one company will not automatically back out the related transaction in the other company, so disallowing this can help lessen the chance of reconciliation problems for intercompany accounts.

- **Update Accelerator Information**: If you are using Advanced Financial Analysis, it is recommended to mark this option if you have frequent changes to the financial report layouts.
- **Reporting Ledgers**: Another feature added in Dynamics GP 2010 is the ability to set up multiple reporting ledgers to meet compliance standards for **IFRS** (**International Financial Reporting Standards**). When **Allow** is checked, **Reporting Ledgers** can be added, and when entering a GL transaction, a reporting ledger will need to be selected.

> Once **Allow** is selected under **Reporting Ledgers**, it cannot be unchecked. Make sure this is a setting you want to enable before selecting **Allow**.

- **User-Defined Field Labels**: These are the labels for the four user-defined fields on the **Account Maintenance** window (**Cards** | **Financial** | **Account**).

The following is an example of the **General Ledger Setup** window with the typical setup options:

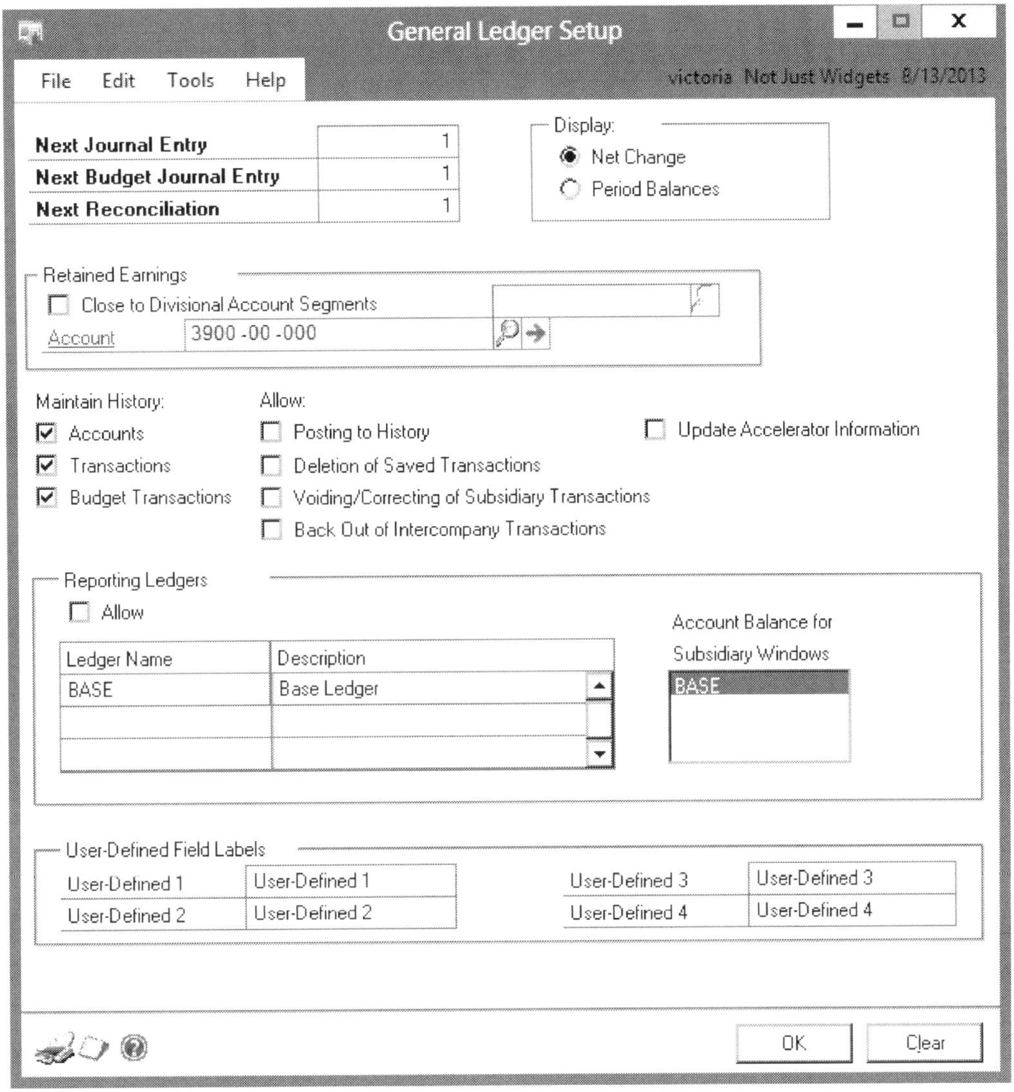


Changes on the **General Ledger Setup** window will not be saved until you click on the **OK** button. The **Clear** button will clear any changes you have made to this window prior to saving them.

# Categories

General Ledger **account categories** in Dynamics GP help identify the function or financial reporting section for each GL account. Categories are used for automatic creation of some of the **Home Page** metrics in Dynamics GP and can sometimes be helpful during financial report creation. However, if all your GL accounts were created with the same category, it would not break any basic functionality within Dynamics GP.

There are 48 predefined General Ledger account categories—they are listed in *Appendix, General Ledger Account Categories* for your reference. You can also create your own categories or rename the existing categories on the **Account Category Setup** window:

1. Navigate to **Microsoft Dynamics GP** | **Tools** | **Setup** | **Financial** | **Category**.
2. To rename an existing category, find it in the list and edit the **Category Description**.
3. To create a new category, scroll to the end of the list and type in a new **Category Description** on the first blank line. The **Number** for all new categories will show as a star (*). However, this will not cause any problems in using them:

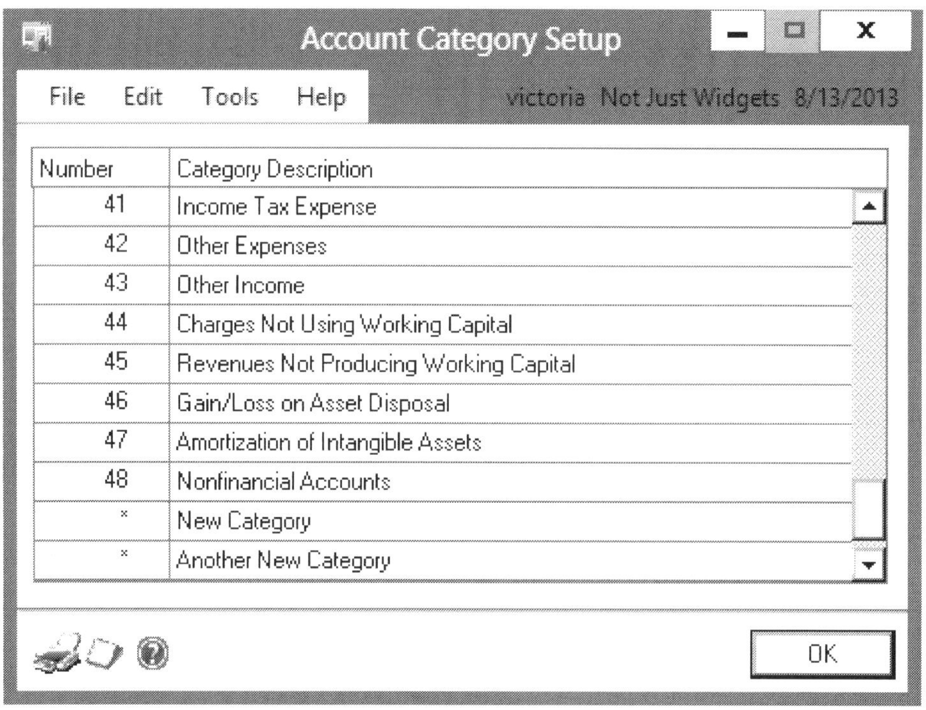

4. To delete a category, right click on the row and choose **Delete Row**. Note that new categories you have created can only be deleted if there are no accounts assigned to them. The predefined categories cannot be deleted.

If you have multiple Dynamics GP companies, it is recommended to have the same list of account categories in each company, so that there is no confusion during reporting or errors during account creation or imports.

# Segments

When setting up your Dynamics GP company account format, you gave unique names to each of your General Ledger account segments. Some of these may have a predefined list of values and names. For example, if one of your segments is Department, your list of departments may look like the following:

| Department Number | Department Name |
|---|---|
| 00 | Corporate/Overhead |
| 10 | Administrative |
| 20 | Sales |
| 30 | Marketing |
| 40 | Information Technology |
| 50 | Customer Service/Support |

When account numbers are entered into Dynamics GP, the unique value for each segment will be identified by the system and you can, optionally, predefine a name for each unique segment value. There are four benefits to naming your segments:

- **Dynamics GP reporting and lookups**: Some reports and lookups in Dynamics GP can be filtered and sorted by GL account segments. If the segments have meaningful names, it is easier to use these filters without having to consult additional documentation. A few examples of this are the GL Trial Balance reports and the Budget Wizard for Excel.
- **Custom reports**: When creating custom reports, segment names assigned in Dynamics GP can be referenced instead of having to hard code names into reports, thus making reports more dynamic.
- **Creation of new GL accounts**: If you have not disabled (or have re-enabled) Dynamics GP's auto-naming functionality, then while creating new GL accounts, the system will automatically populate the appropriate segment names into the account name, thereby possibly speeding up new account creation.

- **Financial reports**: If you create departmental or divisional financial reports, FRx or Management Reporter can automatically populate the names assigned to each segment in Dynamics GP. For one or two reports, this might not make a difference but, as more reports are added, this can significantly simplify and speed up report creation.

To enter names for your GL account segments, navigate to **Microsoft Dynamics GP | Tools | Setup | Financial | Segment**. On the **Account Segment Setup** window, select the **Segment ID**, select the segment **Number**, then type in a **Description**:

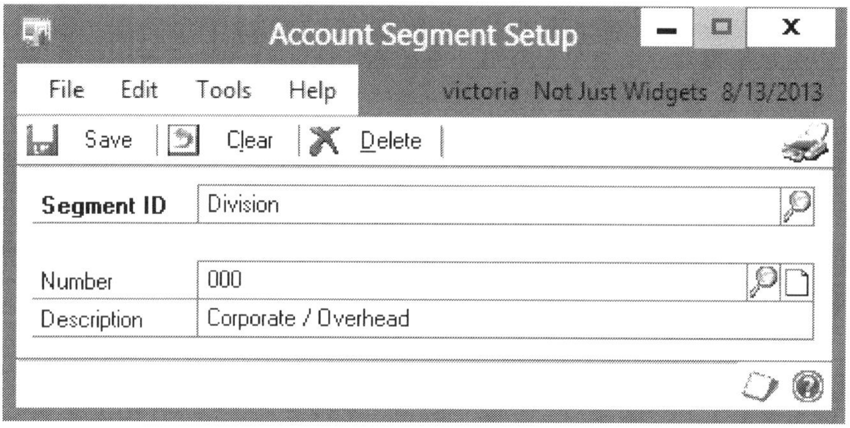


The segment names can be changed at any time.

# Account currencies

Dynamics GP allows you to control what GL accounts can be used with each currency you have enabled. By default, all accounts will be accessible to your functional currency. To allow posting to your GL accounts using currencies other than your functional currency, you will need to set up each account/currency combination. This can be done either for one account or multiple accounts at once.

To assign currencies to one account, perform the following steps:

1. Navigate to **Cards | Financial | Account Currencies** to open the **Select Account Currencies** window.
2. Select the GL **Account** and **Currency IDs** from the available list.

3. Select whether or not you wish to **Revalue Account** when the revaluation process is performed in Dynamics GP. If you decide to revalue, then choose:
    - Whether to revalue using the **Net Change** or **Period Balance** of the account.
    - Where to **Post Result To**—the **Account** itself or to a different **Financial Offset** account.

If you are setting up currencies for multiple accounts, open the **Multicurrency Mass Account Update** window by navigating to **Cards | Financial | Currency Account Update**. On this window, you can select your General Ledger accounts by using the **Segment ID** lookups/ranges and clicking on **Insert**. If you do not enter any restrictions, all accounts will be updated. Use **Mark** or **Unmark** to select the desired options and click on **Update** to make the changes to all the accounts selected.

# Bank Reconciliation

The **Bank Reconciliation** module is also sometimes referred to as **Bank Rec** or **Cash Management** and is part of the Financial series in Dynamics GP. The menu choices for Bank Reconciliation will start with **Financial**, while the SQL tables will start with `CM`. Setup for the Bank Reconciliation module consists of two steps—setting up Checkbooks and Bank Reconciliation Setup.

> Even if you do not own or are not planning to use the Bank Reconciliation module, you will want to perform the checkbook setup in Dynamics GP. This will be used in many other modules throughout the system.

## Checkbooks

A **Checkbook** in Dynamics GP represents a bank account. In a typical company, each individual bank account will have a unique General Ledger account. The Dynamics GP checkbook setup will allow you to link each bank account to a GL account and keep track of the next available check and deposit numbers for the bank account. Most modules in Dynamics GP use a **Checkbook ID** (as opposed to the GL account number) to represent a bank account.

You can create an unlimited number of checkbooks in Dynamics GP. To set up or modify a checkbook, navigate to **Cards** | **Financial** | **Checkbook**. Following are explanations for the fields on the **Checkbook Maintenance** window:

- **Checkbook ID**: The Checkbook ID is alphanumeric (up to 15 characters) and will be used throughout Dynamics GP to identify a bank account. It is recommended to make this ID something easy for users to identify. For example, if you have multiple accounts with the same bank, consider what users typically call them. The IDs might represent their names such as `CHASE CHECKING` and `CHASE SAVINGS`, or might contain part of the account number such as `BOA 1833` and `BOA 5869`. Or you may prefer to call accounts by their function, such as `OPERATING`, `PAYROLL`, or `SWEEP`. If needed, the Checkbook ID can be changed using the Checkbook Modifier tool in the Professional Services Tools Library.
- **Inactive**: Once a bank account is no longer used, you can make it inactive to prevent users from entering transactions to it. Inactive checkbooks still show up on inquiries, but attempting to enter a transaction for one will result in an error.
- **Description**: The name of the bank account, and what will help users identify the correct bank account in a list if the Checkbook ID is not enough. This field allows up to 30 characters. If there are multiple similar accounts, consider putting the account number, or part of it, into the description, especially if it is not part of the Checkbook ID.
- **Currency ID**, **Payment Rate Type**, and **Deposit Rate Type**: Choose the appropriate currency and rate types for the bank account.
- **Cash Account**: The General Ledger account corresponding to this bank account. It is important to have a one-to-one relationship between bank accounts and GL accounts to allow for smooth bank reconciliations.
- **Next Check Number**: Enter the next check number you will be using. Dynamics GP will automatically increment check numbers as checks are printed or entered in various modules. Note that you will need to manually increment the number of digits. For example, if you have set up the check number with four digits, once you reach `9999`, the system will not automatically go to `10000`, it will update to `0000`. While you can add more digits at any time, this will not update check numbers that have already been used, so your check numbers will have different lengths and may not sort properly on lookups or reports. Consider entering an extra zero or two in front of the numbers at the onset, so if your next check number is `6001`, you could start with `06001` or `006001`, depending on the expected volume of checks.

> It is not recommended to leave all the zeros that are originally defaulted on this window. There are many times when users may need to type in a check number, and this will make it much more difficult for them.

- **Next Deposit Number**: Enter the next deposit number you would like to use. Typically, deposit slips are not numbered, so this is more of an internal number. Many companies like to use the prefix `DEP` to clearly identify deposits on a list of bank transactions. As with the check numbers, the deposit numbers will not automatically increment the number of digits, so it is recommended to use a number with enough total digits to last for some time.
- **Company Address ID**, **Bank Account**, and **Bank ID**: These fields are optional and, unless needed by other modules, most companies typically leave these blank.
- **User-Defined 1** and **2**: If there is additional information you would like to track about your bank account, you can use these two fields. The labels for these can be changed on the **Bank Reconciliation Setup** window (**Microsoft Dynamics GP | Tools | Setup | Financial | Bank Reconciliation**).
- **Last Reconciled Balance** and **Date**: These are used to populate your last reconciliation information prior to starting to use Dynamics GP Bank Reconciliation. Leave these blank until you are ready to perform your first bank reconciliation.
- **Payables Options**:
    - **Max Check Amount** and **Password**: With these, you can limit the maximum amount for payables checks and optionally set up a password to override the maximum. Leaving the amount at zero will allow checks of any amount to be created.
    - **Duplicate Check Numbers**: It is recommended to uncheck (disallow) this option so that duplicate check numbers are not inadvertently entered, thus causing problems during bank reconciliation.
    - **Override Check Number**: Usually, it is helpful to leave this checked (allowed), so that when payables checks are printed, the user can override the next check number if for some reason it is not populating correctly.

The following is an example of a typical **Checkbook Maintenance** window:

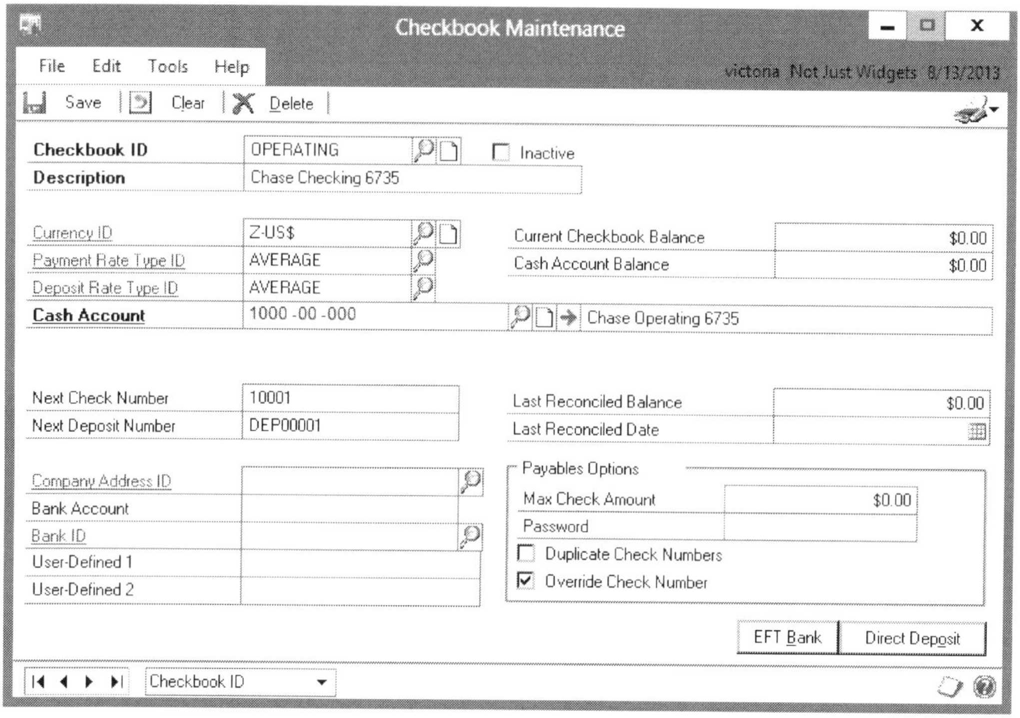


# Bank Reconciliation Setup

Bank Reconciliation setup determines the defaults for the Bank Reconciliation module. If you are not using the Bank Reconciliation module, or not implementing it yet, you can skip this step. To open the **Bank Reconciliation Setup** window, navigate to **Microsoft Dynamics GP | Tools | Setup | Financial | Bank Reconciliation**. Often the only thing that needs to be set up on this window is the default Checkbook ID. The following list explains the fields on this window:

- **Next Number**: This will be the next number used on a bank transaction or bank transfer. This is an internal number and there is typically no reason to change this from the default; it will increment automatically as needed.
- **Transaction Type**, **Description**, and **Code**: These are default descriptions and codes assigned to each type of Bank Reconciliation transaction. It is recommended not to change these descriptions and codes, as having them differ from the defaults will make it difficult to consult with others about any questions you might have on the Bank Reconciliation module.

- **Reconcile Adjustment Type**, **Description**, and **Code**: Similar to the previous option, these are descriptions and codes assigned to Bank Reconciliation adjustments and changing them is not recommended.
- **Maintain History**: This is checked by default; it is recommended to leave it selected and keep all history.
- **Defaults**:
    - **Checkbook ID**: Optionally, you can specify a default **Checkbook ID** for your Bank Reconciliation transactions. This may save time during data entry if most bank transactions use the same bank account. The checkbook has to be set up first to be able to select it as a default. If there are many checkbooks being used, consider leaving this default blank to force users to pick a checkbook for each transaction. Note that if the Multicurrency module is enabled, most Dynamics GP windows will not use this checkbook default.
    - **User-Defined 1** and **2**: These fields allow you to change the labels that appear for the user-defined fields on the **Checkbook Maintenance** window.

The following screenshot shows the **Bank Reconciliation Setup** window:

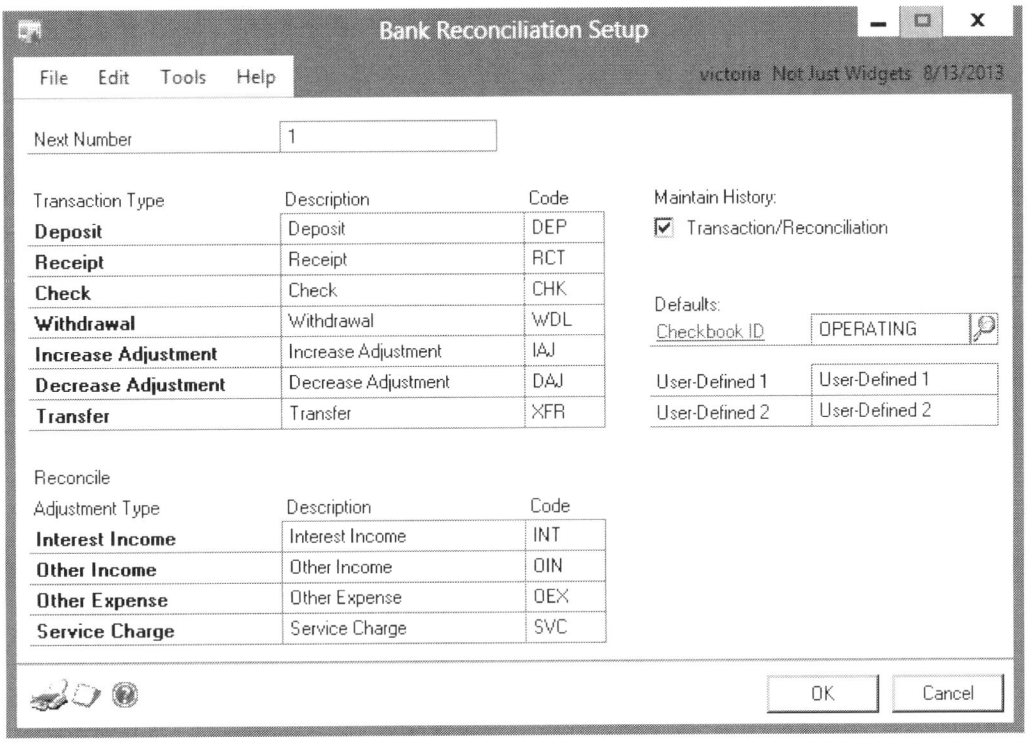

# Payables Management

The **Payables Management** module is commonly referred to as **Payables**, **Accounts Payable**, or **AP**. As it is part of the Purchasing series in Dynamics GP, the menu options for AP will start with **Purchasing**. All the SQL Server tables for the Payables Management module begin with `PM`, so you may also sometimes see it referred to as the **PM module**.

Setup for the Payables Management module includes the following:

- Payables Management Setup
- Payables Setup Options
- Vendor classes
- 1099 setup
- Purchasing e-mail setup
- Vendors

# Payables Management Setup

To open the **Payables Management Setup** window, navigate to **Microsoft Dynamics GP** | **Tools** | **Setup** | **Purchasing** | **Payables**. The following list explains the settings on this window:

- **Aging Periods**: Aging for payables transactions can be done by **Due Date** or by **Document Date** (transaction date). All AP inquiry windows and reports will use this setting when showing aging information for payables transactions. Dynamics GP allows up to seven **Aging Periods**, or buckets, which cannot overlap and cannot exceed 999 days.

  > The out-of-the-box reports in Dynamics GP will only show four payables aging buckets. If you want to use more than four aging buckets, you will need to customize your reports.

  Aging settings can be changed at a later date. However, all open records will need to be reconciled to propagate any changes, which may be a lengthy process and will require all users be out of the system, so it is not something companies will want to do often.

  Typically, companies will have many different payment terms for their vendors, so aging by **Due Date** is recommended.

- **Apply By**: This setting determines if transactions are applied in order of **Document Date** or **Due Date** when the **Auto Apply** button is used on various windows. Auto apply is not very commonly used, so this is not a critical setting. There is no reason why this setting has to be the same as the **Aging Periods** setting.
- **Defaults**:
    - **Default Summary View**: Determines what default view to show on the **Vendor Yearly Summary** and **Vendor Yearly Summary Inquiry** windows. It is recommended to make this either **Calendar Year** or **Fiscal Year**, as this will save users time when inquiring on vendors.
    - **Checkbook ID**: Optionally, you can select a default checkbook to be used for payables transactions. The **Checkbook ID** can be overridden on every transaction; this is simply a default to save users time.
    - **Check Format**: You can save users time and uncertainty during the check printing process by defaulting the check format they will be using. As only one check format can be defaulted per company, if you plan to print checks from multiple checkbooks, consider ordering the same check stock layout for all your accounts so that the same Dynamics GP check format can be used.
    - **List Documents on Remittance**: This setting determines what transactions are listed on the check stub when you print checks. The choices are:
        - **Invoices Only**: Will list only debit transactions (Invoices, Finance Charges, and Misc Charges) on the check stub.
        - **All Documents**: Will list all transactions on the check stub.
        - **Applied Order**: Will also list all transactions, but in the order they were applied.
        - **Totals Only**: Will only show the total being paid and list it as `Prepayment` on the check stub.

      The most commonly used option is **All Documents**.
    - **Print Previously Applied Documents on Remittance**: If this option is checked, any check printed will show all payments and credit memos applied since the last check was printed for the same vendor. For example, if a check is printed, then a wire transfer is entered and a credit memo is applied for the same vendor, the next check to this vendor will show the apply detail for the wire and the credit memo on the check stub.

What setting to choose for this may depend on how your company typically pays vendors. If it is primarily by check, you may want to leave this checked. If it is a combination of payment methods, you may decide to leave this unchecked in order to not clutter up check stubs and create confusion for your vendors.

- **Password**:
    - **Remove Vendor Hold**: If no password is set up, any user with access to the **Vendor Maintenance** window can remove a vendor hold (payments cannot be entered for vendors on hold).
    - **Exceed Maximum Invoice Amount**: If no password is entered and a maximum invoice amount is set for a vendor, the system will not allow a user to save an invoice for more than the maximum. If a password is entered, then the system will prompt for it when saving an invoice that exceeds the maximum invoice amount set for a vendor.
    - **Exceed Maximum Writeoff Amount**: If no password is entered and a maximum writeoff amount is set for a vendor, the system will not allow a user to enter a writeoff for more than the maximum. If a password is entered, then the system will prompt for it when entering the writeoff and allow a writeoff above the maximum.

> Note that all the passwords are stored in plain text, so if a user should not know the passwords, they should be restricted access to this window and any setup reports for this module.

- **Options**:
    - **Override Voucher Number at Transaction Entry**: **Voucher numbers** are Dynamics GP terminology for the automatic numbering assigned to all payables transactions. Typically, you would not want to give users the ability to override this numbering, as it may cause errors during transaction entry.
    - **Track Discounts Available in GL**: If you are planning to set up a Discounts Available account for tracking discounts separately in the General Ledger at the time of transaction posting, select this option. If this option is not selected, discounts can still go to a separate GL account, but only at the time that payments or credits are applied to invoices.

- **Print Historical Aged Trial Balance**: Even if a custom report is used to print the Historical Aged Trial Balance, it may be useful to compare it to the out-of-the-box report, so it is recommended to allow printing of the Historical Aged Trial Balance.
- **Delete Unposted Printed Documents**: This setting applies only to payables documents that are sometimes printed for internal documentation purposes. It does not apply to payables checks—once checks are printed, Dynamics GP will not allow them to be deleted. Most companies choose to allow the deletion of documents and leave this option checked.
- **Print Tax Details on Documents** and **Print Dual Currencies**: These settings are also for internally printed payables documents, which are rarely used in Dynamics GP. If using purchasing taxes, you may want to check these options.
- **Age Unapplied Credit Amounts**: Unapplied credit transactions (Credit Memos, Returns, and Payments) will show in the Current aging bucket on Aged Payables Trial Balance reports unless this option is selected. Most companies choose to age unapplied credit transactions so that they appear in the appropriate aging buckets based on their age.
- **Exclude Expired Discounts from Payments**: If this is selected, when creating a batch of computer checks, any transaction with a discount date prior to the apply date of the check (usually the same as the check date) is not included in the check run. Whether or not to select this should depend on the company's policies for vendor payments and dealing with discounts.
- **Allow Duplicate Invoices Per Vendor**: It is recommended to select **Recurring Transaction Only**, so that Dynamics GP can automatically prevent double entry of invoices by checking for duplicate invoice numbers. Recurring transactions are excluded from this because, by default, they will have the same invoice numbers.

The following illustrates a typical **Payables Management Setup** window:

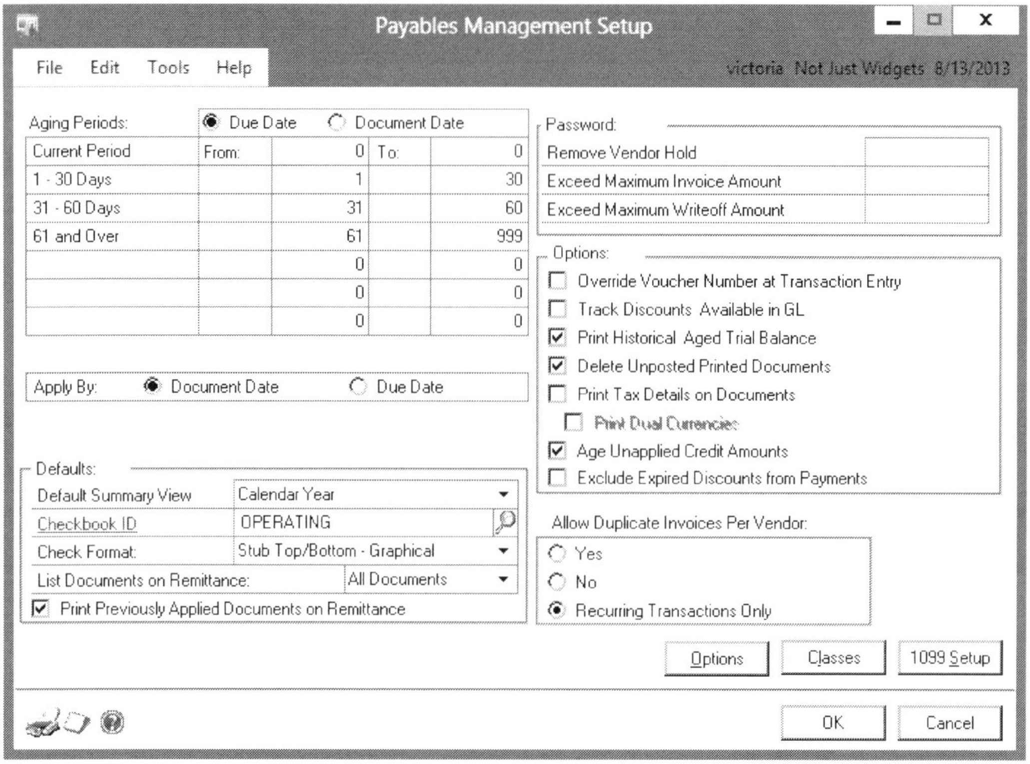


# Payables Setup Options

The **Payables Setup Options** window (**Microsoft Dynamics GP** | **Tools** | **Setup** | **Purchasing** | **Payables** | **Options**) allows you to set:

- Codes used for each payables transaction type
- The numbering scheme and next number for each transaction type
- Tax schedules for payables transactions
- The next temporary vendor ID
- Labels for the user-defined vendor fields

It is not recommended to change the **Descriptions** and **Codes** for transaction types, as that will make support and training more difficult. The **Next Temp. Vendor ID** will set the Vendor ID mask and next number for temporary vendors if they are used.

The default numbers for **Next Voucher Number**, **Next Payment Number**, and **Next Schedule Number** are quite long and most companies will never need so many digits in them, so consider shortening these to make them more user-friendly. Payments and vouchers can have the same numbers; Dynamics GP differentiates between them by the transaction type.

Default **Tax Schedule IDs** can be filled in if you are going to enter purchase taxes. **User-Defined 1** and **User-Defined 2** will change the labels of the two available user-defined fields for vendors.

The following screenshot is an example of the **Payables Setup Options** window:

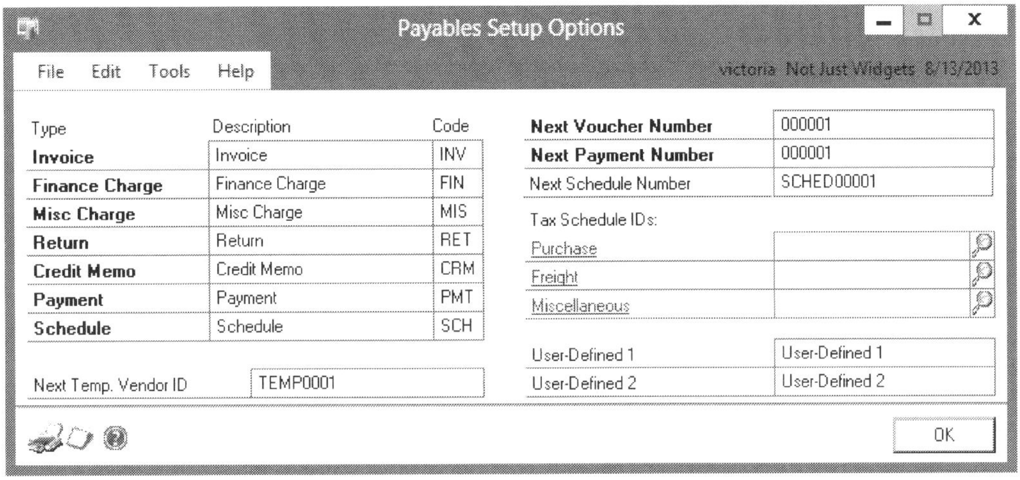


# Vendor classes

**Vendor classes** in Dynamics GP are optional but recommended, as they offer the following three benefits:

- **Time saved when creating vendors**: Classes serve as a template for most of the vendor settings, so they can offer significant time savings when creating vendors in Dynamics GP.
- **Time saved during vendor updates**: Changes to the vendor class can be rolled down to all vendors in that class, making changes to multiple vendors quick and easy.
- **Reporting, filtering, and searching**: Most reports and searches in Dynamics GP offer an option to filter by vendor class. For example, when creating a payables check batch, one of the options is to select vendors for payment by vendor class.

To set up vendor classes, click on the **Classes** button on the **Payables Management Setup** window or navigate to **Microsoft Dynamics GP | Tools | Setup | Purchasing | Vendor Class**. When a new vendor is created and a class is selected, all the settings from the class are defaulted in for the vendor. Any individual vendor setting can be changed later. The following list explains the fields on the **Vendor Class Setup** window:

- **Class ID**: A 10-character ID that cannot be changed once saved. When filtering by vendor class on most reports, there will be one to/from range available. If there are certain vendor classes that will typically be reported on together, consider making their Class IDs start with the same character(s) so they are sorted together in a list. For example, if you have five US and two Canadian vendor classes, and you will typically want to report on all US vendors separately from all Canadian vendors, you could add the prefixes `US` and `CAD` (or `U` and `C`) to all the Class IDs.
- **Default** checkbox: One vendor class can be set as the default class. Once set, newly created classes will copy all the settings from the default class. This can help save time when setting up multiple vendor classes that are similar. The default vendor class can be changed at any time by selecting the **Default** checkbox on a different class. This will automatically uncheck the **Default** checkbox on the class that was previously the default.
- **Description**: A description of what vendors are in this class. This is used to help users identify the proper selection when looking at a list of vendor classes.
- **Currency ID** and **Rate Type ID**: Select the default currency and rate type for the vendors in this class.
- **Payment Terms**: Select the default Payment Terms ID for vendors in this class.
- **Discount Grace Period** and **Due Date Grace Period**: These work together with the **Use Customer/Vendor Grace Periods for Date/EOM Payment Terms** option on the **Payment Terms Setup** window. You can enter up to 99 days for each of these settings.
- **Payment Priority**: This is an additional grouping available for vendors and can be used when selecting payables checks and filtering on some of the Dynamics GP reports. Payment priority can be up to a three-character alphanumeric value, and it is recommended to always use the same number of characters so that you can use ranges of payment priorities for filtering. When sorting reports and lookups, numbers will appear before letters.
- **Minimum Order**: If you have a minimum order amount with vendors, you can enter it here. Note that this is informational only.

- **Trade Discount**: A trade discount is an across-the-board discount on purchases, so if a vendor is set up with a 10 percent trade discount and you enter an invoice or purchase order for $900, a $90 discount will automatically be calculated. Trade discounts are useful in situations where you want to track the discounts/margin from vendors in a separate General Ledger account.
- **Tax Schedule**: If you are using purchasing taxes, enter the default Tax Schedule ID for this vendor class.
- **Shipping Method**: Enter a default Shipping Method ID for this class.
- **Checkbook ID**: It is only recommended to set up Checkbook IDs for vendors or vendor classes when different checkbooks are used for payments to different vendors (for example, if you are using Multicurrency and have a separate bank account for each currency). Otherwise, if the same checkbook is typically used for all payments in a company, leave this blank and transactions will use the default **Checkbook ID** selected on the **Payables Management Setup** window.
- **User-Defined 1** and **User-Defined 2**: If you would like to store generic values for the vendor user-defined fields, you can enter them here. If you have changed the user-defined labels on the **Payables Setup Options** window, you will see those labels here, instead of **User-Defined 1** and **User-Defined 2**.

> It may be useful to know that the **User-Defined 1** field is available as a filter on the Payables Trial Balance reports. So if you need another filter for reports consider using this. **User-Defined 2** is not available as a report filter.

- **Tax Type**: Choose whether this vendor class is for 1099 vendors and, if so, what type of 1099 vendor. If some of the vendors in the class have a different tax type, you will be able to change this during individual vendor setup.
- **FOB**: If desired, select the default FOB type. This is informational only, but will print on POs.
- **Minimum Payment**: This setting can be used with the option to **Pay Only Minimum** when automatically selecting payables checks. Most of the time **No Minimum** is chosen for this option.
- **Maximum Invoice Amount**: This setting can prevent users from entering invoices above a certain amount. If an **Exceed Maximum Invoice Amount Password** was entered on the **Payables Management Setup** window, that password can be used to override this maximum.
- **Credit Limit**: In the Payables module, credits limits are informational only and will not prevent users from entering transactions that would go over the vendor's credit limit. It is assumed that the vendor would be enforcing their own credit limits.

- **Writeoff**: If desired, enter a limit for writeoffs. Note that the default writeoff setting is **Not Allowed**. While it is fairly rare to have writeoffs in Payables, it also doesn't hurt anything to allow them and typically **Unlimited** is selected for this option. If an **Exceed Maximum Writeoff Amount Password** was entered on the **Payables Management Setup** window, that password can be used to override the maximum.
- **Revalue Vendor**: Select whether you will be revaluing transactions for vendors in this class and, if so, whether the gain/loss should go to the **Payables/ Discount Account** or the **Purchasing Offset Account**. **Revalue Vendor** is checked by default, whether or not you are using Multicurrency. Leaving it checked when not using the Multicurrency module will not cause any harm.
- **Maintain History**: It is recommended to keep all history and select all the boxes. If anything other than **Not a 1099 Vendor** was chosen for **Tax Type**, the **Calendar Year** checkbox will be selected and will be non-editable as calendar year history is required to print 1099s.

The following is an example of a typical **Vendor Class Setup** window:

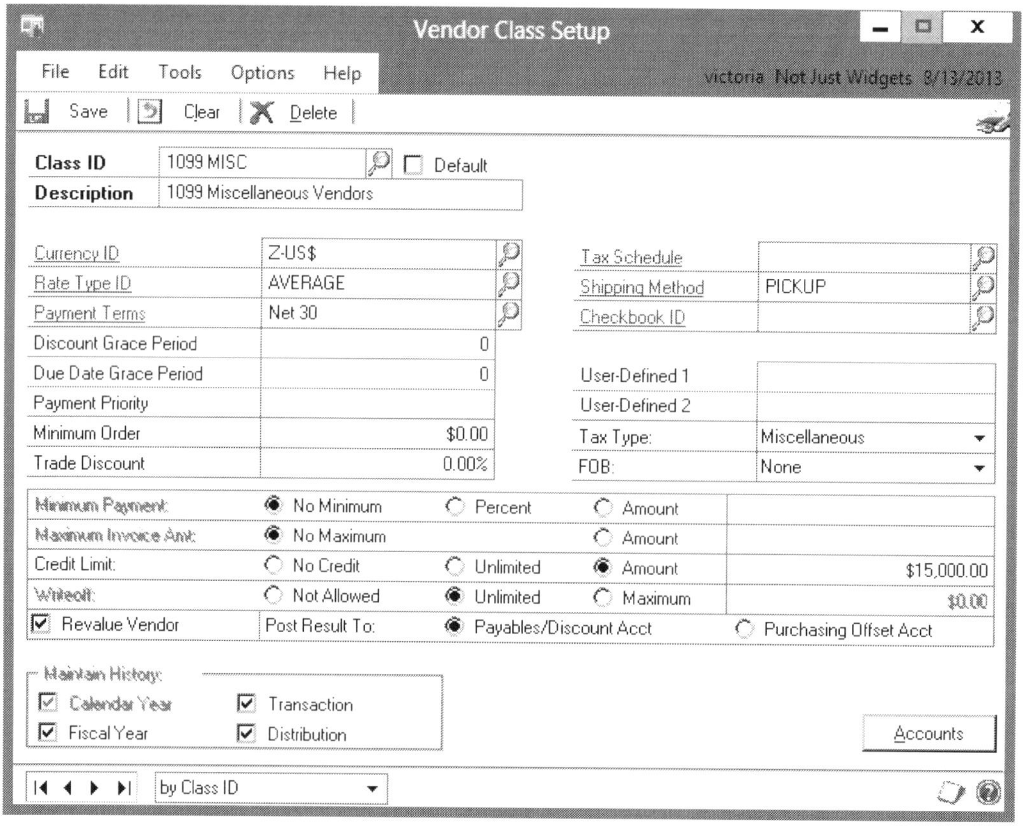

The only required fields for a vendor class are **Class ID** and **Description**, so you can fill in as much or as little detail as you need when setting up a class.

> You can create an unlimited number of vendor classes, but keep in mind that the main goal of classes is to save you time. Creating 100 classes for 350 vendors may not be much of a time saver.

## Accounts for vendor classes

Clicking on the **Accounts** button on the **Vendor Class Setup** window will open the **Vendor Class Accounts Setup** window. These are the default General Ledger accounts that will be populated when you create vendors and assign them to a class. It is recommended to set up accounts at the vendor class level to save time during vendor setup.

Dynamics GP determines GL accounts to be used for payables transactions using the following logic:

1. Use accounts set up for the vendor. These accounts will default in from the vendor class when a vendor is being created, but can be changed for each individual vendor as needed.
2. If any accounts are missing from the vendor setup, use posting accounts for the company (**Microsoft Dynamics GP** | **Tools** | **Setup** | **Posting** | **Posting Accounts**).
3. If any accounts are still missing, leave the accounts blank. Transactions will give a warning and fail to post if any required GL accounts are missing.

> Note that at no time do any transactions in Dynamics GP look at the vendor class to determine what accounts to use. The accounts at the class level are only helpful as defaults when creating vendors or when making changes that will be rolled down to all the vendors in a class.

You do not have to set up every account possible, as many may never be used in your Dynamics GP environment. The most important accounts to default for payables transactions are **Cash**, **Accounts Payable**, and **Purchases**. For the **Cash** account, it is recommended to select **Use Cash Account from Checkbook** to avoid bank reconciliation issues. You can also save considerable time when selecting default accounts by setting up the company posting accounts for any accounts that are always the same for all vendors.

The following is an example of the company **Posting Accounts Setup** window for the **Purchasing** series (**Microsoft Dynamics GP** | **Tools** | **Setup** | **Posting** | **Posting Accounts**):

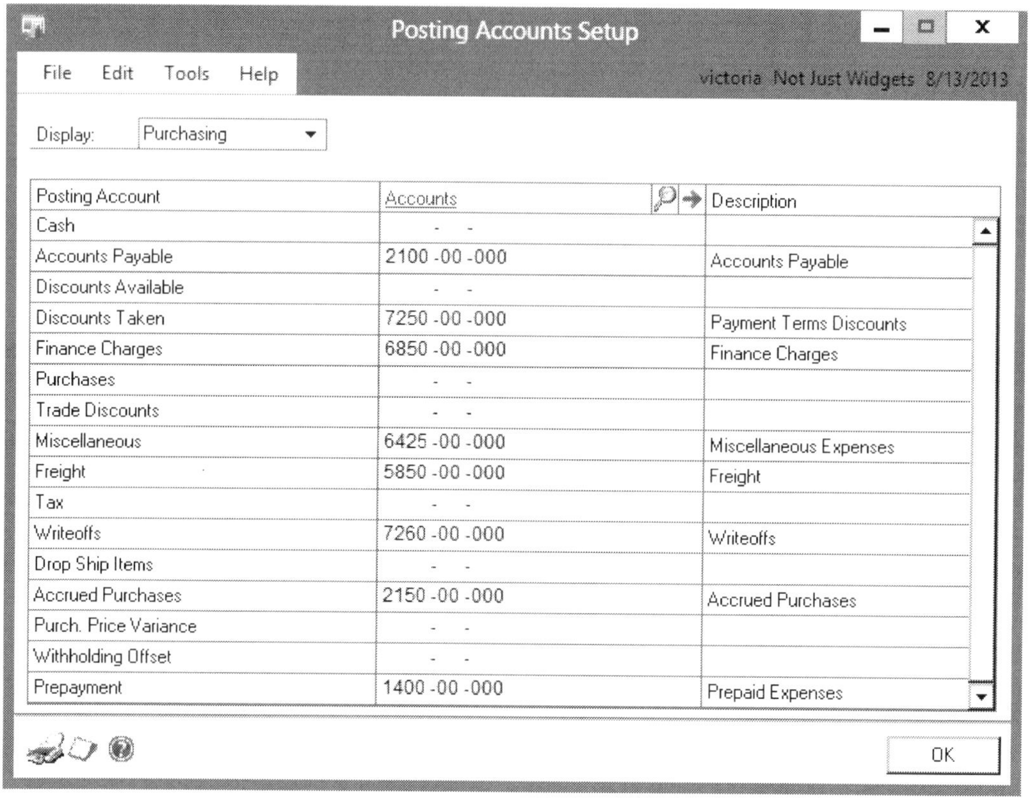


With the posting accounts shown in the previous example, the **Vendor Class Accounts Setup** window might look like the following, with only the **Purchases** account specified:

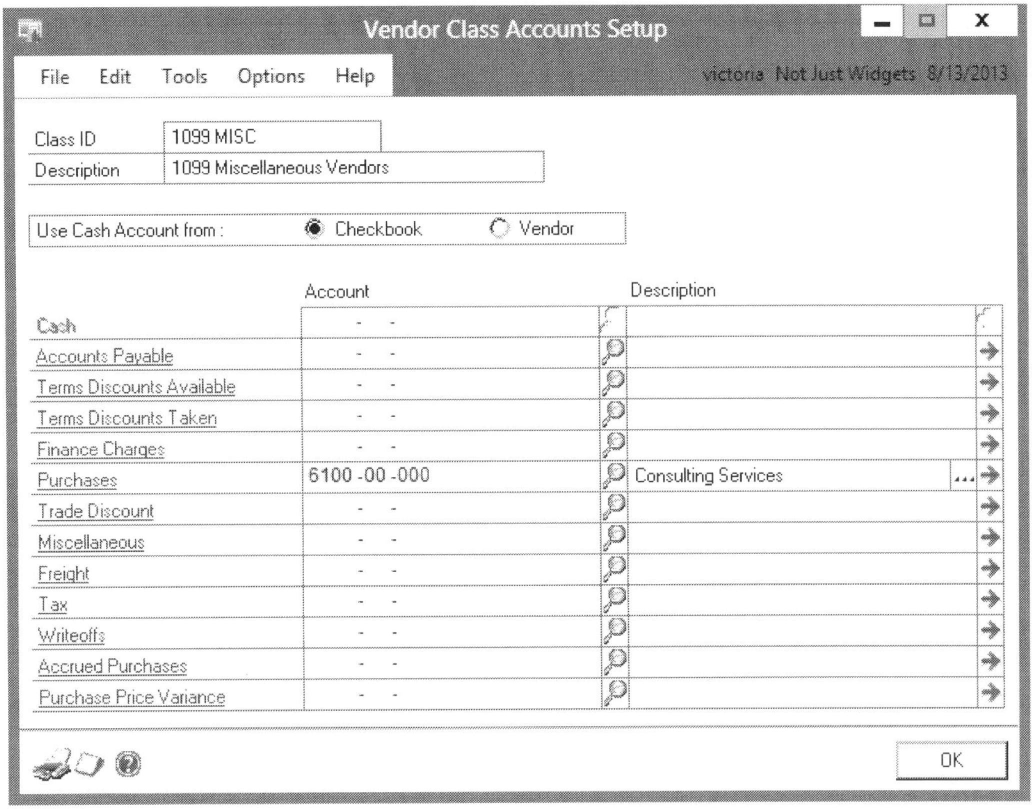


Dynamics GP also offers the ability to set up multiple **Purchases** accounts for vendors. This is a very useful feature for vendors who typically have their invoices go to one of a few accounts or split between multiple GL accounts. To use this feature, perform the following steps:

1. Click on the **ellipsis (...)** at the end of the **Purchases** account line on the **Vendor Class Accounts Setup** window.
2. Add as many accounts as desired in the scrolling list.
3. Check **Default on Trx** for any account that you would like to automatically show on transactions (this is in addition to the **Default Account**, which will always show on transactions). Accounts without **Default on Trx** checked will not show on transactions automatically, but will be available from a lookup during transaction entry.

Typically, during transaction entry, rather than having to search for and manually add all the needed GL accounts, it is easier to have a number of accounts defaulted and simply put amounts in for the accounts needed. Any accounts with no amount entered will be ignored when posting.

The following screenshot illustrates a sample **Additional Vendor Accounts** window:

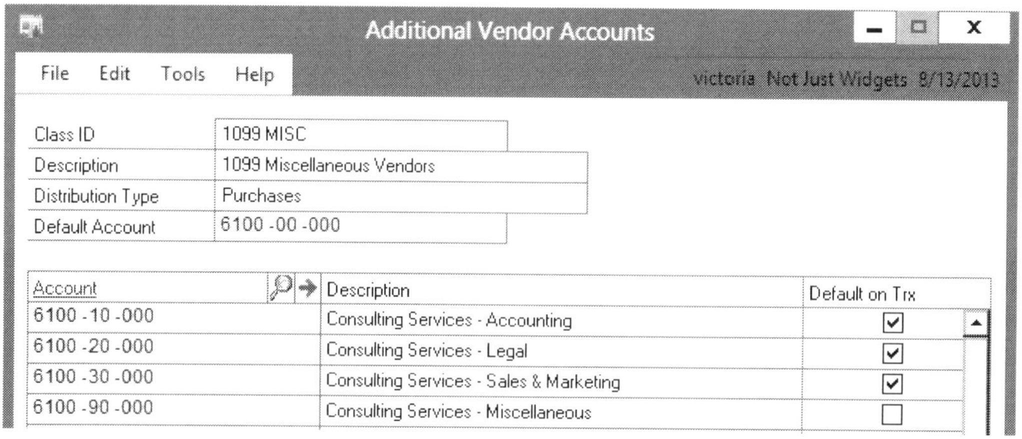


To remove lines that are not needed from the **Additional Vendor Accounts** list, right-click on the line with the account you want to remove and select **Delete Row** or click on the line and select **Edit** | **Delete Row** from the menu.

# 1099 setup

If you have used prior versions of Dynamics GP, you will find that the 1099 functionality has been enhanced significantly starting with Dynamics GP 10.0. As part of the Payables module setup, you can now define the minimum for each 1099 box type and you can even edit the descriptions of the 1099 boxes.

To open the **1099 Setup** window, navigate to **Microsoft Dynamics GP** | **Tools** | **Setup** | **Purchasing** | **Payables** and click on the **1099 Setup** button. Select the **Tax Type** and change the **Descriptions** and **Minimum Amounts** as needed.

# Purchasing e-mail setup

If you would like Dynamics GP to send e-mail to your vendors, you will need to set up Purchasing e-mail options.

> You will need to be on a computer that has an e-mail client to be able to access the **Purchasing E-mail Setup** window.

Navigate to **Microsoft Dynamics GP** | **Tools** | **Setup** | **Purchasing** | **E-mail Settings**. On the **Purchasing E-mail Setup** window, you can determine whether to enable e-mailing of **Purchase Orders** and **Vendor Remittances**, the default **Message ID** to use for each, the default address for **Have Replies Sent to**, and whether to **Allow Changing the 'Reply to' address** and **Update of E-mail** at the time of entering purchase orders. Clicking on **Select Names** will bring up your **Outlook Address Book**.

**Message ID** refers to predefined messages with the subject and text of the e-mail Dynamics GP will generate. You can set up a new message by entering a new **Message ID** and answering **Yes** to the pop-up window asking whether you would like to add this Message ID. You can also set up a new message by navigating to **Microsoft Dynamics GP** | **Tools** | **Setup** | **Company** | **E-mail Message Setup**.

On the **Message Setup** window:

1. Specify a **Message ID**—maximum length is 25 characters.
2. Enter a **Description**—maximum length is 150 characters.
3. Select **Purchasing** under **Series**.
4. Select **Purchase Order** or **Vendor Remittance** under **Doc. Type**.
5. Enter a **Subject** and a **Body** for your message. The **Subject** can be up to 150 characters, the **Body** will allow up to 32,000 characters.

   You can use the **Field** selection under the **Body** section to add global fields like PO number or the vendor's contact name into the **Subject** or **Body** of your email message. To do this, select the **Field** from the drop-down list, position your cursor where you want to add the field and click **Insert**. Click on the **Validate** button to make sure the fields you have selected match the document type assigned to the message.

6. **Have Replies Sent to** will default from the **Purchasing E-mail Setup** window, but can be changed for each individual message.

A sample **Message Setup** window is shown here using the **PO Number** and **Contact** fields:

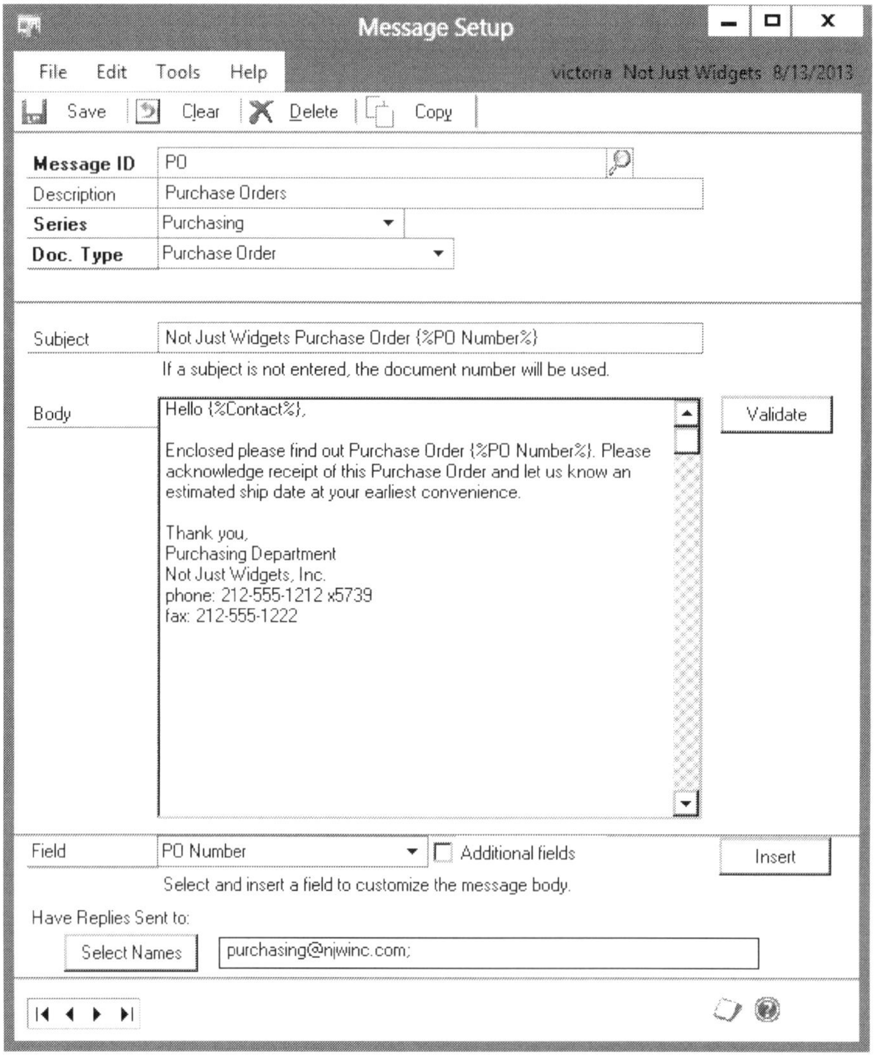


# Vendors

The final step before you can enter payables transactions in Dynamics GP is creating vendors. If you have many vendors to create, you may opt to import them. However, it is still helpful to understand how to set up new vendors manually when planning your import. Creating a vendor includes vendor setup, vendor accounts, vendor options, and vendor e-mail addresses and options.

## Vendor setup

To create a vendor, navigate to **Cards** | **Purchasing** | **Vendor**. The following are descriptions of the fields on the **Vendor Maintenance** window:

- **Vendor ID**: This is the ID that will be used to identify the vendor throughout Dynamics GP—up to 15 characters are allowed.
- **Hold**: A vendor can be put on hold at any time. You cannot enter payments or apply existing payments to a vendor that is on hold. However, any transactions other than payments can still be entered when a vendor is on hold. Holds are useful to automatically exclude a vendor from check runs.
- **Name**: The name that will appear for the vendor throughout Dynamics GP windows and reports. This is what users will see to help them find the vendor if the ID is not enough or if numerical vendor IDs are used.
- **Short Name**: This field is not really used by the application and will default to the first 15 characters of the vendor **Name**. Some companies use this to store other information about their vendors for report filtering or sorting.
- **Check Name**: This is the name that will be printed on payables checks and 1099 forms for this vendor. By default, this will be the same as the **Name** field, but there is no requirement for them to be the same and either can be changed at any time.
- **Primary Address** section: One address for the vendor can be entered directly on the **Vendor Maintenance** window. Additional addresses can be entered by clicking on the **Address** button. There is no limit on the number of addresses that can be entered for a vendor. Even if you are not entering an address for a vendor, it is recommended to create an **Address ID** so that it can be used for the default **Address IDs** below.

> Even though there are three lines available for the **Address**, only the first two address lines will appear on out-of-the-box reports in Dynamics GP. To show the third address line, reports would need to be customized.

- **Address IDs**: Choose the default **Address IDs** to be used on transactions for this vendor. These can be changed at the time of transaction entry.
    - **Purchase**: The vendor address that will be printed on purchase orders for this vendor.
    - **Remit To**: The default address used for checks to this vendor.
    - **Ship From**: Used to store the location where the vendor ships goods from, which may be needed for tax or reporting purposes.

    - **1099**: New in Dynamics GP 2013 is the ability to specify an address that prints on the 1099. This field will only be enabled for 1099 vendors.

- **Status**: There are three possible statuses for a vendor:
    - **Active**: When you create a vendor, the status is defaulted to **Active** and transactions can be entered for this vendor.
    - **Inactive**: Vendors that have historical transactions, but you do not work with anymore, can be set to **Inactive**. Transactions cannot be entered for an inactive vendor, but you can still search and report on past transactions for the vendor. An inactive vendor can be re-activated at any time.
    - **Temporary**: Vendors that you might only do business with once, but still want to track some information for, can be created as temporary vendors. While this is not typically recommended, temporary vendors can be deleted even if they have transaction history. This may be useful for companies that have a large number of temporary vendors.

- **Class ID**: Select the Class ID for this vendor. While classes are optional, they are recommended to simplify setup and reporting. When a Class ID is selected, all settings from that class will populate for this vendor. If any of these settings have already been selected manually for the vendor, they will be overwritten by the settings from the vendor class for any new vendor. For previously saved vendors, you will be asked whether you want to update the vendor information from the class settings.
- **Phone** and **Fax** numbers: Enter any phone or fax numbers you want to track for the vendor. Note that these fields are hard coded for the North American phone format with a four-digit extension. For international phone numbers or longer extensions, many companies use the **Comment 1** and **Comment 2** fields or the vendor note.
- **Tax Schedule**: If you are using purchasing taxes, this is the Tax Schedule ID to be used with this vendor and address. Each address you enter for a vendor will need its own **Tax Schedule**.
- **Shipping Method**: This is the default Shipping Method ID for this vendor and address.
- **UPS Zone**: Most companies do not use the UPS zone and this is informational only. However, if needed, this can store the UPS Zone for this vendor and address.
- **Vendor Account**: You can track your account number with the vendor here. Many companies choose to add this field to their payables checks.

> Note that this field holds 20 characters, while the comment fields hold 30 characters each. If you have long account numbers with some of your vendors, consider using one of the comment fields for this instead.

* **Comment 1** and **Comment 2**: These are additional fields to track information about a vendor. Each allows up to 30 characters.

The following is an example of a typical **Vendor Maintenance** window:

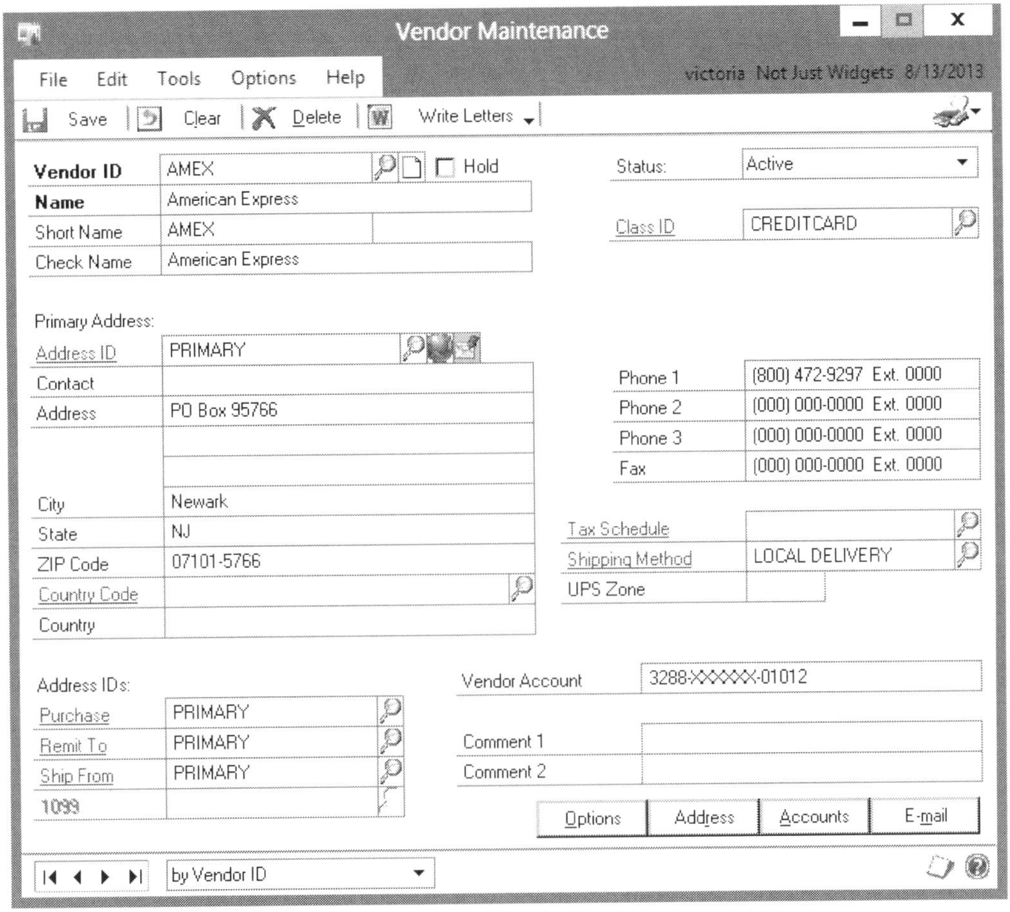

## Vendor accounts

The **Accounts** button on the **Vendor Maintenance** window will open the **Vendor Account Maintenance** window, where vendor-specific General Ledger accounts can be set up. All the settings on the **Vendor Account Maintenance** window are the same as the settings on the **Vendor Class Accounts Setup** window described earlier in this chapter. If a vendor class was entered for the vendor, all the accounts from the class will default in for the vendor. Remember that **Vendor Account Maintenance** is the first place where transactions for each vendor will check for the needed General Ledger accounts.

## Vendor options

The **Options** button on the **Vendor Maintenance** window will open the **Vendor Maintenance Options** window, where you can set up additional information and defaults for the vendor. Almost all of the fields on this window are also on the **Vendor Class Setup** window described previously in the *Vendor classes* section. The fields that are new to this window are:

- **Tax ID**: This field holds the tax ID that will be printed on 1099 forms for this vendor.
- **Tax Registration**: An additional field to hold tax registration information. This field is typically used for GST and VAT taxes and is not used for US implementations.
- **1099 Box**: Depending on the 1099 tax type chosen, you can select the appropriate 1099 box number for this vendor.
- **Language**: This is an informational field that becomes available if you have set up languages for your Dynamics GP system (**Microsoft Dynamics GP** | **Tools** | **Setup** | **System** | **Language**).

The following screenshot shows the **Vendor Maintenance Options** window for a 1099 vendor:

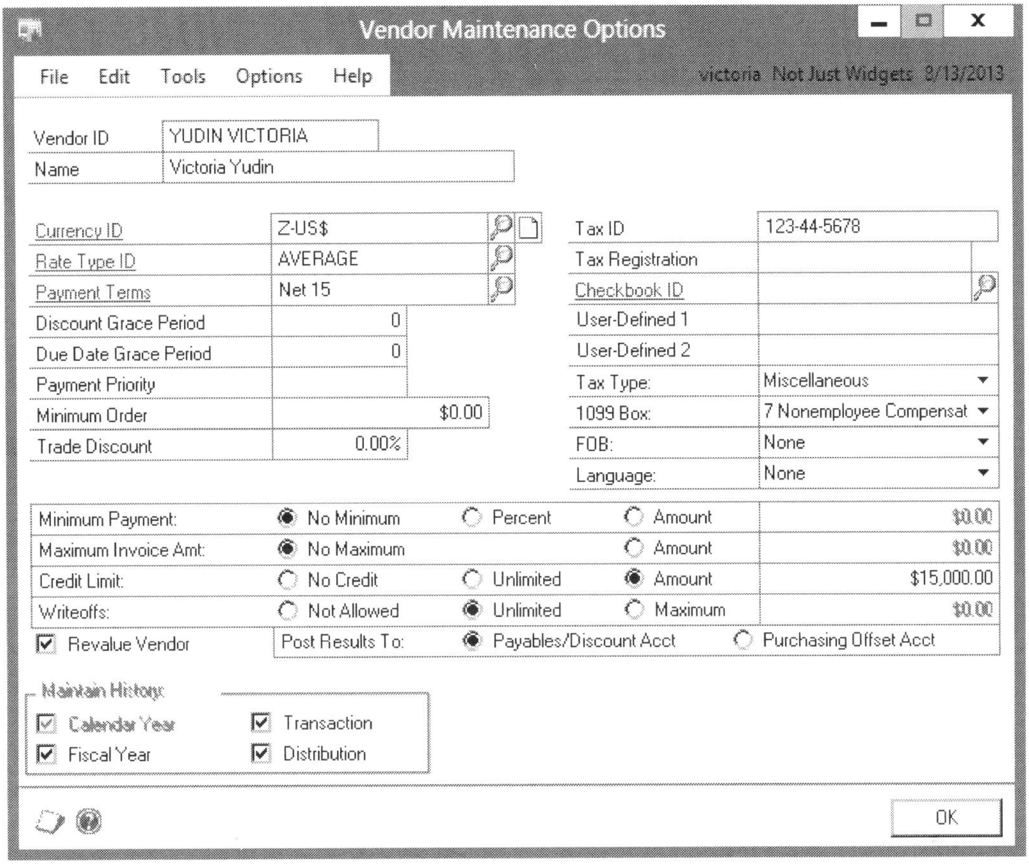

# Vendor e-mail addresses and options

E-mail addresses for vendors are address specific, so each address saved for a vendor can have different e-mail addresses. To set up e-mail addresses for each vendor and address combination, click on the **Internet Information** icon to the right of **Address ID**:

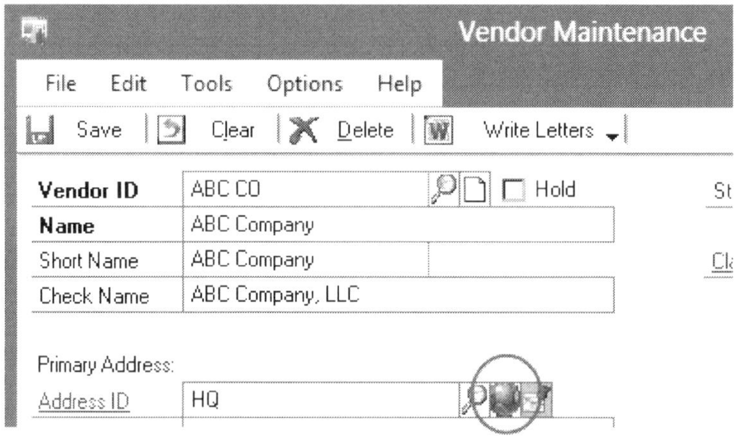


Clicking the **To**, **Cc**, or **Bcc** buttons will open your **Outlook Address Book** and let you choose addresses from there. Alternatively, you can simply enter e-mail addresses separated by semicolons:

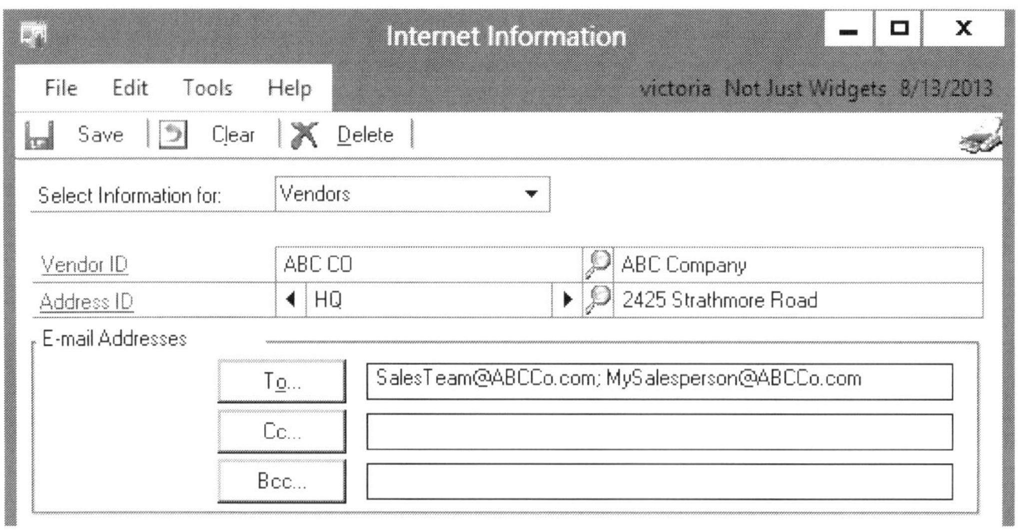

The final step in setting up e-mailing options for vendors is to complete the **Vendor E-mail Options** setup. This can be done individually for each vendor or for a group of vendors at once.

To set up e-mailing for one vendor at a time, click on the **E-mail** button at the bottom of the **Vendor Maintenance** window (**Cards** | **Purchasing** | **Vendor**). As these settings will most likely be the same for all vendors, it may be easier to perform the setup for multiple vendors by navigating to **Microsoft Dynamics GP** | **Tools** | **Setup** | **Purchasing** | **E-mail Settings** and clicking on the **Vendor Setup** button. This will take you to a navigation list with all your vendors.

> If you are on a computer with no e-mail client installed, you will not be able to use the navigation path above. Instead, you can click on **Purchasing** in the bottom left section of the main Dynamics GP window to open the Purchasing menu, and then select **Vendors** from the navigation list at the top left.

Search and filter the vendor list as needed, then click on the **overflow** button (>>) in the **Modify** section of the toolbar, and select **E-mail Settings**:

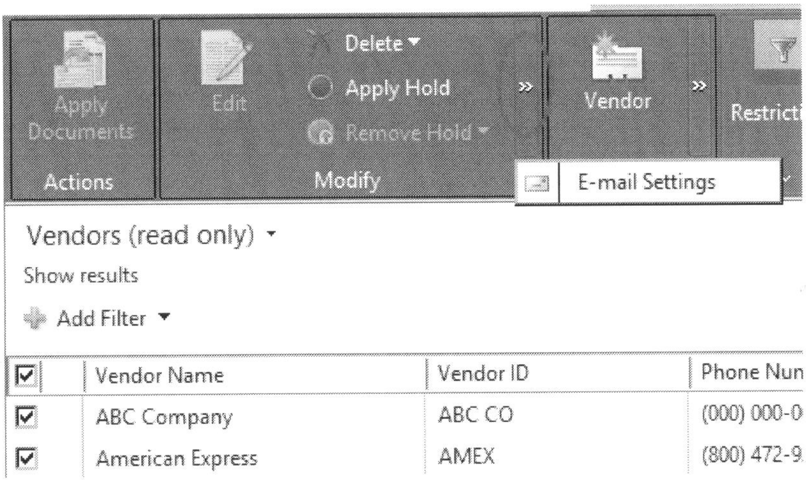


Depending on the options you previously chose on the **Purchasing E-mail Setup** window, some of the fields on the **Mass Vendor E-mail Settings** window will be disabled. Select the desired choices for **Attachment Options**; if **Send Documents as Attachments** is selected, **Multiple Attachments per E-mail** can be chosen and you can **Set Maximum File Size**.

On the **Send Forms as E-mail** section, you can select **Purchase Order**, **Vendor Remittance**, or both, depending on what was enabled on the **Purchasing E-mail Setup** window. If there was already a **Message ID** selected on the **Purchasing E-mail Setup** window, it will default here, but it can be changed as needed. Note that only the **HTML Format** will work for sending Dynamics GP standard Report Writer reports. To use any of the other formats requires Word templates to be set up for Dynamics GP or using a third party product to e-mail documents.

With the Payables module setup completed and vendors created, payables transactions can now be entered into Dynamics GP.

# Receivables Management

The Dynamics GP **Receivables Management** module is also commonly referred to as **Accounts Receivable**, **AR**, or just **Receivables**. It is part of the Sales series, so menu options and navigation for the Receivables module will start with **Sales**. All the SQL server tables for the Receivables Management module begin with `RM`, so you may also see this module referred to as **RM**.

Setup for the Receivables module includes the following:

- Receivables Management Setup
- Receivables Setup Options
- Sales Territories
- Salespeople
- Price levels
- Customer classes
- Sales e-mail settings
- Customers

# Receivables Management Setup

To open the **Receivables Management Setup** window, navigate to **Microsoft Dynamics GP** | **Tools** | **Setup** | **Sales** | **Receivables**. The following are explanations of the settings on this window:

- **Aging Periods**: Aging for receivables transactions can be done by **Due Date** or by **Document Date** (Transaction Date). All inquiry windows and reports will use this setting when showing aging information for receivables transactions. Dynamics GP allows for up to seven **Aging Periods**, or buckets, which cannot overlap and cannot exceed 999 days.

> The out-of-the-box-reports in Dynamics GP will show only four receivables aging buckets. If you want to use more than four aging buckets, you will need to customize your reports.

Aging settings can be changed at any time; however, all open records will need to be reconciled while users are out of the system to propagate the changes, so this is not something companies will want to do often.

If different payment terms are offered to different customers, aging by **Due Date** is recommended.

- **Track Discounts Available in GL**: If you are planning on setting up a Discounts Available account for tracking available discounts separately in the General Ledger at the time of transaction posting, select this option. If this is not chosen, discounts can still go to a separate GL account, but only at the time that payments or credits are applied.
- **Print Historical Aged Trial Balance**: Even if a custom report is used to print the Historical Aged Trial Balance, it may be useful to compare it to the out-of-the-box report, so it is recommended to allow printing the Historical Aged Trial Balance.
- **Delete Unposted Printed Documents**: It is recommended to leave this option unchecked, so that if a receivables document (for example, an Invoice or a Credit Memo) was printed and possibly sent to a customer, users will not be able to delete it. Note that this setting is for the Receivables module only and will not apply to any documents printed from the Sales Order Processing module.
- **Compound Finance Change**: Check this option if you will want to calculate finance charges on overdue finance charges.
- **Pay Commissions After Invoice Paid**: This option is somewhat misleading, as it makes it sound like Dynamics GP has the ability to create commissions payables transactions. In reality, this option only changes behavior of some of the out-of-the-box commissions reports. Dynamics GP can track commission information and generate commissions reports, but the functionality is very limited and many companies either use custom commissions reports or an add-on product to track commissions if they have anything but a very simple commissions structure. Having this option checked will allow you to print commissions reports that show commissions only when customer invoices are fully applied. When using custom commissions reports or third-party products, this option will typically not make any difference.

- **Reprint Statements**: If you decide to use Dynamics GP to print customer statements, all the statement details will be saved so that they can be reprinted when this option is selected. I have not run into any situations where the ability to reprint a statement was something companies wanted to disallow.
- **Print Tax Details on Documents**: This will print the tax summary information on receivables documents. Since taxes are typically printed in the Sales Order Processing module, not in Receivables, most companies do not need this. If selected, you can also select **Print Dual Currencies**, which will show multicurrency detail for taxes.
- **Auto Apply to Finance Charges First**: If the auto-apply feature is used when applying receivables transactions, this option will cause finance charges to be applied before any other sales transactions.
- **Age Unapplied Credit Amounts**: Unapplied credit transactions (Credit Memos, Returns, and Payments) will always show in the **Current** aging bucket unless this option is selected. Most companies choose to age unapplied credit transactions.
- **Passwords**:
    - **Exceed Credit Limit**: If a password is entered here, users will not be able to enter a transaction that exceeds a customer credit limit without entering the password. If there is no password, users will see a credit limit warning, but will be able to ignore it.
    - **Remove Customer Hold**: This label is a bit misleading, making it sound as if this password is needed to take a customer off hold, which is not the case. If a password is entered here and a customer is placed on hold, users will need to type in the password to be able to enter any transaction except a payment for that customer. If no password is entered, transactions for customers on hold will show a warning, but users will be able to enter the transaction. Payments can always be entered, whether or not a customer is on hold.
    - **Exceed Maximum Writeoff Amount**: If no password is entered and a maximum writeoff amount is set for a customer, the system will not allow a user to enter a writeoff for more than the maximum. If a password is entered, then the system will prompt for it when entering the writeoff and allow a writeoff above the maximum.
    - **Waive Finance Charge**: If a password is entered, users will not be able to waive customer finance charges without the password. If no password is entered, users can waive finance charges as long as they have access to the proper window to do this.

> Note that all the passwords will be stored in plain text, so if a user should not know the passwords, they should be restricted access to this window.

- **Apply By**: This setting determines if transactions are applied in order of **Document Number** or **Due Date** when auto apply is chosen during the process of applying a cash receipt, credit memo, or return. Auto apply is not very commonly used, so this setting is not critical and can be changed at any time.
- **Defaults**:
    - **NSF Charge**: Enter the non-sufficient funds charge your company bills customers when a check bounces. This can be changed at the time of entering the NSF transaction.
    - **Checkbook ID**: Optionally, you can select a default **Checkbook ID** to be used for receivables transactions. The Checkbook ID can be overridden on every transaction; this is simply the default to save users time.
    - **Price Level**: Each inventory item in Dynamics GP can have multiple price levels. Customers can be assigned one price level. The price level entered here will be used on transactions for customers with no price level assigned.
    - **Document Format**: Choose the default report format for transactions printed in the Receivables module. Typically, the **Blank Paper** option is selected.
    - **Default Summary View**: This setting determines what view to show by default on the **Customer Summary** and the **Customer Yearly Summary Inquiry** windows. It is recommended to make this either **Calendar Year** or **Fiscal Year** to save users time when inquiring on customer information.
- **E-mailed Statements Status Recipient**: If you will be e-mailing customer statements directly from Dynamics GP using the built-in functionality, a status report will be sent to the e-mail address specified. If no **Status Recipient** is specified, Dynamics GP will send the status report to the e-mail address statements are sent from.

The following screenshot is an example of a typical **Receivables Management Setup** window with all seven of the aging buckets used. Remember, anything over four aging buckets will require custom or modified aging reports.

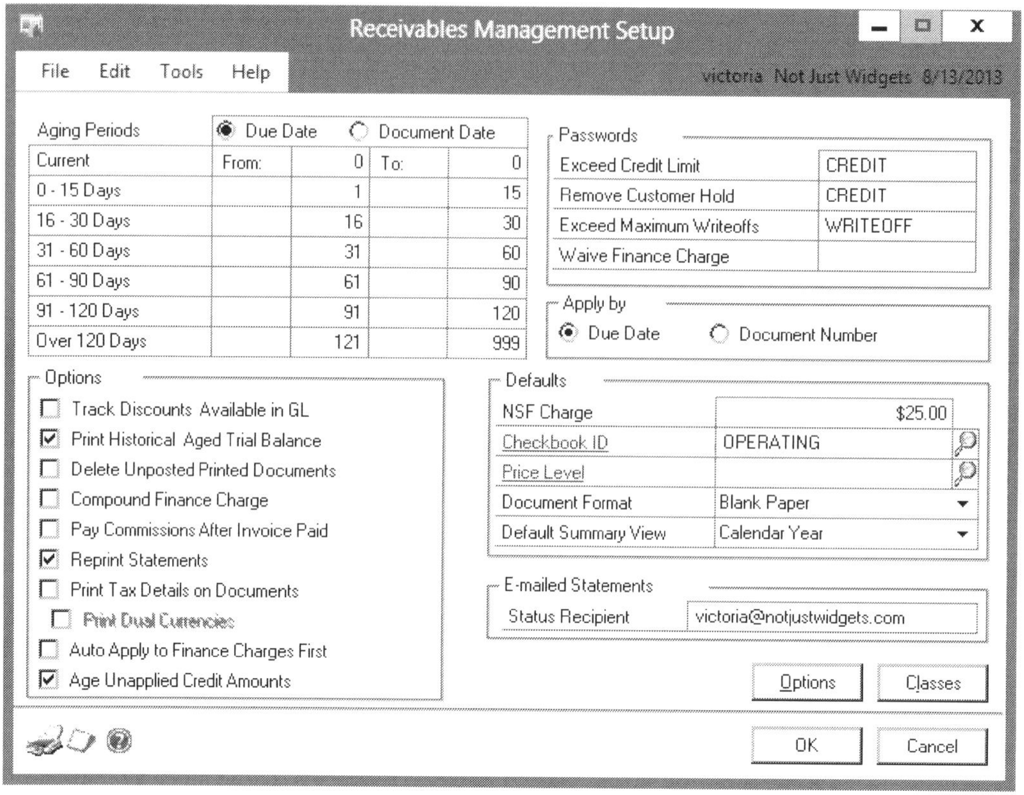

# Receivables Setup Options

The **Receivables Setup Options** window (**Microsoft Dynamics GP** | **Tools** | **Setup** | **Sales** | **Receivables** | **Options button**) allows you to:

- Set up descriptions and codes for each receivables transaction type
- Set up the numbering scheme and the next number for each receivables transaction type
- View the dates when sales routines, such as aging, were last run
- Set the default tax schedules for receivables transactions
- Change labels for the customer and customer address user-defined fields
- Choose what amount types are included in sales history kept for receivables transactions

It is recommended to leave the **Descriptions** and **Codes** for receivables transactions with the default values, to facilitate support and training. The default **Next Number** values for all the transactions are quite long. Many companies will never need so many digits and choose to take out a few zeros to make these numbers easier to work with. Keep in mind that these numbers will not auto-increment the number of digits they use, so after reaching `SALES9999`, the system will not be able to go to `SALES10000` automatically and will instead go to `SALES0000`, then start over with `SALES0001`. Consider the expected volume of each type of transaction before deciding how many digits to leave. The **Next Number** for any transaction type can be changed at any time.

The **Date of Last** section is strictly informational, no changes to the system will occur if these dates are changed. These dates are updated when processes such as aging customer accounts and assessing finance charges are performed in Dynamics GP. To ensure accurate information is available, it is recommended not to change these dates manually.

The **Default Tax Schedule IDs** set on this window will default on all receivables transactions. Even though taxes can be changed as needed on every individual transaction, if you plan on using the Receivables module to routinely enter customer transactions that require tax calculations, filling out this section can save some time and effort during transaction entry. Other modules, such as Sales Order Processing, will have separate tax setup options.

One way of making tax calculations easier is to create two catchall tax schedules—one containing all sales tax details and another containing sales tax details for all jurisdictions that tax freight. To decide what tax details to use on a transaction, Dynamics GP first looks at the shipping method type to determine whether to use the customer Tax Schedule ID or the company Tax Schedule ID. It then uses the tax details that are in both the tax schedule set up for the transaction and the customer/company tax schedule. As an example, suppose you have the following tax schedules in Dynamics GP:

| Tax Schedule ID | Tax Details included |
|---|---|
| ALL | NJ, NY STATE, NYC |
| FREIGHT | NJ, NYC |
| NJ SALES | NJ |
| NYC SALES | NY STATE, NYC |

The following table shows how taxes will be calculated using different setup options when the shipping method is Delivery (meaning the customer's tax schedule is used):

| Customer Tax Schedule ID | Transaction Tax Schedule ID | Tax Details included on transactions |
|---|---|---|
| NJ SALES | ALL | NJ – only NJ is in both NJ SALES and ALL. |
| NYC SALES | ALL | NY STATE, NYC – only these two are in both NYC SALES and ALL. |
| | ALL | No matter what is set up for the transaction, no taxes will be calculated if the customer is not set up to be taxed. |
| NJ SALES | NYC SALES | No taxes will be calculated as there is no Tax Detail that is in both NJ SALES and NYC SALES. |
| NYC SALES | FREIGHT | NYC – as only NYC is in both NYC SALES and FREIGHT, only NYC tax will be calculated. |

**Miscellaneous** charge taxes are separated out to allow the **Miscellaneous** field to be used on transactions for non-taxable items if sales are taxed. This option is rarely used, but is there if needed.

In the **Customer Master User-Defined 1** and **User-Defined 2** fields, you can enter labels that will change what these fields are called on customer setup and inquiry windows, as well as reports. The user-defined fields are used to store additional information about a customer.

[ **User-Defined 1** can also be used as a filter for Receivables Trial Balance reports, whereas **User-Defined 2** cannot. ]

Starting with Dynamics GP 2013, you can now change the labels on the **Customer Address User-Defined 1** and **User-Defined 2** fields. While it may not sound like a big deal, there have been numerous requests on Dynamics GP user forums asking for this.

The **Sales History Includes** section allows you to choose what types of amounts on transactions get stored as part of the sales summary for each customer. The sales summary for customers can be seen on various windows, such as the **Customer Yearly Summary Inquiry** (**Inquiry** | **Sales** | **Yearly Summary**). As an example, consider the following selections on the **Sales History Includes** section:

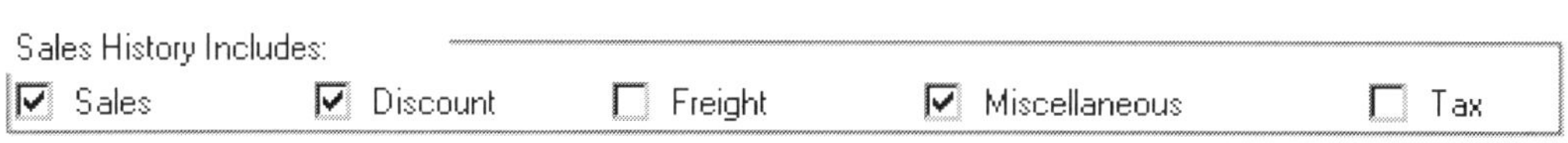

A transaction with a Sales amount of $95, Discount of $5, Freight of $10, and Tax of $7 will add $90 (Sales less Discount) to the customer's sales total. The default setting on this window has only **Sales** selected, but many companies like to include either all or at least the **Discount** and **Miscellaneous** amounts as well.

> It is important to remember that the settings in the **Sales History Includes** section are not what determine whether transaction history is stored for AR transactions; these settings only determine which parts of each transaction get accumulated in the total sales amount stored in summary history tables.

The following screenshot is an example of a typical **Receivables Setup Options** window:

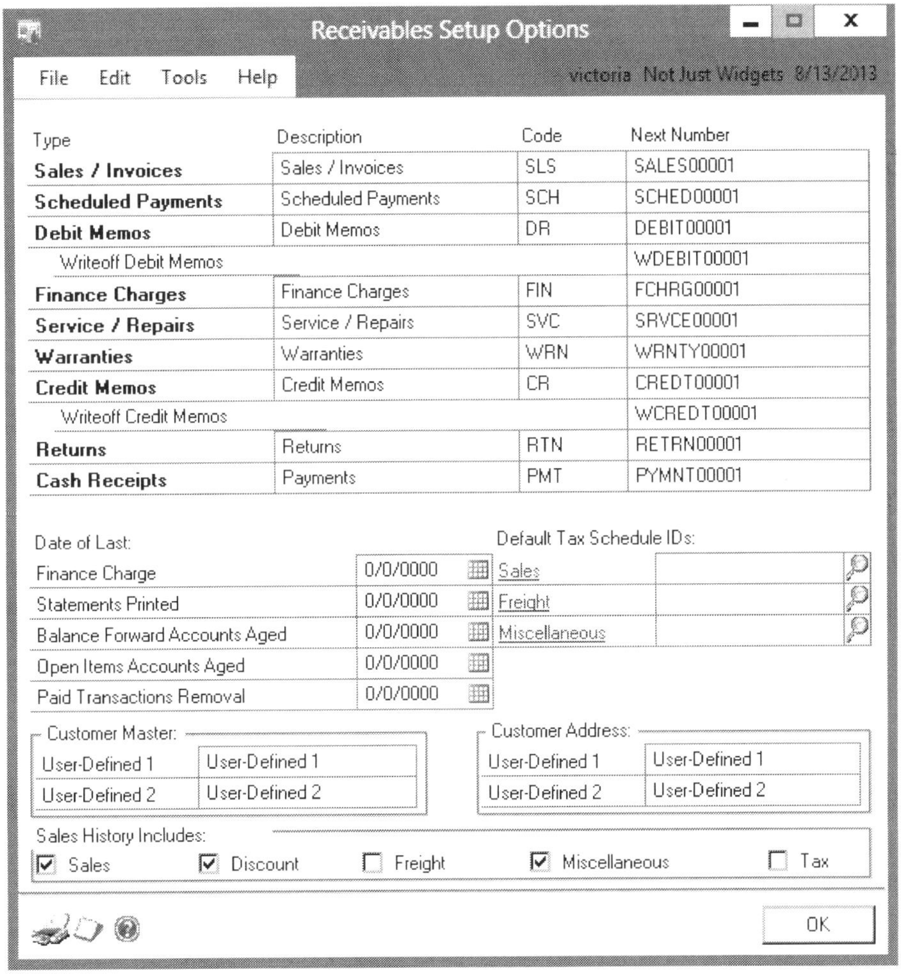

# Sales Territories

**Sales Territories** in Dynamics GP are used for the grouping and reporting of sales transactions. They are not required, but can add another level of available reporting filters and summaries if used. If you are not going to be using sales territories, but want to use **salespeople** in Dynamics GP, you will need to set up one default territory.

To set up a sales territory, navigate to **Cards** | **Sales** | **Sales Territory**. On the **Sales Territory Maintenance** window, the only required field is the **Territory ID**, and the rest are informational only. The **Territory ID** can be up to 15 characters and it is recommended to keep these alphanumeric like other IDs. The lookup available under **Manager** will let you select from salespeople set up in Dynamics GP. All the **Maintain History** checkboxes are marked by default when a new territory is created; it is best to leave these marked in case this history is ever needed.

# Salespeople

Similar to sales territories, salespeople in Dynamics GP are used for the reporting and grouping of sales, as well as calculating commissions. When using the Receivables module to enter sales transactions, salespeople can be assigned per transaction. In the Sales Order Processing module, each line item on a transaction can have a different salesperson. Even if the commissions functionality is not being used in Dynamics GP, it may be helpful to set up all the salespeople in the company so that they can be assigned to transactions for reporting purposes.

To set up salespeople, navigate to **Cards** | **Sales** | **Salesperson**. On the **Salesperson Maintenance** window, the only required fields are **Salesperson ID** and **Territory ID**—this is the reason why you will need at least one sales territory, even if they are not used. If the salesperson is also a vendor or an employee set up in Dynamics GP, you can link the **Salesperson ID** to the **Vendor ID** and/or **Employee ID**. Currently, there is no functionality in Dynamics GP that will use these links for any transactions; it is simply for information and reporting. Similarly, there is a **Commission ID** field that is grayed out and the documentation states that it is for functionality not yet available.

The **Percent** field will determine whether Dynamics GP calculates commissions on sales transactions that are assigned to the Salesperson ID. If a value is entered for **Percent**, General Ledger distributions will be created for Commissions Expense and Commissions Payable accounts on every sales transaction for the salesperson. The **Applied To** setting determines whether the commissions amount is calculated on the **Sales** amount (subtotal, not including any trade discounts, miscellaneous charges, freight, or tax) or the **Total Invoice** amount.

When you create a new salesperson, the **Maintain History** checkboxes will be marked and it is recommended to leave these in case history is needed. The following is an example of a typical **Salesperson Maintenance** window:

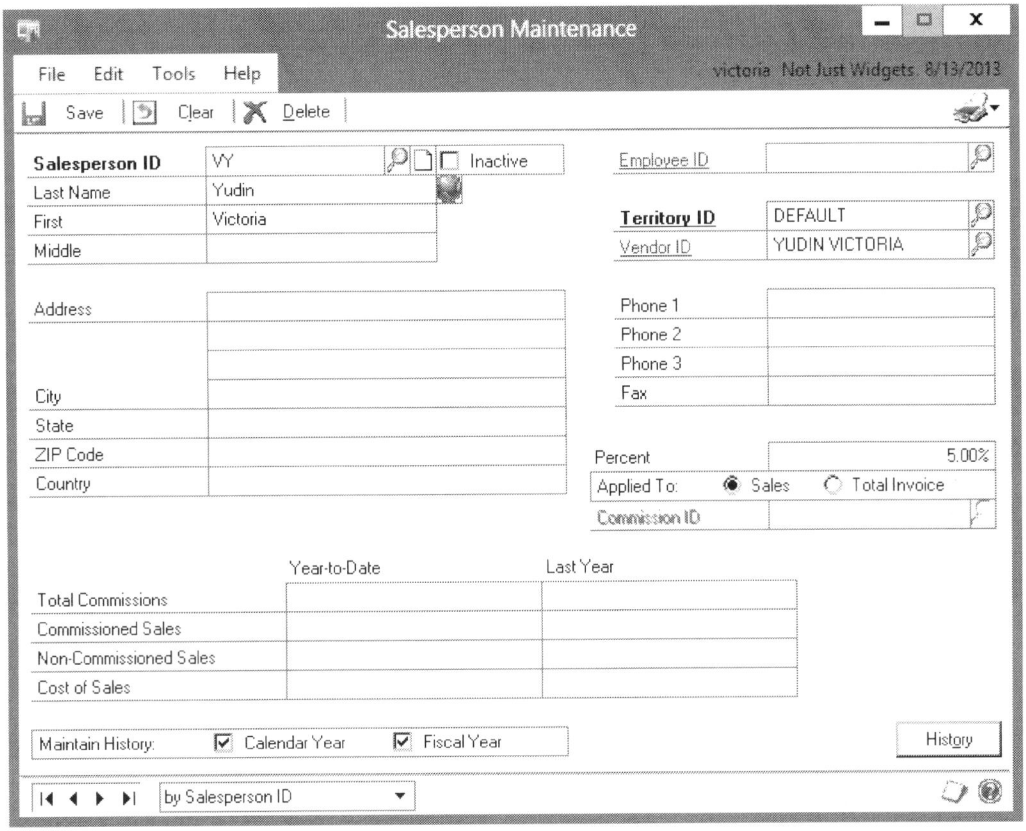


# Price levels

**Price Levels** in Dynamics GP can help automate correct pricing on Sales Order Processing transactions and greatly speed up data entry. A customer is assigned a price level and inventory items can be set up with different prices for each price level. During transaction entry, Dynamics GP will automatically select the item price corresponding to the customer's price level. Price levels and individual item prices can still be changed on any transaction. Using price levels is optional, but you will want to set up a default one, even if you are not going to be using price levels.

To set up price levels, navigate to **Microsoft Dynamics GP** | **Tools** | **Setup** | **Sales** | **Receivables** and click on the **Price Level** hyperlink. The only thing needed to set up a price level is an ID of up to 10 characters. The **Description** is helpful, but optional.

# Customer classes

Customer classes in Dynamics GP are optional, but they are recommended as they offer the following three benefits:

- **Time saved when creating customers**: Classes are used as a template for most of the customer settings, so they can offer significant time savings when creating customers in Dynamics GP.
- **Time saved during customer updates**: Changes to a customer class can be rolled down to all customers in that class, which makes changes to groups of customers significantly faster and easier.
- **Reporting, filtering, and searching**: Most reports and searches in Dynamics GP offer an option to filter by customer class. For example, when printing a Receivables Aged Trial Balance, the customer class or a range of classes can be used as a filter.

To set up customer classes, click on the **Classes** button on the **Receivables Management Setup** window or navigate to **Microsoft Dynamics GP** | **Tools** | **Setup** | **Sales** | **Customer Class**. All the settings for a customer class will be defaulted when a new customer is created with that customer class. Any individual customer setting can be changed at any time, regardless of the customer class assigned. The following list explains the fields on the **Customer Class Setup** window:

- **Class ID**: This is a 10-character ID for the customer class, which cannot be changed once saved. When filtering by customer class on most reports, there will be one to/from range available. If there are certain customer classes that will typically be reported on together, make sure their Class IDs start with the same characters so that they are sorted together in a list. For example, if you have three retail classes and four partner classes, and you will typically want to report on all retail customers separately from all partner customers, you could add the prefixes `R` and `P` to all the Class IDs.
- **Default checkbox**: One customer class can be set as the default class. Once set, newly created classes will copy all the settings from the default class. This can help save time when setting up customer classes that are similar. The default class can be changed at any time by selecting the **Default** checkbox on another class. This will automatically uncheck the **Default** checkbox on the class that was previously the default class.

- **Description**: A description of the customers in this class. This is used to help users identify the proper class to choose when creating customers.
- **Balance Type**: **Open Item** is the balance type most companies use for their customers. This keeps track of all transactions with their individual balances separately. When **Balance Forward** is used as the balance type, transaction details are kept only for transactions that are not yet due and all other transactions are consolidated into one total balance for the customer.
- **Finance Charge**: This setting determines whether customers in the customer class are assessed finance charges and, if yes, whether they are **Percent** or **Amount**.
- **Minimum Payment**: If there is a minimum payment customers must pay, this setting can determine whether it is a **Percent** or **Amount**. The calculated minimum payment based on this setting can be shown on customer statements.
- **Credit Limit**: If a credit limit is set up, users will receive a warning when they enter transactions exceeding the credit limit and will need to type in a password to override the limit if an **Exceed Credit Limit Password** is entered on the **Receivables Setup Options** window (**Microsoft Dynamics GP** | **Tools** | **Setup** | **Sales** | **Receivables**).

  The expansion button (blue arrow) to the right of the **Credit Limit Amount** opens a **Display Credit Limit Warning** window where you can set up additional options for showing a credit limit warning to users during transaction entry, even if the transaction being entered will not exceed the customer's credit limit. This is useful to flag new transactions for customers that are not meeting their payment terms. For example, with the settings shown in the following screenshot, users will see the credit limit warning if a new transaction is going to make the customer's total balance exceed **$10,000**, or if their **31 - 60 Days** and over balance exceeds **$5,000**:

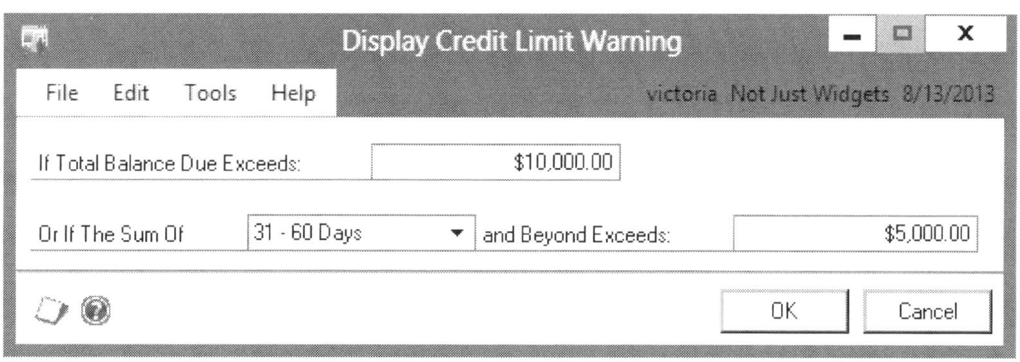

- **Writeoff**: A typical recommendation is to allow users to enter small writeoffs, maybe up to $25, and restrict higher writeoffs with a password that is entered on the **Receivables Setup Options** window (**Microsoft Dynamics GP | Tools | Setup | Sales | Receivables**). If **Not Allowed** is chosen, it may restrict some of the transaction options that users have.
- **Revalue Customer**: Select whether you will be revaluing transactions for customers in this class and, if yes, whether the gain/loss should go to the **Receivables/Discount Account** or the **Sales Offset Account**. **Revalue Customer** is checked by default whether or not you are using the Multicurrency module in Dynamics GP. Leaving it checked when not using Multicurrency will not cause any harm.
- **Order Fulfillment Shortage Default**: Determines the item quantity shortage option that will default on Sales Order Processing transactions. Most companies select **Back Order Remaining** for this option.
- **Trade Discount**: A trade discount is an across-the-board discount on sales, so if a customer has a 5 percent trade discount and you enter a sales transaction for $1,000, a $50 discount will automatically be calculated. Trade discounts are useful in situations where you want to track the discount in a separate General Ledger account or show it separately on an invoice.
- **Payment Terms**: Select the default payment terms for this class of customers.
- **Discount Grace Period** and **Due Date Grace Period**: These work together with the **Use Customer/Vendor Grace Periods for Date/EOM Payment Terms** option on the **Payment Terms Setup** window. You can enter up to 99 days for each of these settings.
- **Salesperson ID**: If you are using salespeople and there is a salesperson that will most often be used for customers in this class, you can enter their **Salesperson ID** here. Typically, the salesperson is set up individually for each customer.
- **Territory ID**: If there is a sales territory that will most often be used for customers in this class, you can select it here.
- **Shipping Method**: Enter a default Shipping Method ID for customers in this class.
- **Tax Schedule ID**: If you are calculating sales taxes and most of the customers in this class use the same Tax Schedule ID, you can enter it here. Unless your customer classes are set up geographically, most often the Tax Schedule ID will be different for each customer and it is easier to leave this blank.
- **Price Level**: Select a default price level for customers in this class.
- **Currency ID** and **Rate Type ID**: Select the default currency and rate type for the customers in this class.

- **Priority**: Priority is an additional grouping available for customers and can be used to determine which customers get orders filled first when automatically allocating inventory for open orders in the Sales Order Processing module. Either **None** or numeric values from **1** to **99** are available for the **Priority** option. If not used for inventory allocation, this is another field that can be used for report filtering or grouping.
- **Statement Cycle**: The statement cycle can be used as a filter when aging receivables transactions or printing customer statements in Dynamics GP. It is unusual for companies to have different statement cycles for different customers but, if it is a need, this setting can be used.
- **Maintain History**: It is recommended to keep all history and leave all the boxes selected for history tracking.

The following screenshot is an example of the **Customer Class Setup** window:

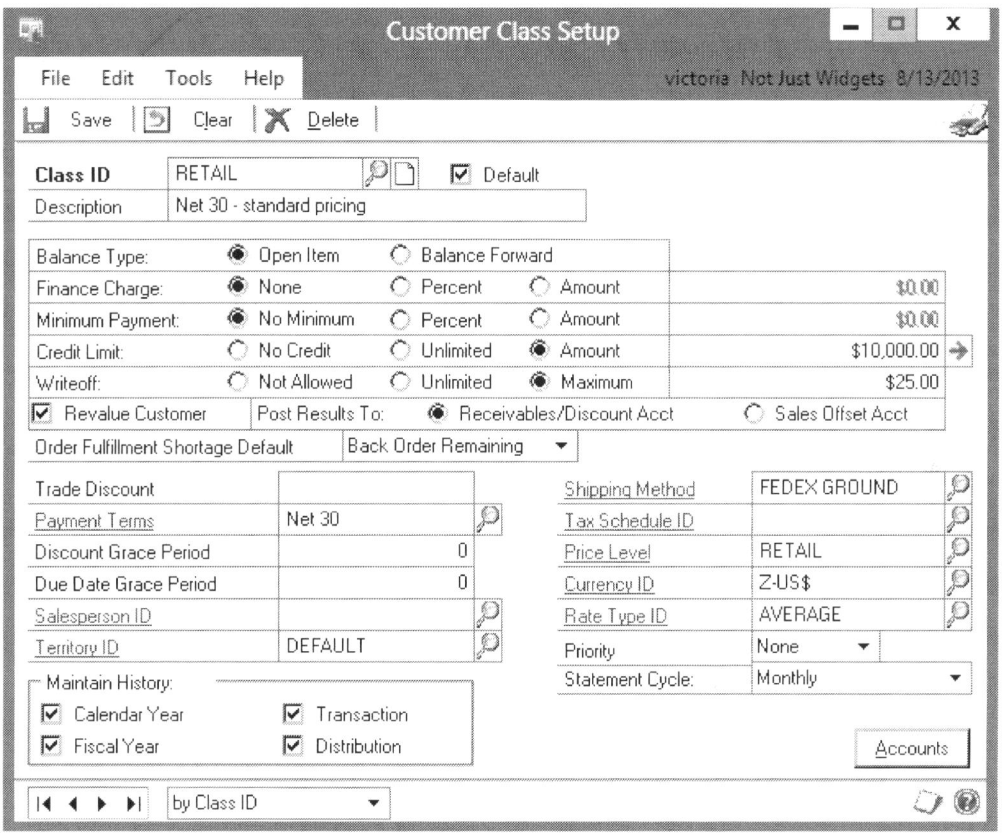


Note that the only required field for a customer class is the Class ID. You can fill in as much or as little detail as you need when setting up a customer class.

# Accounts for customer classes

Clicking on the **Accounts** button on the **Customer Class Setup** window opens the **Customer Class Accounts Setup** window. These accounts are the defaults that will be used for receivables transactions and it is recommended to set these up to save time when creating customers.

If these accounts are the same for all customers in the company, it may be easier to set them up on the **Posting Accounts Setup** window instead (**Microsoft Dynamics GP | Tools | Setup | Posting | Posting Accounts**).

Dynamics GP determines GL accounts to use for receivables transactions using the following logic:

1. Use accounts set up for the customer. These accounts will default from the customer class when a customer is being created, but can be changed for each individual customer.
2. If any accounts are missing from customer setup, use posting accounts for the company (**Microsoft Dynamics GP | Tools | Setup | Posting | Posting Accounts**).
3. If any accounts are still missing, leave the accounts blank. Transactions will give a warning and will not post if any required GL accounts are missing.

> Note that at no time do any transactions in Dynamics GP look at the customer class to determine what accounts to use. The accounts at the class level are only helpful as defaults when creating customers.

Some accounts may never be used for your Dynamics GP implementation. For example, if you are not tracking discounts available in the GL, there is no reason to set up a **Terms Discounts Available** account. However, it is recommended to fill in as many accounts as may be used on transactions to save time and effort during transaction entry.

The **Customer Class Accounts Setup** window also has an option to set up a Checkbook ID. This setting can be useful if you are using multiple bank accounts and certain customer payments always go into one bank account, while others go to a different bank account. If there is one main checkbook used by the company, leave this blank and instead select a default **Checkbook ID** on the **Receivables Management Setup** window. That way, any changes in the future will only need to be made in one place. It is recommended to leave the **Cash Account from** setting on **Checkbook** to avoid bank reconciliation issues.

# Sales e-mail settings

If you would like to use Dynamics GP to send e-mail to customers, you will need to set up Sales e-mail options.

Navigate to **Microsoft Dynamics GP | Tools | Setup | Sales | E-mail Settings**. The **Sales E-mail Setup** window controls e-mail settings for both the Receivables and Sales Order Processing modules. You only need to enable e-mailing for documents you are using and these can be changed at any time.

> You will need to be on a computer that has an e-mail client to be able to access the **Sales E-mail Setup** window.

Select the checkbox next to each document type that you would like to allow e-mailing and choose a default **Message ID** for each. Messages allow you to predefine the subject and text of the e-mail that will be generated by Dynamics GP. You can set up a new message by typing in a **Message ID** and answering **Yes** to the pop-up window asking if you would like to add this Message ID, or by navigating to **Microsoft Dynamics GP | Tools | Setup | Company | E-mail Message Setup**.

On the **Message Setup** window:

1. Specify a **Message ID**—maximum length is 25 characters.
2. Enter a **Description**—maximum length is 150 characters.
3. Select **Sales** under **Series**.
4. Select the appropriate option from the **Doc. Type** drop-down list.
5. Enter a **Subject** and a **Body** for your message. The **Subject** can be up to 150 characters, the **Body** will allow up to 32,000 characters.

   You can use the **Field** drop-down list under the Body section to add global fields like SOP Number or the customer's name into the **Subject** or **Body** of your email message. To do this, select the **Field** from the drop-down list, position your cursor where you want to add the field and click on **Insert**. Click on the **Validate** button to make sure the fields you have selected match the document type assigned to the message.

6. **Have Replies Sent** to will default from the **Sales E-mail Setup** window, but can be changed for each individual message.

Back on the **Sales E-mail Setup** window, you can enter a default reply to e-mail address by typing it under **Have Replies Sent to** or clicking on the **Select Names** button to open your Outlook Address Book. Multiple e-mail addresses should be separated by semicolons. You can also select whether to **Allow Changing 'Reply to' Address at Entry** and **Allow Update of E-mail at Entry** of transactions.

Clicking on the **Customer Setup** button at the bottom will open the customer navigation list showing all your customers. You can search and filter your customers, then click on the overflow button (>>) in the **Modify** section, and select **E-mail Settings**.

This will open the **Mass Customer E-mail Settings** window, where you can define e-mail settings for all the customers you selected on the navigation list. These settings can also be changed individually for every customer.

# Customers

The final step in the Receivables module setup in Dynamics GP is creating customers. If you have many customers, you may decide to import them. However, it is still valuable to know how to set up or change customers manually. Creating a customer includes customer setup, customer accounts, customer options, and customer e-mail addresses and options.

## Customer setup

To create a customer, navigate to **Cards** | **Sales** | **Customer**. The following list explains the fields on the **Customer Maintenance** window. Please note that some of these fields have already been explained in detail in the *Customer classes* section above:

- **Customer ID**: This is the ID that will be used to identify the customer throughout Dynamics GP and it can be up to 15 characters.
- **Hold**: A customer can be put on hold at any time. You can enter payments or apply existing payments for a customer that is on hold, but cannot enter any other sales transactions. If a password was set up for **Remove Customer Hold** on the **Receivables Management Setup** window, then users will need to enter that password before being able to enter any sales transaction other than a payment for a customer on hold. If no password is set up, the user will get a warning, which they can click through, when entering a transaction for a customer on hold.

> Note that this password is not required to actually take customers off hold—anyone with access to the **Customer Maintenance** window can do that.

- **Inactive**: Any customer with no open or unposted transactions can be made inactive by selecting this checkbox. No transactions can be entered for inactive customers. This option is useful when you stop working with a customer and want to prevent users from inadvertently choosing the customer on a transaction, or you want to be able to exclude them from searches.
- **Name**: The name that will appear for the customer throughout Dynamics GP. This is the name that will default on customer invoices and other reports.

> New functionality in Dynamics GP 2013 allows having a different ship to company name for each address for a customer. This can be set up on the **Customer Address Maintenance** window, opened by clicking on the **Address** button or any of the address hyperlinks on the **Customer Maintenance** window.

- **Short Name**: This field is not really used by Dynamics GP and will default to the first 15 characters of the **Name**. Some companies use this to store other information about their customers for report filtering or sorting.
- **Statement Name**: This is the customer name that will default on statements printed from Dynamics GP. When setting up a customer, this will default to be the same as the **Name**.
- **Address ID section**: The address on the **Customer Maintenance** window is typically the primary address for the customer. Additional addresses for the customer can be entered by clicking on the **Address** button at the bottom of the window.

> Even though there are three lines available for the **Address**, only the first two address lines will appear on out-of-the-box reports in Dynamics GP. To show the third address line, reports would need to be customized.

- **Ship To**: This will default as the **Ship To** address on all transactions for the customer.

- **Bill To**: This will default as the **Bill To** address on all transactions for the customer.
- **Statement To**: This will default as the address on the customer statement.
- **Salesperson ID**: This is the primary salesperson for the customer. If there is a salesperson in charge of the customer, you can enter their ID here. If the salesperson changes on every transaction, it may be best to leave this blank. If the salesperson depends on the shipping address, you can add the **Salesperson ID** to each individual address you set up for the customer.
- **Territory ID**: If you have entered a **Salesperson ID**, the **Territory ID** assigned to that salesperson will default in. This is simply to speed up data entry; you can change the **Territory ID** as needed.
- **User-Defined 1** and **User-Defined 2**: These fields can track any additional information you would like for the customer. Each can store up to 20 characters and their labels can be changed on the **Receivables Management Setup** window (**Microsoft Dynamics GP** | **Tools** | **Setup** | **Sales** | **Receivables** | **Options** button).

> The **User-Defined 1** field can be used as a filter on the Receivables Trial Balance reports in Dynamics GP.

- **Parent Customer ID**: This field is used by the **National Accounts** module and is not editable on the **Customer Maintenance** window.
- **Class ID**: Select the **Class ID** for this customer. Classes are optional, but they can speed up setup and simplify reporting. When a new customer is created and a class is selected, all the settings from the class are defaulted in for the customer. While creating a new customer, any of the settings that have already been selected manually will be overwritten with settings from the class. For existing customers, a pop up message will ask whether you want to update the customer settings with the information from the class.
- **Priority**: Optionally, select a priority for this customer.
- **Phone** and **Fax** numbers: Enter any phone or fax numbers you want to track for the customer. Note that the fields are hard coded for the North American phone format with a four-digit extension. For international phone numbers or longer extensions, many companies use the **Comment 1** and **Comment 2** fields or the customer note.

- **UPS Zone**: Not too many companies need to track the UPS zone anymore, but some use this field to store an `R` for residential or `C` for commercial addresses, which may be needed by various shipping software. This field is specific to the primary address on this window and each customer **Address ID** will have its own **UPS Zone** field.
- **Shipping Method**: Select the default Shipping Method ID for the customer's primary address. Each customer address has its own shipping method which can also be changed during transaction entry.
- **Tax Schedule ID**: This is the Tax Schedule ID for the primary customer address on this window. Each address can have a different Tax Schedule ID assigned and the taxes can be changed manually on each transaction.
- **Ship Complete Documents**: This checkbox is for the Sales Order Processing module. If selected, partially-filled orders will not transfer to invoices for this customer. This setting can be overridden on each individual Sales Order Processing transaction.
- **Comment 1** and **Comment 2**: These are additional fields available to track information about a customer. They can store up to 30 characters each.
- **Trade Discount**: Enter a default trade discount percentage for the customer.
- **Payment Terms**: Enter the default payment terms for the customer.
- **Discount Grace Period** and **Due Date Grace Period**: These work together with the **Use Customer/Vendor Grace Periods for Date/EOM Payment Terms** option on the **Payment Terms Setup** window. You can enter up to 99 days for each of these settings.
- **Price Level**: Enter the default price level for the customer—this will be used in the Sales Order Processing module.

The following is an example of the **Customer Maintenance** window:

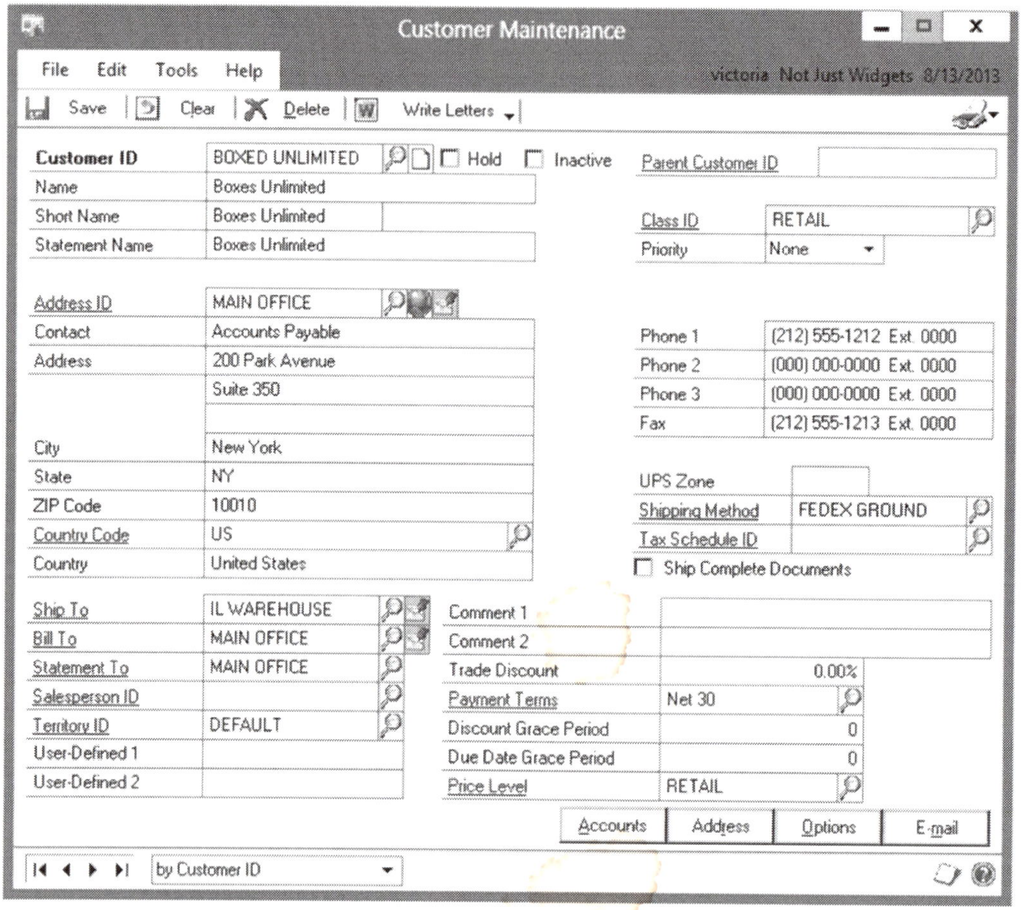


## Customer accounts

Clicking on the **Accounts** button at the bottom of the **Customer Maintenance** window will open the **Customer Account Maintenance** window, where you can set up any General Ledger accounts that are specific to this customer. While account numbers can be changed during transaction entry, it is recommended to have as many accounts as possible default on transactions so that Dynamics GP users do not need to change or add GL distributions manually.

The accounts on the **Customer Account Maintenance** window will be the first ones Dynamics GP looks to use for any receivables transactions. If any accounts are not set up, the posting accounts for the company will be used (**Microsoft Dynamics GP** | **Tools** | **Setup** | **Posting** | **Posting Accounts**).

For any customer assigned to a customer class, the accounts on the **Customer Account Maintenance** window will default from the class settings. If an account for all customers in a class needs to be changed, the change can be made to the class and then rolled down to all customers in that class.

## Customer options

To open the **Customer Maintenance Options** window, click on the **Options** button at the bottom of the **Customer Maintenance** window. Many of the settings on this window are also found on the **Customer Class Setup** window and will all default in when a customer is assigned a **Class ID**. Any of these settings can be changed for an individual customer.

Fields on the **Customer Maintenance Options** window that were not covered in the *Customer classes* section are:

- **Credit Card ID**: If credit cards are used for payment by this customer, you can enter a Credit Card ID that will default onto payment transactions entered for this customer.
- **Credit Card Number**: Anything entered here is stored in plain text, so it is not recommended to enter credit card numbers in this field.
- **Expiration Date**: Expiration date for the credit card entered here. Be careful using this, as many credit card processors now forbid storing customer credit card expiration dates.
- **Bank Name** and **Bank Branch**: These can store the customer's bank and branch—these are not typically used.
- **Language**: This is an informational field that becomes available if you have set up languages for your Dynamics GP system (**Microsoft Dynamics GP** | **Tools** | **Setup** | **System** | **Language**).
- **Tax Exempt 1**, **Tax Exempt 2**, and **Tax Registration**: If you need to track tax exemption numbers for customers, they can be entered in any of these three fields.
- **Send E-mail Statements**: If you are going to use the Dynamics GP built-in routine for sending customer statements, check this box for any customer that should be included when sending statements. Clicking on the **To**, **Cc**, and **Bcc** buttons will open your Outlook Address Book to allow you to select contacts for each. Alternatively, you can enter e-mail addresses separated by semicolons.

## Customer e-mail settings

To enable e-mailing documents other than statements to customers, first set up e-mail addresses for the customer by clicking on the **Internet Information** icon to the right of the **Address ID**:

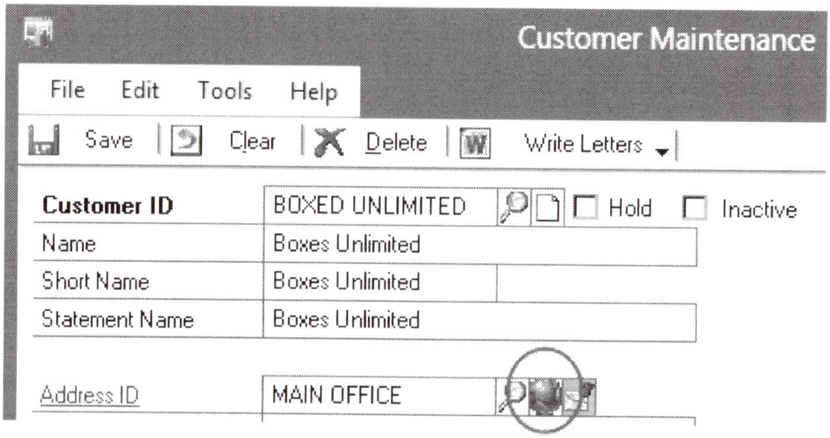


Clicking on the **To**, **Cc**, and **Bcc** buttons on the **Internet Information** window will open your Outlook Address Book, where you can choose from your contacts, or you can type in e-mail addresses separated by semicolons. Every address for a customer will have a separate set of e-mail addresses. Invoices will use the e-mail addresses set up on the Bill To address of the invoice.

To set up e-mail options for the customer, click on the **E-mail** button at the bottom of the **Customer Maintenance** window. This will open the **Customer E-mail Options** window where you can decide on **Attachment Options** and **Size**, enable what **Forms** (documents) can be e-mailed to this customer, and select a **Format** for each. When **Forms** are enabled, the **Message ID** from the **Sales E-mail Setup** window will default in. Note that only the **HTML Format** will work for sending Dynamics GP standard Report Writer reports. To use any of the other formats requires setting up Word templates for Dynamics GP or using a third party product to e-mail documents.

With the Receivables module setup completed and customers created, receivables transactions can now be entered into Dynamics GP.

# Summary

In this chapter, we have described how to set up the General Ledger, Bank Reconciliation, Payables, and Receivables modules. Creating General Ledger accounts, checkbooks, vendors, and customers were discussed in detail. At this point, Dynamics GP can be used to import or create additional GL accounts, customers, and vendors; transactions can also be entered or imported into the system. In the next chapter, we will discuss the setup of additional core Dynamics GP modules.

# 8
# Module Setup – Inventory, SOP, and POP

**Inventory**, **Sales Order Processing** (**SOP**), and **Purchase Order Processing** (**POP**) are commonly referred to as the **Distribution Modules**. These modules integrate with each other and are the modules where the transactions pertaining to inventory quantities and costs, purchases, sales, and transfers are entered.

Dynamics GP offers a great deal of options and additional modules surrounding these core distribution modules. Some very advanced workflows and functionality can be achieved with the additional modules available. For the purpose of this book, we will assume a non-complex distribution environment and go over the basic steps to set up these modules. If advanced distribution functionality is needed, consult with your Dynamics GP resource to make sure you are implementing all the modules you need to accomplish your goals, as well as activating the correct functionality for each module.

In this chapter we will cover basic setup for the following modules:

- Inventory Control
- Sales Order Processing (SOP)
- Purchase Order Processing (POP)

Detailed menu navigation will be provided for each setup window, or you can keep using the setup checklist (**Microsoft Dynamics GP** | **Tools** | **Setup** | **Setup Checklist**).

Typically, each module will have an overall setup window, where global settings and options are chosen, and a few additional windows where the basic objects or templates for the module are set up.

All distribution module settings are company specific. If you have multiple companies in Dynamics GP, you will need to set up each module in each company separately. This is often advantageous, as different companies may require different settings for various features. If you would like to copy module setup from one company to another, Microsoft Dynamics GP KnowledgeBase article 872709 describes how to do this: `https://mbs.microsoft.com/knowledgebase/KBDisplay.aspx?scid=kb;en-us;872709` (CustomerSource or PartnerSource login required). There is also a Company Copy tool available as part of the Professional Services Tools Library; you can read more about this in *Chapter 10, Training, Tools, and Next Steps*.

# Inventory

The Inventory module (also called **Inventory Control**) is a logical place to start setting up the distribution modules, as they all center on the inventory items. Inventory menu options will be under the **Inventory** series, and the SQL Server tables for the Inventory module will start with `IV`.

One common misconception is that the Inventory module is needed only if your company is selling physical goods and needs to track the number of items in stock. In reality, the Dynamics GP Inventory module can also be used in many other situations. The following are two examples of non-conventional inventory uses:

- **Selling services**: A company that sells services to customers can greatly speed up data entry and accuracy, as well as facilitate more meaningful reporting, by setting up each service as an inventory item that does not track quantities. If the services are priced differently for each customer, different price levels can be set up and coded for the respective customers. If sales of different services are tracked in their own GL sales accounts, each item can be coded for the appropriate account. All of this will help ensure that users entering sales transactions can do so with minimal effort and possibility of error.
- **Keeping track of internal use items**: A company that buys large quantities of internally used products may want to know how many items are "in stock" at any time and to charge the expenses to the appropriate internal departments or projects, as the products are used. The items in this case may be stationery and office supplies, or various equipment and materials used in the normal course of business. Setting up the internally used items as inventory items allows for standardization as well as easier integration with the Purchase Order Processing module. It also allows for accurate tracking of expenses incurred by departments and quick visibility into what is in stock.

The setup of the Dynamics GP Inventory module includes the following topics:

- Inventory Control Setup
- Inventory sites
- Unit of Measure schedules
- Item classes
- Inventory item setup

# Inventory Control Setup

To start setting up the Inventory module, navigate to **Microsoft Dynamics GP** | **Tools** | **Setup** | **Inventory** | **Inventory Control**. On the **Inventory Control Setup** window you can set up defaults for the next transaction numbers, set up user categories, and choose a number of additional global settings. The following are explanations of the fields on this window:

- **User Category**: Dynamics GP allows for six user-defined categories to be tracked for inventory items to facilitate reporting and analysis. For example, Not Just Widgets sells software, hardware, and services. They may want to set up a category called **Type** that will hold the values **Hardware**, **Software**, or **Services**. Once you type a category name into one of the **User Category** fields, you can click on the expansion button (blue arrow) next to **User Category** to open the **Item Category Setup** window, where you can fill in the values available for that category:

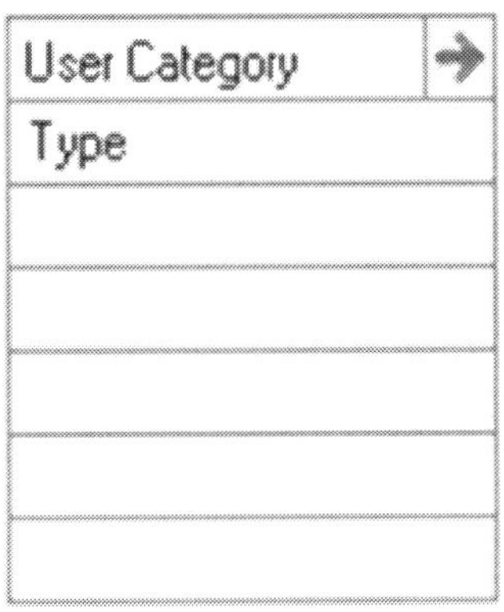


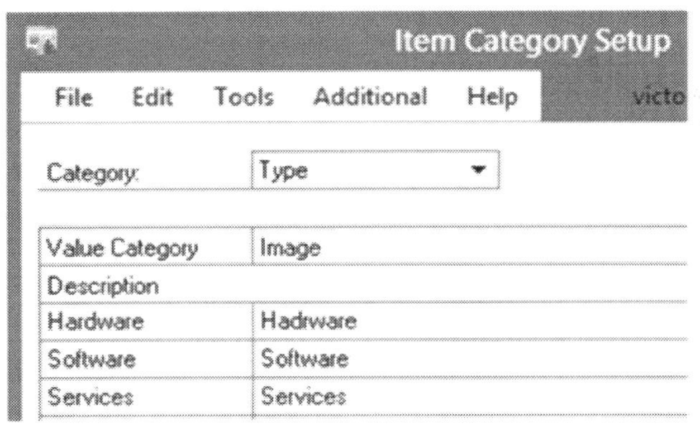

- **Next Document Numbers**: These are the default values for the next available number for each transaction type in the Inventory module. It is recommended to remove some of the zeros to make transaction numbers easier to work with. Keep in mind that these numbers will not automatically increase in size; if the last transaction number was `9999`, the next one will be `0000` and not `10000`. In case you are wondering what a **Production** transaction is, according to the documentation this is for functionality not yet added to Dynamics GP.
- **Segment ID for Sites**: If you intend to use multiple inventory sites (or warehouses) and have different GL accounts that will be used depending on which inventory site is used on a transaction, this setting can help set up Dynamics GP to automatically select the appropriate account number.

  This can be useful in the following scenario:

  Sales from NJ should go to GL account `4000-01-000` and sales from NY go to GL account `4000-05-000`. In that case the **Segment ID for Sites** should be `Segment 2`. When setting up the default Sales account, `4000-00-000` can be used and Dynamics GP will automatically substitute `01` or `05` for the second segment, depending on which site is chosen on every transaction.

> It may be tempting to leave this field blank until such time as this type of functionality may be needed. Unfortunately, without this filled in, you will not be able to create inventory sites in Dynamics GP, which are required to enter transactions for inventory items. Once the first site is created, this setting can no longer be changed.

- **Via Site ID**: Dynamics GP offers the ability to set up an "In-Transit" inventory site, so that if there is a time delay during the transfer of items from one site to another, inventory cannot be sold while it is in transit and there is greater visibility of the items in transit. If you would like to use this functionality, you will need to come back to this window to fill in a **Site ID** after you have created the inventory site you want to use for this.
- **Default Decimal Places**: These are defaults for the number of decimal places for **Quantities** and **Currency** amounts for newly created inventory items. These can be changed for each item created; however, it may be helpful to pick the most commonly used values here. Because there is only one option for **Currency** decimal places on this window, if you have enabled the Multicurrency module, the **Currency** option will be disabled here and will instead be available when setting up individual items or item classes.

- **Allow**: Leaving these options checked allows users to override quantity shortages when entering **Inventory Adjustments**, **Variances**, or **Transfers**. Most of the time, if companies are tracking quantities and want to ensure timely entry of inventory receipts, these should be unchecked. However, there are times when shortages need to be allowed. These settings can be changed at any time.
- **Enable Multiple Bins**: Multiple bins are available in Dynamics GP to allow tracking quantities in multiple locations within one site/warehouse. If you need multiple bins, it is best to perform the setup prior to entering inventory transactions. Multiple bins are explained further in *Chapter 1*, *Overview* of the *Inventory Control* manual. (This manual can be downloaded at: `http://technet.microsoft.com/en-us/library/jj673202(v=gp.30).aspx`.)
- **Enable Picking Shortage Tasks**: With this option selected and a GP **User ID** specified under **Assign To**, when a transaction is entered that would cause an inventory shortage, a task will automatically be created in Dynamics GP for the specified user to deal with the shortage.
- **Autopost Stock Count Variances**: When a stock count is processed, a variance transaction will be created for any differences in quantities. With this option selected, the variance transaction will be posted automatically to the Inventory subledger. This setting can also be changed for each individual stock count, so it is not critical.
- **Use Existing Serial/Lot Numbers Only on Decrease and Transfer Transactions**: With this option selected, a user will not be able to create a new lot or serial number when entering a decrease adjustment or transfer transaction. It is typically recommended to leave this marked so that phantom serial and lot numbers are not created inadvertently.
- **Auto-assign Lot Numbers Based on**: The choice made here will determine which lot number is auto-assigned when entering transactions such as sales orders or invoices. The choices are oldest **Receipt Date** or **Expiration Date**. Users can override lot numbers during transaction entry.
- **Display Cost for Decrease Adjustments**: Unchecking this option would show the cost for items as zero on any decrease adjustments.

> This option is not as useful as it sounds because when an item is selected during transaction entry it automatically shows the cost, only when changing the quantity to a negative would the cost clear to zero.

- **Use Expired Lots in**: Decide whether lot numbers that have expired can be used on **Inventory Adjustments and Transfers** and/or **Other Transactions** and choose a **Password** for one or both. Note that the passwords are not masked, so anyone who should not be able to see or change them should not have access to this window. If an option is allowed and no **Password** is selected, any user will be able to use an expired lot.

The following screenshot illustrates a sample **Inventory Control Setup** window:

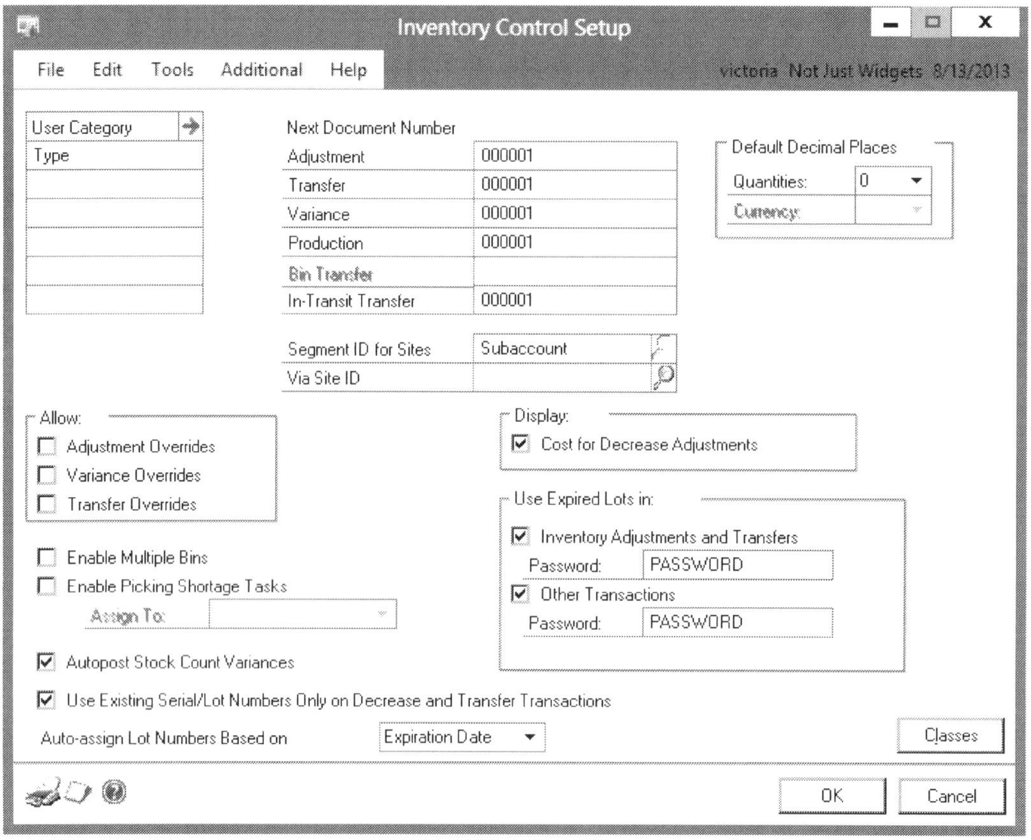


# Inventory sites

**Sites**, sometimes referred to as **Locations**, are Dynamics GP terminology for warehouses or individual locations where you may want to track inventory. You can set up as many sites as you like. However, even if you are not storing any inventory or keeping track of quantities, you must set up at least one inventory site.

To open the **Site Maintenance** window, navigate to **Cards** | **Inventory** | **Site**. The only required fields for creating a new site are a **Site ID** (maximum of 10 characters) and a **Description**, which is a more user-friendly name for Dynamics GP users to identify sites from a list. If you are using the **Segment ID for Sites** functionality described in the previous section, you should also fill in the **Account Segment ID** field at the bottom-left of the window.

The following is a typical **Site Maintenance** window:

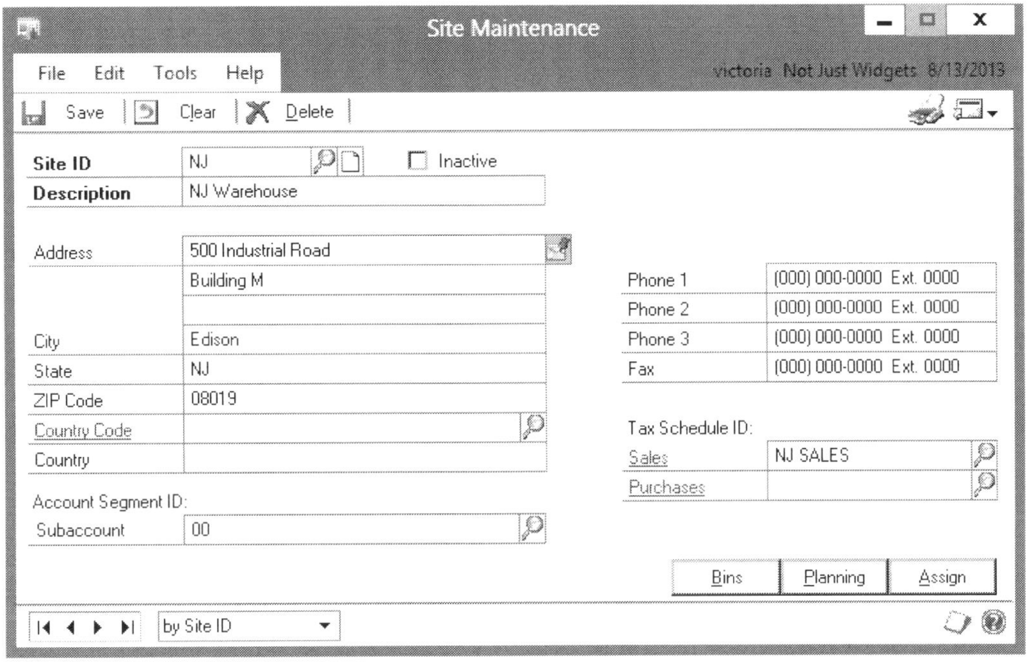


Dynamics GP allows flexible setup of item and site combinations. For example, there may be certain products that are only sold from one warehouse. In that case, you can restrict those items to one site during setup, thus limiting the chances of users mis-keying the **Site ID** during transaction entry. In practice, many companies simply assign all items to each of their sites. Once inventory items have been created, you can return to the **Site Maintenance** window to mass assign all or a range of items to one site at a time by using the **Assign** button.

# Unit of Measure schedules

**Unit of Measure Schedules** in Dynamics GP allow you to set up items that can be purchased or sold in different quantities. For example, you may buy wine in cases, but sell it in half cases or individual bottles. In this scenario, the unit of measure schedule may look like the following screenshot:

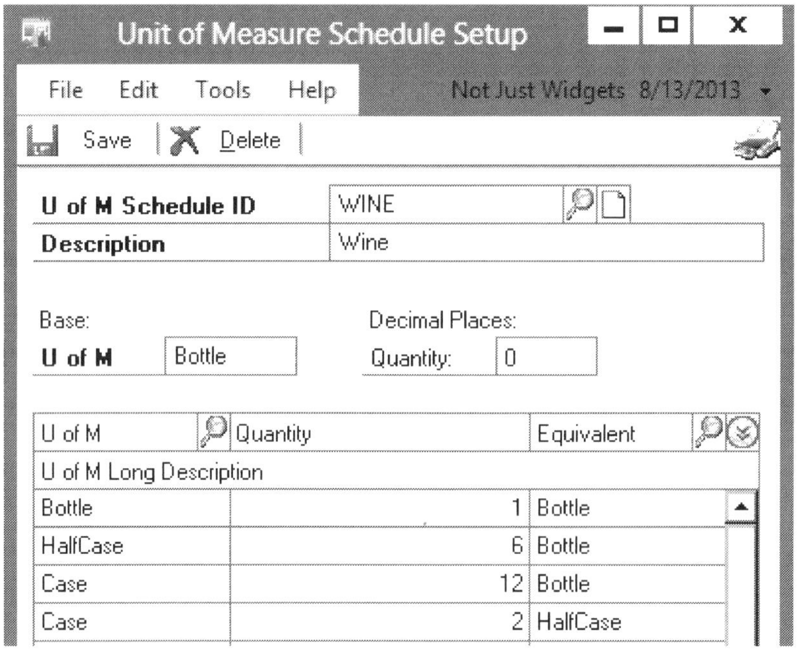


Each unit of measure (often abbreviated **U of M**) for an item can have a separate price, and an item can be set up with default units of measure for purchasing and sales transactions to speed up data entry.

To create a unit of measure schedule perform the following steps:

1. Navigate to **Microsoft Dynamics GP** | **Tools** | **Setup** | **Inventory** | **Unit of Measure Schedule** to open the **Unit of Measure Schedule Setup** window.
2. Enter a **U of M Schedule ID**. This can be up to 10 characters and cannot be changed afterwards.
3. Enter a **Description** that will help users select the proper U of M schedule; this is a required field.
4. Select a **Decimal Places Quantity** for the items that will use this U of M schedule. If you are changing the number of decimal places, do so before entering the **Base U of M**, otherwise you will have to delete and start over.

5. Decide on a **Base U of M**. This will be what inventory is tracked by and will be the unit of measure shown on most reports and inquiries in Dynamics GP.
6. The **Base U of M** will automatically be populated on the first line of the **U of M** scrolling list. Enter additional **U of M** values, **Quantities**, and **Equivalents** as desired. You can add to this list later, if needed.

> Note that every new **U of M** must first be defined in the Base **U of M**. So in the previous example, the **Case** had to be defined as **12** bottles before it could be defined as **2** half cases.

7. Optionally, you can add **U of M Long Descriptions**; these are not used by Dynamics GP but could be added to modified or custom invoices or purchase orders.

The **Copy** button at the bottom of the **Unit of Measure Schedule Setup** window can be used to create copies of existing U of M schedules. To use it, enter a new **U of M Schedule ID**, click on **Copy**, and select the U of M schedule to copy from.

There is no limit on how many unit of measure schedules you can have—some companies have one for each item, others use one for all their inventory items.

> To be able to use inventory items, at least one U of M schedule must exist.

# Item classes

Similar to customer and vendor classes, item classes are optional, but they are recommended for the following three benefits:

- **Time saved when creating items**: Classes serve as a template for many of the item settings, so they can offer significant time-savings when creating new items in Dynamics GP.
- **Time saved during item updates**: Changes to the item class can be rolled down to all items in that class, making changes to groups of items quick and easy. Note that for inventory items there are some settings, such as valuation method that cannot be changed. In that case, changes made to the class will apply only to newly created items in that class.
- **Reporting, filtering, and searching**: Most reports and searches in Dynamics GP offer an option to filter by item class. For example, when generating a list of items in stock, it may make the list much more manageable and useful to be able to filter by item class.

To open the **Item Class Setup** window, navigate to **Microsoft Dynamics GP | Tools | Setup | Inventory | Item Class**. All the settings for an item class will be defaulted when a new item is created and assigned that item class; however, they can all be changed as needed for individual items. The following are descriptions of the fields on the **Item Class Setup** window:

- **Class ID**: A 10-character ID that cannot be changed once the item class is saved.
- **Default checkbox**: One item class can be set as the default class. Once set, newly created classes will copy all the settings from the default class. This can help save time when setting up multiple item classes that are similar. The default class can be changed at any time by selecting the **Default** checkbox for a different class. This will automatically uncheck the **Default** checkbox for the class that was previously the default.
- **Description**: A description of what items are in this class. This is used to help users identify the proper item class during item creation.
- **Generic Description**: An additional 10-character description field for items—this can be another report filter or search criteria.
- **Item Type**: There are six item types available in Dynamics GP and choosing the right one for each item is critical, as this cannot be changed easily after transactions have been entered for an item. The available item types are listed in the following table. **Costs posted** means that when a transaction with this item type is posted in Sales Order Processing, the cost of the item will credit the Inventory General Ledger account and debit the Cost of Goods GL account.

| Item type | Quantities tracked | Costs posted | Notes |
|---|---|---|---|
| **Sales Inventory** | Yes | Yes | This is the most common item type, used for products kept in stock. This can also be used for services that are bought from others and resold to customers if the costs of these need to be tracked and posted with the sales transaction. |
| **Discontinued** | Yes | Yes | When an item reaches the end of its life, the type can be changed from **Sales Inventory** to **Discontinued** to prevent users from creating new purchase orders for it and to filter it out of searches and reports. |

| Item type | Quantities tracked | Costs posted | Notes |
|---|---|---|---|
| **Kit** | No<br>(see notes) | No<br>(see notes) | Kits are a combination of any other item types that are not actually assembled prior to the sale. Consider a store promotion that offers a discounted price for two items bought together. Each item is on a different shelf and can be bought separately. However, together these items have a special price. A Kit allows you to set up that scenario in Dynamics GP. Quantities are tracked and costs are posted only for Sales Inventory and Discontinued Items within a Kit. |
| **Miscellaneous Charges** | No | No | This is typically used for one-time charges and items that are not stocked. |
| **Services** | No | No | This is the typical item type used for any type of service that is performed by internal employees or outside consultants. |
| **Flat Fee** | No | No | Similar to **Services**, but almost never used, as it has some additional limitations when posting. |

- **Valuation Method**: This is a critical setting that determines how costs for items are calculated. The available options are:

| Valuation method | Details |
|---|---|
| **FIFO Perpetual** | This is the most commonly used valuation method. Inventory is valued at actual cost using First In, First Out. |
| **LIFO Perpetual** | Inventory is valued at actual cost using Last In, First Out. |
| **Average Perpetual** | Every increase in inventory causes the cost for all items in stock to be recalculated. This is also referred to as Weighted Moving Average and is the second most commonly used valuation method in my experience. |
| **FIFO Periodic** | Inventory is valued at Standard Cost, which can be adjusted manually as needed or automatically during the year-end closing for the Inventory module. The method used is First in, First Out. |
| **LIFO Periodic** | Inventory is valued at Standard Cost, which can be adjusted manually as needed or automatically during the year-end closing for the Inventory module. The method used is Last In, First Out. |

The valuation method you select will typically be governed by accounting guidelines in your country and for your industry. In most cases all items within the same company will have the same valuation method.

> The valuation method is not something that should be changed simply because you are changing accounting software, as there are tax implications to consider. If you are not sure what method should be used, consult with the company's CPA or auditor for help on this.

- **Track**: Dynamics GP offers the ability to track either **Serial Numbers** or **Lot Numbers** for items. Note that only one or the other can be tracked for an item, as both serial and lot numbers are actually stored in the same field. If you do not want to track either, you can select **None**. Lot or serial number tracking can be turned on after the item is created, but only when there is no on-hand quantity for the item and it is not on any open transactions.
- If **Lot Numbers** are selected under **Track**, you can select a default **Lot Category** and whether to **Warn** if **Days before lot expires** are within the specified number.

> Lot Categories can be set up to track different lot attributes for different types of items. For example, you might want to track receipt or manufacture dates for non-perishable items and expiration dates for perishable items.

- **Sales Tax Option**: If the items in this class are not taxed, choose **Nontaxable**. If the items are taxed depending on the customer tax setup, choose **Base on customers**. There are certain items that may be taxed in some states or localities, but not in others; in that case, you can set up a special tax schedule that contains all the tax details for locations where this item it taxed. Select **Taxable**, in the **Sales Tax Option** field, which will enable the **Tax Schedule ID** field where you can select the special tax schedule you have created.

  Recall from previous chapters that taxes in Dynamics GP are determined by the intersection of all the tax schedules, as well as the shipping method type of a transaction.

- **Allow Back Orders**: Select this option if you want to allow back ordering items in this class. If back orders are not allowed, sales orders can only be entered for quantities on hand.

- **Revalue Inventory for Cost Variance**: This setting determines how the Purchase Order Processing module treats differences between received and invoiced inventory cost. If the inventory has not been sold yet, the cost of the inventory is adjusted for the difference if **Revalue Inventory for Cost Variance** is selected. If the inventory has already been sold, the cost of the goods sold can be adjusted. Here is an example:
    - You order an item priced at $2,000.
    - You receive the item and enter a purchasing receipt transaction into Dynamics GP; at this time, as far as you know, the cost of the item is $2,000.
    - You sell the item to a customer for $3,000. When the sales invoice is posted, the Cost of Goods posted to the GL is $2,000.
    - Now you receive the vendor invoice and it is actually for $1,950 – the item cost decreased by $50.
    - When you enter the vendor invoice into Dynamics GP, you have two options:

        **Revalue inventory**: This posts a $50 credit (decrease) to your Cost of Goods GL account.

        **Don't revalue inventory**: This posts a $50 credit to your Purchase Price Variance GL account.

    Both of these approaches have their place. Revaluing inventory combines any cost variances into Costs of Goods Sold, not revaluing it keeps the variances in a separate account where you can see them more clearly. Large variances may indicate issues with the purchasing process, so some companies may want to track them separately. One important thing to understand is that the variance of $50 in the preceding example may be posted to the General Ledger in a different accounting period than the customer invoice, as you may not receive the vendor invoice right away.

If you choose the **Revalue Inventory for Cost Variance** option, then you can also enter a **Tolerance Percentage** – in this case, inventory will be revalued only if the variance is equal to or greater than the percentage entered. If the **Tolerance Percentage** is left at 0%, all variances will be revalued.

> This option is not available for periodic valuation methods.

- **Quantity Tolerance Percentage**: This is a new feature added with Dynamics GP 2013, available for Sales Inventory and Discontinued item types.
    - **Shortage**: Selecting this and entering a percentage will cancel any remaining quantities on a Purchase Order when the quantity received is within the shortage tolerance. Quantity shortages are rounded down using the number of quantity decimal places for the item. For example:

      An item has 0 quantity decimal places and the shortage tolerance is set to 10%.

      When you order a quantity of 75, the shortage tolerance is 7 (7.5 rounded down to 0 decimal places).

      If you receive 68 of the item, the remaining quantity of 7 will be cancelled.

      If you receive 67 of the item, the remaining quantity is 8, which is above the tolerance and will not be cancelled.
    - **Overage**: Selecting this and entering a percentage will limit the amount that can be received over what was ordered to the quantity ordered plus the overage tolerance. Quantity overages are rounded up using the number of quantity decimal places for the item. For example:

      An item has 2 decimal places and the overage tolerance is set to 15%.

      You order a quantity of 125.25, the overage tolerance is calculated as 18.79 (18.7875 rounded up to 2 decimal places).

      If you receive 144 of the item, that is 18.75 over and within the tolerance, so it will be allowed.

      If you receive 145 of the item, that is 19.75 over and outside of the tolerance, and you will see a message saying that you cannot enter this quantity, as it exceeds the overage tolerance.

- **Maintain History**: By default these are not selected. It is recommended to keep all history and to select all four of the options under **Maintain History**.
- **Quantity Decimals**: This is the default number of decimal places for quantities of items in this class. This will change automatically, depending on the **U of M Schedule ID** chosen for this class, as it has to match the number of decimal places set up for the U of M schedule.
- **Currency Decimals**: The default number of decimal places in currency amounts for items in this class. As there is only one option for **Currency Decimals**, if you have enabled Multicurrency, this option will be disabled and the decimal place setup can be completed by clicking on the **Currency** button at the bottom of the window.
- **U of M Schedule ID**: This is the default U of M schedule for items in this class and can be changed when items are created.
- **Price Group**: Price groups are optional in Dynamics GP and allow for an additional grouping of items for either reporting purposes or price updates.
- **Default Price Level**: Optionally, you can select a default price level for the items in this class. Some companies choose to create a default price level for all items, which can be used in case a customer is not assigned a price level or an item does not have specific pricing for the customer's price level.
- **Price Method**: Dynamics GP has a number of available price methods; however most companies use either the **Currency Amount** (flat amount) or **% of List Price** option. Formulas and further descriptions for the other available methods are listed in the *Price Methods* section in *Chapter 10, Item cards* of the *Inventory Control* manual. (This manual can be downloaded here: `http://technet.microsoft.com/en-us/library/jj673202(v=gp.30).aspx`.)
- **Purchase Tax Option**: Most companies do not pay or record purchase taxes separately, so typically **Nontaxable** is chosen here. If purchase taxes need to be calculated, the **Taxable** option can be selected and a **Tax Schedule ID** specified, or you can select **Base on vendor**.
- **User Category**: If you set up inventory categories on the **Inventory Control Setup** window, they will be automatically populated in this section and you can select from the available values predefined for each category.

The following is a typical **Item Class Setup** window:

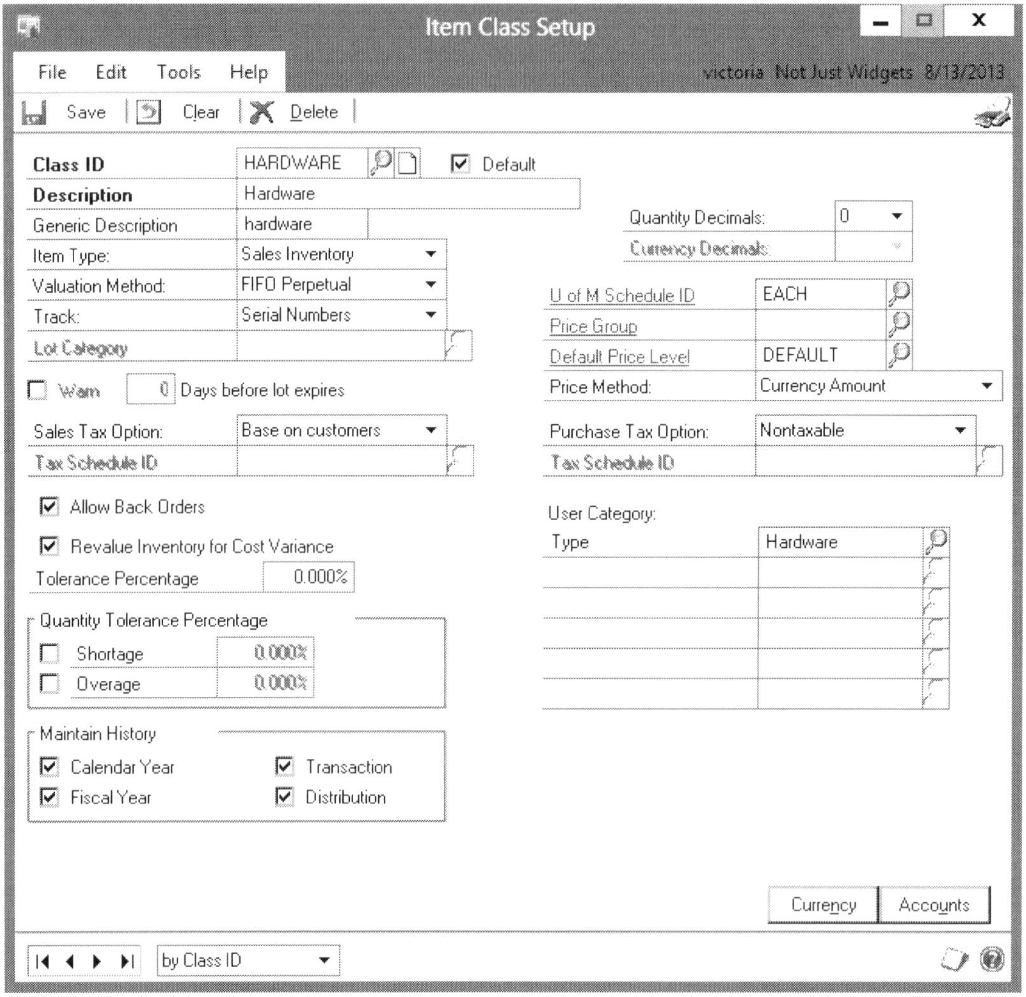


Note that the only required fields for an item class are **Class ID** and **Description**, so you can fill in as much or as little detail as you want when setting up a class.

> You can create as many item classes as you need; however, keep in mind that the main goal of classes is to save time and allow for more meaningful reporting, so plan these out before creating a large number of classes.

## Item class currency setup

Clicking on the **Currency** button at the bottom of the **Item Class Setup** window will open the **Item Class Currency Setup** window where you can specify the number of **Currency Decimals** for each **Currency ID**. The following is a sample of what this setup looks like:

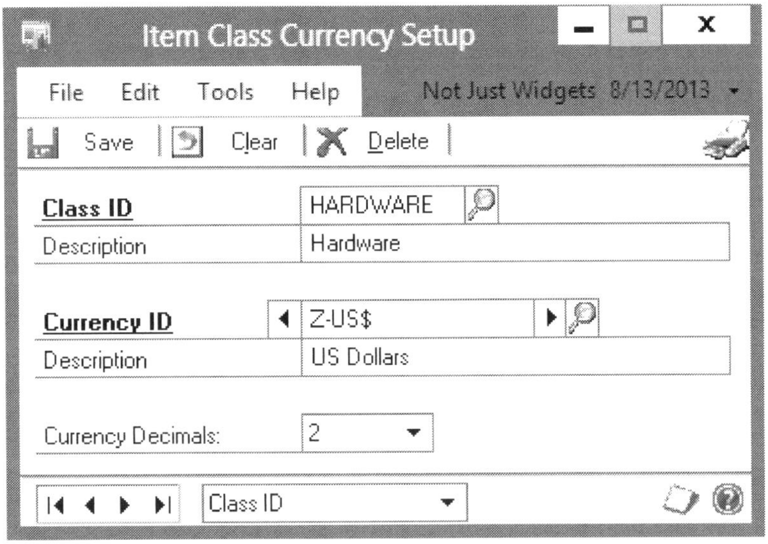


## Item class accounts setup

Clicking on the **Accounts** button at the bottom of the **Item Class Setup** window will open the **Item Class Accounts Setup** window, where you can specify the default GL accounts for each item class. The following list explains the available accounts:

- **Inventory**: Balance Sheet asset account that holds the inventory value. It is debited when inventory increases and credited when inventory decreases.
- **Inventory Offset**: This is a default account used for the other side of inventory transactions if no other account is specified. Most often this is used by inventory adjustment transactions. It is recommended not to use the **Inventory** account for this so that there is greater visibility into posting issues if accounts are not set up properly.
- **Cost of Goods Sold**: This is the Profit and Loss (P&L) account debited for the inventory cost when a sales invoice is posted.
- **Sales**: The P&L account that is credited for the sale amount when a sales invoice is posted.

- **Markdowns**: This is the P&L account debited with the markdown amount (discount on individual line items) on a sales invoice. Some companies choose to make this the same as the **Sales** account; others like to track these discounts in a separate account.
- **Sales Returns**: The P&L account that is debited for the return amount when a sales return is posted in Sales Order Processing (SOP) and the SOP module is set up to use accounts from the item. Many companies choose to make this the same as the **Sales** account, while others like to track returns in a separate GL account for additional visibility.
- **In Use**, **In Service**, **Damaged**, and **Inventory Returns**: When inventory items are returned in Dynamics GP, they can be classified as On Hand, Returned, In Use, In Service, or Damaged. Items can also be transferred from one of these statuses (called **Quantity Types**) to another to offer better control and visibility of the condition of items. These accounts offer the ability to put the inventory asset cost of each inventory status into a separate account; however, in practice, many companies use the **Inventory** account for all of these. The On Hand status is not in the list of options you can select here, as inventory returned to On Hand status will debit the **Inventory** account.
- **Variance:** This account is used for the cost of the item when a variance transaction is posted, usually after a physical stock count.
- **Drop Ship Items**: Balance Sheet asset account to hold the inventory value of drop shipped items. It is debited when a vendor invoice for drop ship items is posted and credited when a sales invoice for drop ship items is posted.
- **Purchase Price Variance**: This account records the difference in receipt versus purchase cost of items if the option to revalue inventory is not used. This account is used for periodic inventory valuation methods or if you are not selecting the **Revalue Inventory** option for non-periodic valuation methods.
- **Unrealized Purch Price Var**: The unrealized portion of a purchase price variance for items with periodic valuation methods is recorded in this account.
- **Assembly Variance**: This account will be used if there is a difference between the planned component cost and final item cost on an Assembly Transaction when using periodic valuation methods.
- **Standard Cost Revaluation**: New in Dynamics GP 2013, this account is used for the Change Item Standard Cost utility, also new in Dynamics GP 2013.

The following is a typical **Item Class Accounts Setup** window:

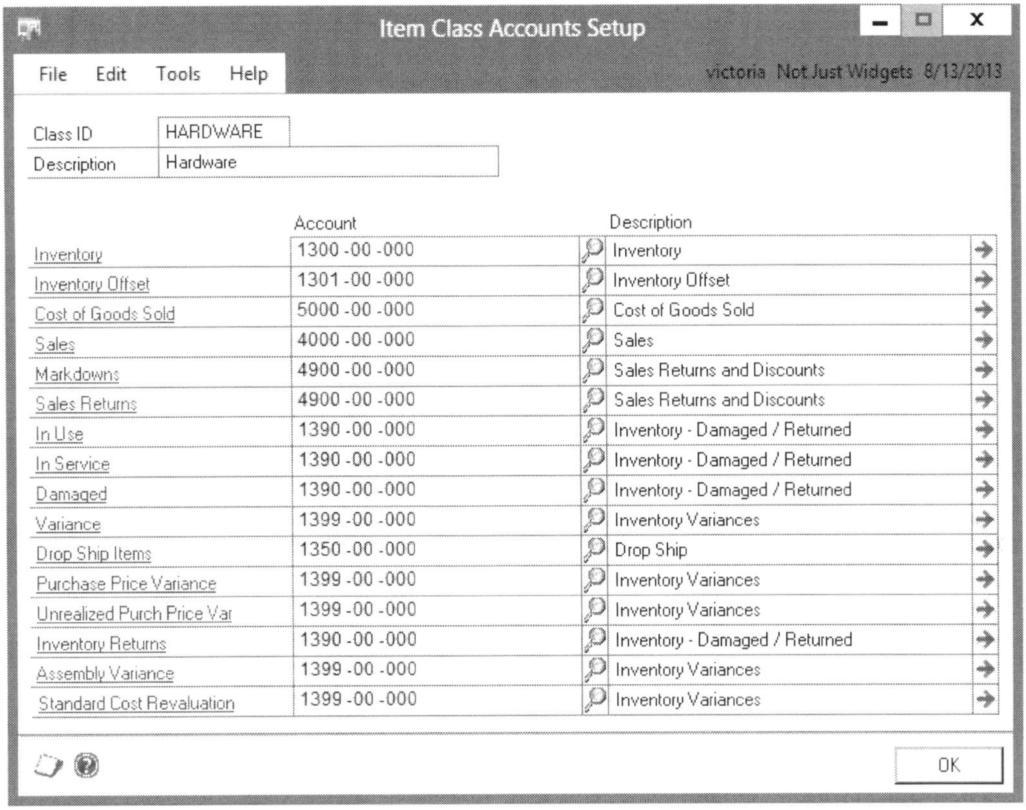


Even though any account can be left blank and then filled in as needed during transaction entry, it is highly recommended to fill in all accounts that may possibly be used on transactions to speed up data entry and avoid errors.

> You can save considerable time by setting up company posting accounts for any accounts that are the same for most inventory items, and then only exceptions need to be set up individually.

When inventory items are used on transactions, Dynamics GP determines the General Ledger accounts in the following order:

1. Use accounts from inventory item.
2. If any accounts are missing from the item setup, use posting accounts for the company (**Microsoft Dynamics GP** | **Tools** | **Setup** | **Posting** | **Posting Accounts**).
3. If any accounts are still missing, leave them blank. Transactions will give a warning and will not post if any required accounts are missing.

> There is an exception to these rules when using the Sales Order Processing module. Part of the SOP module setup has a switch that lets you choose accounts from the customer setup, instead of item setup, when posting SOP transactions.

# Inventory item setup

The last step in setting up the Inventory module is to create items. Even though you may decide to import your inventory items, it is still important to understand what is involved in setting them up manually. There are quite a number of steps to creating items in Dynamics GP:

- Item Maintenance
- Item Internet Information
- Item Maintenance Options
- Item Account Maintenance
- Item Currency
- Price List
- Price List Options
- Purchasing
- Item vendors
- Assigning items to sites
- Kits
- Suggested sales items
- Copying items

# Item Maintenance

To start setting up a new item in Dynamics GP, open the **Item Maintenance** window by navigating to **Cards** | **Inventory** | **Item**. Most of the settings for an item are defaulted from the item class and have been described in the previous *Item class setup* section. The new ones are described here:

- **Item Number**: This is also referred to as the Item ID and will be the main identifier used in Dynamics GP to find the item. The **Item Number** can be up to 30 characters.
- **Description**: The full name of the item (up to 100 characters). This defaults on sales and purchasing transactions unless additional setup for vendor or customer item descriptions is performed.

> The default out-of-the-box reports in Dynamics GP can only show 80 character strings and a customization would be required to show all 100 characters. If you are planning on using out-of-the-box reports for purchase orders, sales invoices, and packing slips, consider not entering more than 80 characters for your item descriptions.

- **Short Description**: This will be the default description that shows up for the item on Dynamics GP lookups, so enter something that will help users identify this item in a list of others. The length is limited to 15 characters.
- **Shipping Weight**: This is informational only and is not used by any Dynamics GP functionality; however, it is often used for calculations on modified or custom reports.
- **Standard Cost**: This is used by some of the pricing methods to calculate item prices. The standard cost is also used for the Cost of Goods calculation with periodic valuation methods.
- **Current Cost**: For perpetual valuation methods, the current cost is updated with every increase transaction for an item. For the Average Perpetual valuation method, this will show the current average cost.
- **List Price**: The list price can be used in the calculation for some pricing methods. If Multicurrency is set up, this field will be disabled and a list price can be entered for each currency on the **Item Currency Maintenance** window.
- **Quantity On Hand** and **Quantity Available**: These are informational only and cannot be changed.

The following screenshot shows a sample **Item Maintenance** window:

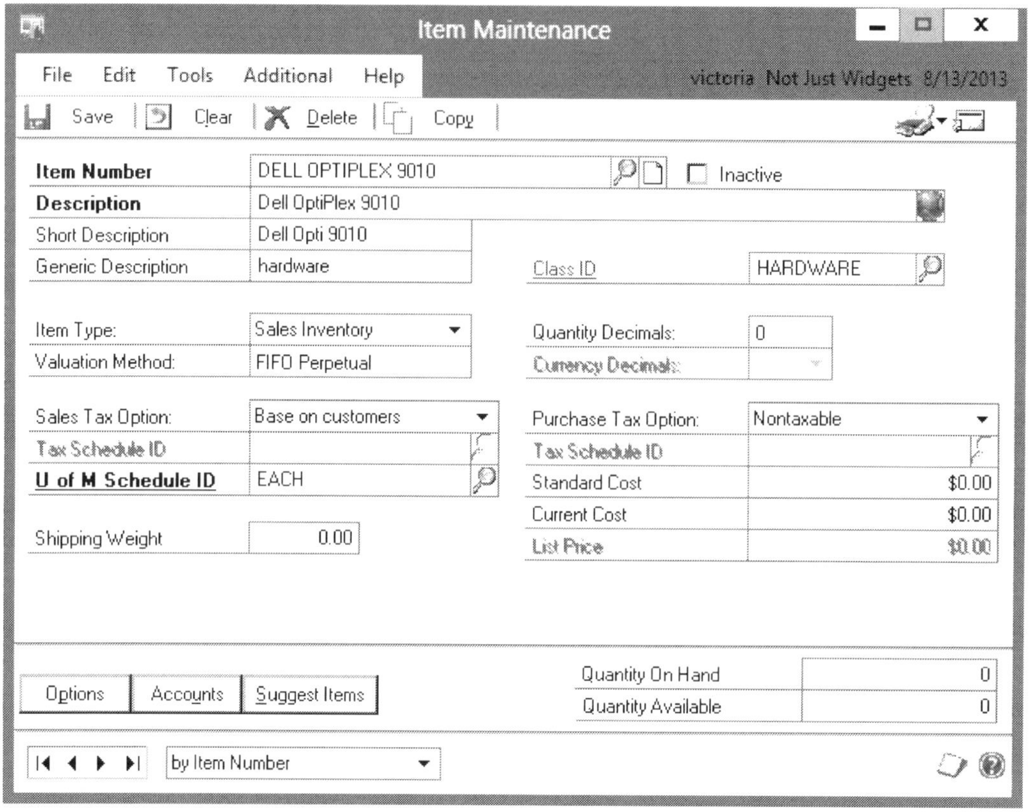


## Item Internet Information

Clicking on the **Internet Information** icon to the right of the **Description** field opens the **Internet Information** window. As this window is common to company, customers, vendors, items, salespeople, and employees, there may be fields on here that do not pertain to inventory items. Some examples of information that can be stored for inventory items are:

- **Website**: This can hold the URL of the item on a vendor's or manufacturer's website, or on your website.
- **Image**: You can store the location of the item's picture.
- **Additional Information**: This is one of the fields that cannot be renamed on the **Internet Information** window and it can hold up to 32,000 characters. Many companies find this to be a good place to store a long description or notes for the item.

## Item Maintenance Options

Clicking on the **Options** button at the bottom of the **Item Maintenance** window will open the **Item Maintenance Options** window. This window also has some settings that will be copied from the item class. In addition, you can select **Substitute Items** to be suggested if this item is out of stock, **Warranty Days**, and an **ABC Code**. If this item is a **Kit** or **Kit Component**, a checkmark will appear next to the appropriate values in the **Item** list at the bottom.

This window is also where you can enter the optional **Category** information for items and change whether to **Track Serial Numbers** or **Lot Numbers**.

> If you are not using item classes it is important to check all the **Maintain History** checkboxes on the **Item Maintenance Options** window, as they are unchecked by default.

## Item Account Maintenance

The **Item Account Maintenance** window opens when you click on the **Accounts** button at the bottom of the **Item Maintenance** window. It is important to make sure that any accounts that need to be different for an item are filled in here. If a change to the accounts needs to be made globally, it can be entered in the **Item Class Accounts Setup** window and rolled down to all items in the class.

> If you are making a change to a class and rolling it down to all items in that class, any item that is opened on a screen at the time you are making the change may not be updated properly.

## Item Currency

On the **Item Maintenance** window, click on the **GoTo** button in the upper-right corner and select **Item Currency** or navigate to **Cards** | **Inventory** | **Item Currency**. This will open the **Item Currency Maintenance** window, where you can specify the number of **Currency Decimals** and a **List Price** for each **Currency ID**. Until you set up the number of currency decimal places for a currency, you will not be able to enter the item on a transaction with that currency.

Once entered, the **Currency Decimals** will be grayed out; however, it is possible to change this setting with a utility within Dynamics GP if you have no open transactions or quantities on hand for an item. As typical items will often have open transactions or stock quantities, the number of currency decimal places should be considered carefully. Selecting more decimal places will allow you more granularity for costs and prices for low cost items. However, the total number of decimal places selected will appear on all windows and reports for that item, potentially making it more cumbersome to work with. Additionally, if your items have different numbers of decimal places for the costs and prices, out-of-the-box reports may be a lot less presentable and may require modifications.

# Price List

A **Price List** in Dynamics GP allows you to set up all the default prices for each unit of measure, price level, currency, and quantity break. To open the **Item Price List Maintenance** window, click on the **GoTo** button in the upper-right corner of the **Item Maintenance** window and choose **Price List** or navigate to **Cards** | **Inventory** | **Price List**.

Choose a **Price Method**—note that only one is available per item. **Price Group** is optional and can be filled in at any time. It is recommended that you specify a **Default Selling U of M** so that users do not have to enter this manually every time they select this item on a sales transaction. The **Default Price Level** will be used if a customer is not set up with a price level. This can be useful if most customers have the same prices, but some receive special pricing. In that case, you only have to set up a price level for customers with the special pricing and others will automatically default to the **Default Price Level**.

The following is an example of a **Currency Amount Price Method** with different prices based on price level:

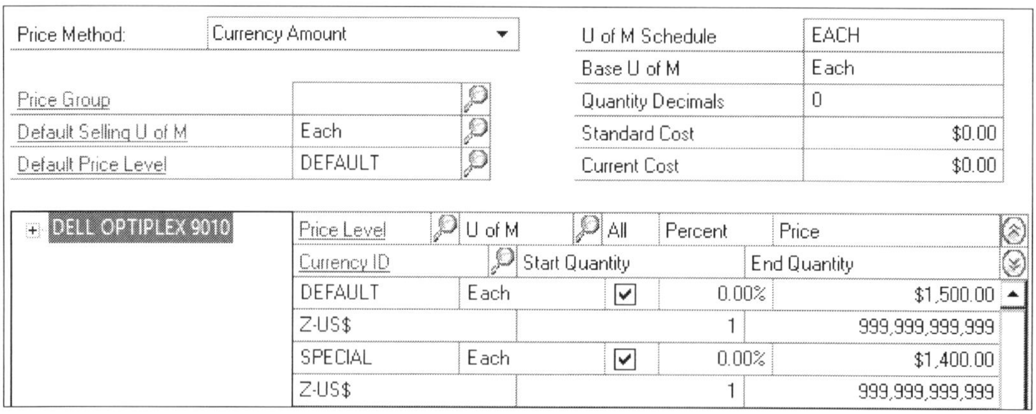

The following screenshot shows an example of a quantity discount, where buying three or more items will result in a lower price, but only for the **SPECIAL** price level:

| Price Level | U of M | All | Percent | Price |
|---|---|---|---|---|
| Currency ID | Start Quantity | | | End Quantity |
| DEFAULT | Each | ☑ | 0.00% | $1,500.00 |
| Z-US$ | 1 | | | 999,999,999,999 |
| SPECIAL | Each | ☐ | 0.00% | $1,400.00 |
| Z-US$ | 1 | | | 2 |
| SPECIAL | Each | ☐ | 0.00% | $1,350.00 |
| Z-US$ | 3 | | | 999,999,999,999 |

This is a final example using % **of List Price** as the price method, where the list price of `$1,500` has been entered on the **Item Currency Maintenance** window:

| Price Level | U of M | All | Percent | Price |
|---|---|---|---|---|
| Currency ID | Start Quantity | | | End Quantity |
| DEFAULT | Each | ☑ | 100.00% | $1,500.00 |
| Z-US$ | 1 | | | 999,999,999,999 |
| SPECIAL | Each | ☐ | 93.00% | $1,395.00 |
| Z-US$ | 1 | | | 2 |
| SPECIAL | Each | ☐ | 90.00% | $1,350.00 |
| Z-US$ | 3 | | | 999,999,999,999 |

There are many scenarios that can be set up with price lists. For situations that cannot be covered by this, there is additional functionality available in Dynamics GP called **Extended Pricing**. You may want to investigate it if you have complex pricing requirements. Extended pricing is covered in *Chapter 11, Standard price lists* of the *Inventory Control* manual. (This manual can be downloaded at: `http://technet.microsoft.com/en-us/library/jj673202(v=gp.30).aspx`.)

# Price List Options

Clicking on the **Options** button at the top of the **Item Price List Maintenance** window will open the **Item Price List Options Maintenance** window. For items with one or more quantity decimal places you can choose whether or not to allow selling fractional quantities under **Selling Option**. For price methods other than **Currency Amount**, you can also set up **Round Policy**, **Round Option**, and **Round Amount** to control the pricing.

For example, using the % **of List Price** example shown previously, if you want all the prices to be rounded to the nearest $50, you would set it up as follows:

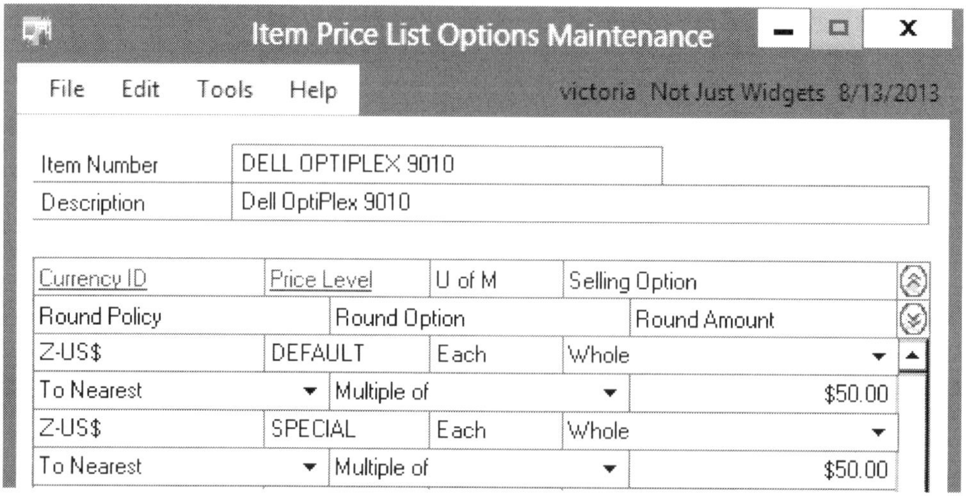


After saving these changes, the resulting price list would look like the following:

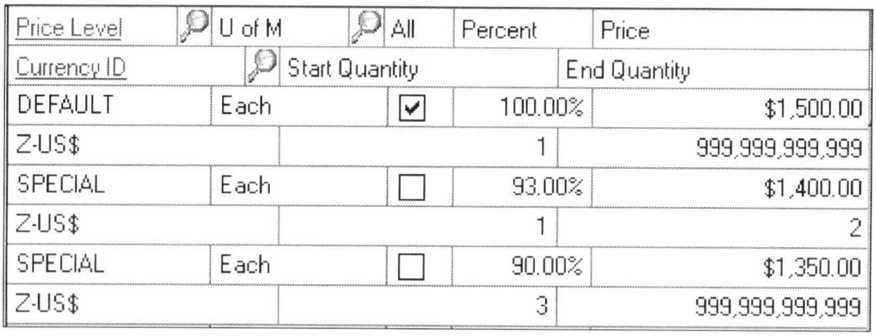


Once you have set up a price list, you can use the **Copy** button at the top of the **Item Price List Maintenance** window to copy the price list to another item.

## Purchasing Options

Setting up purchasing options for an item helps speed up data entry for Purchase Order Processing transactions. To open the **Item Purchasing Options Maintenance** window, click on the **GoTo** button in the upper-right corner of the **Item Maintenance** window and choose **Purchasing**, or navigate to **Cards | Inventory | Item Purchasing Options**.

The **Base U of M** will be filled in automatically, but you can choose something different for the **Default Purchasing U of M**, depending on how you typically purchase this item. Here is an example:

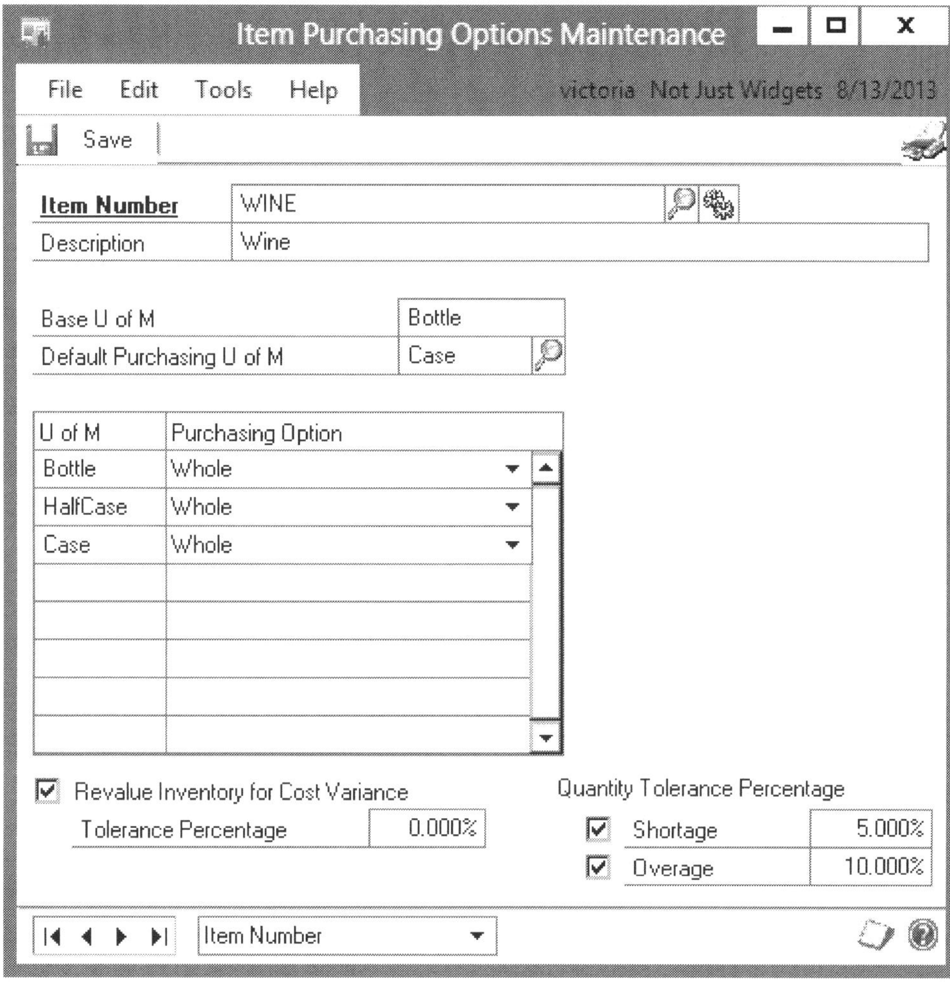


You can also specify whether **Whole** or **Fractional** values are allowed for each possible **U of M**; fractional values will only be possible when your items are set up with one or more decimal places. You can select whether to **Revalue Inventory for Cost Variance** and, if so, with what **Tolerance Percentage**. A **Tolerance Percentage** of `0.000%` means that inventory will be revalued for all variances.

Under **Quantity Tolerance Percentage** you can optionally enter the **Shortage** and **Overage** percentages (the description for these is in the *Item classes* section).

The gears icon to the right of the **Item Number** opens the **Manufacturer's Item Number Maintenance** window, where you can enter the manufacturer's item numbers for your inventory items. Many companies do not use this, but it is a useful option to have, if needed.

## Item vendors

To facilitate the automatic creation of purchase orders from sales orders and keep track of vendor part numbers, lead times, and costs, you can set up one or more vendors for each inventory item.

Navigate to **Cards** | **Inventory** | **Vendors** or click on the **GoTo** button in the upper-right corner of the **Item Maintenance** window and choose **Vendors**. On the **Item Vendors Maintenance** window you can enter a **Vendor ID**, **Vendor Item**, and **Description** for each item. Click on **Save** and repeat the process for as many vendors as you buy the item from.

If the unit of measure you typically purchase the item in is different depending on vendor, you can change that in the **Default Purchasing U of M** section in the bottom-right corner; otherwise, it will default to what has been set up on the **Item Purchasing Options Maintenance** window. The **Originating Invoice Cost** will automatically be updated every time you post an invoice for this item from the selected vendor and this will be the cost defaulted on future purchase orders for this item/vendor combination. If you pre-populate this cost prior to entering purchase orders, that cost will default on the first PO you create.

If you want to have your purchase orders automatically calculate release dates based on a vendor's lead time for this item, you can enter the **Planning Lead Time** in days (up to 9,999 days will be allowed).

Most of the other fields on this window are not used in the modules we are covering in this book and can be used as informational fields for reporting or lookups.

## Assigning items to sites

To be able to purchase or sell an inventory item, you must first assign it to at least one inventory site. This is why even if you only have one inventory location, you must create at least one Site ID in Dynamics GP. If you have multiple sites set up, you can selectively decide what items can be located at each site.

To assign sites for one item at a time, navigate to **Cards** | **Inventory** | **Quantities/Sites** or click on the **GoTo** button in the upper-right corner of the **Item Maintenance** window and choose **Quantities/Sites**. Working with this window is a little counter-intuitive, as everything appears grayed out at first. To assign an item to a site, click on the radio button next to **Site ID** under the **Sites** section. This will enable the **Site ID** lookup and let you pick from your existing sites:

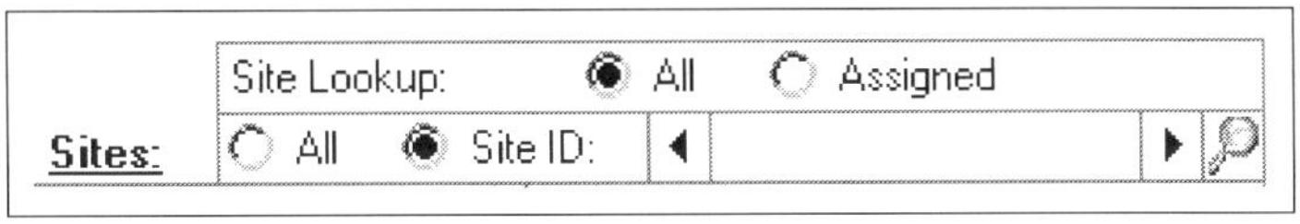


Once you select a site, click on the **Save** button and the item/site combination will be saved. You can repeat this process for as many sites as you want. Changing the **Site Lookup** selection to **Assigned** and then clicking on the looking glass icon will show you only the sites that have been assigned to this item.

There are two other useful features on the **Item Quantities Maintenance** window:

- Specifying a **Default Site ID** can be helpful during purchase order entry if an item is typically ordered to the same site.
- When a **Site ID** is selected, the **Primary Vendor ID** field becomes available. If a vendor is entered here, that vendor will be defaulted when a purchase order for this item is generated from a sales order. This may be helpful when there are multiple vendors set up for an item, but most purchase orders are placed with one particular vendor.

Using the **Item Quantities Maintenance** window is good for assigning sites selectively or when adding just one item. However, more often sites will need to be assigned globally for either all or a large group of items. To accomplish this, navigate to **Cards** | **Inventory** | **Sites** or click on the **Sites** hyperlink on the **Item Quantities Maintenance** window. On the **Site Maintenance** window, select a **Site ID** and click on the **Assign** button at the bottom.

On the **Item Site Assignments** window, the default options will select all your items, or you can filter them by choosing any or all of the available four options. For example, the settings shown in the following screenshot will select all items in the `HARDWARE` class:

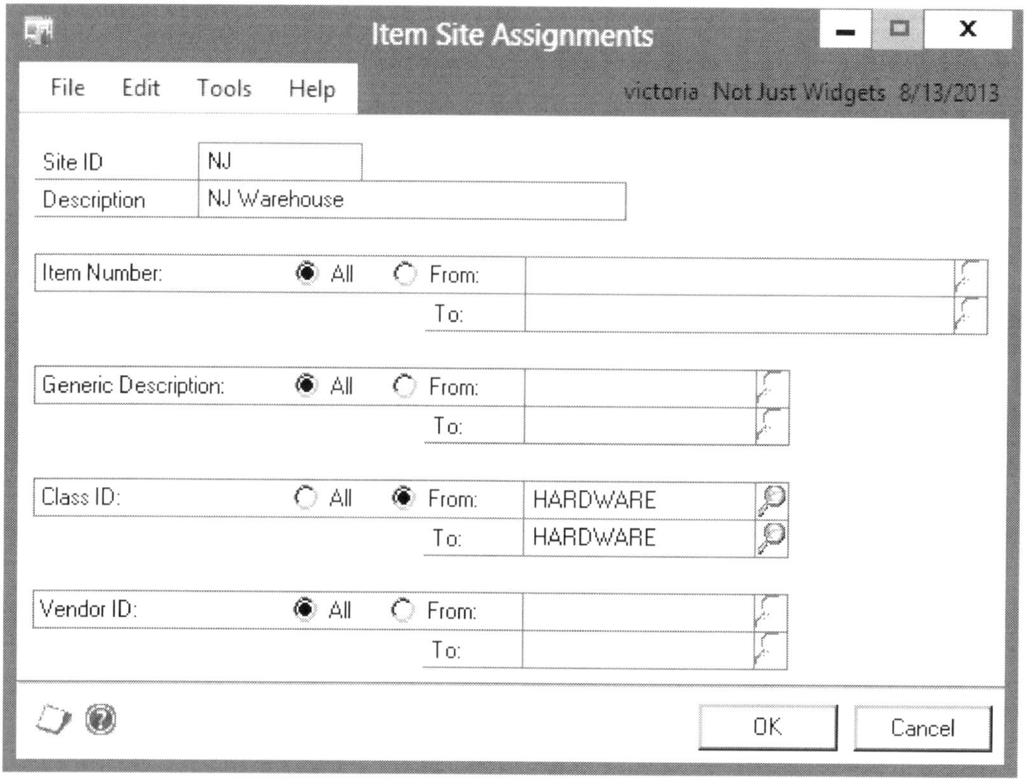


When you click on the **OK** button all the items selected will be assigned to the **Site ID** shown at the top of the window.

# Kits

To use **Kits**, you will need to predefine them. The setup of a kit item is the same as any other item type, with one additional step needed. Navigate to **Cards | Inventory | Kits** or click on the **GoTo** button in the upper-right corner of the **Item Maintenance** window and select **Kits**.

> Note that you will not be able to track serial or lot numbers for kits, but if the kit components contain items that track serial or lot numbers, they will still be tracked for the individual items sold within a kit.

On the **Item Kit Maintenance** window, determine whether the **Cost of Goods Sold Account** for the kit should be used **From Component Item** (so if the components have different accounts, this will create multiple COGS distributions) or **From Kit Item**. In the scrolling list, fill in each **Component Item Number**, **U of M**, and **Quantity** that will make up the kit. If the items have already been received into inventory, the costs will populate, otherwise they will be zero. The following screenshot shows an example of a kit with two components:

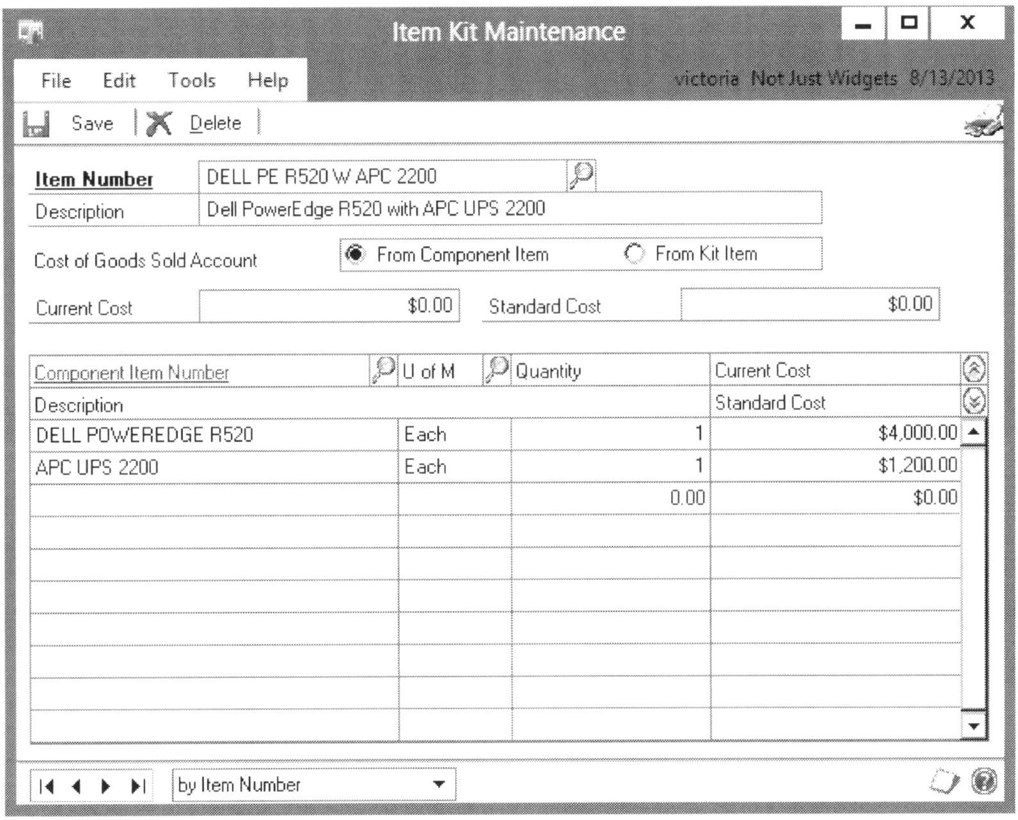

# Suggested sales items

A new feature has been added in Dynamics GP 2013 to allow adding up to five **suggested sales items** to each inventory item. This can be very useful for linking related items or upsell opportunities. When an item that has suggested items is entered on a Sales Order Processing transaction, the user will see a pop-up with the suggested items. They can select any combination of these items to quickly add them to the sales transaction.

To set up suggested sales items, click on the **Suggest Items** button at the bottom of the **Inventory Maintenance** window. You can decide what sales transactions to have the suggestions show up on by selecting the checkboxes under **Document Type**, and then enter the suggested items in the list. The following is an example of the **Suggest Sales Item Maintenance** window:

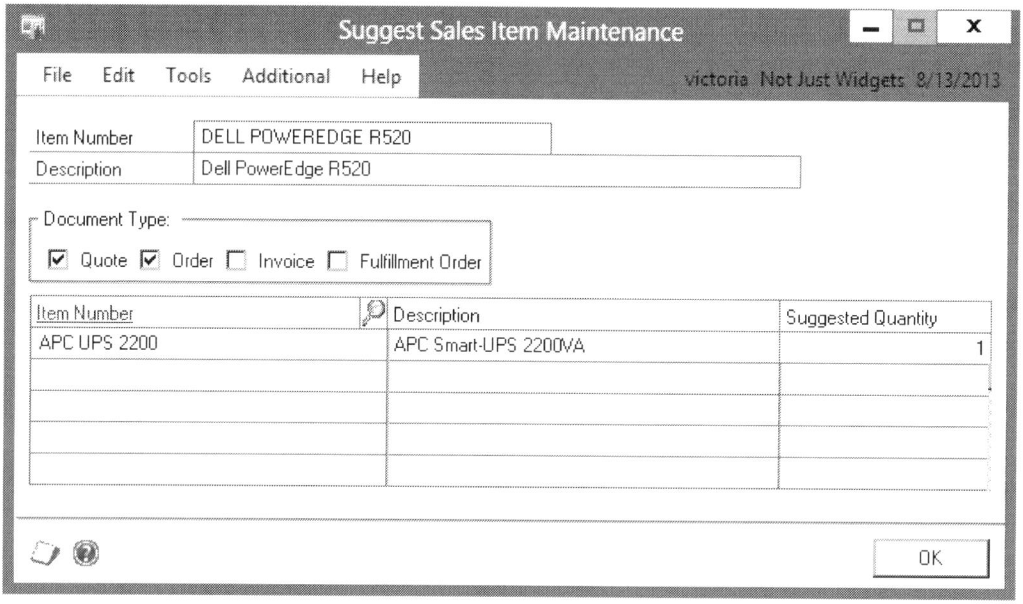


> The inventory items must already exist before they can be added on the **Suggest Sales Item Maintenance** window.

## Copying items

A very useful and often overlooked feature on the **Item Maintenance** window is the ability to copy all the settings from an existing item to a new one. To use this feature follow these steps:

1. Type in a new **Item Number**.
2. Click on the **Copy** button at the top of the window.
3. Select the **Item Number** that you would like to copy from on the **Item Copy** window.
4. Choose the attributes to copy—by default, everything is selected. You may not want to copy **Vendor Assignments** or **List Prices** unless they are very similar with only a few changes needed.
5. Click on **Copy**.
6. This will create an exact duplicate of your existing item with the new **Item Number** entered in step 1. Remember to change the **Description** and **Short Description** fields, as they will also be copied.

Now that you have completed the setup of the Inventory module, you can enter or import items and start entering inventory transactions.

# Sales Order Processing

The **Sales Order Processing** module, also commonly referred to as **SOP**, bridges the gap between the Inventory and Receivables modules in Dynamics GP. It is part of the Sales series, so all the menu options for it will start with **Sales**. The SQL Server tables for the SOP module start with `SOP`.

In SOP, you can enter quotes, orders, back orders, invoices, and returns with detailed inventory and non-inventory items. SOP also integrates to the Purchase Order Processing module with the ability to automatically create purchase orders for sales orders that you do not have adequate stock on hand to fill.

Setup for Sales Order Processing consists of the following steps:

- Sales Order Processing Setup
- Sales document Setup
- User-Defined fields
- SOP document numbers
- Sales Order Processing Setup Options
- E-mail settings
- Customer items

# Sales Order Processing Setup

To begin setting up Sales Order Processing, navigate to **Microsoft Dynamics GP | Tools | Setup | Sales | Sales Order Processing**. The following is a list of the fields on the **Sales Order Processing Setup** window:

- **Display Item Unit Cost**: Unmarking this will show the unit cost of items entered on sales order transactions as zero. Some companies prefer to hide item costs from users; however, this option hides them only on the **Sales Transaction Entry** window, not anywhere else in the system. So, unless a user has extremely limited access in Dynamics GP, this is not as useful as it sounds.
- **Track Voided Transactions in History**: It is recommended to leave this option marked, as there may often be a reason to look at voided sales transactions.
- **Calculate Kit Price Based on Component Cost**: This option applies to pricing methods based on cost, which are not too common. Selecting this option will cause the cost of the kit (and thus the price) to be recalculated based on the cost of each component in the kit.
- **Display Quantity Distribution Warning**: Selecting this enables a warning during transaction entry that helps users avoid mistakes when entering quantities for transactions. It is recommended to leave this checked.
- **Search for New Rates During Transfer Process**: This setting only applies to Multicurrency transactions. If it is checked, then during the transfer of sales documents (for example from quote to order), Dynamics GP will look for an updated exchange rate. If this setting is not selected, the system will still verify that the exchange rate is valid, but will not update exchange rates unless they are expired.
- **Track Master Numbers** and **Next Master Number**: Dynamics GP offers the ability to track related transactions with a **Master Number**. For example, a quote, a resulting order, and two partial invoices may all have their own individual document numbers but share one master number, thus allowing for easy lookups of all related transactions. It is recommended to leave this option selected, even if you do not foresee a need to use master numbers. The **Next Master Number** can be anything you would like, although there is typically no reason to change it from the default value of **1**.

- **Prices Not Required in Price List**: This option works together with the Inventory module and, if selected, allows users to enter items without a price level set up. This may sometimes be needed, but it is better to leave this unchecked and create price lists for all items to keep setup consistent.

  If this option is selected and no **Password** is supplied, any user can enter an item without a price level on a transaction. With a **Password** selected, a user will be prompted to enter the password before they can continue.

- **Convert Functional Price**: This option is only available if **Prices Not Required in Price List** is selected. With this checked, if a price cannot be found for the item in the currency that is being used on the transaction, the functional currency price will be converted as needed using the current exchange rate.
- **Data Entry Defaults**: These are defaults to help speed up data entry:
  - **Quantity Shortage**: Choose what users will see as the default option when they enter a quantity that is greater than what is in stock. The users can change the selection as needed. If the same option is typically chosen, selecting it here will save users a click each time.
  - **Document Date**: When entering a new SOP transaction, the **Document Date** will default to either the **User Date** (this is at the top of every window next to the **User ID** and **Company Name**) or the date of the previously saved transaction. If you typically enter all invoices with the same date (for example, the end of the previous month), set this to the **Previous Doc. Date**. If you want to have the current date defaulted for new transactions, choose **User Date**.
  - **Price Warning**: You can decide whether to warn users if the price being used on a transaction they are entering is a default price for an item because a price has not been set up for the customer's price level. This may be useful if there should be a price set up on the item price list for each customer price level and can help avoid mistakes. If you choose to give a warning, using the **Message** option is recommended, as it will give users an indication of what the problem is. The **Beep** option may not be enough to catch a user's attention when you consider the typical noise level in an office and the number of beeps various applications generate.

    - **Requested Ship Date**: When SOP orders are entered into Dynamics GP, a **Requested Ship Date** automatically populates to help determine when orders should be shipped and when purchase orders may need to be placed. A user can change the requested ship date on each line item for an order; however, if there is a typical default you can use this setting to help speed up data entry. Choices are either **Document Date** (order date) or number of **Days After Doc. Date**. If the latter is chosen, a box will appear next to this option where you can fill in the number of days (up to 999).

- **Document Defaults**: Similar to a customer with multiple address IDs, each document (or transaction) type in SOP can have multiple document IDs set up to follow different rules. During transaction entry, users select which document type and document ID to use for the proper set of rules to be followed. This section allows you to optionally set up the default for each document type, as well as the **Site ID** and **Checkbook ID**, to help speed up data entry. If you decide to set these up, you will need to come back to this section after you have created the various document IDs for each document type. If there is a document type you will not be using, or that you want to make sure users have to proactively select during transaction entry, leave it blank.
- **Posting Accounts From**: If **Item** is chosen, the system will first look at the item's accounts, then at the Inventory series of the company posting accounts to determine what General Ledger accounts to use for SOP transactions. If **Customer** is chosen, the system will first look at the customer's accounts, then at the Sales series of the company posting accounts to determine what GL accounts to use for SOP transactions.
- **Maintain History**: It is recommended to keep all history and leave all of these selections checked.
- **Decimal Places for Non-Inventoried Items**: If non-inventory items are entered on SOP transactions, these settings will determine how many decimal places to use for **Quantities** and **Currency**. If Multicurrency is enabled, use the expansion button (blue arrow) next to the **Currency** field to enter these for each currency.

The following screenshot shows a typical **Sales Order Processing Setup** window:

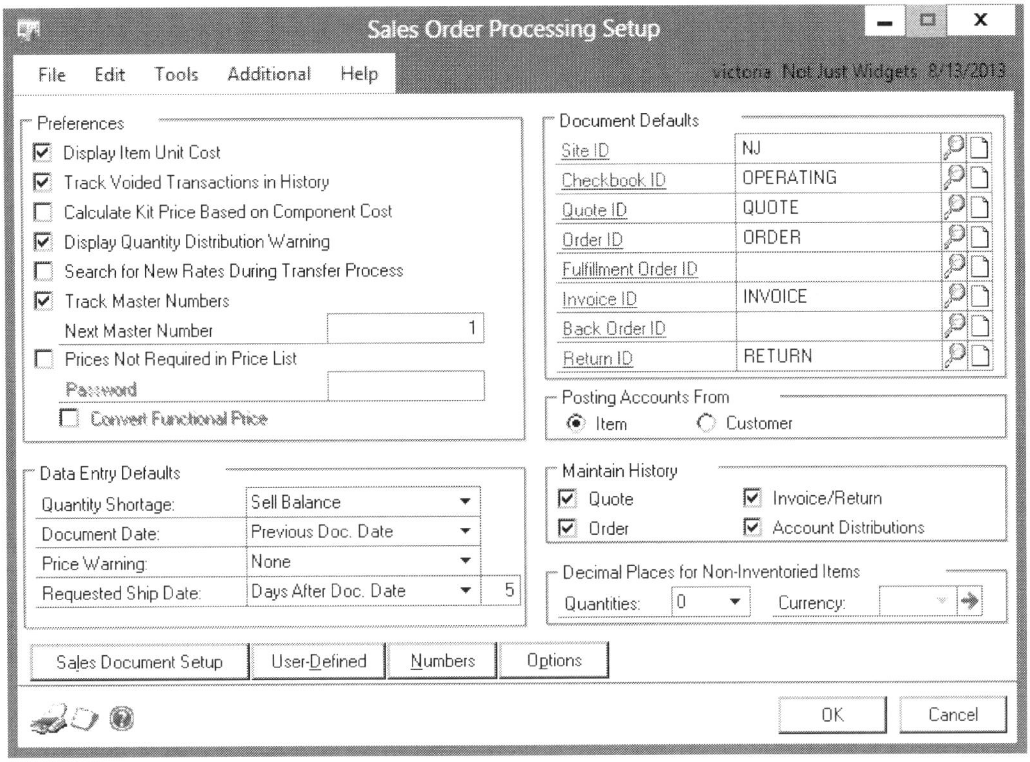


## Sales document setup

You can set up as many document IDs as you need for each Sales Order Processing transaction type. One reason to set up different document IDs is to allow for different transaction rules. Another reason is to use different numbering schemes or be able to segregate transactions for reporting purposes.

Dynamics GP has two types of transactions that are basically the same—a fulfillment order and an invoice. In most places you will see these listed together as **Fulfillment Order/Invoice**. When using **Workflow** with the SOP module, a fulfillment order becomes a separate transaction type that, once completed, turns into an invoice automatically.

To start setting up document IDs, click on the **Sales Document Setup** button at the bottom of the **Sales Order Processing Setup** window. You will see a list of the available documents types:

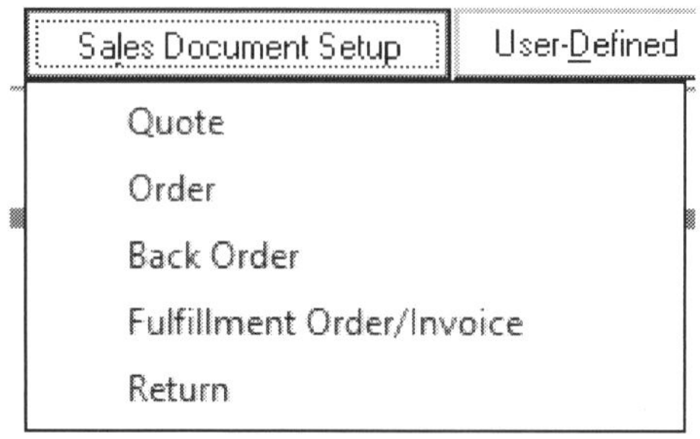


The following sections will go over the setup for each transaction type.

# Quote

**Quotes** are typically the start of the sales process and can be entered for customers or prospects.

> **Prospects** can be created "on the fly", as they are needed in Dynamics GP, and then transferred to customers if they accept a quote and place an order.

The following list explains the fields on the **Sales Quote Setup** window:

- **Quote ID**: This is an ID for this quote document—up to 15 characters. This is what users will need to type or select on a sales transaction when using this quote document ID.
- **Quote ID Next Number**: If you are setting up multiple quote IDs and would like for each to have its own numbering scheme, you can enter the next quote number here. Otherwise, if all quotes share one numbering scheme that can be entered on the **Sales Document Numbers Setup** window, so you can leave this blank.
- **Days to Expire**: This is the default number of days a quote is valid for. After expiration, users will not be able to transfer quotes to orders. Users can change the expiration days as needed on individual quotes.

- **Comment ID**: This is the default comment for a quote. For example, if all quotes are set to expire in 30 days, you could create a comment that says `Prices are guaranteed for 30 days from quote date` and enter the corresponding **Comment ID** here. The comment would automatically populate on every quote created with this quote ID.
- **Format**: Dynamics GP has four report formats available for each SOP transaction type: **Blank Paper**, **Short Form**, **Long Form**, and **Other Form**. If you need to set up multiple quote IDs that show different information when printed, each quote ID can be defaulted to use a different report format. The format being printed can always be changed by the user when printing an order, but this will be the default format suggested.

> Only the **Blank Paper** format can be used if you are going to e-mail quotes.

- **Transfer Quote to Order**: If this quote can be transferred to an order, check the box and enter an **Order ID**.
- **Transfer Quote to Fulfillment Order/Invoice**: If this quote can be transferred to a fulfillment order or invoice, check the box and enter a **Fulfillment Order/Invoice ID**.
- **Default Quantities**: This determines whether the item quantities on the quote default to **Quantity to Invoice** or **Quantity to Order**. This setting will depend on whether you plan to typically transfer a quote to an order or an invoice.
- **Use Prospects**: Leave this checked if you want to allow prospects to be used on quotes, otherwise only customers will be allowed.
- **Allow Repeating Documents**: A quote can be set up to repeat. This is more typical for orders, but may be needed at times for quotes. This setting determines whether this quote ID will be allowed to repeat.
- **Options** and **Password** scrolling list: Each of the **Options** listed has an optional **Password**, saved in clear text:
    - **Delete Documents**: With this unchecked, once saved, a quote cannot be deleted. It is recommended to leave this unchecked, so that users must void quotes that have been saved, thus keeping a record of them.
    - **Edit Printed Documents**: With this unchecked, once a quote is printed, it cannot be changed.

    ◦ **Override Document Numbers**: If you want the users to be able to change the quote numbers when they are creating them, check this option. Note that, once entered, a quote number cannot be changed.
    ◦ **Void Documents**: Select this if users are allowed to void quotes. If so, make sure that you have selected **Track Voided Transactions in History** on the **Sales Order Processing Setup** window.

## Order

In Dynamics GP, a sales transaction can start out as an order or back order, or a quote can be transferred to an order. Depending on setup, orders can allocate inventory items, thus making them unavailable for other orders or invoices. The following is a list of the fields on the **Sales Order Setup** window:

- **Order ID**: An ID for the order document—the maximum length allowed is 15 characters. This is what users will need to type or select when using this order document ID on a transaction.
- **Order ID Next Number**: If you are setting up multiple order IDs and would like for each to have its own numbering scheme, you can enter the next order number here. Otherwise, if all orders will share one numbering scheme that can be entered on the **Sales Document Numbers Setup** window, so you can leave this blank.
- **Comment ID**: This is the default comment you would like to populate automatically on orders with this order ID.
- **Format**: Dynamics GP has four report formats available for each SOP transaction type: **Blank Paper**, **Short Form**, **Long Form**, and **Other Form**. If you need to set up multiple order IDs that show different information when printed, each order ID can be defaulted to use a different report format. The format can always be changed by the user when printing an order, but this will be the default suggested.

> Only the **Blank Paper** format can be used if you are going to e-mail orders.

- **Allocate by**: This setting determines how (or if) inventory is allocated for this order ID. Allocated inventory is still considered on-hand stock, but it is not available for other orders or invoices.
    ◦ **Line Item**: Select this if you want to allocate inventory as each line is entered. Users will need to choose an action on each line with a quantity shortage, which could significantly slow down order entry if most of the orders being entered do not have inventory in stock.

- **Document/Batch**: Inventory is not allocated as orders are entered and a separate allocation process is run either for each order or batch of orders. This gives less visibility of inventory availability during order entry; however, this can greatly speed it up because each line item is not checked and dealt with individually.
- **None**: Orders are not allocated at all and only after an order is transferred to an invoice or fulfillment order is inventory allocated.

- **Transfer Order to Back Order**: If this order ID can be transferred to a back order, check this selection and enter a **Back Order ID**. Many companies do not use back orders, and simply use the back ordered quantity on orders to track back ordered items.
- **Transfer Order to Fulfillment Order/Invoice**: There is no checkbox here, as the basic functionality of an order is to transfer to an invoice. The only choice is what **Fulfillment Order/Invoice ID** to use.

> The **Fulfillment Order/Invoice ID** is a required field and you will not be able to save the order ID without a valid **Fulfillment Order/Invoice ID** filled in. What you can do to get around this is type in the **Fulfillment Order/Invoice ID** you would like to use, click on **Add** on the message that comes up asking if you want to add it, then click on **Save**. You can go back to the **Fulfillment Order/Invoice ID** later to finish setting it up.

- **Options** section:
    - **Allow Repeating Documents**: If this order ID can be set up to be repeated, mark this checkbox. **Allocate by** has to be set to **Document/ Batch** or **None** to enable this option.
    - **Use Separate Fulfillment Process**: If this option is checked, a separate step to fulfill orders will be needed prior to being able to transfer them to invoices.
    - **Allow all Back Ordered Items to Print on Invoice**: If this is selected, all back ordered items will be transferred to an invoice with a fulfilled quantity of zero, allowing them to print on the invoice. If you want to only show items that are being shipped/billed on invoices, leave this option unchecked.
    - **Credit Limit Hold ID**: Holds can offer an additional level of control in Sales Order Processing. Setting up **Process Holds** is explained in *Chapter 2, Module setup* of the *Sales Order Processing* manual. (This manual can be downloaded at: `http://technet.microsoft.com/en-us/library/jj673202(v=gp.30).aspx`.)

- **Override Quantity to Invoice with Quantity Fulfilled**: Marking this option will change the **Quantity to Invoice** on orders with the quantity fulfilled. This may be useful if you often have orders that are partially fulfilled.

  If this option is checked, **Enable Quantity Cancelled in Sales Order Fulfillment** becomes available. This will allow cancelling the remaining quantities when orders are partially fulfilled during the fulfillment process.

  If **Transfer Order to Back Order** is selected, **Enable Quantity to Back Order in Sales Order Fulfillment** will also be enabled.

- **Options** and **Password** scrolling list: Each of these **Options** has an optional **Password**, saved in clear text on this window.

  - **Allow Invoicing of Unfulfilled or Partially Fulfilled Orders**: This option is activated only when the **Use Separate Fulfillment Process** option is selected. Otherwise, if **Use Separate Fulfillment Process** is not selected, invoicing an unfulfilled or partially fulfilled order will not be allowed, even though you can select this option.
  - **Delete Documents**: With this unchecked, a saved order cannot be deleted.
  - **Edit Printed Documents**: With this unchecked, once an order is printed, it cannot be opened or changed.
  - **Override Document Numbers**: If users can change the order numbers when they are creating them, check this option (once entered, an order number cannot be changed).
  - **Void Documents**: Select this option if users are allowed to void orders. If so, make sure that you have selected **Track Voided Transactions in History** on the **Sales Order Processing Setup** window.

The following screenshot shows a sample **Sales Order Setup** window:

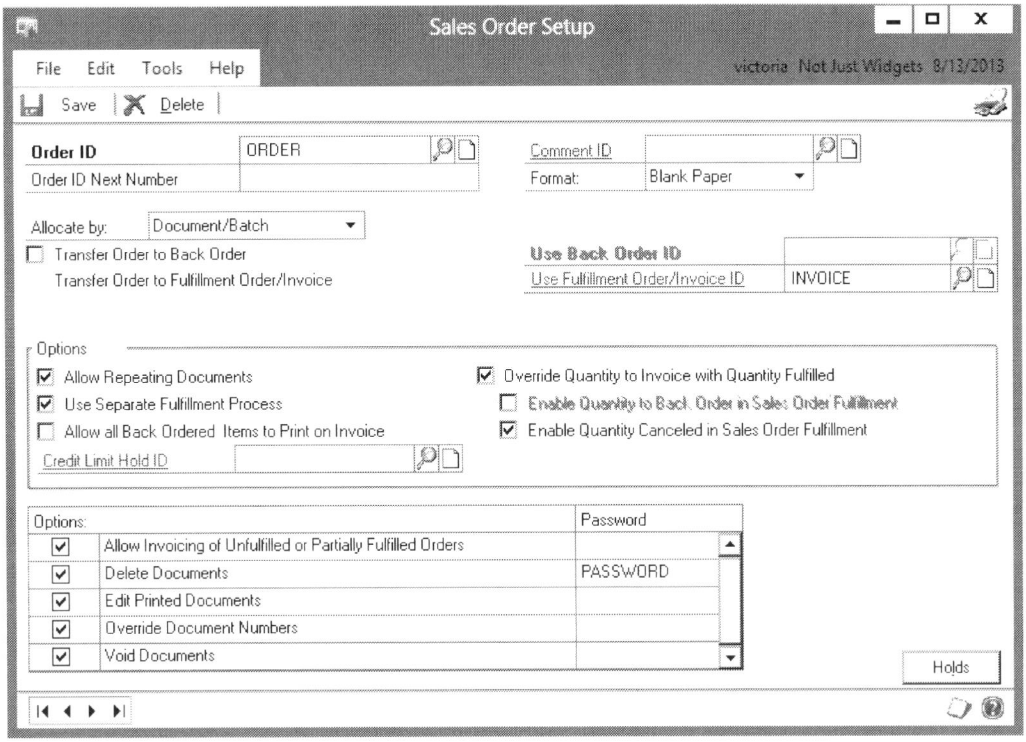


## Back Order

Back orders allow companies to transfer unfulfilled line items from orders or invoices to a separate transaction. Many companies do not use back orders and simply use the back order quantity on orders for back ordered items. If you choose to use back orders in Dynamics GP, refer to the setup options under the preceding *Quote* section for an explanation of the fields on the **Sales Back Order Setup** window.

## Fulfillment Order/Invoice

Fulfillment orders and invoices share the same setup window because they are basically the same transaction. All the options on the **Sales Fulfillment Order/Invoice Setup** window have been explained under the *Order* section, with the following new fields: **Enable Fulfillment Workflow**, **Update Actual Ship Date During Confirm Ship**, and **Update Invoice Date on First Print**. These fields are used with **Sales Fulfillment Workflow**, which offers additional functionality for the SOP module. Setting up a fulfillment workflow for sales is detailed in *Chapter 4, Sales fulfillment workflow setup* of the *Sales Order Processing* manual. (This manual can be downloaded here: `http://technet.microsoft.com/en-us/library/jj673202(v=gp.30).aspx`.)

A sample **Sales Fulfillment Order/Invoice Setup** window is shown here:

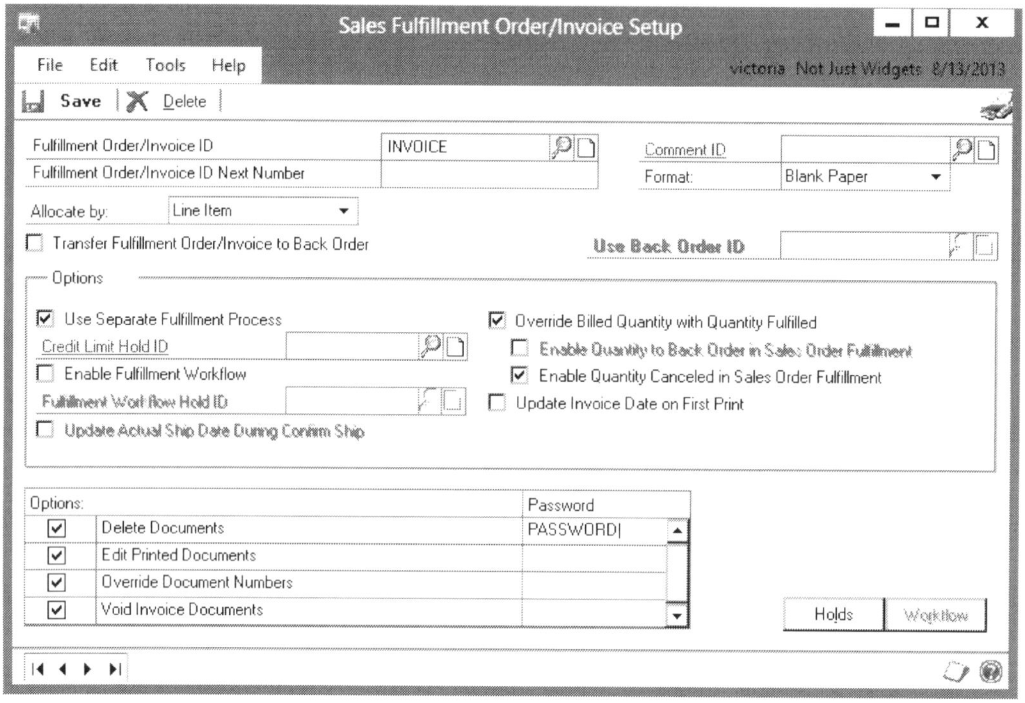


> Note that even if you mark the **Delete Documents** option, once an invoice is printed users will not be allowed to delete it. This option only applies to unprinted invoices and fulfillment orders.

## Return

A sales return transaction allows the return of inventory and non-inventory items to be entered. There are just a few options on the **Sales Return Setup** window compared to the other sales document types. All of these options have been explained in previous sections except the following:

- **Use next number from Fulfillment Order/Invoice ID**: If you would like your returns to use the same numbering scheme as your invoices, choose this option and provide an **Invoice ID** with the desired numbering scheme. With this selected, if the last invoice number was `1234`, a new return transaction will be numbered `1235`, and the next invoice will be `1236`.
- **Override Item Unit Cost for Returns**: The default item cost on returns will be the current cost of the item. If this option is selected, users can override the costs on returns.

Some of the fields on the sales document type setup windows are difficult to give recommendations for, as they very much depend on the exact workflow and needs of your organization. Textbook explanations of these options are often not enough to get a full understanding. Use your Dynamics GP resource to help you determine the best settings for your specific situation, and perform tests to verify that your selected settings will behave as desired.

# User-Defined fields

During sales transaction entry, users have a window of user-defined fields available to them for entering additional data you want to track for transactions. Additionally, prospects and customer items have some user-defined fields available. The labels for all of these fields can be changed on the **Sales User-Defined Fields Setup** window, accessed by clicking on the **User-Defined** button at the bottom of the **Sales Order Processing Setup** window.

There are three sections of fields you can set up labels for:

- **User-Defined Field Entry**: These fields are accessed from the **Sales Transaction Entry** or **Sales Transaction Inquiry** windows. There are three lists that can hold predefined values (up to 20 characters), two date fields, and five text fields that can hold up to 20 characters each.
- **Prospect Maintenance**: These fields are available when entering or changing a prospect. Two text fields of 20 characters each are available.
- **Customer/Item Maintenance**: If you will be using customer items, five text fields holding 20 characters each will be available on the **Customer Item Maintenance** window.

You can change these labels at any time and the corresponding field names on the windows showing them will change.

# SOP document numbers

Clicking on the **Numbers** button at the bottom of the **Sales Order Processing Setup** window opens the **Sales Document Numbers Setup** window. Here you can set the **Code**, **Next Number**, and **Format** for each sales transaction type, as well as **Packing Slips** and **Picking Tickets**.

It is not recommended to change the default **Codes**, as that will make it more difficult for training and ongoing support. The **Next Number** selections on this window will only be used if no numbering scheme is set up for a **Document Type ID**. Some companies like to have letters at the beginning of transaction numbers, so that by looking at a transaction list they can quickly identify the transaction types, while other companies prefer to use only numbers. In either case, make sure to leave enough digits for growth, as the number of characters will not auto increment. After reaching `999`, the next number will be `000`, not `1000`. However, after reaching `00999`, the next number will be `01000`.

> Dynamics GP will allow the same number to be used for different sales transaction types. This means you can have Order # 12345, Invoice # 12345, and Return # 12345 all co-existing in the system with no conflicts. A unique transaction is determined by the combination of transaction type and number. Even though it is allowed by the system, users may find it confusing to have the same numbers for different transaction types and this is typically not recommended.

Packing slips and picking tickets can either have their own numbering schemes, or use the number of the transaction they are being printed for. The following screenshot shows a typical **Sales Document Numbers Setup** window where the invoice numbers will start with **005500** to continue from a previous system, but all the other transaction types will have a new numbering scheme starting with a different digit for somewhat easier identification:

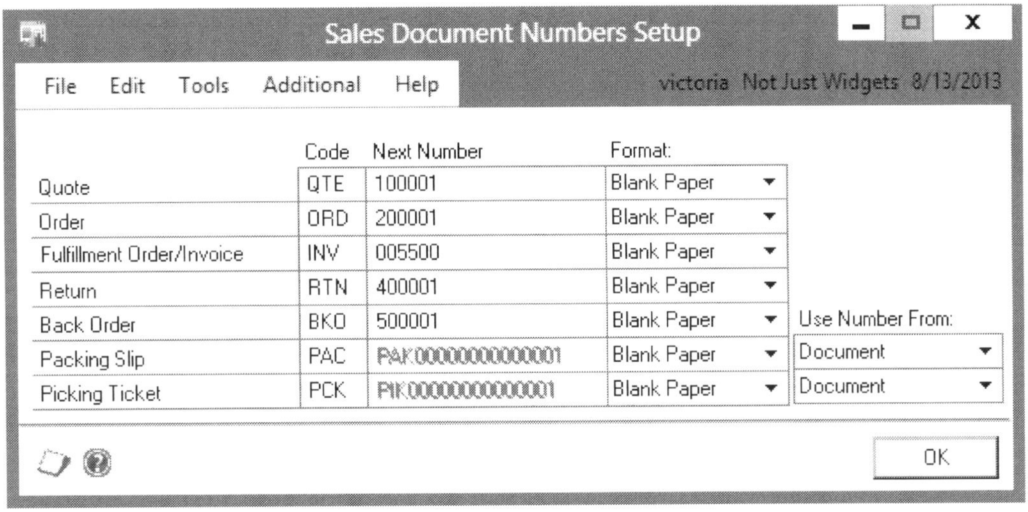


Note that you can also default a **Format** for each sales transaction type on this window. If the **Next Number** for a transaction is taken from this window, the **Format** selected here will be defaulted. If a **Next Number** is entered for a specific document ID, that will override the **Next Number** and **Format** on this window.

# Sales Order Processing Setup Options

The **Sales Order Processing Setup Options** window can be opened by clicking on the **Options** button at the bottom of the **Sales Order Processing Setup** window. This window holds additional setup selections for the SOP module, such as tax defaults and defaults for how POs are created from SOP transactions. The following is a list of the fields on this window:

- **Tax Calculations**: If **Single Schedule** is chosen, you can specify one tax schedule to be used on SOP transactions. Typically, if a company is selling taxable products and services, the **Advanced** setting is recommended so that you can control taxes with more granularity.

- **Tax Options**: When **Advanced Tax Calculations** is selected, this section is enabled and you can set up **Tax Options** for **Non-Inventory Items**, **Freight**, and **Miscellaneous** amounts. Typically, non-inventory and miscellaneous amounts are taxed based on the customer's tax setup, and whether freight is taxed depends on each state. If you have a tax schedule called **FREIGHT** containing all the tax details where freight is taxed, the setup would look like the following:

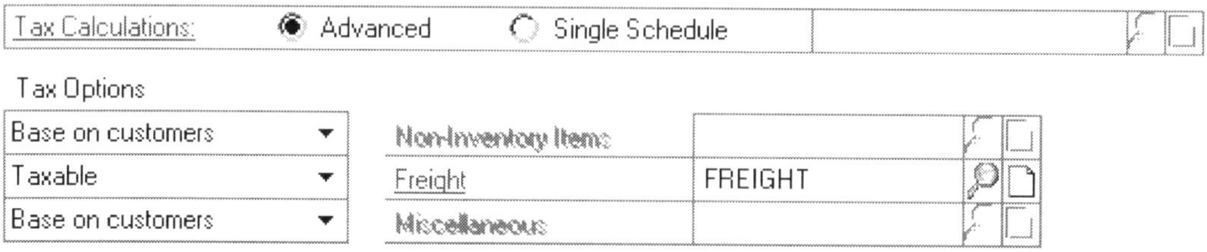


- **Defaults for Picking Ticket**: These options will work only for **Advanced Picking** and when using multiple bins. Setting up **Advanced Picking** is covered in *Chapter 2, Module setup* of the *Sales Order Processing* manual. (This manual can be downloaded at: `http://technet.microsoft.com/en-us/library/jj673202(v=gp.30).aspx`.)
- **Defaults for Purchase Order**: These settings control the behavior of purchase orders that are created directly from sales order transactions:
    - **Site Preference**: If you use different Site IDs for line items on the same sales invoice (which is not very typical), you can choose between:

      **Combine Items with Different Sites on Same PO**: If a sales order has items shipping from more than one site, all the items will be placed on the same purchase order, with different sites for each line. This is not typical for most companies.

      **Don't Combine Items with Different Sites on Same PO**: If a sales order has items shipping from more than one site, separate purchase orders will be created for each site. This selection is the most common.

      **Use a Single Site for All POs**: This will enable a **Site ID** field where you can choose what site to use. This is useful for companies that always receive items to one location.
    - **Required Date**: Purchase orders can store and print required dates. Choose between **Requested Ship Date** from the order and **Days Prior to Requested Ship Date**, which will enable you to enter the number of **Days**.

- ◦ **U of M**: Select whether to use the **Sales Line Item's U of M** or the **Item's Default Purchasing U of M**.
- ◦ **Combine Similar Items Into a Single PO Line**: If the same item exists on multiple lines, they will be combined into one PO line with this option selected. Often there is a reason why the same item is on separate lines on an order, so this is typically unchecked to preserve the separate line items on the PO.
- ◦ **Drop-Ship Sales Items**: Choose whether you would like to **Combine Different Ship-To Addresses into one PO** and, if so, whether you also want to **Combine Different Ship-To Addresses from Different Sales Orders into one PO**.

The following is a sample **Defaults for Purchase Order** setup, where POs are always received at the NJ site and the PO **Required Date** is set to **3 days** before the required ship date for the sales order:

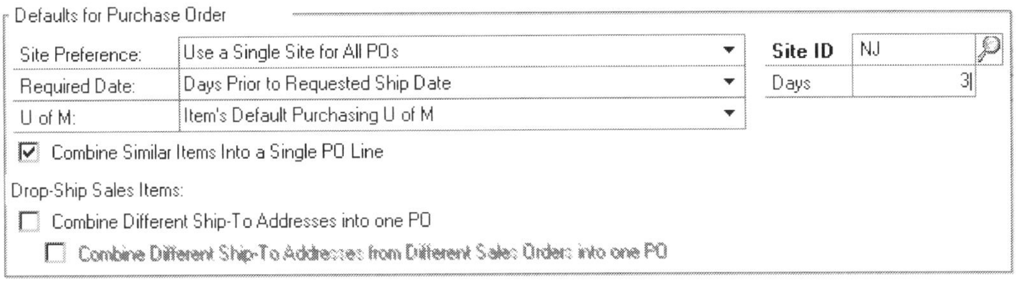


- **Options**: This section has a list of actions that you can allow or disallow during sales transaction entry. You can also enter a **Password** for each of these so that only a user who knows the password will be allowed to complete the action. Note that the passwords are not masked.
  - ◦ **Allow Markdown**: Mark this option if you want to allow markdowns on individual items on sales transactions.
  - ◦ **Auto-Assign Lot Numbers**: With this option marked, items that track lot numbers will automatically assign lot numbers to sales transactions by either receipt date or expiration date, depending on what was chosen on the **Inventory Control Setup** window. If receipt date was selected, lot numbers will be assigned based on the item valuation method. If expiration date was selected, the lots with the oldest expiration dates will be used first, and lots without expiration dates will not be auto-assigned. Expired lots would also not be auto-assigned.

- **Auto-Assign Serial Numbers**: With this option marked, items that track serial numbers will automatically assign the next serial number item based on the item valuation method.
- **Enter Non-Inventoried Items**: Mark this option if you want to allow users to enter non-inventory items on sales transactions. Often companies choose to not allow this, so that any items sold must be properly set up as an inventory item first.
- **Allow Prices Below Cost**: Mark this option if you want to allow items with a price that is below cost on sales transactions. This may be needed if your company sends out samples at zero cost.
- **Override Prices**: If users are allowed to change prices on sales transactions, mark this option. If this is not allowed, all prices must be set up properly prior to entering sales transactions.
- **Override Quantity Shortages**: Mark this if you want to allow users to override quantity shortages. If this option is not selected, users will only be able to sell items currently on hand.
- **Override Price Levels**: Mark this option if you want to allow changing the price level from what is defaulted on sales transactions.
- **Allow Deletion of PO Commitments**: PO commitments are created when a purchase order is created from a sales order and they can also be manually added to "commit" items on a purchase order to a specific sales order. Mark this option if you want to allow these commitments to be deleted to be able to re-allocate or re-commit the items to different sales orders.
- **Allow Sale of Discontinued Items**: Mark this option if you want to be able to sell inventory items that have been changed to the **Discontinued Item Type**.

# E-mail settings

If you are planning on e-mailing sales documents to customers from Dynamics GP, you will need to make sure that e-mailing for Sales Order Processing transactions is enabled and set up. To do this, navigate to **Microsoft Dynamics GP** | **Tools** | **Setup** | **Sales** | **E-mail Settings**. You may have already completed this setup as part of the Receivables module setup. If you need to add to or change it, please refer to *Chapter 7, Module Setup: General Ledger, Bank Reconciliation, Payables, and Receivables*, for more details on e-mail setup.

# Customer items

Dynamics GP allows you to set up customer-specific part numbers for your inventory items. This may be needed for larger customers who want to order using their own part numbers and want to see these numbers on their invoices. When entering sales transactions, if a customer item number is typed in, the system will automatically substitute it with your inventory item number.

Customer items allow you to set up a one-to-one relationship between each customer and item you have set up in Dynamics GP. To start this setup, navigate to **Cards | Sales | Customer Items**. The fields on the **Customer Item Maintenance** window are:

- **Customer ID** and **Name**: When you select a **Customer ID**, their **Name** will automatically be displayed.
- **Item Number** and **Description**: Select the **Item Number** you want to set up a customer item for and the **Description** will be displayed.
- **Customer Item**: Enter the customer part number for the item.
- **Customer Item Description**: This will default to your **Item Description**, but if you would like the customer to see a different description, enter it here.
- **Customer Item Short Name** and **Customer Item Generic**: These will be blank by default. If there is any other information you want to save about the customer item, you can store it in these fields.
- **Text Fields 1**, **2**, **3**, **4**, and **5**: These are user-defined fields and can store any other information you need about the customer item. The labels for these fields can be changed on the **Sales User-Defined Fields Setup** window, accessed by clicking on the **User-Defined** button at the bottom of the **Sales Order Processing Setup** window.
- **Substitute Item Number**, **Description**, and **Effective Date Range**: Optionally, you can set up an item to be offered as a substitute if the item being ordered is out of stock. This is a customer-specific substitute, as opposed to generic substitutes that can be set up for each item in the Inventory module.

Now that the setup of the Sales Order Processing module is complete, you can start entering SOP transactions in Dynamics GP.

# Purchase Order Processing

The **Purchase Order Processing** module, often referred to as **POP**, integrates the Inventory and Payables modules in Dynamics GP. It is part of the Purchasing series, so all the menu choices for it will start with **Purchasing**. The SQL Server tables for the POP module start with `POP`.

In POP you can enter purchase orders, returns, receipts of inventory, and corresponding vendor invoices. Purchase Order Processing also works together with Sales Order Processing to link purchase orders to sales orders with back ordered items.

Setup for Purchase Order Processing includes the following steps:

- Purchase Order Processing Setup
- Purchase Order Processing Options
- Receivings User-Defined
- E-mail settings

# Purchase Order Processing Setup

To start the setup of the POP module, navigate to **Microsoft Dynamics GP** | **Tools** | **Setup** | **Purchasing** | **Purchase Order Processing**. The following is a listing of the fields on the **Purchase Order Processing Setup** window:

- **Code** and **Next Number**: It is recommended to leave the **Code** unchanged for all transactions. For the **Next Number** settings, consider making these a bit shorter so they are more user-friendly. Only one purchase order numbering scheme is available in Dynamics GP. Receipts are used for both receipts of inventory and matching vendor invoices in Dynamics GP and receipt numbers are typically only used internally.

  As with other number schemes in Dynamics GP, these will not add more digits when they run out, so if the PO numbering is set to `001`, when it reaches `999`, the next number will be `000`, then `001` again.

- **Purchase Order Format**: Two purchase order report formats are available in Dynamics GP: **Blank Paper** and **Other Form**. Users can pick which report format to print during transaction entry; this setting simply controls the default.

> Only the **Blank Paper** format can be used for e-mailing POs.

- **Non-Inventoried Items**: These settings will only be used for non-inventory items. For inventory items, the decimal places and quantity tolerance settings from each item will be used.
    - **Decimal Places**: If users enter non-inventory items on POs, the **Quantities** and **Currency** decimal places set here will control how those items show up. If Multicurrency is enabled, clicking on the expansion button (blue arrow) next to the **Currency** field will open the **Purchasing Non-Inventoried Currency Decimals Setup** window where you can set the number of **Currency Decimals** for each **Currency ID**.
    - **Quantity Tolerance**: If you want to set quantity tolerance options for non-inventory items on POs, enter them here. For a detailed description of these options, please refer to the *Item class setup* section in this chapter.

> There is no way to disallow non-inventory items in Purchase Order Processing. However, the Default Add Item tool available in the Professional Services Tools Library may help prevent inadvertently entering non-inventory items by popping up a message asking if the user wants to add the item when a non-inventory item is entered.

- **PO Document Date:** Choose between **User Date** (also called the GP date) and **Previous Doc. Date** to set what defaults as the purchase order date during transaction entry. Typically POs are not back dated, so **User Date** is more commonly picked for this option.
- **PO Line Site ID**: If **Previous Line's Site ID** is chosen, a user will always have to fill in a Site ID on the first line item when creating a new PO. All subsequent lines will default to the same site as the previous line. Choosing **Item's Default Site** will fill in the **Default Site ID** selected on the **Item Quantities Maintenance** window for each item. This may result in one PO with multiple sites, which Dynamics GP allows; however, most companies do not choose to do this.
- **Display Item During Entry By**: If you have set up vendor item numbers during inventory item setup, you can choose **Vendor Item** here to have the vendor's part number display during PO entry. Otherwise, choose **Item** so that your item numbers are displayed.

- **Allow Editing of Purchase Orders On Hold**: Select this to allow users to edit POs while they are on hold. This option will be available only when **Allow Hold/Remove Hold of Purchase Orders** is selected in the **Options** list at the bottom of this window. Typically, there is no reason to prevent editing POs on hold (a PO on hold cannot be printed or released).
- **Place Purchase Orders Created From Sales Order Processing on Hold**: If this is selected, POs created from sales orders are automatically placed on hold. This may be useful if someone first needs to check all POs created from sales orders before releasing them.
- **Search for Uncommitted PO Quantities From Sales Order Processing**: When creating a PO from a sales order with back ordered items, if this option is selected, the system will first search for any existing POs for these items that are not already committed to other sales orders. If this is not selected, a new PO will always be created from a sales order.
- **Transfer Line Comments from Sales Document**: Selecting this option will copy any line item comments from sales orders to the POs created from the SOP module. This setting should depend on what is typically entered in the SOP line item comments on orders.
- **Calculate Line Item's Release By Date Based on Vendor Lead Time**: Selecting this will use the number of days entered for the **Planning Lead Time** of a vendor/item combination on the **Item Vendors Maintenance** window.
- **Maintain History**: It is recommended to keep all history and leave all these choices selected.
- **Prepayment Setup**: A new, and highly requested, feature in Dynamics GP 2013 is the ability to enter prepayments on purchase orders. Unfortunately, this option is only available if the following is true:

| Module | Registered |
|---|---|
| Payables Management | Yes |
| Purchase Order Processing | Yes |
| Project Accounting | No |
| Multidimensional Accounting | No |
| Analytical Accounting | No |

This limitation may rule out the use of PO prepayments in many implementations of Dynamics GP. However, if you happen to meet these criteria and you want to be able to enter prepayments on POs, mark the **Allow Purchase Order Prepayment** option, which will enable the rest of the choices in this section.

Selecting **Create manual prepayment from Purchase Order Processsing** will enable manual prepayments to be entered; otherwise only computer checks can be used to enter prepayments. Even if you typically send computer checks, there should be no harm in allowing this option.

If you would like to control who can enter the prepayments with a password, enter one here. For **Prepayment Account**, enter the account that will be debited when a PO prepayment is entered.

- **Options**: Each one of the following options can have a password set up, so that only users who know the password can perform the associated task. Note that the passwords are not masked.
    - **Allow Receiving Without a Purchase Order**: If this option is selected, a receipt transaction can be entered without first having to enter a PO. Some companies choose to disallow this to ensure better control of the purchasing process.
    - **Change Site ID in Receiving**: Selecting this option will allow users to change the site that items are being received to during the entry of a receipt transaction. If this option is not selected, the receipt will have to be entered for the site specified on the purchase order.
    - **Allow Hold/Remove Hold of Purchase Orders**: Hold functionality will be available for POs if this option is checked. Use the **Password** to control which users can create or remove a hold.
    - **Allow Editing of Costs in Receiving**: If this is allowed, users will have the ability to change costs for inventory items being received if they are different from the costs on the purchase order.
    - **Warn when Purchase Order Line Item is Not Fully Invoiced**: This is a new option added in Dynamics GP 2013. If selected, users will see a warning if they are closing a purchase order that has remaining quantities to invoice.

The following illustrates a sample **Purchase Order Processing Setup** window:

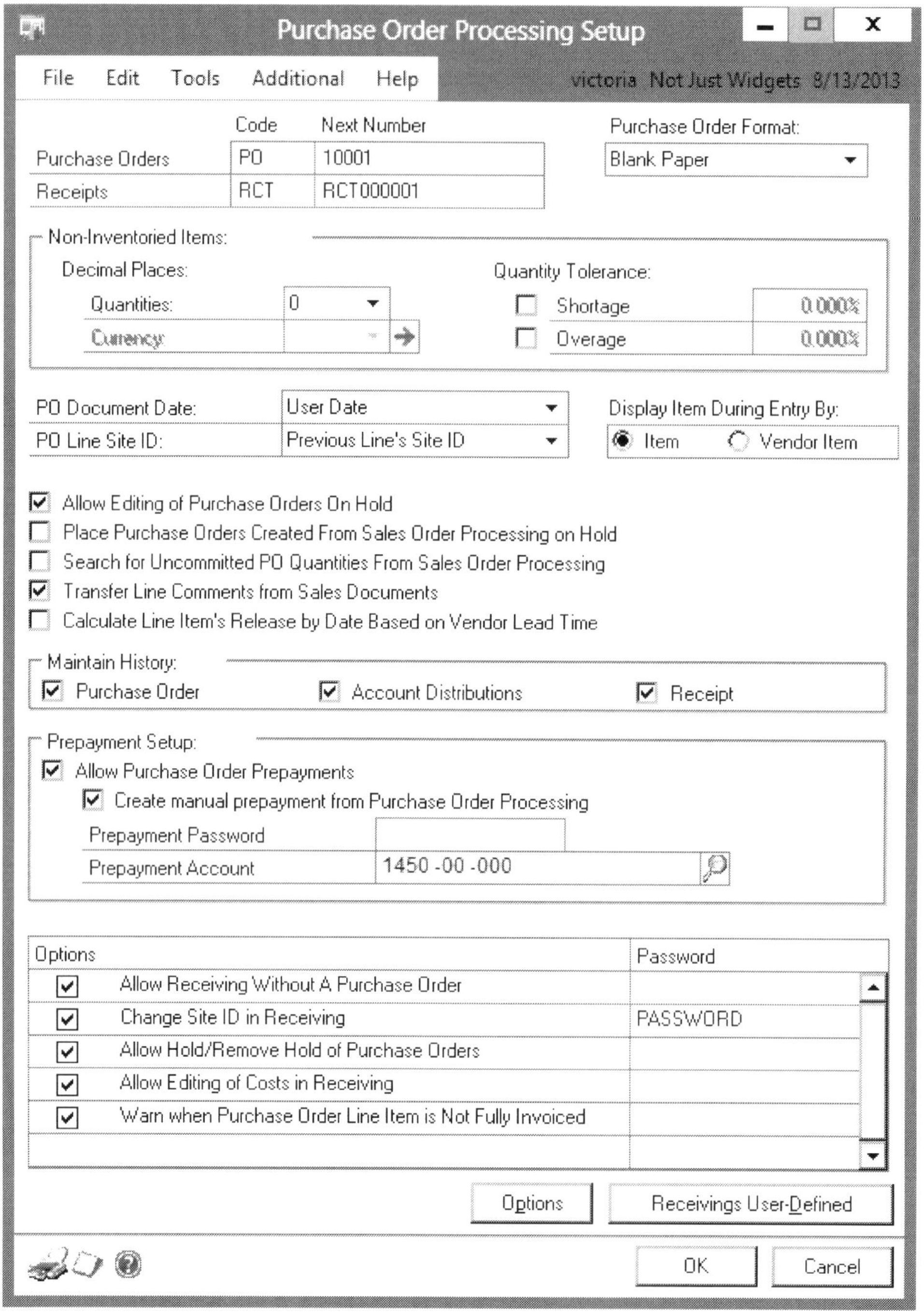

# Purchase Order Processing Options

Clicking on the **Options** button at the bottom of the **Purchase Order Processing Setup** window opens the **Purchase Order Processing Setup Options** window, where you can set up defaults for taxes and the Purchase Order Generator functionality.

While most companies do not use purchase taxes, if this is something you need to set up, choose **Single Schedule** and a **Tax Schedule ID** under **Tax Calculations** if all items, freight, and miscellaneous amounts on POs will be using the same tax schedule. Choosing **Single Schedule** will look like the example shown in the following screenshot, with the other options disabled:

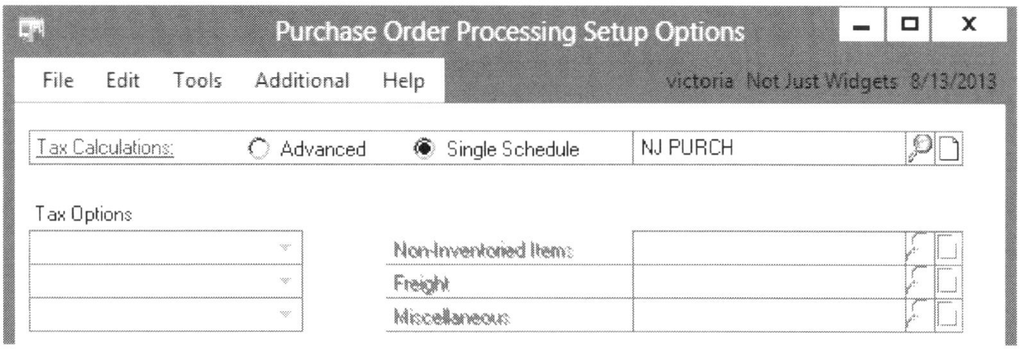


If the **Advanced** option is chosen, you can specify different **Tax Options** and **Tax Schedule IDs** for **Non-Inventoried Items**, **Freight**, and **Miscellaneous** amounts.

For details on setting up Purchase Order Generator functionality please refers *Chapter 3*, *Purchase order generator setup* of the *Purchase Order Processing* manual. (This manual can be downloaded at: `http://technet.microsoft.com/en-us/library/jj673202(v=gp.30).aspx`.)

# Receivings User-Defined

During the entry of POP receipts, users can track additional details about the receipt, with 35 user-defined fields available. Many companies never use this, but for those that want to take advantage of this functionality, labels for each field can be set up on the **Receivings User-Defined Fields Setup** window.

To set up these labels, click on the **Receivings User-Defined** button at the bottom of the **Purchase Order Processing Setup** window—five list fields with predefined values (up to 30 characters long), 10 text fields, and 20 date fields are available. The labels for each can be up to 30 characters.

# E-mail settings

If you are planning on e-mailing purchase orders to vendors from Dynamics GP, you will need to make sure e-mailing options for POs are enabled and set up. To do this, navigate to **Microsoft Dynamics GP | Tools | Setup | Purchasing | E-mail Settings**. You may have already completed this setup as part of the Payables module setup. If you need to add to or change it, please refer to *Chapter 7, Module Setup – General Ledger, Bank Reconciliation, Payables, and Receivables*, for more detail on e-mail setup.

Once the setup of the Purchase Order Processing module is complete, you can start entering purchase orders, inventory receipts, and invoices in Dynamics GP.

# Summary

In this chapter, we discussed the setup of the distribution modules—Inventory, Sales Order Processing, and Purchase Order Processing. We went over the details of selections on setup windows and discussed the importance of using classes for inventory items. At this point, Dynamics GP is ready to be used to enter master records and transactions.

In the next chapter we will go over populating initial data into Dynamics GP using Integration Manager.

# 9

# Populating Initial Data

Before starting to use your Dynamics GP system, you will typically need to populate some initial data such as General Ledger accounts, vendors, customers, and open transactions or balances. While all of these can be entered manually, it is often more efficient to import them. Each Dynamics GP license sold today includes an **Integration Manager** license for up to 240 days from your GP purchase.

In this chapter, we will go over the basics of using Integration Manager to import data into Dynamics GP and look at an example of each of the following types of imports:

- General Ledger accounts
- General Ledger transactions
- Vendors
- Open payables transactions
- Customers
- Open receivables transactions
- Inventory items
- Inventory transactions

## Basics of Integration Manager

In *Chapter 2, Planning – Business Requirements*, we went over various tools and methods available for importing data into Dynamics GP. Because Integration Manager is included with the initial Dynamics GP purchase and is fairly easy to use without any complex coding, many companies choose Integration Manager for their initial data imports.

When Integration Manager is installed, a number of sample imports (also called integrations) are installed, as well. It is often easier to start with these rather than create your own imports, or to at least look at these samples if you have questions when setting up your own imports.

# Components of an integration

There are four parts to setting up an import in Integration Manager:

- Integration properties
- Source(s)
- Destination
- Destination mapping

## Properties

The properties of an import specify whether the import will be inserting records, updating them, or both, how many errors or warnings are allowed before the import automatically stops, and settings for the log files created by the import. To access the **Properties** window, navigate to **Integration** | **Properties** on the top menu or right-click on the name of the import and select **...Properties...** at the bottom. Note that your integration name will show as part of the menu choice:

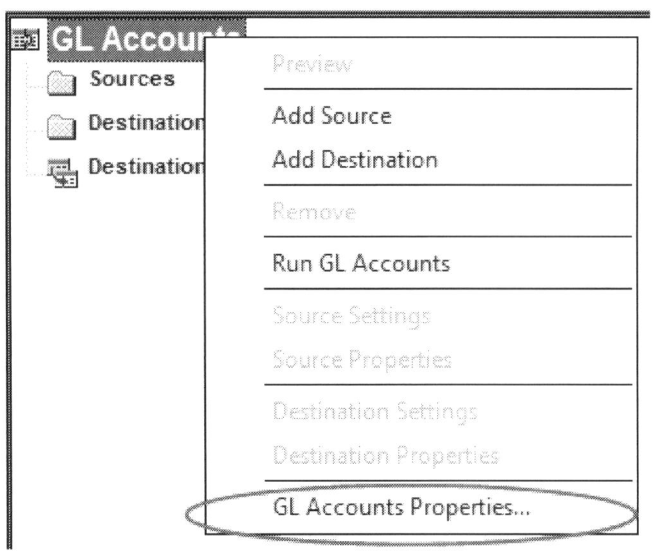

The following is a sample **Properties** window for a GL account import:

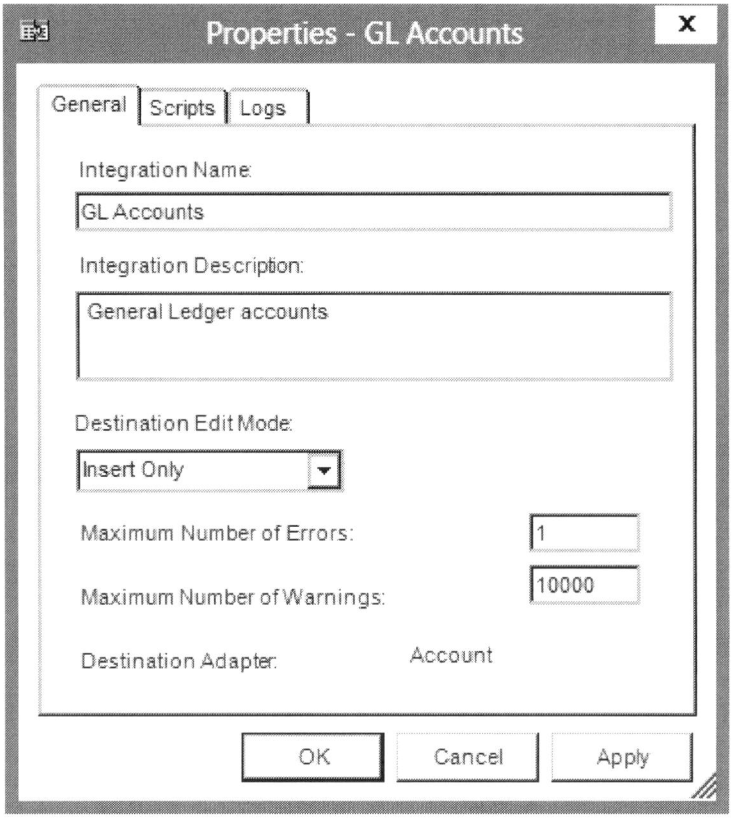


The settings shown will automatically stop the import if there is more than one error; however, 10,000 warnings will be allowed before stopping the import. Warnings are typically fine to allow, as they are usually simply informational. However, you still will want to look through all the warnings after your import to make sure there are no corrections needed. An error is something that violates the business logic of Dynamics GP and all errors must be fixed for the import to work.

To get the most detailed level of log files, so that you can see as much information as possible about all the errors and warnings, change the **Level** on the **Logs** tab to **Trace**. Changing the **Storage Type** field to **File** will save the log file in a text file that can easily be opened afterwards. You will need to specify an existing **File Directory** by clicking on the ellipsis button (**...**) to the right of the **Storage Type** field:

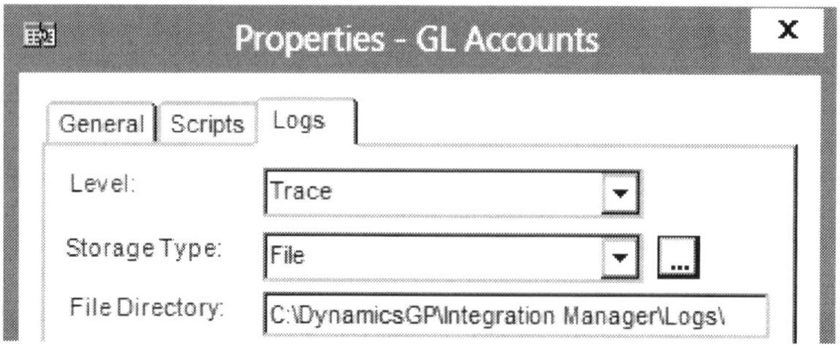


Log files will be stored in the specified directory until manually deleted.

# Source(s)

A **source** is a pointer to your source data for the import. Sources can be made up of one or more files or database queries. If multiple data sources are used for the same import, a relationship will need to be set up between them. For the examples in this chapter, we will use tab delimited text files as the sources for our imports. Typically, these are first created in Excel, then saved as a `Text` (`Tab delimited`) file with a `.txt` file extension.

To create a new source for an import, click on **Add Source** on the top menu or right-click anywhere in the **Integration** window and select **Add Source** to open the **Add Source** window. For a text file, select **Text** under **Adapters** on the left, select **Define New Text** under **Sources** on the right, and click on **Open**. This will open a new window where you can **Name** your source and point to the **File** with your data.

If the first row of your source file contains labels, be sure to check **First Row Contains Column Names**. You can switch to the **Columns** tab to see the columns in your source file.

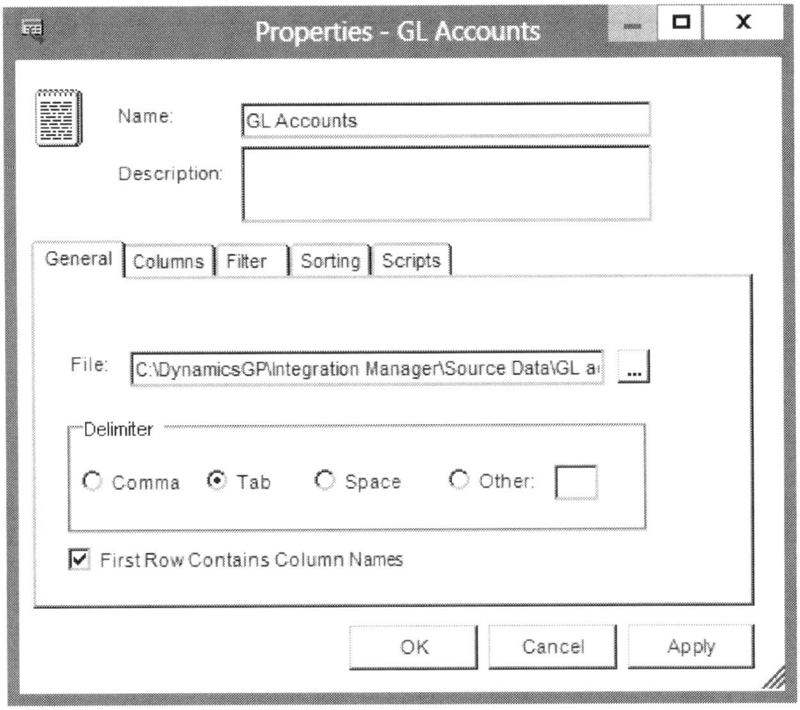


## Destination

**Destination** determines the type of Dynamics GP data that will be imported. To specify a destination, click on **Add Dest.** on the top menu, or right-click anywhere in the **Integration** window and select **Add Destination**. Expand **Microsoft Dynamics GP** under **Adapters** on the left and choose the series for your import. From the list of **Destinations** on the right, select the type of data you want to import and click on **Open**:

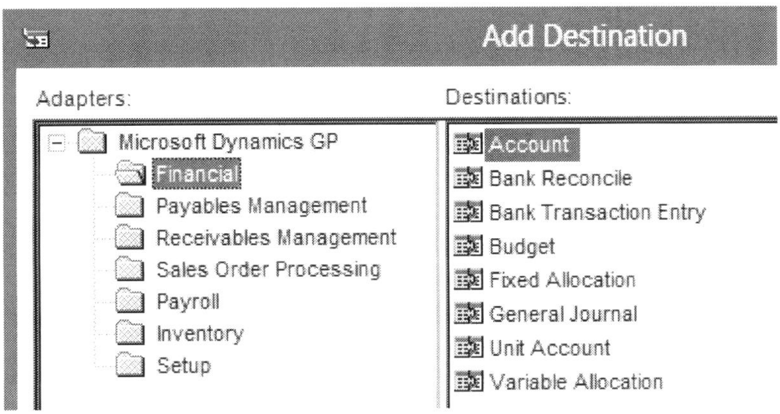

The following is a list of the series and destinations for each of the imports we are discussing in this chapter:

| Import | Series | Destination |
|---|---|---|
| GL accounts | Financial | Account |
| GL transactions | Financial | General Journal |
| Vendors | Payables Management | Vendor |
| Payables transactions | Payables Management | Payables Transaction |
| Customers | Receivables Management | Customer |
| Receivables transactions | Receivables Management | Receivables Transaction |
| Inventory Items | Inventory | Inventory Item |
| Inventory transactions | Inventory | Inventory Transaction |

# Destination mapping

**Destination mapping** is where you define how each column of data in your source(s) maps to the information that Dynamics GP expects for each type of import. The mapping will also include rules for each Dynamics GP column; for example, what to do if the data is missing or if a string is longer than the maximum allowed. The columns and rules available will change depending on the import destination.

# Running an import

Once an import is set up in Integration Manager, you will first need to log in to Dynamics GP on the same computer where you are running Integration Manager in order to run it. Make sure to log in as a user that has been granted access to all the windows that may be used by the import. These would be the windows needed if you were manually entering the data instead of importing it.

> Make sure that all Dynamics GP windows except the main one are closed prior to running an import. If any windows are open, you will receive an error.

A few recommendations for imports:

- Test any newly created import with just a few records. An import will read through all the records first, so testing with just a few records will let you know if there is a problem much faster than waiting for the entire dataset to be read.

- Make a backup of your company database prior to running any imports. This is especially important when you are first learning to use Integration Manager and may encounter unexpected results. This also means all users should be out of Dynamics GP when you are importing or you should be testing your import against a test company. As you get more comfortable with imports and can reuse existing integrations, this may not be as critical.
- Throughout the following sections, you will see notes about making sure imported amounts have the right number of decimal places. This is important because all currency fields in Dynamics GP can accept up to five decimal places. If your source data has more decimal places than the currency setup in Dynamics GP, the import may not give a warning or error about this, and will import the additional decimal places. This can cause reconciliation issues in the future, as there will be no way to fix this (or even see it) using the Dynamics GP user interface.
- After each import, validate your data—both the number of records imported as well as totals for amounts, to make sure you have imported what you expected to import.

When you have set up and saved your import, click on the **Run** button on the top menu to start the import into Dynamics GP. Once the import starts, you will not be able to use Dynamics GP, as Integration Manager will hide it. A **Progress** window will open to show you details about your import. If there are errors, you can click on **View Log** to see more details.

# Open transactions

All open transactions should already be recorded in the General Ledger of your old system, so these will presumably be imported as part of the balances and/or net changes in the General Ledger. Thus, any subledger open transactions (such as Payables, Receivables, and Inventory) should not be posted to the GL, because it would cause duplicate GL entries. There are three options to avoid this:

- Prior to posting the imported batch of open transactions to the subledger, turn off posting of that type of transaction to the GL. This is done on the **Posting Setup** window (**Microsoft Dynamics GP** | **Tools** | **Setup** | **Posting** | **Posting**) and has to be done while no other users are posting current transactions in that module, to make sure no new transactions are affected.

> If using this method, be sure to turn the posting to the General Ledger back on once you are done.

- On the **Posting Setup** window (**Microsoft Dynamics GP | Tools | Setup | Posting | Posting**), make sure that the subledger transactions are not set to post through to the GL automatically, and that a new GL batch is created for each posted subledger batch. Post the subledger batch and then delete the resulting GL batch prior to posting it. Be very careful with this method, as it is very easy to inadvertently delete the wrong batch or post a batch that was not meant to be posted.
- Import the open subledger transactions with the same GL accounts for debits and credits. The transactions can be posted to the GL; they will simply cause a net zero change. The account numbers for distributions can be hard coded in the import; however, it is an extra step that needs to be remembered and tested. This is the method I typically choose, because it does not involve any setup changes or deleting of batches.

> Even though there is a net zero change, some companies may not like to see these additional ins and outs in the General Ledger. If this method is used, make sure to clearly label these as beginning balance imports.

# General Ledger account import

During your module setup, you may have already created some General Ledger accounts. Instead of manually creating the rest, you could import them.

The following table lists the fields needed for a General Ledger account import:

| Field | Notes |
|---|---|
| **Account Number** | This should be your entire account number, including delimiters. For example: `1100-00-000`. |
| **Account Name** | This is also called Account Description in GP. The maximum length is 50 characters. |
| **Category** | This must be one of the existing categories in your GP company. *Appendix, General Ledger Account Categories* has a list of all the default account categories. For example: `Cost of Goods Sold`. |
| **Posting Type** | Valid options are **Balance Sheet** or **Profit and Loss**. |
| **Typical Balance** | While this is not too critical, you need to pick one and selecting the proper choice can help save time during transaction entry. Valid options are **Debit** or **Credit**. |

For a file with these fields, the destination mapping would look like the following screenshot:

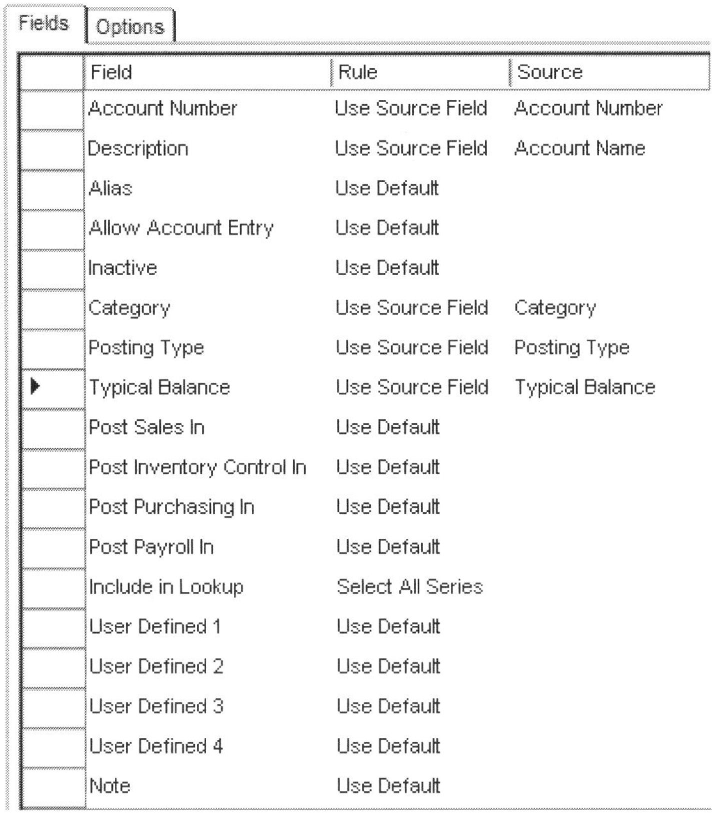

Fields | Options

| Field | Rule | Source |
|---|---|---|
| Account Number | Use Source Field | Account Number |
| Description | Use Source Field | Account Name |
| Alias | Use Default | |
| Allow Account Entry | Use Default | |
| Inactive | Use Default | |
| Category | Use Source Field | Category |
| Posting Type | Use Source Field | Posting Type |
| Typical Balance | Use Source Field | Typical Balance |
| Post Sales In | Use Default | |
| Post Inventory Control In | Use Default | |
| Post Purchasing In | Use Default | |
| Post Payroll In | Use Default | |
| Include in Lookup | Select All Series | |
| User Defined 1 | Use Default | |
| User Defined 2 | Use Default | |
| User Defined 3 | Use Default | |
| User Defined 4 | Use Default | |
| Note | Use Default | |

As you select each field on the right, a section for rules is activated at the bottom of the left side of the mapping window. The following is an example for the **Account Number** field:

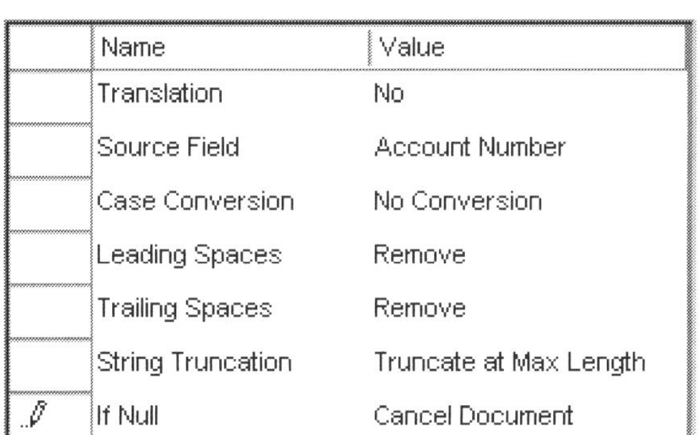

| Name | Value |
|---|---|
| Translation | No |
| Source Field | Account Number |
| Case Conversion | No Conversion |
| Leading Spaces | Remove |
| Trailing Spaces | Remove |
| String Truncation | Truncate at Max Length |
| If Null | Cancel Document |

These rules are specific to the field selected on the right (shown under **Source Field**), so each of these rules can be different for every field. For example, if an account number or name is missing, you may want to skip that account by selecting **Cancel Document** under **If Null**, as shown in the preceding screenshot. However, if the typical balance is missing, you may decide to choose **Use Default**, which will pick the first value available (in this case **Debit**). Another useful setting is **String Truncation**—if you have not checked the length of your account names and simply want to import the first 50 characters, selecting **Truncate at Max Length** will give you a warning, but will continue with the import.

> Once you have completed the import of General Account Numbers, you can verify the imported data in Dynamics GP using the **Accounts** SmartList.

# General Ledger transactions

In *Chapter 2, Planning – Business Requirements*, we discussed some typical scenarios for importing General Ledger opening balances, as well as data for comparative financial statements into Dynamics GP.

The following fields are needed for a basic GL transaction import:

| Field | Notes |
|---|---|
| **Transaction Date** | The GL date, typically in the following format: `MM/DD/YYYY`. If your regional settings are different, make sure to test your import to verify your dates are being imported as expected. |
| **Reference** | A transaction description—this is required for GL transactions, however it can be set to be a constant (for example, `Imported Balances`) in the integration mapping. It is recommended to include some indication that this was imported, so that users will be able to see this when looking up the transactions later. Maximum length is 30 characters. |
| **Account Number** | This should be your entire account number, including delimiters. For example: `1100-00-000`. |
| **Amount** | Positive number for debit values and negative number for credit values. It is important to make sure that none of your amounts are using more decimal places than you have set up for your currency.<br><br>It is possible to have separate columns for debits and credits, but in my experience it is easier to have just one amount column. |
| **Batch ID** | This is optional because it can be hard coded as part of the import. However, if you want to import GL transactions into multiple batches, you will need to specify a Batch ID of up to 15 characters. Batch IDs should be in all capital letters. |

Only one transaction date and reference are needed per transaction. However, there will be multiple account numbers and amounts for each transaction, so one way to set up this import is with two source files:

- A header file with each unique **Number**, **Transaction Date**, and **Reference**:

GL header.xlsx

| | A | B | C |
|---|---|---|---|
| 1 | Number | Transaction Date | Reference |
| 2 | 1 | 12/31/2012 | Import - 2012 balance |
| 3 | 2 | 01/31/2013 | Import - Jan 2013 net change |
| 4 | 3 | 02/28/2013 | Import - Feb 2013 net change |
| 5 | 4 | 03/31/2013 | Import - Apr 2013 net change |
| 6 | 5 | 04/30/2013 | Import - May 2013 net change |

- A detail file with each **Account Number** and **Amount**:

GL detail.xlsx

| | A | B | C |
|---|---|---|---|
| 1 | Number | Account Number | Amount |
| 2 | 1 | 1000-00-000 | 256,895.56 |
| 3 | 1 | 1100-00-000 | 1,598,356.23 |
| 4 | 1 | 1100-20-000 | 20,492.19 |
| 5 | 1 | 1110-00-000 | (1,689.82) |
| 6 | 1 | 1300-00-000 | 52,288.88 |
| 7 | 1 | 1400-00-000 | 20,766.25 |
| 8 | 1 | 3900-00-000 | (1,947,109.29) |
| 9 | 2 | 1000-00-000 | 25,632.58 |
| 10 | 2 | 1100-00-000 | (12,357.27) |
| 11 | 2 | 1100-20-000 | 2,598.36 |
| 12 | 2 | 1300-00-000 | (5,689.52) |
| 13 | 2 | 1400-00-000 | 246.89 |
| 14 | 2 | 3900-00-000 | (10,431.04) |
| 15 | 3 | 1000-00-000 | 25,632.58 |

The **Number** column is in both of these files and will be used by Integration Manager to link the detail lines with the headers.

In Integration Manager, set up two sources, one for each of these files. Once they are both set up, a new section called **Query Relationships** will appear on the integration and the **Relationships** icon on the top menu will become active. Click on **Relationships** and drag your mouse from **Number** under the **GL header** to **Number** under the **GL detail**. This will create an arrow from the header to the detail:

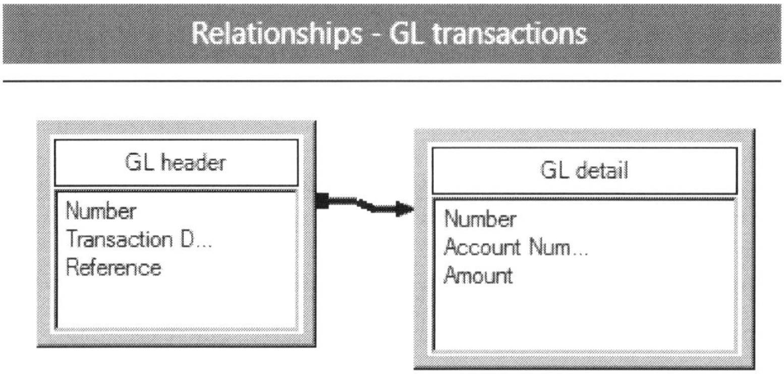


Right-click on the arrow and select **Properties** to open the **Select Relationship Type** window. The default is typically correct; it should look like the following screenshot:

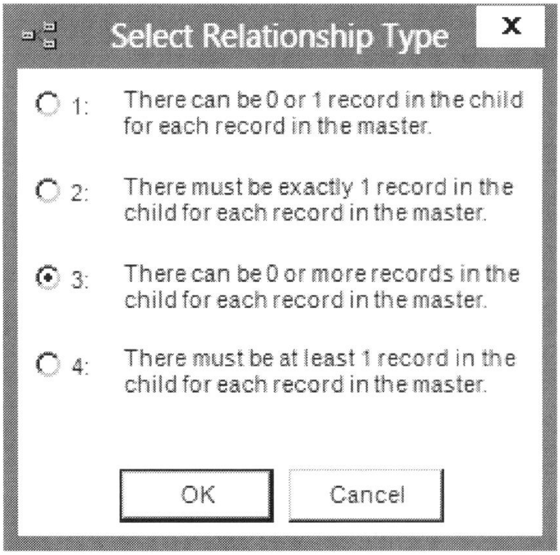

When you open the **Destination Mapping** for this import, you will notice it has a few different choices listed on the top left. This is because there are multiple sections of a General Ledger transaction, which may or may not be needed depending on the specifics of your import. You only need to fill out the sections you are using. Selecting each option on the left will open a different set of fields on the right. The following are the steps to set up a GL transaction import:

1. Click on **General Journal** on the left.
2. For the **Batch ID** field, change **Rule** to **Use Constant** and type in a Batch ID under **Source**. This can be up to 15 characters and should be all in capitals.
3. While on the **Batch ID** field, switch to the **Options** tab and select **Add New Batch** under **Rule** next to **Missing Batch**:

   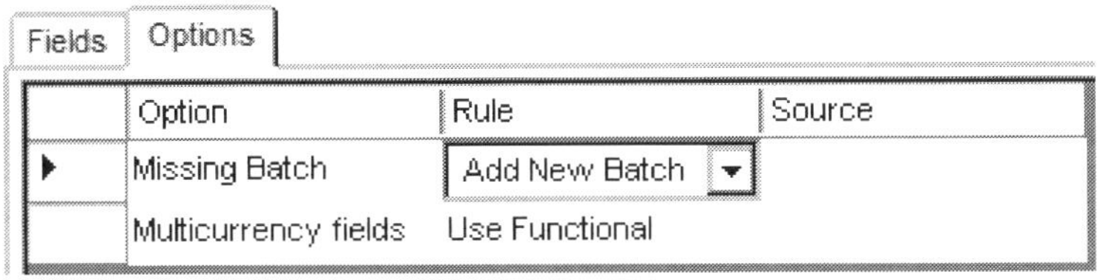
   

   This will tell Integration Manager to create a new batch if there is no batch already in Dynamics GP with the name you have specified. Note that at the bottom left the selections will change to allow you to enter a **Comment** and other options for the batch.

4. Switch back to the **Fields** tab and map **Transaction Date** and **Reference** to the corresponding fields in the GL header source:

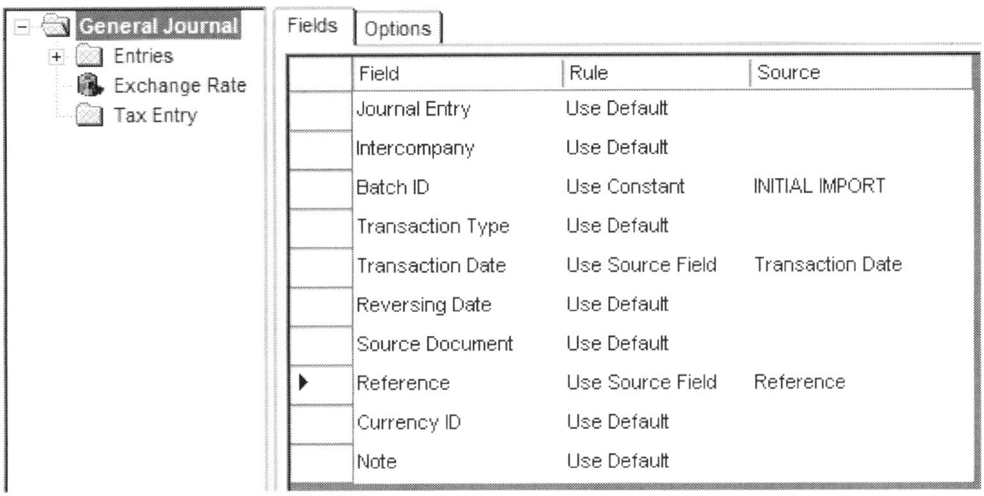

5. Click on **Entries** on the left, and switch to the **Options** tab. Select **Use Source Recordset** under **Rule** and **GL detail** under **Source** on the **Record Source** line:

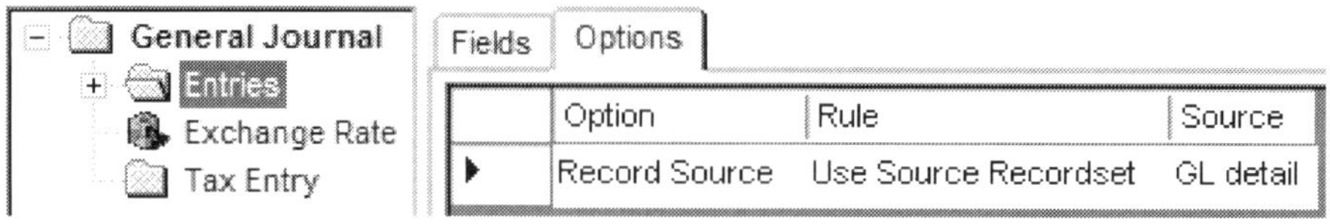


6. On the **Fields** tab for **Entries** map the **Account Number**, **Debit Amount**, and **Credit Amount** fields to the **GL detail** source as shown in the following example. Note that **Debit Amount** and **Credit Amount** are pointing to the same **Source** field, but have a different **Rule**:

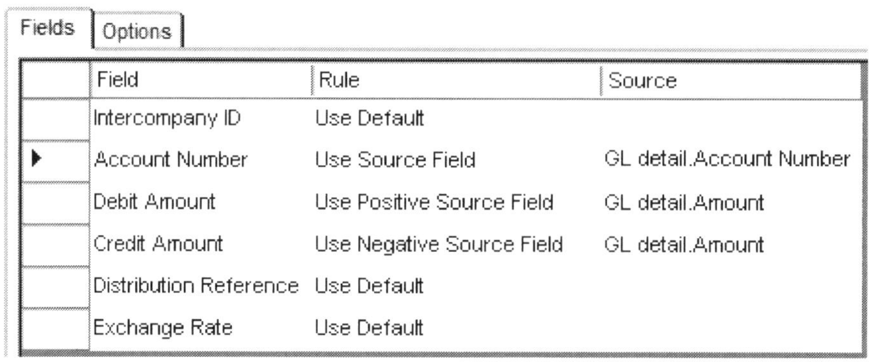


All the other defaults can be left as they are, however, if you need to add additional fields, such as **Distribution Reference**, be sure to keep an eye on the selections at the bottom left when you are setting up each new field.

> Once you have imported your General Ledger transactions, you can validate the data by checking the **Account Transactions** SmartList.

# Vendors

Importing vendors into Dynamics GP can mean bringing in just the minimal information or a lot of details about each vendor. This is a great example of a situation where vendor classes can help enormously, as most of the details about a vendor can be defaulted from the class and there is no need to import them. The following example will show a vendor import with just a few basic fields of data and one address.

Columns used for import:

<table>
<tr><th>Field</th><th>Max. Length</th><th>Notes</th></tr>
<tr><td>Vendor ID</td><td>15</td><td>This is required and must be unique. It is recommended not to use special characters in IDs. Vendor IDs should all be in capitals.</td></tr>
<tr><td>Vendor Name</td><td>64</td><td>Required field – this will automatically copy to the Check Name, and the first 15 characters will copy to the Short Name.</td></tr>
<tr><td>Class ID</td><td>10</td><td>Optional, but recommended. This should be a Class ID that already exists in Dynamics GP.</td></tr>
<tr><td>Primary Address ID</td><td>15</td><td>Even if there is no address for some vendors, import an Address ID to avoid issues during transaction entry. The Purchase, Remit To, and Ship To Address IDs will also be set to this by default if no other Address IDs are specified.<br><br>If you are importing multiple addresses for vendors, you can set up an additional file with the addresses, similar to the previous example of a header and detail file for General Ledger transactions.</td></tr>
<tr><td>Contact</td><td>60</td><td rowspan="6">All the address fields are optional. Even if there is an Address ID used, there is no requirement to have an address.<br><br>The Address 3 field is not included in this list, as the out-of-the-box computer checks and reports in Dynamics GP will not show it. However, if you are planning on custom reports, Integration Manager is capable of importing Address 3, as well.</td></tr>
<tr><td>Address 1</td><td>60</td></tr>
<tr><td>Address 2</td><td>60</td></tr>
<tr><td>City</td><td>35</td></tr>
<tr><td>State</td><td>29</td></tr>
<tr><td>Zip Code</td><td>10</td></tr>
<tr><td>Country Code</td><td>2</td><td>Use the two character country code for this and Dynamics GP will automatically populate the country properly. You can see a list of the country codes by opening the Vendor Maintenance window in Dynamics GP (Cards | Purchasing | Vendor) and clicking the lookup icon next to Country Code.</td></tr>
<tr><td>Phone 1</td><td>14</td><td rowspan="2">Phone and fax numbers need to be formatted as numbers only – a 10 digit number and a four digit extension. Example: <code>21255512120123</code> will represent (212) 555-1212 x0123.</td></tr>
<tr><td>Fax</td><td>14</td></tr>
</table>

Using the listed fields, the following are the steps to set up a vendor import destination mapping:

1. Select **Vendor** on the left and map the following fields to the fields in your source file:
    - **Vendor ID**
    - **Vendor Name**
    - **Class ID**
    - **Primary Address ID**

    Leave all the other default settings. The screen will look like the following:

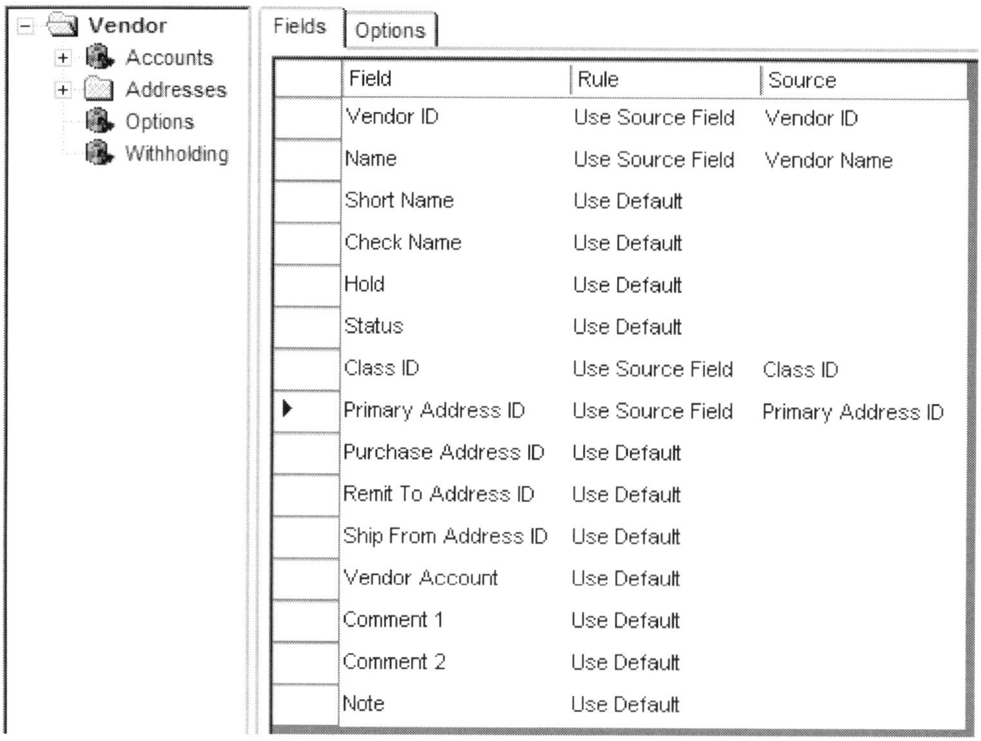

2. Select **Addresses** on the left and map the address fields from your source data:

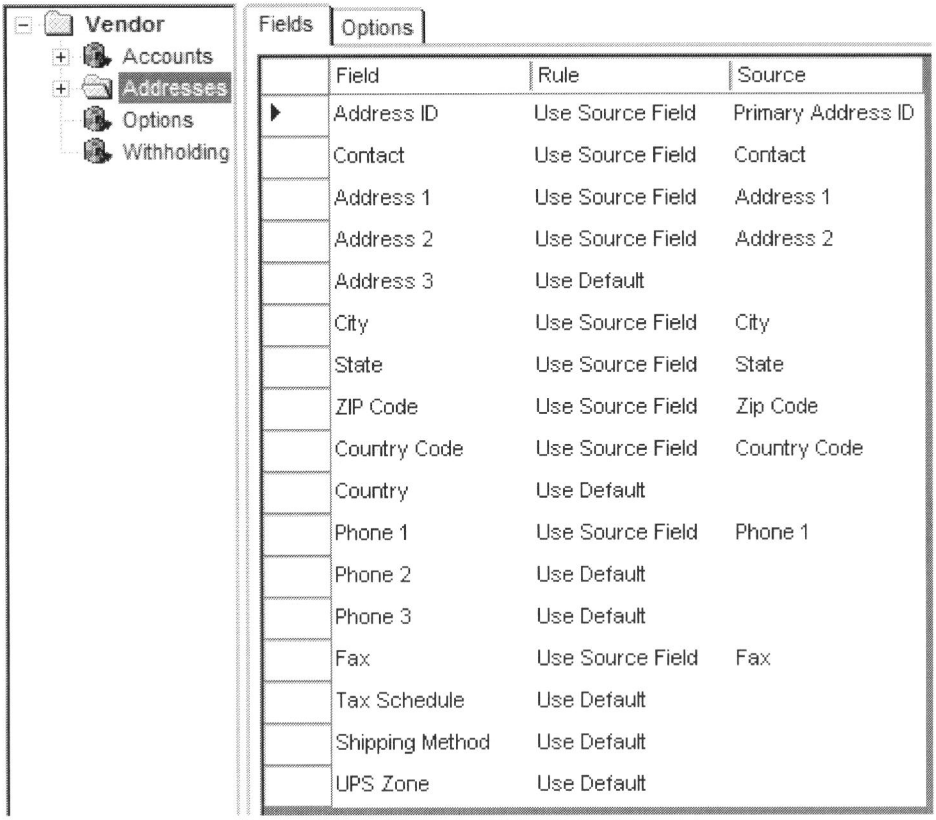


All the other settings can be left as they are defaulted by Integration Manager. If you are bringing in a Tax ID for 1099 vendors, this will be under the **Options** section on the left.

> You can check your imported vendors using the **Vendors** SmartList.

# Open payables transactions

Once you have manually entered or imported vendors into Dynamics GP, you will most likely want to bring in open (or unpaid) payables transactions from your previous system. In a typical implementation, all open invoices will be imported individually and any unapplied payments will be imported as credit memos.

The following is a list of the fields needed for a payables transaction import:

| Field | Notes |
|---|---|
| **Vendor ID** | This must be a Vendor ID that already exists in Dynamics GP. |
| **Document Date** | This is the invoice or credit memo date—typically, the real date of the open transaction is used here. Dates can be formatted regularly, with slashes. Example: `10/15/2013`. |
| **GL Posting Date** | This is the General Ledger date that will be used when the payables transaction is posted. As these transactions should not be hitting the GL anyway, this date is not critical. However, it must be in a fiscal period that is set up and open to avoid errors during import and posting. Example: `10/15/2013`.<br><br>Note that if your posting settings are set to use the batch date for the GL posting date, you may want to create the batch prior to your import and specify the GL posting date you want to use. If this is not specified or if the batch is created by the import, the GL posting date will default to the current Dynamics GP user date shown in the bottom left corner of the main Dynamics GP window at the time of the import. This date can be changed prior to posting, but may be easy to forget. |
| **Document Type** | While there are a number of payables transaction types in Dynamics GP, for the open transaction import typically only Invoice and Credit Memo are used. Any unapplied payments or negative invoices should be imported as credit memos. |
| **Document Number** | The invoice or credit memo number. These must be unique per vendor unless you have allowed duplicate vendor invoices during the Payables module setup, which is not recommended. Dynamics GP also cannot have an invoice and a credit memo with the same number for the same vendor. The maximum length is 20 characters and any letters should be all in capitals. Example: `2013-08 RENT`. |
| **Description** | This is an optional field where you can enter up to 30 characters for a description. It is typically useful to put a short note in the description indicating that this transaction has been imported—that way users can easily differentiate these from transactions entered directly in Dynamics GP. |
| **Amount** | All amounts should be positive, whether you are importing an invoice or credit memo. In Dynamics GP the type of transaction determines whether the amount is added or subtracted from the vendor balance. It is important to make sure that the number of decimal places is not greater than the number of decimal places set up for the currency you are using for each transaction. Example: `1,234.56`. |

| Field | Notes |
|---|---|
| **Currency ID** | If Multicurrency is used, specify an existing Currency ID for each transaction. If the same Currency ID is used for all transactions, this is something that can be defaulted in the destination mapping. |
| **Batch ID** | This is optional because it can be hard coded as part of the import. However, if you would like to import payables transactions into multiple batches, you will need to specify a Batch ID of up to 15 characters. Batch IDs should be all in capitals. |

To set up the destination mapping with the preceding fields in Integration Manager, you only need to fill in fields for the **Payables Transaction** option on the left as all the others can be left as defaulted. The following is what the mapping would look like:

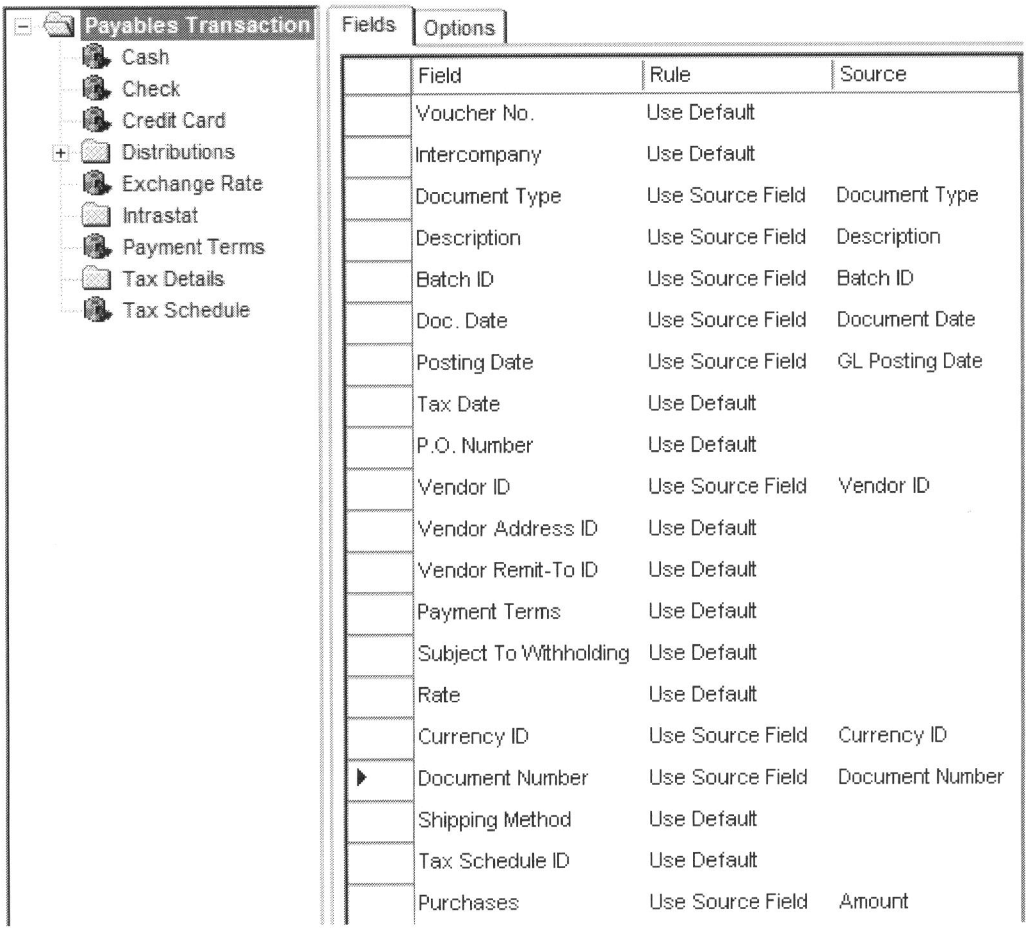

If you are using a Batch ID that does not yet exist in Dynamics GP, click on the **Batch ID** field, go to the **Options** tab and change the **Rule** next to **Missing Batch** to **Add New Batch.**

> Once imported, you can check your transactions in SmartList. They will be under **Payables Transactions** with a **Document Status** of **Unposted**.

# Customers

Similar to vendors, when importing customers into Dynamics GP you can decide to bring in just the minimal information or a lot of detail for each customer. This is another example where classes can be used to default much of the information and save a lot of work during the import. The following example shows a customer import with just a few basic fields of data and one address.

Columns used for import:

<table>
<tr><th>Field</th><th>Max. Length</th><th>Notes</th></tr>
<tr><td>Customer ID</td><td>15</td><td>This is required and must be unique. It is recommended not to use special characters in IDs. Customer IDs should all be in caps.</td></tr>
<tr><td>Customer Name</td><td>64</td><td>Required field – this will automatically copy to the Statement Name and the first 15 characters will copy to the Short Name.</td></tr>
<tr><td>Class ID</td><td>15</td><td>Optional, but recommended. This should be a Class ID that is already created in Dynamics GP.</td></tr>
<tr><td>Primary Address ID</td><td>15</td><td>Required. Even if there is no address for some customers, import an Address ID to avoid errors. The Ship To, Bill To, and Statement To Address IDs will also be set to this by default if no other Address IDs are specified.<br><br>If you are importing multiple addresses for customers, you can set up an additional file with the addresses, similar to the preceding example for GL transactions.</td></tr>
<tr><td>Contact</td><td>60</td><td rowspan="6">All the address fields are optional. Even if there is an Address ID used, there is no requirement to have an address.<br><br>If default Dynamics GP reports will be used, it is recommended not to populate the Address 3 field. Out-of-the-box reports, including customer invoices and statements, will not show Address 3. However, if you are planning on custom reports, Integration Manager is capable of importing Address 3, as well.</td></tr>
<tr><td>Address 1</td><td>60</td></tr>
<tr><td>Address 2</td><td>60</td></tr>
<tr><td>City</td><td>35</td></tr>
<tr><td>State</td><td>29</td></tr>
<tr><td>Zip Code</td><td>10</td></tr>
</table>

| Field | Max. Length | Notes |
|---|---|---|
| **Country Code** | 2 | Use the two character country code for this and Dynamics GP will automatically populate the country properly. You can see a list of the country codes by opening the **Customer Maintenance** window in Dynamics GP (**Cards \| Sales \| Customer**) and clicking the lookup icon next to **Country Code**. |
| **Phone 1** | 14 | Phone and fax numbers need to be formatted as numbers only – a 10 digit number and a 4 digit extension.<br>Example: `21255512120000` or `2125551212` will represent (212) 555-1212 with no extension. |
| **Fax** | 14 | |

Using the listed fields, the following are the steps to set up a customer import destination mapping:

1. Select **Customer** on the left and map the following fields to the fields in your source file:
    - **Customer ID**
    - **Customer Name**
    - **Class ID**
    - **Primary Address ID**

   Leave all the other default settings. The screen will look like the following:

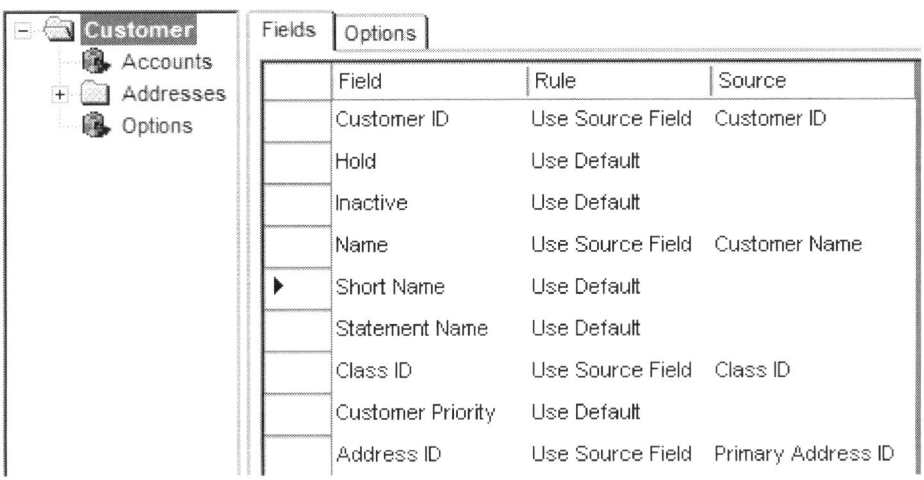

2. Select **Addresses** on the left and map the address fields from your source data as illustrated in the following screenshot:

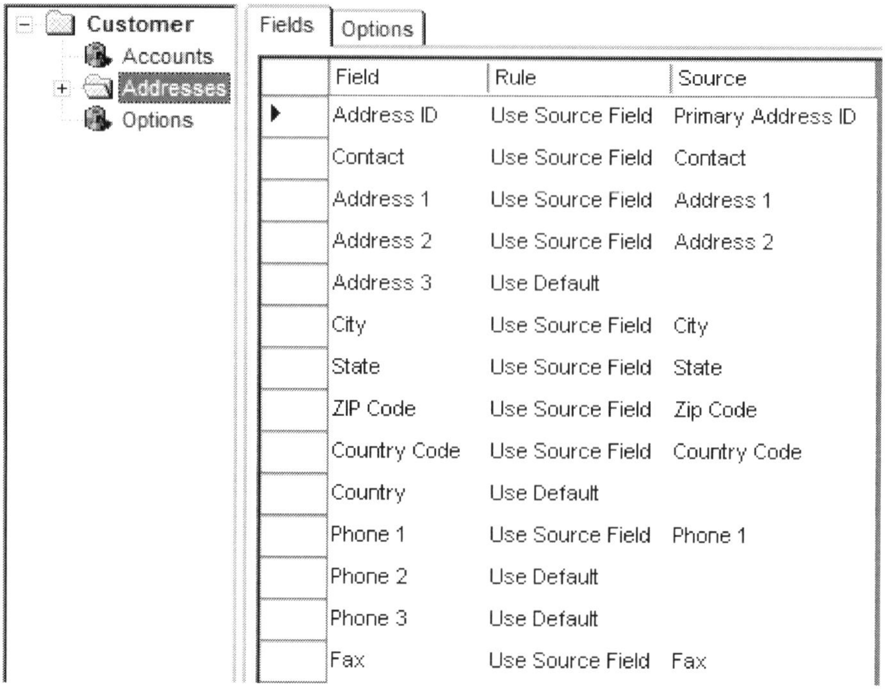


All the other settings can be left as they are defaulted by Integration Manager.

[ You can check your imported customers using the **Customers** SmartList. ]

# Open receivables transactions

Once you have manually entered or imported customers into Dynamics GP, you will most likely want to import open (or unpaid) receivables transactions from your previous system. In a typical implementation, all open invoices will be imported individually and any unapplied payments will be imported as credit memos.

The following is a list of the fields needed for a receivables transaction import:

| Field | Notes |
|---|---|
| **Customer ID** | This must be a Customer ID that already exists in Dynamics GP. |
| **Document Date** | This is the invoice or credit memo date—typically the real date of the open transaction is used here. Dates can be formatted regularly, with slashes. Example: `10/15/2013`. |
| **GL Posting Date** | This is the General Ledger date that will be used when the receivables transaction is posted. As these transactions should not be hitting the GL anyway, this date is not critical. However, it must be in a fiscal period that is set up and open to avoid errors during import and posting. Example: `10/15/2013`.<br><br>Note that if your posting settings are set to use the batch date for the GL posting date, you may want to create the batch prior to your import and specify the GL posting date you want to use. If this is not specified or if the batch is created by the import, the GL posting date will default to the current Dynamics GP user date shown in the bottom left corner of the main Dynamics GP window at the time of the import. This date can be changed prior to posting, but may be easy to forget. |
| **Document Type** | While there are a number of receivables transaction types in Dynamics GP, for the open transaction import typically only Sales/Invoices and Credit Memo are used. Any open payments or negative invoices should be imported as credit memos. |
| **Document Number** | The invoice or credit memo number. These must be unique per customer and type of transaction—Dynamics GP will allow an invoice and a credit memo with the same number. The maximum length is 20 characters and any letters should be all in capitals. Example: `INV123456`. |
| **Description** | This is an optional field where you can enter up to 30 characters for a description. It is typically helpful to indicate that this transaction has been imported in the description—that way users can easily differentiate these from manually entered transactions when looking these up at a later date. |
| **Amount** | All amounts should be positive, whether you are importing an invoice or credit memo. In Dynamics GP, the type of transaction is what determines whether the amount is added or subtracted from the customer balance. It is important to make sure that the number of decimal places is not greater than the number of decimal places set up for the currency you are using for each transaction. Example: `1,234.56`. |

| Field | Notes |
|---|---|
| **Currency ID** | If Multicurrency is used, you will need to specify an existing Currency ID for each transaction. If the same Currency ID is being used for all imported transactions, it can be defaulted in the destination mapping. |
| **Batch ID** | This is optional because it can be hard coded as part of the import. However, if you would like to import receivables transactions into multiple batches, you will need to specify a Batch ID of up to 15 characters. Batch IDs should all be in capitals. |

To set up the destination mapping with these fields in Integration Manager, you only need to fill in fields for the **Receivables Transaction** option on the left, all the others can be left as they are defaulted. The following is what the mapping would look like:

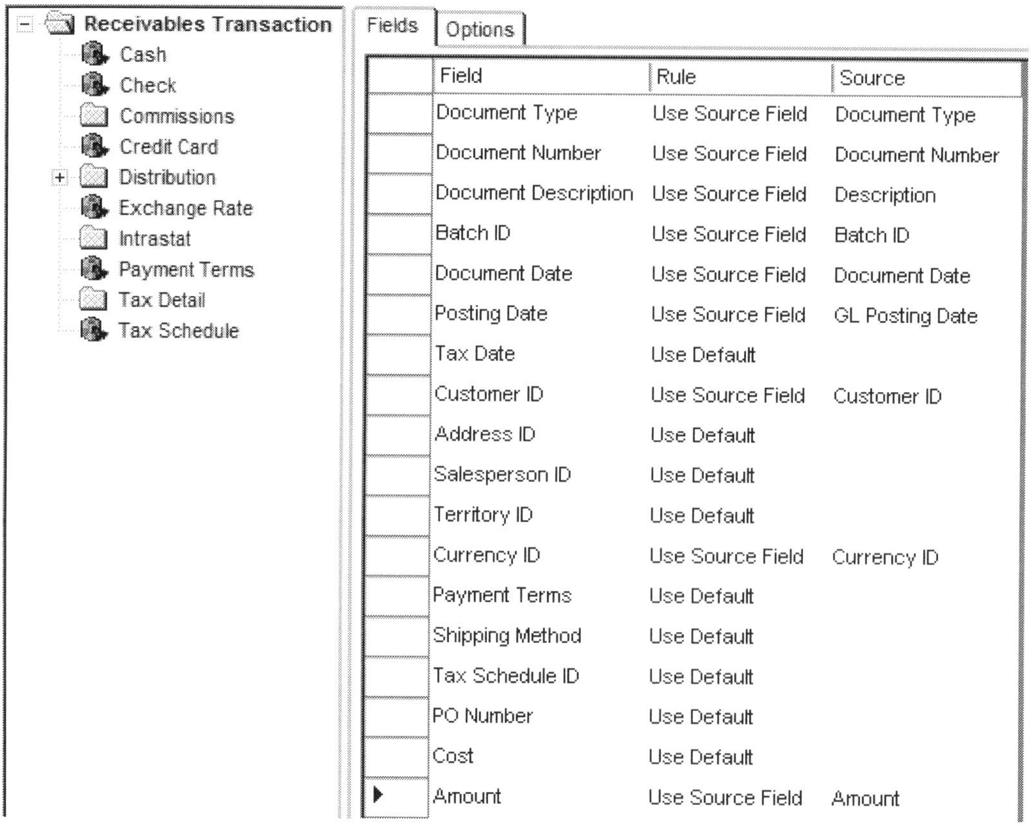


If you are using a **Batch ID** that does not yet exist in Dynamics GP, click on the **Batch ID** field, go to the **Options** tab and change the **Rule** next to **Missing Batch** to **Add New Batch**.

> Once imported, you can check your transactions in SmartList. They will be under **Receivables Transactions** with a **Document Status** of **Unposted**.

# Inventory items

Just like for customers and vendors, setting up classes for inventory items will save you a great deal of effort when importing new items. With all the options filled out for an item class, importing inventory items can be fairly easy. The following example will use two source files: `Items` and `Prices`.

The following is a typical listing of fields for the `Items` source file. This file will have one line per inventory item:

| Field | Max. Length | Notes |
|---|---|---|
| **Item Number** | 30 | This is required and must be unique. Item numbers should all be in capital letters and it is recommended not to use special characters. |
| **Description** | 100 | Required field - using all 100 characters here may make it difficult to use some of the out-of-the box Dynamics GP reports without modifications. |
| **Short Description** | 15 | This field is optional, but recommended as it is used for lookups in Dynamics GP. Unlike short names for customers and vendors, this will not automatically default from the Description and will be blank if not specified. |
| **Class ID** | 10 | Optional, but recommended. This should be a Class ID that already exists in Dynamics GP. |
| **Standard Cost** | | Costs are optional. However you may want to import them if you are basing pricing on cost or need this for reporting purposes. Be sure not to use more decimal places than the item is set up for. |
| **Current Cost** | | |
| **List Price** | | If you are bringing in a list price in one currency only, this can be done in one source file, otherwise you will need multiple source files with a listing of each Currency ID and List Price. The decimal places should be the same as the number of currency decimals set up for each item and currency combination. |
| **List Price Currency ID** | 15 | |
| **Default Selling U of M** | 8 | This should be a unit of measure that is already set up in Dynamics GP for the U of M schedule that will be assigned to this item. |

If you want to bring in the main vendor for each item as part of this import, you can add the following five fields. If you will be setting up multiple vendors for each item, you will need to create a separate source file with the vendor details.

| Field | Max. Length | Notes |
|---|---|---|
| **Vendor ID** | 15 | This must be a Vendor ID that already exists in Dynamics GP. |
| **Vendor Item Number** | 30 | Both the Vendor Item Number and Vendor Description are optional. If they are not specified, they will default to the Item Number and Description from the item. |
| **Vendor Description** | 100 | |
| **Purchasing U of M Type** | | This corresponds to the Default Purchasing U of M Type and can have values of **From Item** or **From Item Vendor**. |
| **Purchasing U of M** | 8 | If **From Item Vendor** is used for the Default Purchasing U of M Type, then this Default Purchasing U of M must be imported, otherwise it is not needed. The U of M selected here must already exist in Dynamics GP. |

The following is a listing of fields for the `Prices` source file. This file will have one line for each item/price combination:

| Field | Max. Length | Notes |
|---|---|---|
| **Item Number** | 30 | This field must correspond to the list of Item Numbers in the `Items` source file and will be used to link the two source files. |
| **Price Level** | 10 | This should be a price level that already exists in Dynamics GP. |
| **U of M** | 8 | This is a unit of measure that is already set up in Dynamics GP for the U of M schedule that is being assigned to this item. |
| **Percent** | | Either one or the other of these should be used, but not both. If **Price** is used, it should have the same number of decimal places as are set up for the item and currency combination. Percentages can have up to two decimal places. |
| **Price** | | |
| **Currency ID** | 15 | This should be an existing Currency ID. |

Once you have created your source files and set up the `Items` and `Prices` sources in Integration Manager, follow these steps to import your items:

1. Create a relationship between your two source files by clicking on **Relationships** on the top menu and dragging your mouse between the **Item Number** fields:

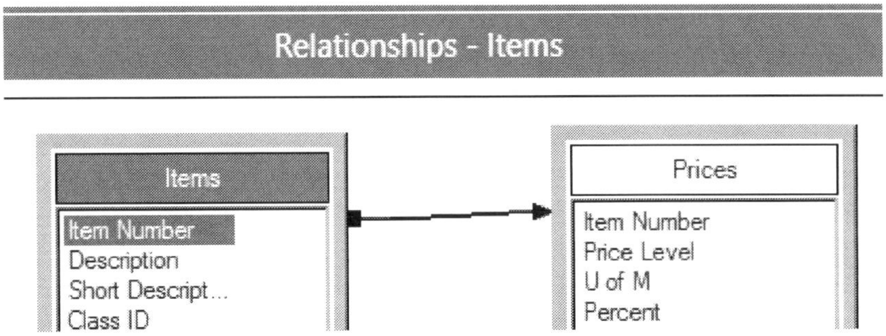


2. Open the **Destination Mapping**, select **Inventory Item** on the left, and fill out all the fields you have included in your source file as follows:

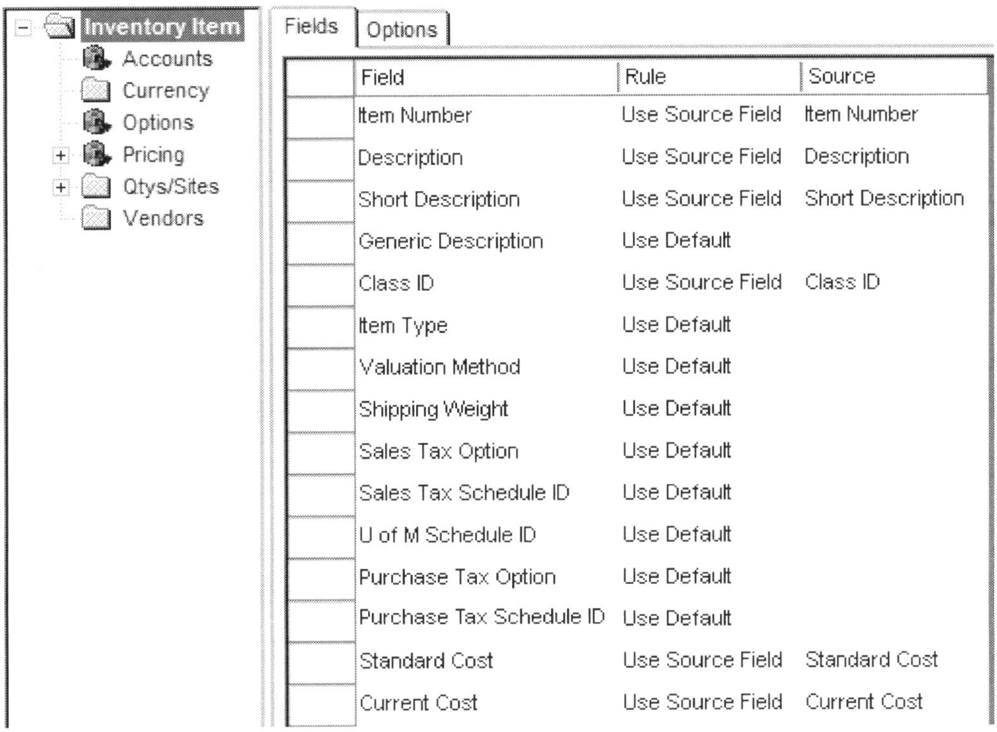

3. If you are using Multicurrency and are importing a list price, select **Currency** on the left and map the **Currency ID** and **List Price**:

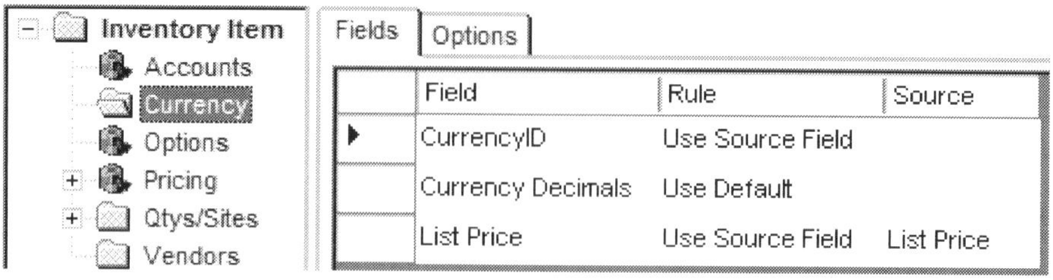


4. Select **Pricing** on the left and map the **Default Selling U of M**:

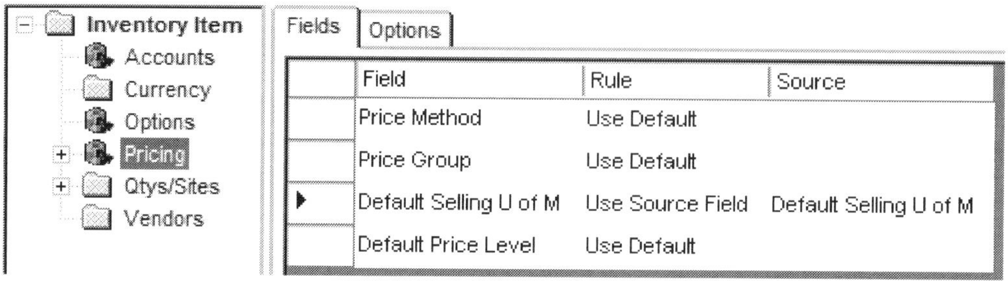


5. While in the **Pricing** section, switch to the **Options** tab and make sure the **Rule** for **Record Source** is **Use Field Rules**:

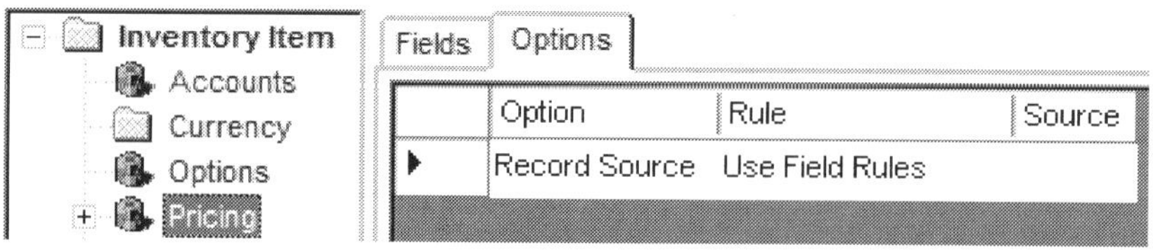


6. Select **Items** (under **Pricing**) on the left, switch to the **Options** tab, change the **Record Source Rule** to **Use Source Recordset**, and select **Prices** (or the name of your source with the prices) as the **Source**:

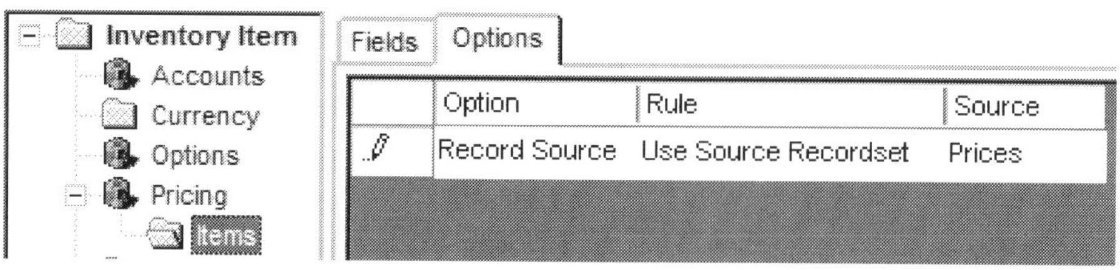

7. While still on the **Items** selection on the left, switch to the **Fields** tab and map the price detail fields. The following example shows importing amounts. If percentages are being used, then the **Price** field should have **Use Default** under **Rule**. If both percentages and prices are selected, most often you will not receive an error but the prices will not be imported.

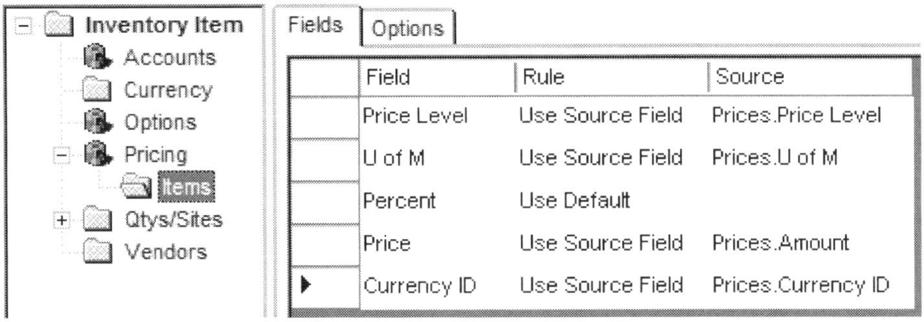


8. If you are importing vendor information for your items, select **Vendors** on the left. Switch to the **Options** tab, change the **Record Source Rule** to **Use Source Recordset**, and select **Items** (or the name of your source with the items) as the **Source**:

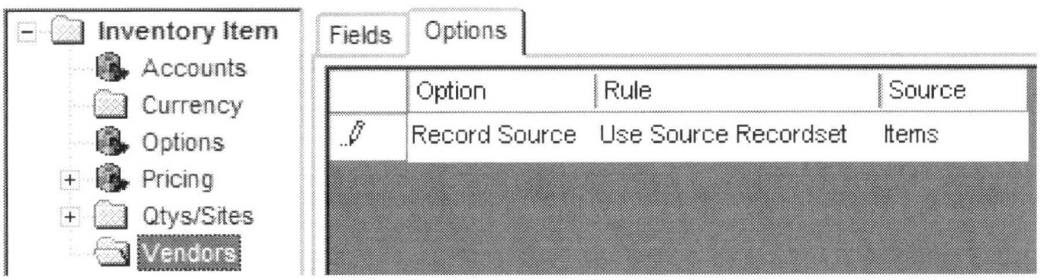

9. While still on the **Vendors** selection, switch to the **Fields** tab and map the fields you are importing for the vendors:

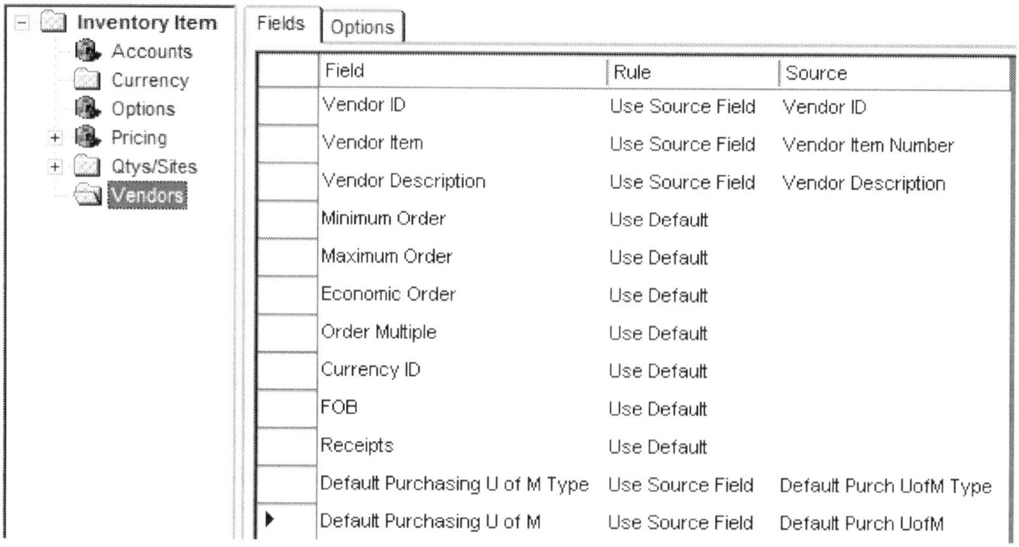


Two additional notes about the preceding import example:

- This does not assign the imported items to any sites. Typically, items are assigned to all sites after they are imported and the steps for this are outlined in *Chapter 8, Module Setup – Inventory, SOP, and POP*.
- There is no ability to bring in different pricing depending on quantities for the same price level using Integration Manager. Only one price per price level is possible.

> Once imported, there are two inventory SmartLists you can check to see your data: **Items** will have the main information and **Vendor Items** will show the vendor details. There is no SmartList to show price levels, however you can create a view to see them using the code from this blog post: `http://victoriayudin.com/2010/08/09/sql-view-for-inventory-price-levels-in-dynamics-gp/`.

# Inventory transactions

Once you have imported or created inventory items in Dynamics GP you will typically need to populate the beginning inventory quantities and costs. The easiest way to accomplish this is to enter or import an inventory adjustment transaction. The following are the fields needed for an inventory adjustment import:

| Field | Notes |
|---|---|
| **Date** | This should be the date of the physical inventory count or cut-off. Dates can be formatted regularly, with slashes, for example: `06/30/2013`. |
| **Item Number** | This must be an Item Number that already exists in Dynamics GP. |
| **Unit of Measure** | This must be a Unit of Measure that already exists in Dynamics GP and is assigned to the item. |
| **Site ID** | Site ID must already exist in Dynamics GP. If you are entering items at one site only, you can hard code this during the import mapping. |
| **Quantity** | Quantity in the unit of measure specified. If using decimal places, make sure not to use more decimals than what the item is set up to use. |
| **Cost** | Per unit cost for the item—if there are items with multiple cost layers in your current inventory, you can enter multiple lines for them, one for each cost layer. Make sure to use the correct number of decimal places for the currency you are using. |
| **Serial/Lot Numbers** | If you are importing items that are tracking serial or lot numbers, you will need to add an additional source file with the serial and lot numbers. The following mapping example will show importing items that are not tracking serial or lot numbers. |
| **Batch ID** | You can specify a Batch ID if you are importing to multiple batches, otherwise this can be hard coded in the import. The batch can be created as part of the import; it does not have to exist in Dynamics GP yet. |

Using a source file with the preceding fields, if you create one source in Integration Manager, your import will work, but you will end up with an individual transaction for each line item in your source file. If you would like to import one transaction with multiple line items instead, you will need to set up two sources which are pointing to your source file. The following are the steps to do this:

1. Create a **New Integration**.

2. Add a source, for example, **Inv Adj header**, pointing to your source data and uncheck all the columns except for **Date** on the **Columns** tab:

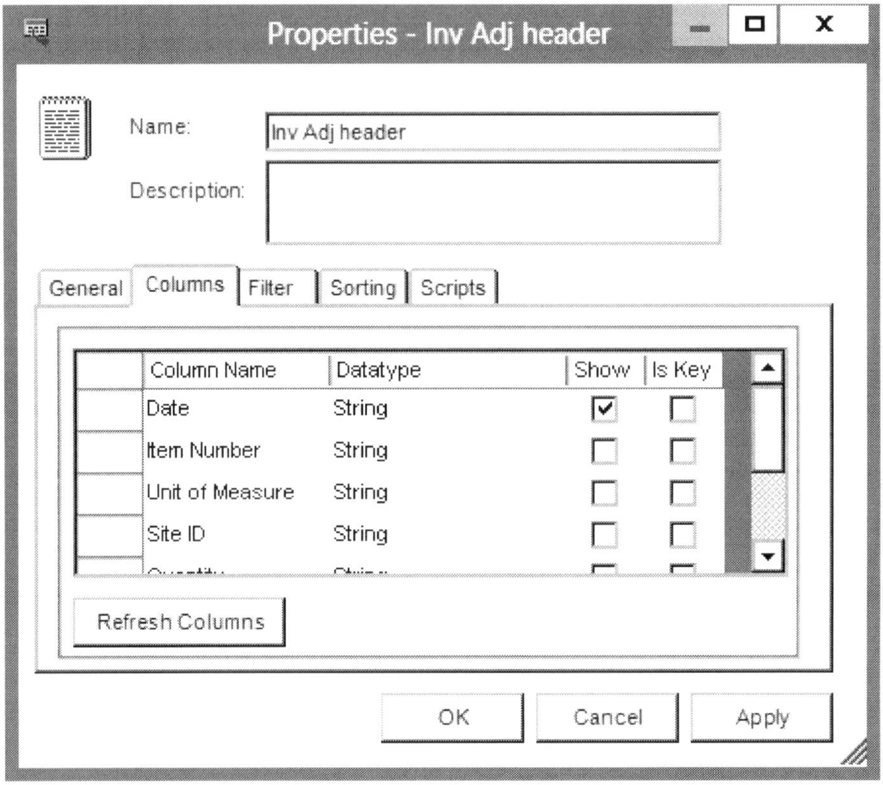


3. Create another source, for example, **Inv Adj detail**, pointing to the same source file. This one can be left with all the columns selected (this is the default behavior).
4. Create a **Query Relationship** between the two sources linking on the **Date**:

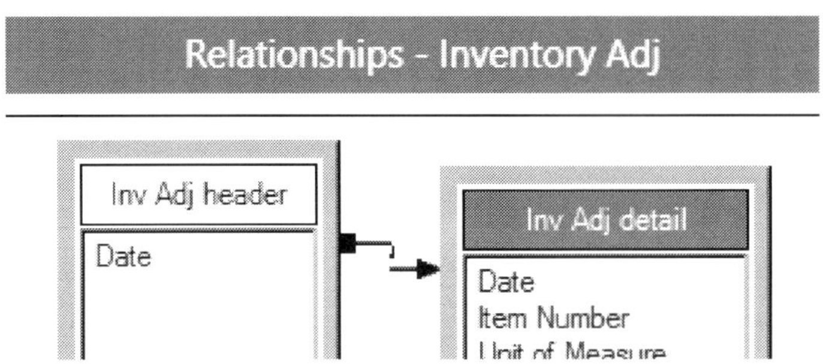

5. Create the **Destination Mapping** using these two sources:

   1. Select **Inventory Transaction** on the left, map the **Date** to the **Date** in your **Inv Adj header** source file and either hard code or map the **Document Type** and **Batch ID**:

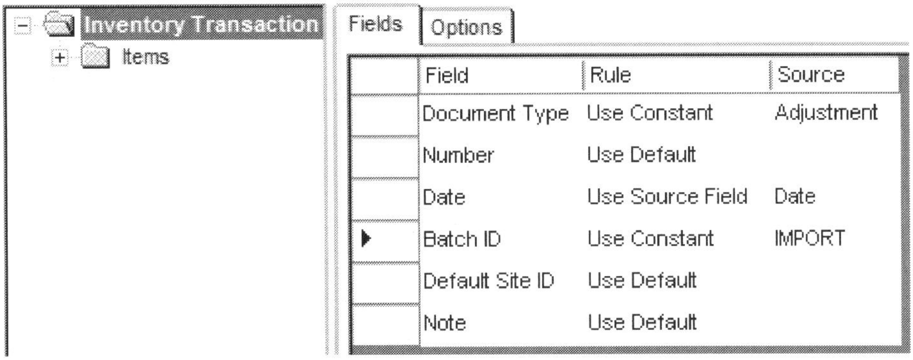


   2. If the batch does not yet exist in Dynamics GP, on the **Options** tab, change the **Rule** for **Missing Batch** to **Add New Batch**.
   3. Select **Items** on the left and change the **Record Source** on the **Options** tab to point to **Inv Adj detail** (or the name of your data source).
   4. With **Items** still selected on the left, map the fields from your source file on the **Fields** tab:

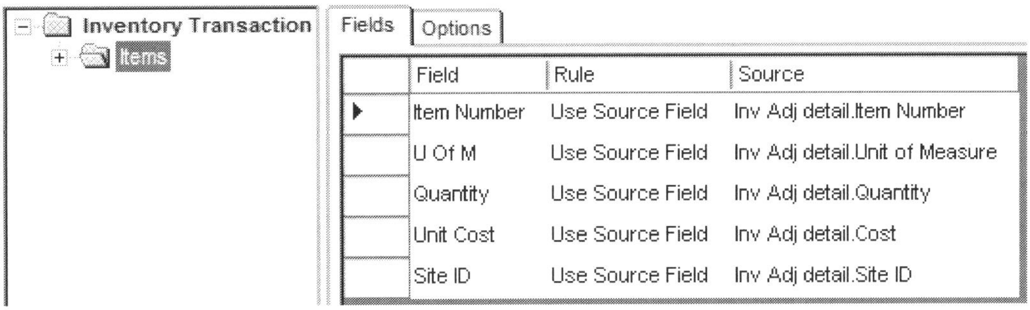


> You can check your import using the **Inventory Transactions** SmartList in Dynamics GP. Once posted, this will update the inventory quantities and you can see them in the **Item Quantities** SmartList.

# Summary

In this chapter, we have gone through the basics of using Integration Manager to import master data and open transactions into Dynamics GP. We have shown detailed examples for importing General Ledger accounts, GL transactions, customers, vendors, and inventory items as well as payables, receivables, and inventory transactions. Now, your Dynamics GP should be populated with master records and open transactions, and ready for Go Live.

In the next chapter, we will go over some additional tools and resources that are available as you start using Dynamics GP, as well as some training recommendations.

# 10
# Training, Tools, and Next Steps

Now that your Dynamics GP system is installed, set up, and you have populated master records and your initial data, what's next?

Most likely, you have already started training users. For many companies training is an ongoing process, so this chapter will go over some ideas for planning your initial, as well as ongoing, training. We will also discuss tools available from Microsoft for your Dynamics GP system. Finally, some troubleshooting tips and additional resources will be listed to help you maintain and get the most out of Dynamics GP.

## Training

There are many different training methods, and users may respond differently to training depending on their level of comfort with technology and accounting, as well as their prior experience with similar applications. The following sections discuss ideas to consider when deciding how and when to train users on Dynamics GP, grouped into these topics:

- How to train and who should be the trainer?
- How much training and for whom?
- When to train?
- Notes for the trainer.
- Available training resources.

# How to train and who should be the trainer?

This is by no means a complete guide to training. However, having trained many users over the years, there are a few concepts that have proven true time and time again:

- Make sure you have a trainer that knows their stuff. Nothing can be worse than being trained from a script with no ability to have a meaningful discussion or ask follow up questions. If the trainer has textbook knowledge of a system, but no real life experience with it, they will not have as much knowledge to share, which could result in incomplete training and lost credibility with the users. If you do not have someone on your team that is a good training resource for Dynamics GP, bring a trainer in.
- If you are bringing a training resource in from outside your team, help them by explaining what the company does, what Dynamics GP modules will be used, and the basics of the setup that has been performed. With this knowledge, the trainer will be better equipped to train your users.
- Focus the training on the functionality that will be used. For example, if Purchase Order Approvals are not being used, it can certainly be mentioned that this functionality is available, but why spend time on it? Most likely, if it is implemented six months later, re-training will be required.
- Set up a training schedule that is reasonable. Some companies may be able to close an accounting department for a whole week to perform training for all users of the new system. Given today's busy working environments, this is often not a realistic option.
- Keep the number of users in a training session to no more than four or five, anything else can get unruly very quickly. If there are many users that need to be trained on the same functionality, hold two or more sessions for the same topic.
- Keep training sessions to no more than three hours. This will typically be the most users can absorb at one time. It will also give the company's employees an opportunity to get some of their regular work done on training days.
- Make the system available to users during training if at all possible. If Dynamics GP is already installed and the sample or test company is set up, give users access to log in during and after training to experiment with what they have just learned.
- Some companies like the idea of training the trainer—taking a more advanced user who will be using most of the Dynamics GP functionality and training them, so they can train the rest of the users. While this may be a cost saving option in the short term, this can easily become similar to the broken telephone game and is not something that is recommended for most companies.

# How much training and for whom?

Often training classes and manuals for Dynamics GP modules will start with the setup of the module, then go into detail for each type of transaction possible, and then cover routines and utilities available in the module.

Think about the users for your Dynamics GP system. How many of them will need to change setup options, or even have the permissions to do so? How many of them will be performing maintenance if there are issues? Typically the answer is one or two (we will call them super users). The rest of the users (regular users) will be entering transactions, inquiring on them, printing reports, and analyzing data.

One idea for training your super users on the setup options of Dynamics GP is to do it at the same time as the module setup. That way, as you are going through all the settings, you can explain the available options to them and at the same time get their feedback on the most appropriate settings for the company. Super users thus become part of the implementation process, benefiting them as they get more knowledge of the system, and benefiting the implementation as the modules are set up with all the available knowledge of key accounting personnel.

For regular users, make a concise list of the users and what functions they typically perform as part of their job. Only include users in the sessions that they need for their work. Breaking out the training sessions by functionality and keeping them short will afford the best chance of users retaining knowledge. If a user is moved to a different area or gets more responsibility, it is usually best to train them on the additional functionality they need at that time.

There is a fine line between too much and too little training. With too much, most of the training is not retained because users can get overwhelmed. With too little training, users may not understand enough of how Dynamics GP works and the repercussions of their actions throughout the system. The key is to find just the right amount of training, and that's where an experienced trainer can really add value to your implementation.

# When to train?

It may be appealing to set aside time for training users before the implementation really gets started. Everyone has more time and is more relaxed, schedules are more open. I strongly recommend against this. Training users and having them not use the training for several weeks to a month will render that training almost useless for many of the users. To maximize the chances of success, plan to do the bulk of the training right before the users need to start using Dynamics GP. This is another reason why a phased approach often makes more sense than implementing all the functionality at once.

Plan to keep training users through at least the first few days of the Go Live. Users that are not very computer savvy, or are more resistant to change, may need some hand-holding during the Go Live to ensure a smooth transition. If you can identify these users and plan for this ahead of time, you will increase your chances of a successful implementation.

Keep in mind that training is not a discrete process. While the bulk of the training may be done right before the Go Live, make plans for retraining regularly. If there is high turnover in the company's GP users, put together a plan for training new users as they are hired. Many companies have employees that are leaving train their replacement. While this may work for some aspects of a job, this is not always a good idea for systems such as Dynamics GP, especially if it has not been in place long.

Once employees start using Dynamics GP they will have questions that need to be answered right away, as they are stopping critical work, but there will also be many non-critical questions. Make sure your users have a resource to ask the critical questions and let them know how to access this resource. For the non-critical issues, ask users to make a list of these as they go about their daily work and plan for periodic refreshers on the training. This will give users a chance to get familiar with the system and let them know they have a resource to answer any questions that might come up.

# Notes for the trainer

Each trainer will have their own technique and methodology. This is not meant to teach someone how to train Dynamics GP users, just a few things to keep in mind if you are the one performing the training:

- **Understand your audience**: Are they experienced accountants that have used Dynamics GP or a similar ERP system in the past? Or are they mostly clerical users that simply key in transactions without too much accounting experience or computer knowledge? The answer may change how you present or explain things. It will also help you understand and answer their questions better. Often you will have a mix in the audience—try to involve more experienced users in answering the questions about company accounting policy and practices for the others. You will get the benefit of their experience with the company and make them feel more involved in the process.
- **Be flexible, but firm**: If users want to ask questions during training, be flexible enough to veer a little off course to accommodate them. However, if the discussion starts getting too far off topic or taking an inordinate amount of time, make a note if you need to follow up later, but get back to the scheduled training.

- **Start each training session with a brief introduction to navigation in Dynamics GP and some of the basic terminology**: For users that have not seen Dynamics GP before, a lot of the terminology and navigation may take some getting used to. Reinforce this throughout the training—certain icons appear on almost every window and have the same functionality—remind users of this. For example, clicking on the looking glass icon will always give you a list of choices for the field you're on, or a note icon will add a note to the item it is right next to, but a note icon in the bottom right corner of a window will be a window level note.
- **Follow up**: If there were questions left open during training, make notes and follow up via e-mail or in the next training session with the same users.

# Available training resources

If you have no trainer available on your team and are looking for classroom or pre-recorded training, the following are some Dynamics GP training resources:

- **E-Learning**: Microsoft E-Learning offers a comprehensive list of pre-recorded training sessions for various Dynamics GP modules. Currently E-Learning is available to all Dynamics GP customers on a maintenance plan at no additional charge. To access your E-Learning, log onto CustomerSource (`https://mbs.microsoft.com/customersource/`) and navigate to **Readiness and Training | E-Learning** from the menu on the left.
- **Training available from Microsoft**: Other training options, including instructor-led classroom and online training, are available from Microsoft. As the offerings and schedules change often, it is best to use Microsoft's Training Catalog (`http://learning.microsoft.com/Manager/Catalog.aspx`) to find the training you are looking for.
- **Manuals**: Many modules in Microsoft Dynamics GP have printable guides available, found at the following URL: `http://technet.microsoft.com/en-us/library/jj673202(v=gp.30).aspx`.

While all of these resources can help with training, both initially and on an ongoing basis, typically best results are accomplished by using a dedicated trainer as opposed to a canned resource to train your users prior to a Go Live. This allows the training to be geared specifically to your company's needs, which usually saves time and offers the best return on your company's Dynamics GP investment.

# Tools for Dynamics GP

There are a number of tools available from Microsoft to help troubleshoot and add functionality to Dynamics GP. In this section we will go over the following tools:

- Professional Services Tools Library
- Tools from Microsoft's Professional Services Team
- Support Debugging Tool

# Professional Services Tools Library

The **Professional Services Tools Library** (**PSTL**) is a suite of tools originally created by the Microsoft Dynamics GP support, development, and professional services teams to add functionality to Dynamics GP. For many years most of the tools in the PSTL were sold for anywhere from $750 to $1500 each and the entire suite cost $5,000. On March 26, 2012 Microsoft announced that the PSTL would be available to all customers using Dynamics GP 10.0 or later at no additional cost.

The PSTL can be installed during the Dynamics GP application installation or added as an additional component later. Dynamics GP partners can download the PSTL at the following URL: `http://bit.ly/18qHTH3` (requires PartnerSource access). Customers can ask their Dynamics GP partner to download this for them.

There are currently 40 tools in the PSTL. The following sections lists them all with a brief description of each, grouped by series.

## System tools

These are tools that are global to the entire Dynamics GP system:

| Tool name | Description |
|---|---|
| **Database Disabler** | Allows an administrator to temporarily disable any existing Dynamics GP companies. This is a great tool to use when running maintenance or other updates, to prevent users from logging into selected companies. (*Requires* `sa` *login.*) |
| **Shortcuts Copy** | This tool will copy shortcuts from one user to another. |
| **Toolkit** | The Toolkit is used to rebuild the GL Account Master Index table (GL00105), re-create Dex Procs, rebuild indexes, recreate tables, and check identities of tables. This will typically only be needed when working with support. (*Requires* `sa` *login.*) |

| Tool name | Description |
|---|---|
| **Menu Inquiry Utility** | Allows you to see detailed technical information for each menu item in your Dynamics GP. |
| **Update User Date** | If this tool is enabled, the Dynamics GP User Date will automatically increment the date at midnight if the Dynamics GP application is open. Note that this tool requires a setting in the `Dex.ini` file of `SuppressChangeDateDialog=True`. More `Dex.ini` settings with detailed explanations can be found here: `http://dynamicsconfessions.blogspot.com/2011/02/dexini-downloadable-file-updated.html`. |

## Financial tools

These are tools for the General Ledger and Bank Reconciliation modules:

| Tool name | Description |
|---|---|
| **Account Modifier / Combiner** | This incredibly useful tool will go through all posted and unposted transactions throughout Dynamics GP and change or combine General Ledger account numbers. Often this tool is used after a reorganization, when the chart of accounts needs to be changed to accommodate the new company structure. It can also be helpful to clean up a chart of accounts when many new accounts have been added. (*Requires* `sa` *login*.) |
| **Checkbook Modifier** | Allows you to change a Checkbook ID. This will update all transactions in the system. |
| **Fiscal Period Modifier** | This tool is used to change the Year number for closed years. Often this is needed when changes to the fiscal years are made, for example to align them to calendar years. |
| **GL Master Triggers** | With this tool General Ledger accounts created in a master company can be set up to replicate to some or all of your other companies. |

## Purchasing tools

These are tools for the Payables Management and Purchase Order Processing modules:

| Tool name | Description |
|---|---|
| **1099 Modifier** | This tool will update 1099 amounts for vendors that were not set up as a 1099 vendor, but should have been. |
| **PM Master Triggers** | With this tool vendors created in a master company can be set up to replicate to some or all of your other companies. |

| Tool name | Description |
| --- | --- |
| **PM Minimum Check** | If this tool is enabled, a new option to set a minimum check amount will be available on the **Additional** menu during the Select Checks process in the Payables module. |
| **Select Checks Combiner** | If this tool is enabled, when users add payments to existing check batches, payments for the same vendors will be combined into one check instead of creating multiple checks for the same vendor. |
| **Vendor Combiner** | This tool allows combining multiple vendors into one. You may find this tool useful if multiple users are creating vendors and may have inadvertently created multiple Vendor IDs for the same vendor. (*Requires* sa *login*.) |
| **Vendor Modifier** | This popular tool will change the Vendor ID for all unposted, open and historical records throughout Dynamics GP. You may find this tool useful if you are using the vendor name as part of the Vendor ID and the vendor changes their name or a mistake was made when creating the Vendor ID. (*Requires* sa *login*.) |
| **Vendor Name Modifier** | Allows changing the vendor name on all existing transactions in Dynamics GP. (*Requires* sa *login*.) |
| **Minimum PO/ Receipt #** | If this tool is enabled, you can specify minimum Purchase Order and Receipt numbers, so that the system does not go back and try to use numbers that are below what you have specified. |
| **POP Cost Disabler** | If this tool is enabled, you can specify the Current Cost or Standard Cost of inventory items to be defaulted onto Purchase Orders instead of the standard Dynamics GP behavior of using the Last Invoice Cost per vendor. |

# Sales tools

These are tools for the Receivables Management and Sales Order Processing modules:

| Tool name | Description |
| --- | --- |
| **Customer Combiner** | This tool allows combining multiple customers into one. You may find this tool useful if customers merge or multiple users are creating customers and may have inadvertently created multiple Customer IDs for the same customer. (*Requires* sa *login*.) |
| **Customer Modifier** | This popular tool will change the Customer ID for all unposted, open, and historical records throughout Dynamics GP. You may find this tool useful if you are using the customer name as part of the Customer ID and the customer changes their name or a mistake was made when creating the Customer ID. (*Requires* sa *login*.) |

| Tool name | Description |
|---|---|
| **Customer Name Modifier** | Allows changing the customer name on all existing transactions in Dynamics GP. (*Requires* sa *login.*) |
| **RM Master Triggers** | With this tool customers created in a master company can be set up to replicate to some or all of your other companies. |
| **RM Transaction Unapply** | When receivables transactions are moved to history they can no longer be unapplied or voided. This very useful tool allows historical receivables transactions to be unapplied and moved back to an open status to allow voiding, entering an NSF, or changing apply information. |
| **Salesperson Modifier** | Allows changing a Salesperson ID on all transactions in Dynamics GP. (*Requires* sa *login.*) |
| **SOP Customer Item Lookup** | With this tool enabled, users can look up customer specific item sales history quickly during sales transaction entry. This can be helpful to show what a customer purchased in the past and at what prices. |
| **Territory Modifier** | Allows changing a Territory ID on all transactions in Dynamics GP. (*Requires* sa *login.*) |
| **Territory Combiner** | This tool is used to combine territories. As with the other tools, all existing transactions are updated. (*Requires* sa *login.*) |
| **SOP PO Number Check** | With this tool enabled you can set up your Dynamics GP to check for duplicate customer PO numbers and either not allow them, or show a warning message to the user. |

# Payroll tools

These are tools for the Payroll module:

| Tool name | Description |
|---|---|
| **Certified Payroll Report** | Enabling this tool with the US Payroll module allows you to add a project number to employee transactions. |
| **Employee Modifier** | Allows changing an Employee ID on all transactions in Dynamics GP. |

# Inventory tools

These are tools for the Inventory module:

| Tool name | Description |
|---|---|
| **Inventory Site Combiner** | Allows combining inventory sites. This may be useful if a new site was created by mistake. |
| **Inventory Site Modifier** | This tool allows you to change the ID of an inventory site on all transactions in Dynamics GP. |
| **Item Description Modifier** | This tool changes the name of an inventory item based on an item number on all transactions in Dynamics GP. This should be used very carefully, as some companies change the item descriptions on both sales and purchasing documents on purpose and may want to keep those changes in their historical data. |
| **Item Number Combiner** | One of the more popular tools, this allows inventory items to be combined into one. (*Requires* `sa` *login.*) |
| **Item Number Modifier** | Another of the tools used often, this allows you to change the number of an inventory item on all transactions in Dynamics GP. This is very useful when changing inventory numbering. (*Requires* `sa` *login.*) |
| **Item Reconciler** | This tool runs the same Inventory Reconcile process that is available in the Inventory module in Dynamics GP; however, it only runs for the items that need to be reconciled. If you have a large number of items and transactions, this tool may increase performance of the reconcile process. |

# Miscellaneous tools

Additional tools that do not fit into the previous categories, or were added recently:

| Tool name | Description |
|---|---|
| **Fixed Asset Modifier** | Allows changing an Asset ID on all transactions in Dynamics GP. |
| **Default Add Item POP/SOP** | With this tool enabled, if a user types in an item number that does not exist on either a POP or SOP transaction, they will see a prompt asking them if they want to add the item. This is very useful to quickly alert users that they have typed in a non-inventory item. |

| Tool name | Description |
|---|---|
| **Doc Date Verify** | This is arguably one of the most useful tools available and I recommend that it be enabled for every Dynamics GP installation. With this tool enabled, when a user types in a transaction date, Dynamics GP checks to see if it is in an existing or closed fiscal period. Transactions will not be allowed for non-existing fiscal periods and will be allowed with a warning for closed fiscal period. Doc Date Verify works with the following transaction windows:<br>• Payables Transaction Entry<br>• Payables Manual Payment Entry<br>• Purchase Order Entry<br>• Receivings Transaction Entry<br>• Purchasing Invoice Entry<br>• Receivables Transaction Entry<br>• Invoice Entry<br>• Sales Transaction Entry<br>• Cash Receipts Entry<br>• Inventory Transaction Entry |
| **Decimal Place Tool** | With this tool enabled, the Check Amount in words on Payables and Payroll checks will be shown with two decimal places. |
| **Company Copy** | This tool allows copying module setup and/or data from one Dynamics GP company to another. This can be very useful when creating a new Dynamics GP company that needs to have similar setup to an existing company. (*Requires* `sa` *login*.) |

You can find more information and detailed instructions for each tool listed in the preceding table from the Professional Services Tools Library manual, included with the PSTL download. Note that some of the tools require that the user be logged in as `sa` for the tool to work. Many of the tools that offer the ability to change IDs or names have the option of importing a list of the changes instead of having to manually enter them one at a time.

> While many of these tools have become invaluable to Dynamics GP users and administrators, it is important to test these to make sure they will accomplish what you need and to see how they work. If you have implemented customizations or third-party products for your Dynamics GP, make sure the PSTL tools will work with them, as this is not always the case. It is also recommended to keep detailed records of changes made, as there is no audit trail maintained for these by Dynamics GP.

# Tools from Microsoft's Professional Services Team

Microsoft's Professional Services Team has created many customizations for Dynamics GP customers over the years. Some of these customizations have been packaged into tools that have also been made available for free. Similarly to the PSTL, Dynamics GP partners are able to download these tools from the following URL: `http://bit.ly/18qHTH3` (requires PartnerSource access). Dynamics GP customers would need to ask their partners for the tools.

Following is a list of these tools with brief descriptions:

| Tool name | Description |
|---|---|
| **AutoDim** | This tool allows you to launch Dynamics GP, run one or more integrations or integration groups, and have Dynamics GP exit upon completion of the integrations. This product also supports integration into several different companies. |
| **AutoPost** | DLL that uses the Continuum API to call the posting processes in Dynamics GP. The Dynamics GP application must be opened with a user logged into the appropriate company for this to work. AutoPost works for transactions entered on the following windows:<br>• General Ledger Transaction Entry<br>• Inventory Item Transaction Entry<br>• Inventory Item Transfer Entry<br>• Receivables Cash Receipts Entry<br>• SOP Sales Transaction Entry<br>• POP Receivings Transaction Entry<br>• Payables Transaction Entry |
| **Detail Payroll Activity Tracking** | Allows you to track all employee changes made in Microsoft Dynamics GP. |
| **PO Returns** | When invoicing a receipt in POP, this tool will check the previous quantity invoiced and the quantity returned for the line item. The maximum quantity allowed to be invoiced is based on the following formula: Quantity Shipped *minus* (Previous Quantity Invoiced *plus* Quantity Returned). This tool will not allow invoicing for more than the maximum quantity allowed. |
| **RM Auto Apply** | Allows you to mass apply posted receivables credit documents (payments, returns and credit memos) to posted receivables debit documents. You can select ranges of customers, transaction dates and document types. |

| Tool name | Description |
|---|---|
| **Shipment Notification** | This tool allows drop ship sales orders to be transferred to invoices prior to invoicing the purchase order. |
| **SOP Default per Site Line** | This tool defaults the site from the **Cards** \| **Inventory** \| **Quantities/ Sites** window for each line item entered on an SOP transaction. |
| **SOP Sort Line Items** | Allows you to define custom sorting options to display line items in Sales Order Processing. |
| **SOP to POP Line Reordering Utility** | This tool will reorder the line items of Purchase Orders generated by the SOP to POP transfer process to be in the same order as they originally were on the Sales Order document(s). |

More details and instructions are included with the download for each of these tools.

# Support Debugging Tool

The **Support Debugging Tool** for Dynamics GP was created by David Musgrave (`http://social.msdn.microsoft.com/Profile/david%20musgrave`), a key contributor to the Dynamics GP community. The Support Debugging Tool is written in Dexterity and contains a number of very useful utilities for helping with support, troubleshooting, and reporting in Dynamics GP.

Dynamics GP partners can download the Support Debugging Tool for Dynamics GP 2013 on PartnerSource (login required): `https://mbs.microsoft.com/partnersource/support/selfsupport/productreleases/MDGP2013_SupportDebuggingTool`. Customers can ask their Dynamics GP partner to obtain the Support Debugging Tool for them.

Some additional links for the Support Debugging Tool:

- Installing and frequently asked questions: `http://bit.ly/18qLzbZ`.
- How to configure SQL Profile Tracing using the Support Debugging Tool: `http://bit.ly/18qLIMh`.
- 21 Reasons why every workstation should have the Support Debugging Tool installed: `http://bit.ly/18qLOnd`.
- One of my personal favorites: Differentiating companies in Dynamics GP: `http://bit.ly/18qLVzi`.
- How to use the Support Debugging Tool to get resource information:
    - One resource at a time: `http://bit.ly/18qM19Y`.
    - Building a file of all resources: `http://bit.ly/18qLZin`.

# Troubleshooting tips

Troubleshooting can be a difficult and lengthy process and often, without enough information, can become iterative and frustrating. This section offers a list of tests to attempt and information to collect when troubleshooting or asking for support.

## Tests

One of the key factors in identifying and fixing a problem is being able to reproduce it. Before trying to look up an issue or error, or asking others for help with it, consider running through some of the following tests on your own:

- Are the results the same when logged into Dynamics GP as another user on the same computer?
- Are the results the same when logged into Dynamics GP as the same user on a different computer (or, even better, the Dynamics GP server, if possible to test there)?
- Are the results the same when logged into Dynamics GP as `sa`?
- Are the results the same in all Dynamics GP companies?
- Are the results the same when logged into Windows as a user in the local administrators group?
- If you have multiple Windows operating systems running Dynamics GP, are the results the same on a different operating system?
- If the issue is on a Terminal Server, are the results the same when running Dynamics GP locally on the Terminal Server and/or locally on another computer?
- Are the results the same when logged into Windows as the local administrator (built-in account for administering the computer/domain)?

> Note that this is different from a user in the local administrators group.

- If printing a report is not working:
    - Are the results the same when choosing to print to screen only, instead of choosing printer or export?
    - Has a new printer been added recently?
    - Has anything changed in the printer setup?

# Important information

The following is a list of information that is helpful to provide when asking for help:

- Dynamics GP version and service pack (or build number).
- Windows operating system and service pack.
- SQL Server version and service pack.
- What are the steps to reproduce the issue?
- If you are getting an error, capture a screenshot or the exact wording of the error message and the exact steps that lead to it.
- Describe the steps you have already taken to troubleshoot and their results.

Running through some tests yourself and providing as much information as possible when asking for support will help you get to a resolution much faster. Often the results of the tests will actually lead you to see what is causing the issue even before calling for support.

# Additional resources

There are many additional resources available for Dynamics GP. This section will discuss the following resources:

- Knowledge base
- Forums
- Blogs

## Knowledge base

The Dynamics Knowledge Base requires a login to either CustomerSource or PartnerSource and can be found at the following URL: `https://mbs.microsoft.com/knowledgebase/search.aspx`. This Knowledge Base is for all Microsoft Dynamics products, so be sure to select **Microsoft Dynamics GP** under **Select Product** when searching.

As there are a great number of articles in the Knowledge Base, it is often best to start with the exact and complete text of the error message you are trying to troubleshoot and choose **All of the words entered** or **Exact phrase entered** under **Using**. If that does not provide results, you can always take some of the words out.

> Note that often the Dynamics GP versions listed under the **Applies To** section of the Knowledge Base articles are not updated right away for a new Dynamics GP version. Many of the resolutions will still apply to a newer version, so it may simply be that the article has not been updated yet to include all versions.

Some additional tips on searching the Dynamics Knowledge Base can be found in this blog post and its comments: `http://bit.ly/18qMHMI`.

# Forums

There are a number of Microsoft and non-Microsoft forums, also sometimes referred to as newsgroups, where you can search for answers and ask for help on Dynamics GP. The top four that I have used are:

- Microsoft Dynamics GP Community Forum (requires Windows Live login): `https://community.dynamics.com/gp/f/32.aspx`.
- Microsoft Dynamics GP Partner Forum (requires Windows Live login and affiliation with a partner organization): `http://partnersupport.microsoft.com/en-us/mpndynamics/forum/mpndyngp?tab=QnA`.
- Tek-Tips Dynamics GP Forum (requires Tek-Tips login): `http://www.tek-tips.com/threadminder.cfm?pid=632`.
- Experts Exchange MS Dynamics GP Zone (requires a paid subscription to Experts Exchange or answering questions to accumulate points): `http://www.experts-exchange.com/Microsoft/Applications/Microsoft_Dynamics/`.

This is by no means an exhaustive list and there are other Dynamics GP forums on the internet. Keep in mind that if your issue is urgent, it may be better to contact Microsoft Dynamics GP support or your Dynamics GP partner.

# Blogs

Blogs are now a regular part of supporting and maintaining an application and there are quite a number of blogs dedicated to Microsoft Dynamics GP. Some focus on a specific functionality or aspect of Dynamics GP, while others point out other Dynamics GP-related resources and articles. A few representative blogs are listed as follows:

- Victoria Yudin—Ramblings and musings of a Dynamics GP MVP (yes, this is my blog): `http://victoriayudin.com/`.
- Inside Microsoft Dynamics GP (official Dynamics GP blog): `http://blogs.msdn.com/b/gp/`.
- David Musgrave—Developing for Dynamics GP: `http://blogs.msdn.com/b/developingfordynamicsgp/`.
- Steve Endow and Christina Phillips—Dynamics GP Land: `http://dynamicsgpland.blogspot.com/`.
- Leslie Vail—Dynamics Confessor Blogspot: `http://dynamicsconfessions.blogspot.com/`.
- Mariano Gomez—The Dynamics GP Blogster: `http://dynamicsgpblogster.blogspot.com/`.
- Mark Polino—DynamicAccounting.net: `http://mpolino.com/gp/`.
- Frank Hamelly—GP2theMax: `http://gp2themax.blogspot.com/`.
- Jan Harrigan—Simplify FRx and Management Reporter: `http://www.frxbuzz.com`.
- Jivtesh Singh—About Dynamics, Development and Life: `http://www.jivtesh.com/`.
- Vaidy Mohan—Dynamics GP - Learn & Discuss: `http://vaidymohan.com/`.
- Ian Grieve—Ramblings of a Dynamics GP Consultant: `http://www.azurecurve.co.uk/`.

For other Dynamics GP blogs, take a look at the blog links on any of the blogs listed.

# Summary

In this chapter, we discussed various aspects of training your Dynamics GP users and provided some tips on how and when to train. We also went over tools available from Microsoft for Dynamics GP, troubleshooting steps, and listed a number of resources for further Dynamics GP information.

# General Ledger Account Categories

General Ledger Account Categories help identify the function or financial reporting section for each GL account. The following is the list of predefined Dynamics GP categories and their numbers:

1. Cash
2. Short-Term Investments
3. Accounts Receivable
4. Notes Receivable
5. Inventory
6. Work in Process
7. Prepaid Expenses
8. Long-Term Investments
9. Property, Plant and Equipment
10. Accumulated Depreciation
11. Intangible Assets
12. Other Assets
13. Accounts Payable
14. Notes Payable
15. Current Maturities of Long-Term Debt
16. Taxes Payable
17. Interest Payable
18. Dividends Payable

19. Leases Payable (Current)
20. Sinking Fund Payable (Current)
21. Other Current Liabilities
22. Long-Term Debt
23. Common Stock
24. Preferred Stock
25. Additional Paid-in Capital - Common
26. Additional Paid-in Capital - Preferred
27. Retained Earnings
28. Treasury Stock
29. Common Dividends
30. Preferred Dividends
31. Sales
32. Sales Returns and Discounts
33. Cost of Goods Sold
34. Selling Expense
35. Administrative Expense
36. Salaries Expense
37. Other Employee Expenses
38. Interest Expense
39. Tax Expense
40. Depreciation Expense
41. Income Tax Expense
42. Other Expenses
43. Other Income
44. Charges Not Using Working Capital
45. Revenues Not Producing Working Capital
46. Gain/Loss on Asset Disposal
47. Amortization of Intangible Assets
48. Nonfinancial Accounts

# Index

## Symbols



## A



## B

## C

## D

## E



## F

# G



# H

## I

## J



## K

## L



## M



## N

## O



## P

## Q



## R

## T



## U

## W

Thank you for buying

# Microsoft Dynamics GP 2013 Implementation

## About Packt Publishing

Packt, pronounced 'packed', published its first book "Mastering phpMyAdmin for Effective MySQL Management" in April 2004 and subsequently continued to specialize in publishing highly focused books on specific technologies and solutions.

Our books and publications share the experiences of your fellow IT professionals in adapting and customizing today's systems, applications, and frameworks. Our solution based books give you the knowledge and power to customize the software and technologies you're using to get the job done. Packt books are more specific and less general than the IT books you have seen in the past. Our unique business model allows us to bring you more focused information, giving you more of what you need to know, and less of what you don't.

Packt is a modern, yet unique publishing company, which focuses on producing quality, cutting-edge books for communities of developers, administrators, and newbies alike. For more information, please visit our website: `www.packtpub.com`.

## About Packt Enterprise

In 2010, Packt launched two new brands, Packt Enterprise and Packt Open Source, in order to continue its focus on specialization. This book is part of the Packt Enterprise brand, home to books published on enterprise software - software created by major vendors, including (but not limited to) IBM, Microsoft and Oracle, often for use in other corporations. Its titles will offer information relevant to a range of users of this software, including administrators, developers, architects, and end users.

## Writing for Packt

We welcome all inquiries from people who are interested in authoring. Book proposals should be sent to author@packtpub.com. If your book idea is still at an early stage and you would like to discuss it first before writing a formal book proposal, contact us; one of our commissioning editors will get in touch with you.

We're not just looking for published authors; if you have strong technical skills but no writing experience, our experienced editors can help you develop a writing career, or simply get some additional reward for your expertise.

35136198R00240

Made in the USA
Middletown, DE
21 September 2016